TRANSCENDING POLITICS

A Technoprogressive Roadmap
to a
Comprehensively Better Future

By
David W. Wood

Executive Director, Transpolitica

> Politics is broken.
>
> Technology risks making matters worse.
>
> But transhumanism can fix it. Comprehensively.

Paperback ISBN 978-0-9954942-2-0

Published by Delta Wisdom

Printed and bound in Great Britain by Marston Book Services Ltd, Oxfordshire

The real problem of humanity is the following: we have Palaeolithic emotions, medieval institutions, and god-like technology. And it is terrifically dangerous, and it is now approaching a point of crisis overall.

– Edward O. Wilson, Harvard, 2009[1]

Mother Nature, truly we are grateful for what you have made us. No doubt you did the best you could. However, with all due respect, we must say that you have in many ways done a poor job with the human constitution. You have made us vulnerable to disease and damage. You compel us to age and die – just as we're beginning to attain wisdom. You were miserly in the extent to which you gave us awareness of our somatic, cognitive, and emotional processes. You held out on us by giving the sharpest senses to other animals. You made us functional only under narrow environmental conditions. You gave us limited memory, poor impulse control, and tribalistic, xenophobic urges. And, you forgot to give us the operating manual for ourselves!

What you have made us is glorious, yet deeply flawed. You seem to have lost interest in our further evolution some 100,000 years ago. Or perhaps you have been biding your time, waiting for us to take the next step ourselves. Either way, we have reached our childhood's end.

We have decided that it is time to amend the human constitution.

We do not do this lightly, carelessly, or disrespectfully, but cautiously, intelligently, and in pursuit of excellence…

– Max More, *Letter to Mother Nature*, 1999[2]

Table of Contents

Foreword

Advance praise for *Transcending Politics*

Politics plays a significant role in the possibility of our future survival and flourishing. But politics today is largely broken.

In response, Wood urges us to embrace transhumanism – to use technology to overcome the limitations of brains formed in the Pleistocene. For without greater intelligence, emotional well-being, and better political institutions, we are doomed.

This carefully and conscientiously crafted work defends this thesis with vigour, and it is a welcome relief from the ubiquitous nonsense that passes for political dialogue today. Let us hope that it informs that dialogue and fuels action.

> – John G Messerly, Author of "Reason and Meaning", "Top 100 Philosophy Blogs on the Planet"

In the big question 'If politics is broken, what's the Alternative', David Wood gives us a short-cut to the answer. The first clue is in the title 'Transcending Politics' because in order to reap the benefits of all that is coming down the line in terms of biology, technology and AI, what we currently understand as politics has to be left behind.

From homo economicus to transhumanism and the abolition of aging. From knocking on doors every five years to liquid democracy and citizens' assemblies. From nations competing in global markets to transnational networks sharing artificial intelligence and energy sources. It's all there – and with heart.

This book will be a key text for The Alternative UK political platform.

> – Indra Adnan, Co-initiator, The Alternative UK

For anyone interested in whatever comes next for a truly technoprogressive society, David Wood lays out in clear, accessible language not only the case for why the politics of the future must be transformed, but also the way in which we might want to go about it. The topics he covers represent some of the most important conversations we need to be having as a society, today, here and now, before it's too late.

> – Gareth John, Independent Researcher, Aberystwyth, UK

Most transhumanism advocates wish to 'transcend' politics in the sense of replacing it – that is, when they're not trying to avoid it altogether. Their utopian visions may be clear but they haven't a clue about how to achieve them. David Wood is relatively unique in addressing this matter head on. A particularly refreshing feature of his approach is that he is willing to accept people as they are before attempting to foist a radical future on them. Wood combines the right balance of enthusiasm and sobriety to take forward a truly 'technoprogressive' vision for transhumanism.

– Prof Steve Fuller, Auguste Comte Chair in Social Epistemology,
University of Warwick

Politics is broken. If it ever worked, it did so poorly. We live in amazing times where tools to analyze and fix our problems are now available. Why not apply them to politics?

In this fascinating and informative book, David Wood takes us on a tour of the near future. He explores what's happening, why and how we can harness the promise of technology to move beyond red team/blue team bickering to a place where government decisions have transparency and effect.

– Toby Unwin, Chief Innovation Officer, Premonition LLC

Jeremy Bentham meets Charlie Stross in David Wood's creative patchwork of classical politics and radical transhumanist transformation.

– Giulio Prisco, Board Member, IEET

Humanity has reached a bifurcation point where we either develop significantly more advanced capabilities, including better politics and better humans powered by better algorithms and tech, or descend into a new Dark Age – but this time with WMDs, global surveillance systems etc. Rampant short-termism, together with attempts to preserve the status quo at any price, is leading to the latter. The ideas and suggestions laid bare in this book advance the former. As the final outcome is not set in stone and depends on everyone's thoughts, attitudes, and actions, I sincerely hope this work will steer readers towards contributing to the desired positive technoprogressive solution. The healthy dose of idealism and measured positivity in the book could be just what we need in these times of turmoil and upcoming radical change.

– Andrew Vladimirov, Co-founder and Chief Information Security Officer,
Arhont Information Security

David Wood's *Transcending Politics* frames the transformation of our politics around the breadth of today's technological opportunities. It looks at how governance could maximally benefit from technological advances but also how a failure to govern and to integrate them exposes us, humanity, to much more serious existential threats.

If there is any problem with the book it is that it makes too much good sense compared to the level of political discourse that we are living in. So depending on where you come from you will think the book is either too ideal to be practical, a parachute, or a breath of fresh air.

— Yates Buckley, Technical Partner, UNIT9, London

David Wood's scenarios for the future are so engaging that *Transcending Politics* will become a must-read for anyone engaged in politics or interested in the future of humanity. Readers will be captivated by the author's description of potential impact of exponential growth of technology on human progress, and the changes needed in the relationships between the governed and the governing if we are to mitigate successfully the plethora of existential risks facing humanity.

— Tony Czarnecki, Managing Partner, Sustensis

David Wood has already written one extraordinary book concerning the future impact of technology: *The Abolition of Aging*. His important new book *Transcending Politics* advances an even richer mix of ideas concerning the hopes, fears and possibilities of our collective future. It will help people and organizations to reach a clearer understanding of the main political and technological issues of our time – and to accelerate steps towards a truly healthy society.

— Didier Coeurnelle, Director of the International Longevity Alliance and Vice-President of the Association Française Transhumaniste Technoprog

Note to the reader

In order to advance the conversation, short sections of text from other writers are introduced from time to time throughout this book.

So that they are easier to recognise, these paragraphs are formatted distinctively, in blocks like this, indented and with a smaller font.

1. Vision and roadmap

There's no escape: the journey to a healthier society inevitably involves politics.

That's a message many technologists and entrepreneurs are unwilling to hear. They would prefer to ignore politics. They wish, instead, to keep their focus on creating remarkable new technology or on building vibrant new business. Politics is messy and ugly, they say. It's raucous and uncouth. It's unproductive. Some would even say that politics is unnecessary.

But putting our heads in the sand about politics is a gamble fraught with danger. Looking the other way won't prevent our necks from being snapped when the axe falls. As eruptions from broken politics grow more intense, they will afflict everyone, everywhere.

On their present trajectory, technology and business are actually making politics worse, rather than better. Together, without intending it, they are fuelling increasing dysfunction within politics. In such a setting, technological innovations and aggressive business corporations might end up harming humanity much more than they help us.

You'll find many examples in the pages ahead of how flawed politics leads to a string of bad outcomes. You'll hear about perverse economic incentives, regulatory institutions that are caught in lethargy and inertia, vested interests that hold disproportionate power, self-perpetuating industrial complexes, spiralling arms races, and much more. These outcomes, exacerbated by almighty technology put to sinister use, are likely to lead in turn to a hurricane of adverse consequences – to an epic disaster of social disintegration and humanitarian tragedy.

Indeed, fixing politics is the central challenge of our time – and hence the central theme of this book. If we can fix politics – if we can transcend its messiness and ugliness to enable its true purpose – we can facilitate profound positive progress in many other areas of life. But if politics remains broken, it could lead us to collective ruin.

The necessity of politics

There's no intrinsic reason for politics to be messy or ugly, raucous or uncouth. Nor should it be seen as some kind of unnecessary activity.

Politics arises wherever people gather together. Whenever we collectively decide the constraints we put on each other's freedom, we're taking part in politics.

Consider some examples where constraints on freedom are needed. Someone in the thralls of a mid-life crisis wants the freedom to drive his car along public roads at high speed, even though it's been years since any mechanic has checked the roadworthiness of the vehicle, and the driver has recently been imbibing some experimental new drugs. A factory owner wants the freedom to dump the raw effluent of her factory into the local wildlife lake, rather than spending lots of money to sanitise the waste before disposing of it. A young married couple want the freedom to select the sex of their firstborn child, to ensure they start their family with a son rather than a daughter. A colonel wants the freedom to "modernise" the army's airborne missile defence system so that engagement decisions can be taken by software without slowing down the process by requiring human review.

Consider further: A mother has read on the Internet that vaccinations may have side-effects, and wants the freedom to absent her daughter from the local vaccination programme. An academic has discovered a tweak to the smallpox virus that makes it more deadly than the original, and wants the freedom to publish his research openly on the Internet. An industrialist wants the freedom to use new drilling technologies deep underground, to extract oil and gas that have previously been inaccessible, whilst discounting fears that these new techniques might trigger earthquakes. An entrepreneur wants the freedom to shower particles high in the atmosphere, to counter the effects of rising global temperatures, even though some critics worry about massive unintended side-effects.

In each of these cases, the rest of us probably feel uneasy. We want to say that freedom needs to operate within limits.

But how are these limits agreed? How are they enforced? And – especially important in a time of accelerating change – how are alterations introduced, when the assumptions underpinning a set of limits no longer pertain? *Welcome to politics.*

Of course, the subject of politics extends beyond *constraints* (the limits to freedom). Politics also covers *incentives* – the encouragements we apply to each other to take action we believe will be in our collective good interest. Politics provides carrots as well as sticks. Road tax may be reduced if a car uses a greener form of energy. Financial assistance may be provided for companies providing various sorts of apprentice training. Governments may top up pension contributions. Some jurisdictions provide monetary incentives to couples with certain demographic features to have children. Public funding may encourage companies to set up factories in deprived areas. Prizes can be offered, to stimulate ideas in areas lacking attention.

The same questions arise as before: *how are these incentives agreed, operated, and updated?*

Ideally, political decision processes will draw on the best insights of the entire community. Ideally, society's regulatory and legal frameworks, which constrain how we all operate, will serve society as a whole, rather than narrow cliques. Where there are conflicts of interest, these should be addressed and resolved rationally, rather than by brute power or hidden skulduggery.

In today's fast-changing world, the legal frameworks that stipulate which activities are restricted, and which are, instead, encouraged, need updating more and more quickly. As new technological possibilities arise, laws and standards that made good sense in previous times no longer make such good sense. As technological innovation becomes more pervasive, legal reform needs to accelerate. In some cases, frameworks need loosening; in others, tightening; in yet others, whole new concepts are required. But how will these changes be agreed and overseen? And how can we prevent powerful vested interests from defining and manipulating these regulatory and legal frameworks for their own narrow benefits? These are key tasks for twenty-first century politics.

The bad news is that politics is failing at this task – due in part to incompetence, and in part to malice. Misconceived actions by out-of-touch politicians threaten to derail necessary reforms in these frameworks. Obstructive actions by self-serving politicians further hinder the reform process. The sorry result will be to stunt or even strangle important positive humanitarian initiatives – initiatives in multiple fields of life, involving engineers, scientists, entrepreneurs, futurists, community-builders, and other social reformers. Not for the first time in history, what is mediocre about humanity will obstruct what is potentially best about humanity.

That's only the start of what's wrong with contemporary politics. It's not just that bad politics can impede vital civil improvement projects.

Equally worrying, political machinations can distract society's attention, sideline critical resources, provoke divisions rather than unity, inflame the disaffected into acts of gross sabotage, and, in the worst case, plunge nations into cataclysmic war with each other.

In short, we ignore politics at our peril. We need to take our heads out of the sand, fast.

Nevertheless, I write this book not to condemn politics but to commend it. Politics, done well, can be a powerful ally in the quest to elevate humanity to our true potential.

The good news is that a better politics awaits us, beckoning us forward. It's up to us – all of us – whether we recognise that call and take the required actions. Key to these actions will be to harness technology more wisely and more profoundly than before.

By the phrase "better politics", I'm thinking not just of *individual politicians becoming more responsive and more knowledgeable* – welcome though such a development will be. Nor is my vision limited to the advent of *new, future-savvy political parties* – something, again, that is long overdue. Critically, what I have in mind is the emergence of a reinvigorated *political system* – a twenty-first century *arena* which, aided by twenty-first century technology, facilitates political debate that is better informed, more engaged, more productive, and genuinely beneficial. This improved new mode of conduct will transcend the short-sightedness, self-justifications, and other deep-seated obstructions that so widely bedevil present-day political interactions.

In this envisioned possible new politics of the near future, decisions can take place informed by the best insight of the population as a whole, rather than being subverted by partisan vested interests. Viewpoints and information that deserve more attention will rise to the top of political discussion, untarnished, rather than being pushed aside or deviously distorted by those who find them inconvenient. Political discourse will become authentic, rather than contrived. Our politics will become animated by the spirit of constructive curiosity and open collaboration.

Evidently, that's a far cry from the present situation. Our politics has grown dysfunctional in recent times – frustratingly, *dangerously* dysfunctional.

The underlying reason for this dysfunction is because our mainstream mental worldviews and cultural frameworks are unable to handle the accelerating pace of change. To cope with this intense twenty-first century pace, we sorely need new worldviews and new frameworks. We are overdue for a decisive move beyond formerly dominant thought patterns such as economic neoliberalism, market-led capitalism, worker-led socialism, nation-state conservatism, technological determinism, and backward-looking "natural is best" eco-primitivism. We urgently require a twenty-first paradigm that can supersede and transcend these ailing predecessors.

The necessity of transhumanism

In response to our current conceptual crisis, I offer transhumanism. Just as I believe that the journey to a healthier society inevitably involves politics, I also believe that journey inevitably involves transhumanism.

That's a message many observers may be unwilling to hear. But it's a message that deserves attention. To persevere with outdated mental and cultural frameworks, without absorbing the full transformational insights and energy of transhumanism, is, again, to risk social disintegration and humanitarian tragedy.

If you're unsure about transhumanism – if the word disturbs you, or you've heard weird things about apparently naive transhumanists – I ask you to put these critical thoughts temporarily on hold. Hopefully you'll find in the pages ahead a description that makes more sense than you expected.

The essence of transhumanism is captured in this succinct definition by Swedish polymath Anders Sandberg[3]:

> Transhumanism is the philosophy that we can and should develop to higher levels, physically, mentally, and socially, using rational methods.

And here's a formulation from 1990 by the founder of the modern transhumanist movement, philosopher Max More[4]:

> Transhumanism is a class of philosophies of life that seek the continuation and acceleration of the evolution of intelligent life beyond its currently human form and human limitations by means of science and technology, guided by life-promoting principles and values.

Throughout this book, I'll be highlighting the special relevance of transhumanism to the project of enhancing politics. Don't worry: I won't be presuming any prior knowledge of transhumanism. However, if you're interested, you can read many of the movement's foundational articles in the collection *The Transhumanist Reader*[5]. Another good starting point to explore the overall concept is the online H+Pedia wiki[6].

For now, I'll extend Sandberg's definition as follows. Transhumanism asserts that humanity can and should take wise and profound advantage of technology to transcend the damaging limitations and drawbacks imposed by the current circumstances of human nature. As a result, humans will be able to transition, *individually and collectively*, towards a significantly higher stage of life – a life with much improved quality.

As in the short video "An Introduction to Transhumanism"[7] – which, with approaching a quarter of a million views, is probably the most widely watched video on the subject – transhumanism is sometimes expressed in terms of the so-called "three supers":

- *Super longevity*: significantly improved physical health, including much longer lifespans – overcoming human tendencies towards physical decay and decrepitude

- *Super intelligence*: significantly improved thinking capability – overcoming human tendencies towards mental blind spots and collective stupidity

- *Super wellbeing*: significantly improved states of consciousness – overcoming human tendencies towards depression, alienation, vicious emotions, and needless suffering.

My advocacy of transhumanism actually emphasises one variant within the overall set of transhumanist philosophies. This is the variant of transhumanism known as *technoprogressive transhumanism*.

The technoprogressive variant of transhumanism in effect adds one more "super" to the three already mentioned[8]:

- *Super democracy*: significantly improved social inclusion and resilience, whilst upholding diversity and liberty – overcoming human tendencies towards tribalism, divisiveness, deception, and the abuse of power.

But I'm getting ahead of myself. Before saying more about technoprogressive ideas, there's some additional context I need to set. The following remarks – about power and technology – should help make clear the deep inadequacies of existing mainstream political thinking.

Power and corruption

Power tends to corrupt, warned Lord Acton, the nineteenth century historian and politician. *Absolute power corrupts absolutely.*[9] Power can corrupt the clarity of our thinking, and our sense of moral duty. It can lead us to forget our social binds to our fellow citizens. It can cause us to think of ourselves as much more worthy and deserving than our former kith and kin. *We might gain the whole world, but lose our soul.*[10]

What is worrying is that never before have we humans held so much power in our hands. Science and technology have provided us with spectacular capabilities. We can redirect mighty rivers, hasten the formation of storm clouds, cool down the earth by blotting out sunlight using aerosols, and, through hydraulic fracturing, trigger massive earthquakes. We may soon recreate in the midst of our countrysides the same sustained nuclear fusion as takes place deep inside stars. We can cut and splice genetic solutions from one species into others that are far distant on the tree of life. And, grown emboldened from re-engineering nature, we are now poised to re-engineer *human nature*.

Whether these near-absolute powers will corrupt humanity, ruinously, or instead uplift humanity, gloriously, remains an open question. Given the pace at which breakthrough change hurtles around the world, frequently with cascading unintended consequences, it's also an *urgent* question.

We may not like to be reminded of this, but our increasingly powerful superhuman capabilities coexist, precariously, with ugly subhuman proclivities carried forward from prehistoric times. This potent, deadly combination may be on the point of veering completely out of control.

Eminent biologist Edward O. Wilson has put it well[11]:

The real problem of humanity is the following: we have Palaeolithic emotions, medieval institutions, and god-like technology. And it is terrifically dangerous, and it is now approaching a point of crisis overall.

Ages-old primal human traits, such as vanity, envy, self-righteousness, tribalism, and alienation, are being aggravated by the blistering pace of modern-day social change. These traits are being fanned by divisive ideologies of retrenchment and separation. They're being magnified by all sorts of accelerating technological breakthroughs and societal dislocation. With their newfound unprecedented vigour, these traits are poised to wreak existential havoc. All that we hold dear could perish.

That forecast may seem melodramatic. But observe that, as humanity becomes smarter, it's far from clear that we're also becoming wiser. Greater strength doesn't automatically bring greater kindness. More intelligence can make us more narrow-minded, rather than more thoughtful. It gives us a terrifying capability to discover or invent new reasons to justify us doing whatever it is that we've already decided we want to do.

Sadly, we often choose to harness our intelligence to bolster our biases and reinforce our prejudices. Lacking a compelling bigger vision, people wrap themselves in small-minded cleverness.

Without a better understanding of the layout of the landscape ahead – without a trustworthy vision of how technology can best serve human needs – we risk unwittingly stumbling our way into some kind of Armageddon. Through blinkered haste and collective naivety, we could trigger hideous twenty-first century equivalents of the Four Horsemen of the Apocalypse.

Each of us is already under frequent hostile attack, if not from apocalyptic equestrians, then from multiple commercial and political forces that seek to exploit us, manipulate us, or diminish us. We are the victims of ingenious pressures that operate on our minds as well as on our bodies – weapons, if you like, that warp not only our physical infrastructure but also our cultural fabric and our perceptual frameworks. It is no wonder that so many people perceive they are losing control of their lives. Escalating competitive arms races mean that these pressures are more likely to intensify than to diminish.

These pressures cannot be turned off. But they can be steered.

The first task in steering is to establish the appropriate direction. That direction cannot simply be "more technology", "more trade", or "more wealth". I'll argue in this book that the vision should be "more humanity" – an increase in human flourishing – with a strong emphasis on quality rather than quantity. I'll also argue that technology, wisely guided, has an enormous positive role to play in the fulfilment of this vision.

Indeed, technology has a huge potential to elevate and improve the operation of politics. It can enable us to transcend the blockages and myopia of present-day politics. In short, technology can fix politics, and open the way to a comprehensively better future. But only if we learn to handle it properly.

Floods ahead

It's time to talk frankly about technology.

Technology is eating the world[12], at an accelerating pace. Technology is changing everything, but not necessarily for the better. We've been embracing new powers with insufficient forethought. Like the animated broom in Goethe's fable of the sorcerer's apprentice, technology initially promises so much, but has the potential to unleash floods of damage.

Consider the disruptions that are already in progress: ubiquitous surveillance; always-on 24x7 Internet connectivity; carefully targeted individualised messaging that knows how to catch each of us at our weakest; hardware and software robots that transform the workforce and threaten human redundancy; pills that profoundly modify personal mood; therapies and implants that radically alter the health of body, brain, mind, and spirit; vast virtual worlds that entice us to become immersed in alternative realities; pervasive new infrastructures that are vulnerable to large-scale hacking and distortion as never before; engineering capabilities at both the genetic and planetary scale which have the potential, if they go wrong, to devastate our shared ecosystem; new tools and weapons that put unparalleled power in the hands of terrorists, criminals, demagogues, and tyrants; all kinds of arms races intensifying as competing interests frantically seek to keep one step ahead of their perceived foes.

As all these changes take place at an intensified pace, converging with and impacting each other, present-day problems and concerns will soon fade into comparative insignificance. They'll be surpassed by much larger issues: vast new opportunities and monstrous new threats. Sensing these impending changes – sometimes dimly, sometimes more clearly – voters around the world are rebelling from conventional wisdom. Our social and political landscapes, with their long-familiar mix of tensions and conflicts, are morphing before our eyes into surprising new configurations. These new configurations are riven with fault lines of their own, and are likely to spiral and splinter into yet stranger alliances. In short, we can expect the future of politics to be increasingly turbulent.

Technology is already a highly significant influence on our social wellbeing – both for good and for ill. That influence is getting stronger all the time. Without wise guidance, technological excesses threaten to multiply environmental destruction, social division, personal alienation, and political chaos. We need to take charge of technological change, before technological change takes charge of us.

More precisely, we need to step up before various hotheads or ideologues or naïfs, whether with malign motivations or misguided intentions, take charge of technology and use it, wittingly or unwittingly, to plunge society into a new dark age. We also need to ensure that no-one manages to throw a big 'Off' switch for technological progress, effectively sabotaging all the vitally useful development that's underway.

For all these reasons, it's critically important to fix the problems that beset politics. If we cannot discuss big issues rationally, we should not be surprised if irrational choices transpire. If our politics remains broken, there's little hope for humanity.

Steering technology

The future of politics is intimately tied up with the future of technology. We cannot hope to free politics from the destructive pressures it faces – the drowning of collective reason by collective rancour, and the industrial-scale manipulation of the public mood by nefarious behind-the-scenes forces – without highlighting, understanding, and actively directing the huge transformational potential of technology. We have to focus attention on that huge transformational potential, and show how technology can be used to dramatically improve politics, rather than continuing to degrade politics.

Fixing politics will become *much* easier once a compelling, integrative vision of a sustainable transhumanist future has become widespread – a convincing account of how technology can be harnessed for profound positive progress; an energising account that inspires coordinated action in support of that future.

This book sets out such a vision. I call it the Transpolitica vision.

The vision is *transhumanist*: it envisions all humans having the freedom to experience greater health, greater wisdom, and greater wellbeing than has been possible in history so far. We will be free as never before.

The vision is *technoprogressive*: it involves humanity actively and collectively steering the progress of technology so that society can take deep advantage of the resulting innovations – so that society will be able to progress to a radically better configuration, for the clear benefit of everyone, with no one left behind.

The vision is *sustainable*: the envisioned future lifestyles won't drain or waste resources: human society will be poised to grow and evolve far into the future, in ongoing harmony with the natural environment.

The vision is *integrative*: it will be able to accept and acknowledge diverse points of view, allowing people to collaborate deeply, despite having conflicting backgrounds and different temperaments.

But such a vision, by itself, will be insufficient to transform politics. Something else is needed, namely, a credible roadmap by which society can move, step by step, from its present troubled status towards the envisioned sustainable positive future.

That roadmap needs to acknowledge the very serious risks and obstacles that lie en route to the envisioned better future – vested interests, institutional inertia, short term thinking, power dynamics, obstructive media, debilitating fears, dysfunctional political structures, and much more. Crucially, the roadmap also needs to indicate solutions to these risks and obstacles.

You can find my suggestions for these solutions in the chapters that follow. These chapters spell out the Transpolitica roadmap alongside the Transpolitica vision.

The roadmap encompasses progress in multiple different fields of technology:

- The next-generation *greentech* which can provide an abundance of clean energy, from the likes of sun, wind, wave, and geothermal

- The nature-enhancing *synthetic biotech* which can provide an abundance of healthy food and drink

- The atomically-precise *nanotech* which can provide an abundance of all sorts of material goods, including low-cost 3D-printed housing

- The restorative and preventive *rejuvenation tech* which can provide an abundance of affordable healthcare, with people able to become "better than well" and even, if they choose, youthful again

- The brain-boosting *cognotech* which can provide an abundance of all-round intelligence: emotional, rational, social, spiritual, and more

- The labour-saving *automation tech* which can provide us with an abundance of time for creativity

- The world-transforming *geotech* which can address the threats of natural disasters such as tsunamis and supervolcanoes

- The world-transcending *space tech* which will allow us to explore and find purpose in the vast terrains of both outer and inner space

- The resource-enhancing *fintech* which can empower society to make best use of our collective energies, without risk of economic chaos

- The bridge-building *collabtech* which can enable us to cooperate better, in pursuit of our technological and social progress

- The sorely-needed *politech* which will improve our political processes – leveraging elements of the other technologies listed above.

It should go without saying that each of these fields of technology has the potential for radically bad outcomes, as well as the positive ones I've just listed. For example, modifications to the genomes of organisms could result in fast-spreading pathogens. Misapplications of geoengineering could plunge the planet into a new ice age even as we seek to avoid global warming. Powerful new sources of energy, such as low-cost nuclear fission, could find their way into terrorist weaponry. And once we have put more of our human systems under the watchful eye of software supervision, these systems could become vulnerable in new ways to unexpected bugs in that software.

It's because of these risks of technology-going-wrong that we must collectively seek to actively steer the progress of technology, rather than leaving its development in the hands of industrialists, entrepreneurs, scientists, and engineers. Much though we can admire the positive accomplishments of these groups of people, we should also be aware of examples when good intentions have led to dreadful outcomes.

Think about the unexpected drawbacks arising from the use of asbestos in buildings, corn fructose syrup in numerous foods, the insecticide DDT, leaded petrol, tobacco as a stress reducer, plastic bags for convenience, aerosols that caused the hole in the ozone layer, and much more. Now think about forthcoming similar problems that could have one hundred times the impact and take effect one hundred times more speedily.

For that reason, the Transpolitica vision is techno*progressive* more than it is techno*libertarian*. I admire and champion liberty, but argue that we have to impose important constraints on our collective freedom in order to secure a future state where freedom flourishes more fully. Greater liberty arises *as a consequence of* wise social coordination, rather than existing primarily *as a reaction against* such coordination. Selecting and enforcing social constraints is the proper task of politics.

Anyone interested in the transformative potential of technology will naturally be apprehensive about possible adverse impacts of collective constraints and incentives on new technologies. The wrong constraints will unnecessarily impede the development of much-needed innovative solutions. The wrong incentives will keep in place obsolete systems that have outgrown their previous usefulness.

But to be clear: despite these potential drawbacks, I fully support the existence of *well-chosen* constraints and incentives. I'm no libertarian apprehensive of all such social interventions. I see that social constraints and incentives have vital positive roles to play, in helping to provide people with an environment in which they can flourish more fully.

If we dislike the way politicians are intervening in the development of new technology, that's no reason to say, "Let's keep politicians out of this". Instead, it's a reason to ensure that we have a better quality of political involvement. Rather than saying "There should be *no* regulations", we should say, "We need *smarter* regulations" – regulations that are more transparent, lighter weight, harder to "game", and self-policing. We should also be designing systems whereby all players are naturally incentivised to follow the regulations, rather than seeking to work around them.

Critics might respond that politicians are, somehow, inherently prone to becoming bad regulators. Politicians will inevitably be tempted towards empire-building. Given their all-too-human personal frailties, they'll pursue "white elephant" vanity projects to glorify their own names. Lacking appropriate knowledge of technology or industry, they'll be vulnerable to being misled by vested interests. Any hope on my part for better politicians and for better politics is misguided, a libertarian might assert.

But in this book, I will argue the contrary. Not only do we need better politicians and better politics, but there is a roadmap to achieve these outcomes. By taking judicious advantage of technology, we can improve both politicians and politics, step by step.

Roadmap ingredients

The French philosopher Joseph de Maistre may have overstated matters when he wrote in 1811 that[13] "Every nation gets the government it deserves", but there's more than a gist of truth in the saying.

Politics is the result of the actions of many different kinds of people – including lots of people who would not think of themselves as politicians. If we dislike how politics operates, it's probably not just politicians who are at fault. Fixing politics involves more than seeking to change the behaviour of individual politicians.

Likewise, the regulations under which technology is steered – sometimes encouraged, sometimes restricted, sometimes for better, sometimes for worse – arise from the contributions of people in many different roles:

- As well as the elected politicians, who come to power on receiving the support of the voters, there are many civil servants and other public officials, who tend to remain in their roles even when there is a change in ruling party

- Some of these public officials primarily administer regulatory policies assigned to them by elected politicians; others act as advisors who can recommend changes in regulations for consideration by elected politicians

- Ideas about changes in regulations arise from external consultants, academics, think tanks, the politicians themselves, and others

- Ideas about changes in regulations receive support or criticism from journalists and other public analysts

- Many of these external influences on politicians are driven by financial interests or other power considerations; this can lead them to distort (knowingly or unknowingly) the information they present to politicians – or to offer bribes for favourable decisions

- The frameworks under which politicians of all sort operate are defended or challenged from time to time by lawyers and judges

- Whether or not politicians proceed with particular policy ideas often depends on the feedback they receive from the electorate as a whole, and from loud voices within the electorate. Indeed, the same voices will influence whether these politicians resolve to continue working in the political field, or instead quit politics to transfer their focus to other kinds of activity.

The Transpolitica roadmap for better politics involves, accordingly, the following ingredients:

- *Transparency systems*, so that the deliberations of decision-makers are visible, and can be judged more easily and accurately

- *Fact-checking systems* to determine more quickly and clearly, via an online lookup, if some information is misleading, deceptive, biased, or in any other way suspect or substandard

- *Thinking training systems* to help everyone understand and routinely practice the skills of critical thinking, hypothesis formulation and testing, and independent evaluation of sources

- *Accountability systems* to hold people and organisations to account whenever they pass on damaging misinformation – similar to how codes of conduct already operate in the fields of advertising and investment communications

- *Bridging systems* to encourage people with strong disagreements to nevertheless explore and appreciate each other's points of view, so that shared values can be identified and a constructive dialog established

- *Educational systems* to keep politicians of all sorts informed, succinctly yet reliably, in timely fashion, about the trends that could require changes in regulations

- *Simulation systems* to help politicians of all sorts creatively explore possible new policy frameworks – and to gain a better idea in advance of likely positive and negative consequence of these new ideas

- *Monitoring systems* to report objectively on whether regulatory policies are having their desired effect

- *Concentration systems* to boost the ability of individual politicians to concentrate on key decisions, and to reach decisions free from adverse tiredness, distraction, bias, or prejudice

- *Encouragement systems* to encourage greater positive participation in the political and regulatory processes by people who have a lot to contribute, but who are currently feeling pressure to participate instead in different fields of activity.

Key to many of these ingredients will be the smart design, development, and deployment of new technological systems. Collectively, these systems can be called "politech". As mentioned previously, politech can take advantage of improvements in fields such as cognotech and collabtech.

But I expect that two further considerations are already forming in readers' minds:

1. Would a focus on technological solutions blind us to important non-technological factors influencing politics?

2. What's going to prevent the *misuse* of these new technologies, by politicians who are self-serving or narrow-minded, or by powerful corporations who want to pull the strings of politicians?

Here are my answers to these questions:

1. Indeed, we do need to keep human factors high in our minds, rather than just the technological possibilities. I'll return to the question of motivations and incentives in the next chapter.

2. Agreed, the maxim that all technologies can be applied for destructive purposes as well as constructive ones, applies for politech as much as in any other field. We're all going to need to keep our eyes wide open. The price of liberty is vigilance. You'll find plenty on that topic in the chapters ahead too.

Transcending left and right?

The Transpolitica vision of "transcending politics" does *not* foresee the abolition or eradication of politics. There's nothing intrinsically undesirable about the central purpose of politics – the process whereby collective decisions are taken on the constraints we put on each other's freedom. What *is* undesirable, however, is a great deal of the *practice* of current politics. Transpolitica aims to leave that bad practice behind, thereby raising the quality of the decisions taken and overseen by politics.

One of the most destructive elements of current politics is its divisiveness. Politicians form into warring parties which then frequently find fault with each other. They seek to damage the reputation of their adversaries, throwing lots of mud in the hope that at least some of it will stick. Whereas disagreement is inherent in political process, what would be far better is if politicians could disagree *without being disagreeable*.

The division between "left" and "right" is particularly long-established. The pioneering transhumanist philosopher F.M. Esfandiary, who later changed his name to FM-2030, lamented this division in his 1977 book *Up-Wingers*[14]:

> To transcend more rapidly to higher levels of evolution we must begin by breaking out of the confinement of traditional ideologies.
>
> We are at all times slowed down by the narrowness of Right-wing and Left-wing alternatives. If you are not conservative you are liberal. If not right of centre you are left of it or middle of the road.
>
> Our traditions comprise no other alternatives. There is no ideological or conceptual dimension beyond conservative and liberal – beyond Right and Left.
>
> Right and Left – even the extreme Left – are traditional frameworks predicated on traditional premises striving in obsolete ways to attain obsolete goals.

Esfandiary's answer was a different dimension: "Up" – the optimistic embrace of radical technological possibility for positive human transformation:

> How do you identify Space scientists who this very day are working with new sets of premises to establish communities in other worlds? Are they Right-wing or Left? Are they conservative or liberal?
>
> How do you categorize radio astronomers now scanning the galaxies in search of Intelligent Life? Or scientists working on the implantation of devices in the human body enabling the individual to control its own pain and pleasures – emotions and dreams? Or those working on telefarming systems which can provide endless quantities of food? Or computerers developing cybernated systems to free people of the primitive ordeals of perpetual work and of leadership government? Or bio-engineers striving to conquer death?
>
> These and other breakthroughs are outside the range of all the traditional philosophical social economic political frameworks. These new dimensions are nowhere on the Right or on the Left. These new dimensions are Up.

Up is an entirely new framework whose very premises and goals transcend the conventional Right and Left...

The Right/Left establishment wants to maintain an evolutionary status quo. It is resigned to humanity's basic predicament. It simply strives to make life better within this predicament.

Up-Wingers are resigned to nothing. We accept no human predicament as permanent, no tragedy as irreversible; no goals as unattainable.

The term "Up" dovetails with Esfandiary's evident interest in the exploration of space. We should raise our thinking upwards – towards the stars – rather than being constrained with small-mindedness.

Professor Steve Fuller of the University of Warwick and legal expert Veronika Lipinska take these ideas further in their 2014 book *The Proactionary Imperative: A Foundation for Transhumanism*[15], in which they explore "the rotation of the ideological axis", from left/right to up/down. Fuller and Lipinska provide some fascinating historical background and provocative speculations about possible futures – including a section on "the four styles of playing God in today's world".

I share the view that there are more important questions than the left-right split that has dominated politics for so long. Esfandiary was correct to highlight the question of whether to embrace ("Up") or to reject ("Down") the potential of new technology to dramatically enhance human capabilities.

But the "Up" decision to embrace the potential for transhuman enhancements still leaves many other decisions unresolved. People who identify as being up-wing are torn between being "right-leaning upwingers" and being "left-leaning upwingers":

- The former admire the capabilities of a free market
- The latter admire the safety net of a welfare system
- The former mistrust the potential over-reach of politicians
- The latter mistrust the actions of profit-seeking corporations
- The former wish to uphold as much individual freedom as possible
- The latter wish to uphold as much social solidarity as possible
- The former are keen to reduce taxation
- The latter are keen to increase equality of opportunity

- The former point to the marvels that can be achieved by competitive-minded self-made individuals
- The latter point to the marvels that can be achieved by collaboration-minded progressive coalitions.

I've already identified myself as a technoprogressive more than a technolibertarian. Individual freedoms are important, but the best way to ensure these is via wise collective agreement on appropriate constraints. Rather than seeking minimal government and minimal taxation, you'll see in the pages ahead that I argue for *appropriate government* and *appropriate taxation*.

However, I'm emphatically *not* going to advocate that left-leaning transhumanists should somehow overcome or defeat right-leaning transhumanists. The beliefs I listed as being characteristic of right-leaning transhumanists all contain significant truths – as do the beliefs I listed for left-leaning transhumanists. The task ahead is to pursue policies that respect both sets of insights. That's what I mean when describing the Transpolitica initiative as "integrative". Rather than "either-or" it's "both-and".

Technocracy and its limits

There's a long history to the idea that political decisions should be taken, not on the basis of ideology (such as left-wing or right-wing), nor on the basis of party loyalty, but on the basis of independent rational thinking, empirical evidence, and scientific methods.

The Greek philosopher Plato argued against using principles of democracy to decide the direction of government[16]. He saw this as analogous to deciding how a boat should be steered through choppy seas and low-lying rocks. That's not the kind of decision you leave up to a vote between passengers – some saying raise the sails, some saying lower the sails, some urging turning port, others demanding starboard. It's far better to employ a trusted expert for the role – especially someone who would be impervious to bribes and threats.

Under the heading "technocracy", similar ideas were promoted in the United States and Canada in the 1930s, by a movement that still exists today. Here's an extract from the website of Technocracy Inc[17]:

> Technocracy wants the people who are designated excellent in their fields,
> by their direct peers, to make the vital societal decisions.

Do we want a farmer telling the doctors how to do their business? Do we want a production manager to tell the farmers what is the best crop for their land?

Do we want profit driven politics to make our decisions on anything?

Technocracy has always wanted the 'Experts' to make decisions.

More recently, Michigan physician Peter Ubel has promoted the idea of "scientocracy", which he describes as "a government of the people, but informed by scientists"[18]:

The key to good policy-making is to understand human nature.

Want to increase how much money people save? You better know what they will do if you change the tax code. Want to reduce the threat of terrorism? All the security in the world won't suffice if you don't, at the same time, find ways to confront the behavioural forces that lead people to commit acts of terror. Want to make health care affordable to all? Policy won't achieve this goal unless policymakers understand the ways doctors and patients make decisions about what healthcare services to use.

In my new blog – Scientocracy – I plan to explore important policy debates through the lens of human behaviour. I intend to not only show why psychological science is relevant to a whole range of policy debates, but to also imagine what policies might look like if they were better aligned with human nature.

Ubel provides this clarification:

When I talk about Scientocracy… I'm not talking about a world ruled by behavioural scientists, or any other kind of scientists. Instead, I am imagining a government of the people, but informed by scientists. A world where people don't argue endlessly about whether educational vouchers will improve schools, whether gun control will reduce crime, or whether health savings accounts can lower health care expenditures, but one instead where science has a chance to show us whether vouchers, gun control laws, and health savings accounts work and, if so, under what conditions.

Political decision-making via the scientific process: what could go wrong with that? And what's the problem with putting politics into the hands of experts in economics, financial systems, psychology, and so on?

Nowadays, the term "technocrat" is often applied as a kind of insult. The implication is that someone may well have elite qualifications, but that's not enough to provide authority over the affairs of state.

Specifically, here are concerns over rule by technocrats and scientocrats:

- Experts often get things wrong. Communities of experts often reinforce each other's views, as a herd mentality. This observation lies behind the infamous remark by UK Conservative politician Michael Gove[19], "people in this country have had enough of experts", referring dismissively in the run-up to the Brexit referendum to professional economics forecasters

- In other cases, different groups of experts reach diametrically opposed answers. Distinguished Nobel prize winning economists prescribe starkly different policies from each other

- Particular scientific principles that have a good track record in one field of science may be less applicable in a different field of science – for example, requiring a repetition of double blind tests. It's by no means always agreed what it means to "apply scientific method"

- Citizens dislike having policies imposed on them by apparent elites, without their involvement or discussion

- A focus on phenomena that are measurable – such as the GDP metric of economic performance – may result in less attention paid to other phenomena that are ultimately more important

- Although science can in principle explain the best way to achieve a particular outcome, it cannot by itself tell us whether that outcome is worth achieving

- Scientists and other experts are by no means immune from distorting their theories – and their evidence – in order to match the inclinations of their political masters. Thus, to gain favour with Joseph Stalin, Soviet biologist Trofim Lysenko championed anti-Darwinian "socialist genetics" theories of inheritance for agricultural products; the resulting famines caused millions to die from starvation[20].

The Technocratic movement ran into public ridicule in the United States in the 1930s when it became clear that the movement's spokesperson, Howard Scott, lacked the academic credentials which he had claimed, and was by no means the distinguished engineer he had portrayed himself as being[21]. What's more, independent analysts found many problems with the movement's proposal to replace the free market "price system" (including the dollar) with a new set of calculations based on the energy required to create goods.

Despite these issues, I stick with the proposal that, *as far as possible*, methods of rationality, empirical observation, scientific analysis, and expert review should be applied to political decisions. To that extent, I see the ideals of technocracy (with a lower-case 't') as one of the pillars of technoprogressive thought. But I say this with two caveats:

- Rationality, empirical observations, scientific analysis, and expert review are often harder than people expect; we definitely should not trust the first few self-proclaimed experts who offer their opinion as to whether something is indeed rational, empirically-grounded, and/or scientific
- Technocracy is only one of *four* pillars.

The four technoprogressive pillars

As this chapter has progressed, I've gradually introduced the notion of technoprogressive thinking. As a summary, I'll break down that thinking into four pillars:

1. *Technocracy*: the use, as far as possible, of principles of independent rationality and scientific analysis
2. *Transhumanism*: the pillar that sets the direction for policy, namely the profound ongoing elevation of all-round human health, human wisdom, human wellbeing, and human freedom
3. *Democracy* – or, better put, *super-democracy*: the active involvement of the entire population, both in decision-making, and in the full benefits of transhumanism; I'll have a lot more to say about democracy in Chapter 10, "Democracy and inclusion"
4. *Urgency* – which might be expressed as *exponential urgency*: the accelerating pace of technological innovation threatens to hurl humanity within just a few short years into a bewildering no-man's land between pitiful existential disaster and a magnificent sustainable abundance. We need to hasten our understanding of the possible trajectories ahead, and equip ourselves to progress at full speed in the required direction.

In case you're wondering: although the terms 'transhumanism' and 'technoprogressive' each go back several decades, the name 'Transpolitica' is relatively new. I coined it in January 2015[22], as my recognition increased for the need for a new think tank dedicated to a different approach to politics.

The Transpolitica manifesto has the following preamble[23]:

Transpolitica holds that human society should embrace, wisely, thoughtfully, and compassionately, the radical transformational potential of technology.

The speed and direction of technological adoption can be strongly influenced by social and psychological factors, by legislation, by subsidies, and by the provision or restriction of public funding. Political action can impact all these factors, either for better or for worse.

Transpolitica wishes to engage with politicians of all parties to increase the likelihood of an attractive, equitable, sustainable, progressive future. The policies we recommend are designed:

- To elevate the thinking of politicians and other leaders, away from being dominated by the raucous issues of the present, to addressing the larger possibilities of the near future

- To draw attention to technological opportunities, map out attractive roads ahead, and address the obstacles which are preventing us from fulfilling our cosmic potential.

I chose the name 'Transpolitica' as a deliberate riff on the word "transhumanism". Transhumanism anticipates tomorrow's humanity:

- It envisages the positive qualities and characteristics of future intelligent life

- It takes steps towards achieving these qualities and characteristics

- It identifies and manages risks of negative characteristics of future intelligent life.

Similarly, Transpolitica anticipates tomorrow's politics:

- It envisages the positive qualities and characteristics of future social structures

- It takes steps towards achieving these qualities and characteristics

- It identifies and manages risks of negative characteristics of future social structures.

Three years after these foundational ideas appeared on the Transpolitica website[24], the need is stronger than ever for joined-up thinking to anticipate the better political practices of the future and to transcend the quagmire of current politics. Hence the book you now hold in your hands.

The next step forwards is a candid assessment of how bad things have become.

2. Battles and bewilderment

Politics has grown nasty – *dangerously* nasty.

In recent times, political topics such as immigration, sovereignty, the EU, Jeremy Corbyn, Nigel Farage, Donald Trump, Hillary Clinton, and Vladimir Putin have become increasingly toxic. Personal relationships fractured, as long-time acquaintances found themselves unexpectedly on opposite sides of spiralling bad-tempered political disagreements. Former friends dismayed each other by championing views previously thought to be beyond the pale. "How can you believe such nonsense?" they gasped to each other, in mutual bewilderment. "Have you taken leave of your senses?"

For many people, social gatherings have become more delicate experiences. We have had to learn to tread gently on eggshells. A *Private Eye* cartoon captured this sour turn of events as it depicted guests arriving for a wedding ceremony. The guests were asked: "Which side of the family: Brexit or Remain?" Sitting with the wrong camp might provoke a bitter dispute that would overshadow what should be a happy occasion.

With political discussions dominated by hostility and suspicion, it's no surprise that the conclusions of these discussions fail to take full advantage of the collective insight latent in the community. Our best ideas are drowned out by the loudest voices or flashy distractions. The unwarranted certainty of true-believers leaves little space for the collaborative exploration of more nuanced solutions. "The people have spoken", we hear. "You lost. Get over it!"

Politics at the speed of light

Some might say that there's nothing new here. Politics has long had its unpleasant side. Ours is far from the first generation in which people have been deeply troubled by the political opinions of their erstwhile favourite uncles or nieces.

However, six factors deserve special attention as we hurtle towards 2020.

1. The numerous ways in which news items can nowadays spread rapidly around the world, aided by multiple connections on social media

2. The proportion of these news items which are deliberately *designed* to mislead, being partially or totally false

3. The way in which these news stories frequently tug on our emotions, triggering and amplifying feelings of "us versus them" warring tribes; these stories set fire to our hearts and smother our rational minds in clouds of confusion

4. The power of software to deliver individually-tailored messages that are particularly effective in amending our political outlook; this software gains its strength by mining our online social media footprints (for example our "likes" and our "shares") and by selecting the optimal time and place to intrude in our news feeds

5. The degree to which participants in debates care little about the truthfulness of the stories they share; instead, in a so-called *post-truth era*, participants care much more about whether these stories will draw applause from fellow members of their own tribe, and whether they will cause anger or annoyance to their opponents

6. The speed of adoption of new ideas that formerly lay outside the bounds of "respectable opinion": the unthinkable becomes thinkable much more quickly than before.

Taken together, these factors mean politics is likely to become worse before it becomes better. They mean that we risk fiercer animosity, harsher irrationality, more trenchant silencing of critical thinking, more draconian restrictions on our freedoms, and sharper spirals into conflict and chaos.

Behind these six factors lies the increasing pace of change of technology. The Internet was widely expected to herald an age of unprecedented knowledge. You've no doubt heard the claim that "A teenager with a smartphone has access to more knowledge than the president did a few decades ago"[25]. But it turns out that the Internet can spread falsehoods just as reliably as it spreads truths. The ideas which leap across social media, propagating like viruses, gain their potency from their "clickability" rather than their accuracy.

It's similar to the way that the "earworm" pieces of music that we find going round and round in our head are frequently far from being our absolute favourite pieces of music. These earworms thrive because of their catchiness, rather than their profundity.

The essayist Jonathan Swift lamented as long ago as 1710 that "Falsehood flies, and the Truth comes limping after it"[26]. Swift sagely pointed out that even when people realise they have been deceived, it is often "too late": the falsehood has already had an effect on them. Their opinions and dispositions have adjusted. They may have altered their loyalties, without consciously realising the factor responsible for that change. As Swift remarked, "If a lie be believed only for an hour, it has done its work, and there is no further occasion for it."

Three hundred years after Swift's essay, falsehoods can fly much faster than before: they circulate at the speed of light. They can also benefit from the fearsome ingenuity of one of the largest, cleverest industries on the planet, namely advertising – an industry that pays some of the world's brightest people huge salaries if they find new ways to capture viewers' attention and change their opinions. In turn, this ingenuity depends on an increasingly rich understanding of the factors that motivate human action. The sad outcome of this richer understanding is that social media progressively amplifies confirmation bias, groupthink, bandwagon effects, and other cognitive biases. Rather than us becoming smarter, we have grown more befuddled.

Falsehoods on the rise

Not only are falsehoods spreading more quickly nowadays, but they exist in greater number. The Washington Post reported in November 2017 that Donald Trump had made "made 1,628 false or misleading claims" over the course of the preceding 298 days – an average of 5.5 such claims each day[27]. The New York Times performed a comprehensive comparison between the false or misleading claims of Donald Trump and Barack Obama while president[28]:

> We applied the same conservative standard to Obama and Trump, counting only demonstrably and substantially false statements. The result: Trump is unlike any other modern president. He seems virtually indifferent to reality, often saying whatever helps him make the case he's trying to make.

> In his first 10 months in office, he has told 103 separate untruths, many of them repeatedly. Obama told 18 over his entire eight-year tenure. That's

an average of about two a year for Obama and about 124 a year for Trump.

The New York Times further explored the difference between Trump and previous presidents Obama and George W. Bush:

> If we had used a less strict standard, Trump would look even worse by comparison. He makes misleading statements and mild exaggerations – about economic statistics, his political opponents and many other subjects – far more often than Obama. We left out any statement that could be plausibly defended even if many people would disagree with the president's interpretation. We also left out modest quantitative errors, such as Trump's frequent imprecision with numbers.
>
> We have used the word "lies"… If anything, though, the word is unfair to Obama and Bush. When they became aware that they had been saying something untrue, they stopped doing it…
>
> Trump is different. When he is caught lying, he will often try to discredit people telling the truth, be they judges, scientists, F.B.I. or C.I.A. officials, journalists or members of Congress. Trump is trying to make truth irrelevant. It is extremely damaging to democracy, and it's not an accident. It's core to his political strategy.

These tabulations of the unprecedented extent of falsehoods by Trump produce vitriolic responses by Trump's fan base. The mainstream press, they reply angrily, are the ones who are publishing "fake news" as never before. Chillingly, the language they use echoes that of Joseph Goebbels, the Reich Minister of Propaganda of Nazi Germany from 1933 to 1945. Trump's term "fake news" recalls Goebbels' use of "Lügenpresse", meaning "lying press." Professor of Marketing Philip Kotler commented in an article in March 2017[29]:

> Trump's aim to subvert the press is clear. He calls the "liberal" news media FAKE NEWS. He says the New York Times and the free press are not his enemy. They are "the enemy of the American People!"
>
> Is this familiar? Isn't it reminiscent of Dr. Joseph Goebbels, Hitler's chief of propaganda? Goebbels job was to use propaganda to prepare Germans to need a demagogue like Hitler to set right their grievances. Goebbels believed that if you repeated falsehoods often enough, they became facts in the minds of the ignorant and aggrieved. Goebbels needed to create a hated "other," non-Aryans and Jews, who threatened the jobs and wellbeing of German Aryans. Ultimately Goebbels managed to get compliance from political, academic, commercial and military Germans

through inculcating fear of being unpatriotic. After all, Hitler's mission was to "Make Germany Great Again."

Goebbels needed the German public to see the press as the common enemy, not just of Nazis but of the German people. Opposing the Nazis was equivalent to opposing the German people. Shortly afterwards, Goebbels shut down all Jewish newspapers and other "messengers of decay." Later he took over the radio stations to spread the Nazi message and vision. Still later, he used the film industry to further Nazi ideas.

In reality, supporters of Donald Trump are generally well aware of the president's larger-than-life character flaws: his "grabbing" womanising, his self-obsession, his unbridled nepotism, the long string of bankruptcies experienced by his businesses, and his torrent of unreliable statements. But they don't seem to mind. They have different criteria for choosing to stand behind Trump. BBC reporter Katty Kay put it like this, in an article entitled "Why Trump's supporters will never abandon him"[30]:

> To understand why somewhere between 35-38% of Americans consistently approve of the job Mr Trump is doing, you need to reframe the way you look at his voters.
>
> It's not what they are for that matters, it's what they are against.
>
> So it's not that a third of US voters are fervently on the side of Donald Trump – what's more relevant is that they are adamantly on the opposing side of a culture war that's been brewing here since the 1980s.

Kay continued:

> Look at it like that and you can see why it doesn't really matter what Mr Trump achieves or doesn't achieve.
>
> He defies the normal metrics for success because his voters don't so much support him for what he does as they adore him for what he's against.
>
> Mr Trump is against the political establishment (the media, the Republican Party, political grandees like the Bushes and the Clintons) and change (which encompasses everything you had but fear you are losing) and he's against the world (which has taken jobs and sent immigrants to take over America)…
>
> If you believe America is engaged in a life-or-death battle over its identity, in which the past looks golden and the future looks, well, brown-ish, then Mr Trump sounds like he's on your side.

We cannot counter the escalation of unpleasant politics simply by appealing for participants to be more considerate, or more rational, or more conciliatory. Instead, we need to address the underlying motivations which are driving people into warring tribes. These motivations arise deep within human nature. These motivations extend far beyond goals of mere material improvement; critically, they include an earnest search for meaning and purpose – a search to see oneself as being "one of the good guys" on the right side of human history.

American author Upton Sinclair wrote in 1935[31] that "It is difficult to get a man to understand something, when his salary depends upon his not understanding it!" That quote rightly emphasises how economic motivation (to earn a salary) can interfere with someone's reasoning abilities. But it's the same with other kinds of motivation. An amended form of Sinclair's quote would read as follows: *It is difficult to get a man to understand something, when the ideas that underpin his sense of self-worth depend on his not understanding it.*

These human motivations are neither intrinsically positive nor intrinsically negative. Like technology, these motivations are two-edged swords. They can lead to greater human flourishing, but can also lead to greater human alienation.

As technology becomes more powerful, and as technology changes more quickly than in previous times, the likelihood increases for these underlying human tendencies to cause dramatic changes in human social structures. Technology will magnify effects that previously had lesser impact.

We urgently need to recognise and harness these motivations, before they trample us into a new dark age.

Beyond homo economicus

We humans cannot live by bread alone. Even when we have plenty of healthy food, pleasant shelter, and an abundance of material possessions, we frequently feel a strong yearning in our hearts for *something more*. We would be foolish to ignore that yearning.

Psychologist Abraham Maslow postulated a "hierarchy of needs": alongside our physiological needs we also have deep-seated desires for friendship, belonging, intimacy, esteem, and meaning. We can argue about which needs might be more "important". But any approach to society that regards all participants as "homo economicus" – people who single-mindedly pursue their own financial wellbeing – is storing up problems.

Any political policy aimed at maximising GDP (gross domestic product) – the monetary value of all the goods and services produced – risks leaving voters deeply unsatisfied. Regardless of how much bread, cakes, designer clothing, electronic gadgets, package holidays, and entertainment gizmos voters possess, these voters remain vulnerable to promises of would-be leaders who seem to offer a route to *something more* – the chance to attain meaning in some kind of historic or cosmic sense.

This helps to explain the ongoing success of fundamentalist religious preachers. It also speaks to the success of new social movements that display at least some of the same "other worldly" trappings.

One striking feature of the Brexit debate in the UK was the way in which many people said they would prefer to leave the EU, even if that imposed financial drawbacks. They could accept a short-term drop in the wellbeing of the economy, as a price worth paying for what they saw as more desirable outcomes. Far better, they said, to be in control of our own destiny – to regain national sovereignty from "unelected officials in Brussels" – even if that move would (for a while at least) reduce trade. And far better to reduce what was perceived as a bewildering flow of immigration, even if these immigrants were, on the whole, adding to the national GDP due to their skills and industriousness. For these voters, there were more important factors to weigh up than economic prosperity.

For a different example of personal motivations that rejoice in an adverse turn of events, consider this kick-in-the-teeth joke recounted by analyst Ronald Bailey of Reason[32]:

> An old Russian joke tells the story of a peasant with one cow who hates his neighbour because he has two. A sorcerer offers to grant the envious farmer a single wish. "Kill one of my neighbour's cows!" he demands.

Bailey comments as follows:

> Research by two British economists, Daniel Zizzo of Oxford University and Andrew Oswald of Warwick University, suggests there is a good bit of truth behind that joke. In a recent study[33], Zizzo and Oswald ask, "Are People Willing to Pay to Reduce Others' Incomes?" "The short answer to this question is: yes," they report. "Our subjects gave up large amounts of their cash to hurt others in the laboratory."

Another Russian joke has an even harsher punchline:[34]

A genie says to a peasant, "I will grant you any wish, but remember that I will give your neighbour twice what I give you." The peasant thinks for a while and responds, "Poke out one of my eyes."

A different version of this joke has the peasant asking to be deprived of one of his testicles.

Lurking behind the malice in these jokes is an important truth of human society. Progress depends not just on the heroics of individual performers, but also on the cooperation of people within groups. In turn, cooperation depends not just on reciprocity ("I'll scratch your back if you scratch my back") but on the willingness of group members to punish free-riding cheaters in their midst – the people who take (or appear to take) more than their fair share of group spoils. Without individuals being able to punish these free-riders – even at potential cost to themselves – the group would become torn apart by the selfish-individualism of these free-riders. Having lost its effectiveness, everyone in the group would suffer. For groups to survive, the *wellbeing of the group* sometimes needs to trump the *wellbeing of the individual*. Individuals with too many cows, who threaten group harmony, sometimes need to be taken down a peg.

We notice strangers jumping forwards in a queue, and we shout out to them to decry their behaviour, even if we're not directly impacted by the cheater. We may chase a mugger in the street, at considerable risk to our own personal safety, because our blood boils with indignation at the callous selfishness of the perpetrator, even if we have never seen him (or his victim) before.

Similarly, if the apparent elites of society apparently take too large a share of national wealth to themselves, or seem to disregard the opinions and needs of large sections of the electorate, then, once again, our blood may boil. Frustrated and overheated, we give our vote to those would-be leaders of society who draw attention to these issues, and who claim that they'll do something about it. They promise to shake up the system. And even if our cool reason might tell us there is personal danger in trusting such leaders – just as there is personal danger in chasing muggers – our deep-seated instincts tell us that this is our human duty.

These instincts are a critical part of our human makeup. They can be a force for good as well as a force for ill. Alas, politicians of all stripes have grown increasingly savvy in leveraging these instincts for their own electoral gains. They deliberately stir up resentment and grievance. Provoked and outraged, electors are becoming *more* frustrated and *more* overheated. Cool reason is losing out.

In search of status

As I said, we humans cannot live by bread alone. We also need the support of social groups with whom we can identify. John Donne put the sentiment in verse back in 1623:[35]

> No man is an island, entire of itself;
>
> Every man is a piece of the continent, a part of the main

When members of our social group suffer, that's something which concerns us as well. Writing whilst seriously ill and facing death himself, Donne memorably phrased that insight as follows:

> Any man's death diminishes me…
>
> Therefore never send to know for whom the bell tolls;
>
> It tolls for thee.

Of course, we don't all articulate sentiments like John Donne. Many of us feel alienated from members of the groups in which we find ourselves located. We dislike their personalities, their prejudices, their quirks, and their hypocrisies. We may particularly dislike the apparent freeloaders and deceivers amongst them. We may actually rejoice at their misfortune – as per the misanthropic jokes mentioned earlier.

But that doesn't negate our social tendencies. Disliking one group, we seek another, more suited to us – perhaps smaller, and perhaps more geographically dispersed. Social media makes it much easier to find such groups nowadays. We are drawn to these new groups, not specifically because they'll help us economically, but because we feel at home with them. They validate us. They speak to our inner needs. They give us a sense of belonging, even as we feel estranged from the other people in our surrounding. They help us find meaning, even as we lack sympathy for the stated goals of our previous companions. They make us feel cool, or part of a vanguard. They're in touch with a purpose seemingly far more worthy than the commonplace concerns of "the mainstream".

Because we value these new groups, we want to secure our bonds to them. It's not sufficient that we happen, for a while, to be part of such a group. Loose connections are subject to unravelling. Instead, we have profound human desires for *status* in the groups that matter most to us. With increased status, our longer-term security has deeper roots:

- We're less likely to be driven out of these groups
- We're more likely to benefit from whatever fruits can be shared in these groups – physical rewards, social relations, intimacies, privileged knowledge, and control over the evolution of the group.

Our actions, therefore, often have the purpose of heightening our status in the groups that matter most to us. If we have a choice of banners to hold high – or a choice of which messages to publicise on social media – we reach a decision based, not on whether a particular message strikes us as being *true*. Instead, what matters is the *usefulness* of a message *as a signal*. Will that message mark us as a valuable member of the group where we care to have good status? If so, then our subconscious mind will get to work, and the rational parts of our brains will adapt to these messages.

It's as one of my friends-of-a-friend said on Facebook, explaining why she passed on a particular photograph seemingly validating a rumour concerning past homosexual preferences of VP-elect Mike Pence:

I have not verified this, but wouldn't be surprised....

Sharing just because even if fake it would piss this f*cker off.

A cursory online check quickly indicated that the photo in question had nothing to do with Pence[36]. The photo featured a gay porn actor, Brad Patton, who actually only bore a passing resemblance to Pence. Nevertheless, sharing the photo served the dual purpose of:

- Annoying members of political tribes opposed by my friend-of-a-friend
- Drumming up excitement and approval in the tribe she identified with – the tribe objecting to the election of Pence and Trump.

This is only one of very many examples of "striking below the belt" in recent political discussions. In such encounters, veracity limps far behind the fast-flying falsehoods. By the time any retraction might appear, confusion has multiplied, and the various tribes despise each other even more than before. Perversely, people felt good that they had strengthened their status within their own favoured tribes. But political division and dysfunction had accelerated.

A battle worth fighting

To fix politics, we have to work *with* these aspects of human motivation, rather than trying to block them or stunt them. We cannot simply tell people to value truthfulness higher than status within their social networks. That would be like trying to eliminate the spread of sexually transmitted diseases by persuading everyone to sign up for chastity. It's not going to happen. Instead, we have to recognise the reality of human drives, and design systems in which these drives can co-exist with better politics.

Rather than asking people to suppress their inner desire to battle against perceived foes, we have to attract them to a battle that will channel their energies in a truly positive direction. Rather than asking people to compromise on their drives for meaning, community, and purpose, it would be far better to provide a vision in which these desires serve tangible social and political progress. *Step forwards to the Transpolitica vision.*

The Transpolitica vision identifies an immense battle to be fought. This is the battle to grasp the radically better future which technology is placing within our sight. Taking part in this battle will provide participants with a profound sense of value – and with a community of great significance.

But in this case, the battle is no longer against a separate group of people. It's not against a nationality, such as "foreigners" or "immigrants". Nor is it against people from a different class in society, such as "elites" or "capitalists". Instead, the "enemies" in this battle are bad ideas and bad systems. The enemies also include the inherited aspects of human nature which make all of us prone to trip up in our reasoning – serious cognitive flaws[37] such as "confirmation bias", "status quo bias", "bandwagon effect", "gambler's fallacy", "base rate fallacy", "hot hand fallacy", "survivorship bias", "false memory", "anchoring", and the "Barnum effect" (which is one reason people too readily give credence to horoscopes).

Another enemy that the Transpolitica vision needs to battle against is fear. The growth of fear drives people to identify more tightly with the groups they see as providing their identity and security. As such, fear polarises communities and poisons the climate of political debate. In the next chapter, we'll explore the deep sources of these fears, and explore how to turn these underlying sources into a positive rather than negative force.

3. Fear and outrage

One important reason why politics is in trouble is because so many people are afraid. They have become preoccupied with risks of bad outcomes ahead. The resulting fear constricts their minds. It pushes them away from expansive, conciliatory politics. Instead, it encourages righteous indignation, lingering resentment, impulsive reactions, and doubling down on perceived certainties. In a fight-or-flight mode, their brains have reduced ability to regulate emotions or pick up subtle cues from the environment. They grab hold of one insight and stick to it through thick and thin.

The real problem here isn't simply that there are things which make us afraid. After all, humans have lived throughout history in the shadow of violence, plunder, famine, disease, aging, and death. We've had ample reason to be scared witless. Literature the world over is full of twisted tales of brother plotting against brother, lovers being unfaithful, allies betraying each other, and leaders failing to keep the promises they made to their supporters. *Only the paranoid survive*, warned Andy Grove, co-founder of IT giant Intel[38]. That phrase is a modern encapsulation of ages-old wisdom. Fear has been our constant companion.

Violence declines, but outrage increases

Strikingly, it can be argued that we have fewer reasons to be fearful, nowadays, than in the past. That's the argument made in, for example, the 802 pages of Steven Pinker's 2011 book *The Better Angels of our Nature: Why Violence has Declined*[39]. And in his 2016 book *Homo Deus: A Brief History of Tomorrow*[40], Yuval Noah Harari declares with gusto that humanity's epic quest against the three great scourges of plague, famine, and war is close to conclusion:

> For the first time in history, more people die today from eating too much than from eating too little; more people die from old age than from infectious diseases; and more people commit suicide than are killed by soldiers, terrorists and criminals combined.

I essentially agree with the interpretations placed by Pinker and Harari on the data they review. Plague, famine, and war are on the back foot. You'll find further evidence to back up these trends in *Abundance* by Singularity University co-founder Peter Diamandis[41].

But that's not the end of the story. Here are some critical complications:

1. For most of history, there were accepted social and philosophical responses to the fears that pervaded human life. For example, life is full of suffering, but people learned from their elders that they ought to accept that reality. The shocks and surprises of life were part of some divine plan or karmic retribution. For the faithful, there was a hope for a better life in some hereafter. Even for the irreligious, there was a role to be accepted in the circle of life. April showers would lead to May flowers.

2. In present times, people are much less willing to accept slings and arrows of fortune as being outside of human influence. Forget passive acquiescence. If a person dies, then someone – another person – is likely responsible. If famine sweeps a region, it's viewed, not as an act of savage nature, but, probably, as a consequence of political failure. If someone is struck down by cancer, it could be due to an over-stressed life, or a bad choice of diet, or contaminants in the environment – all of which are outcomes of human individual and social choices. That's all the more reason to feel... angry.

3. Today's media magnifies and highlights individual cases of human misery, misfortune, and inequity, as never before. The unpleasant maxim attributed to Stalin, "A single death is a tragedy; a million deaths is a statistic"[42], speaks loudly. It's our human nature to respond viscerally to the graphic images that parade on our screens, depicting specific wretched victims of poverty, malnutrition, squalor, infection, conflict, or abuse. Our rational minds might know that, in absolute terms, fewer people than before are victims of such circumstances. But our emotional, feeling selves react differently. Once bitten, twice shy. Once outraged, we remain upset and afraid, long after the trigger for that outrage has gone from sight. For that, we can thank our 24x7 rolling news channels and our omnipresent Internet.

4. Most cultures have had myths of forthcoming apocalypse. The end of the world has been nigh, or so people have thought, ever since the beginning of human storytelling. Societies that ignored divine commandments or natural hierarchies could expect to be destroyed

by flood, pestilence, volcanic eruption, fire from the heavens, or barbarian invaders. These fables long predate recent worries about modern-day existential risks such as nuclear Armageddon, a complete meltdown of the global financial system, or runaway global warming. But what's new is the apparent randomness and complexity of these modern-day risks. Apocalypse is no longer part of some overarching cosmic plan where humans can intercede by taking well-known steps (prayers, rituals, contrition, good deeds, etc). It will arise instead as the accidental outcome of a fiendishly complicated set of connections. That's all the more reason to be... profoundly nervous.

5. The greater set of choices available nowadays paradoxically increases the level of stress that many people experience. No longer are people's careers and lifestyles primarily determined by the circumstances of their birth. This apparent abundance of choice can provoke greater anxiety – "fear of missing out" – and, subsequently, a visceral sense of disillusionment and betrayal if it turns out that various roles in society aren't actually feasible.

6. Perceptions of inequity matter as much as the realities. Even if the poor are better off, in absolute terms, than their predecessors of several generations past, they can still be roused to anger when they contemplate a widening relative gap to the ultra-rich in society. Even if the poor have access to large flat-screen TVs and hyper-connected smartphones, with capabilities their grandparents could not even have imagined, they can become aggrieved by the differential access of the wealthy to superior healthcare or top-notch personalised coaching. If those born into poorer families have life expectancies nine years less than their more fortunate neighbours, that's cause for indignation. And when the glamorous possession-laden lifestyles of the wealthy are visible for all to see on so-called reality TV, it's no surprise that the indignation surges.

7. Indignation at inequality is particularly intense when someone who is well off is believed to have gained their fortune, not through admirable talent or heroic personal enterprise, but through trickery, deception, expropriation, or other manipulation of a rigged system.

8. The Internet has spread not only news of apparent injustices and atrocities, but also an extraordinary set of *theories* about the causes

of these apparent injustices and atrocities. These outrages are the fault, we hear, of all kinds of shady individuals, organisations, corporations, and systems – who have been operating, we hear, with all kinds of perverse motivations. These theories mix (in various degrees) points of fact, points of conjecture, crude fabrications, sophisticated fabrications, suggestive analogies, solid lines of argument, dubious jumps of logic, and downright fallacies. Fictitious examples created as jokes or as satire can take on a life of their own, becoming claimed as evidence in favour of various theories, with their original genesis being overlooked. New theories are constantly emerging, combining elements of previous theories in novel ways. Most of these theories are quickly discarded, but that still leaves large numbers in active circulation, beguiling and horrifying the people who choose to believe them. Some of these theories can be called "conspiracy theories", owing to their suggestions that groups of people have actively conspired to hide facts or to distort their true motivations. Some of these theories may even be essentially correct. To the extent that these theories refer to powerful villains, they provide yet more reasons for the general public to become both fearful and angry.

Of course, ours is not the first age to have experienced populist panics. Previous moral certainties were upturned during, for example, the era of the Black Death. But that's hardly a reassuring precedent.

What makes populist panics particularly dangerous in the present time is the amount of power that our systems of governance have placed in the democratic process. Previously, society's rulers had some flexibility to ignore surges of irrational fear that swept over the populace as a whole. That's no longer the case today.

Debunking, distracting, describing, doubting

How should leaders (and would-be leaders) of society respond to the fact that large numbers of citizens feel strong mixtures of fear and outrage? These citizens may generally appear mannerly and friendly, but underneath their politeness lurks anger and frustration. They're ill at ease in the world as they see it, and they're prone to take rash action. In extreme cases, they may run off to join overseas terrorist organisations. In less extreme cases, they can cast protest votes in large numbers, giving the finger to the so-called elites. In either case, they contribute to the winds of bad-tempered frustration which whistle around discussion forums. So how should leaders respond?

A first possible response is to try to *debunk the theories that motivate citizens' feelings of anger and dissent*. No, the EU has not dictated rules about the shapes of bananas. No, 9/11 was not an inside job. No, the Qur'an does not require all pious Muslims to pick up lethal armaments in a fight against the unbelievers. No, the scientists who produce reports about global warming are not all part of a conspiracy to hide evidence of sunspot activity from the public. No, immigrants don't lower the economic wellbeing. No, poverty isn't on the up-and-up; it's actually declining, worldwide. So relax. The world's not as wicked as you've been told.

Note, however, that this kind of debunking, by itself, makes little headway on people immersed in countercultural thinking. Each debating point made in the previous paragraph can quickly be met with a counterpoint. For example, the EU may not have dictated the shapes of bananas, but there are plenty other poor EU policies that could be highlighted. 9/11 may not have been an inside job, but Osama bin Laden was for a long time a darling of some parts of the Western establishment. And so the discussions run, and run, and run. After all, the arguments offered in the course of these discussions are often rational confabulations for feelings that are deeply lodged in someone's subconscious mind. These arguments aren't the *cause* of the feelings, but are instead an *outgrowth* of someone's personal dissatisfaction and self-identity. Refuting the argument generally won't cause any positive change of heart; if anything, it might provoke greater bitterness.

A second kind of response, therefore, is to try to *distract citizens away from any preoccupation with radical oppositional politics*. OK, there are bad things happening in the world, but there are plenty of ways for citizens to have a good life. Don't rock the boat. Enjoy unprecedented amounts of low-cost multicultural food, exhilarating streaming music, comic online videos, wonderfully plotted box set dramas, engaging computer games, free online education, discount package holidays, easy Internet hook-ups with new intimate partners, and numerous career opportunities for those willing to work hard and work smart. This is the modern-day equivalent of the "soma" drugs[43] provided to citizens in Aldous Huxley's dystopian novel, *Brave New World*. Indeed, near-future politicians may have at their disposal new mood-drugs that leave everyone happier and more blissful all the time. The distraction would be complete. However, we're not there yet, and present-day distractions are limited in their effectiveness.

A third response, accordingly, is to *describe step-by-step improvement projects that are intended to alleviate the actual grounds for fear and outrage*. This is the approach taken, for example, by Theresa May in the speech she delivered outside Number 10 Downing Street just after being appointed the UK's Prime Minister[44]. Whatever you may think about her subsequent actions (and inactions), it's a speech full of fine sentiment. It's worth quoting at some length, especially for its seemingly candid recognition of many of the problems being experienced by citizenry:

> We believe in a union not just between the nations of the United Kingdom but between all of our citizens, every one of us, whoever we are and wherever we're from.
>
> That means fighting against the burning injustice that, if you're born poor, you will die on average nine years earlier than others.
>
> If you're black, you're treated more harshly by the criminal justice system than if you're white.
>
> If you're a white, working-class boy, you're less likely than anybody else in Britain to go to university.
>
> If you're at a state school, you're less likely to reach the top professions than if you're educated privately.
>
> If you're a woman, you will earn less than a man. If you suffer from mental health problems, there's not enough help to hand.
>
> If you're young, you'll find it harder than ever before to own your own home.

Prime Minister May then proceeded to address the people who "just about manage" to cope with the struggles of life:

> The mission to make Britain a country that works for everyone means more than fighting these injustices. If you're from an ordinary working class family, life is much harder than many people in Westminster realise. You have a job but you don't always have job security. You have your own home, but you worry about paying a mortgage. You can just about manage but you worry about the cost of living and getting your kids into a good school.
>
> If you're one of those families, if you're just managing, I want to address you directly.

I know you're working around the clock, I know you're doing your best, and I know that sometimes life can be a struggle. The government I lead will be driven not by the interests of the privileged few, but by yours…

We will make Britain a country that works not for a privileged few, but for every one of us.

That will be the mission of the government I lead, and together we will build a better Britain.

These improvement projects lie within the broad mainstream of existing politics. In the United States, presidential candidate Hillary Clinton anticipated taking a broadly similar approach: *reform from within.*

But many people *doubt whether such politics-as-usual projects will succeed.* They worry as follows:

- Are the politicians who make such statements being genuine, or are they just paying lip service to notions which they will not pursue?

- Will these politicians be constrained by powerful vested interests, such as media barons, multinational corporations, and various industrial complexes?

- Are today's political institutions, with their traditions stretching hundreds of years into the past, sufficiently suited to the fast-changing needs of contemporary issues?

- Even if improvements are made, might other things get worse even faster than the improvements are being applied?

- Are mainstream political initiatives really capable of getting to the roots of the problems facing society?

I share these doubts. As I see things, humanity is facing a number of fundamental risks. Keeping calm and carrying on may have been good advice in the past[45], but it's no longer viable. The onrushing tsunami of technological and social disruption cannot be tamed by diplomatic hand-waving, adjusting tax rates, or tweaking the budget for welfare provision.

Many others evidently feel the same way as well – though we might articulate our understanding of these risks in very different ways. That widespread deep disquiet provides fertile ground for conspiracy theories and other "explanations" of the status quo. Even if some these theories are debunked, people hunger for more; so new theories arise to fill the void. Even if the distracting marvels of fine living appear in adverts all around us, we remain dissatisfied, yearning for a sense of justice and purpose that mere material luxury cannot provide. Even if mainstream politicians try to embrace us into their pragmatic projects for incremental change, we feel alienated, and we find solace instead in dissident groups. Even in the face of evidence of progress in dealing with poverty and disease, we think to ourselves: *it's too slow, and too little, and probably too late.*

Reasons to be outraged

At the close of 2016, many articles appeared, declaring that year to have been the best ever. Kevin D. Williamson urged readers in National Review to "Stop complaining about 2016, you sissies"[46]:

> 2016 was the best year in human history, and 2017 almost certainly will be better...
>
> In the past 30 years, the worldwide rate of extreme poverty has been halved. In the past ten years, new diagnoses of HIV in the United States were reduced by 20%, and the number of Americans who die from AIDS is today about 14% of what it was at its high point in the 1990s...
>
> Howard Hughes was one of the richest men in the world, but he never drove a car as good as yours. Most of your grandparents never set foot in a house as nice as an ordinary new house in 2016. And the children who are born in 2017 will one day look back on us as *poor*.

Marshalling a suite of statistics, contrarian environmental analyst Bjørn Lomborg addressed the same theme[47]:

> Reading the opinion pages, there is a sense that the world is facing a malaise that exceeds any individual events, and that people are becoming increasingly – and dangerously – divided. But if we take a step back, it is clear that there are many reasons to be optimistic. Indeed, in many ways, we are alive at the best time in history...
>
> Consider rising inequality, one of the year's most frequently addressed topics. To be sure, over the last two centuries or so, the gap between the highest and lowest incomes has grown. But that is because pretty much everyone was equally dirt poor in 1820. More than 90% of humanity lived in absolute poverty.
>
> Then the Industrial Revolution arrived, bringing rapid income growth wherever it spread, with China since 1978 and India since 1990 recording particularly high rates. As a result, last year, less than 10% of the world's population was living in absolute poverty.

Furthermore, developing economies are now contributing to a burgeoning global middle class, whose numbers have more than doubled, from around one billion people in 1985 to 2.3 billion in 2015. This tremendous reduction in poverty has sustained a decline in global income inequality over the last three decades.

Inequality has fallen by other measures as well. Since 1992, the number of hungry people worldwide has plummeted by more than 200 million, even as the human population grew by nearly two billion. The percentage of people starving has been nearly halved, from 19% to 11%.

In 1870, more than three-quarters of the world was illiterate, and access to education was even more unequal than income. Today, more than four out of five people can read, and young people have unprecedented access to schooling. The illiterate come mostly from older generations.

The story is similar in health. In 1990, almost 13 million children died before the age of five each year. Thanks to vaccines, better nutrition, and health care, that number has fallen below six million. More broadly, lifespan inequality is lower today, because medical breakthroughs that were available only to the elite a century or so ago are now more broadly accessible.

In short, the world is not going to hell in a handbasket.

Lomborg's article ends with a rallying cry:

Most of the important indicators show that life is better today than it was in the past. We should celebrate the progress we have made against disease, famine, and poverty. And we should continue to advance that progress, by focusing on the smart development investments needed to resolve the real problems we face.

I echo that rallying cry. But the statistics quoted in such articles paint only a part of the overall picture. A fuller view needs to recognise signs of setback as well as signs of progress; risks as well as opportunities. It's as expressed by futurist Ramez Naam in his excellent book *The Infinite Resource: the Power of Ideas on a Finite Planet*[48]:

"It was the best of times, it was the worst of times." The opening line of Charles Dickens's 1859 masterpiece, *A Tale of Two Cities* applies equally well to our present era. We live in unprecedented wealth and comfort, with capabilities undreamt of in previous ages. We live in a world facing unprecedented global risks— risks to our continued prosperity, to our survival, and to the health of our planet itself. We might think of our current situation as *A Tale of Two Earths*.

The most systematic collation of statistics about trends impacting future social wellbeing is probably the *State of the Future* analysis conducted every year (since 1997) by the Millennium Project. The State of the Future Index comprises 28 separate variables. The authors of the *State of the Future v19.1* report, published in 2017, noted the following in their Executive Summary[49]:

> The State of the Future is a comprehensive overview of the present situation and prospects for humanity, integrating forecasts, trends, and judgments of thought leaders and scholars from around the world sharing important future possibilities to improve strategies today.

> The 2017 State of the Future Index shows that we are winning more than losing, so we have no right to be pessimistic; however, where we are losing is very serious, so we cannot fall asleep either.

The authors proceed to reject both pessimism and naïve optimism:

> After updating global developments and trends within the 15 Global Challenges for over 20 years, it is clear that humanity has the means to avoid potential disasters described in this report and to build a great future. Pessimism is an intellectually cowardly position that need not prove anything and can stunt the growth of innovative idealistic minds. Yet idealism untested by pessimism or unaware of the depth and magnitude of global problems fosters naiveté that can waste our time — and time is not on our side.

> We need hard-headed pragmatic idealists willing to understand the depths of human depravity and heights of human wisdom. We need serious, coherent, and integrated understandings of mega-problems and mega-opportunities to identify and implement strategies on the scale necessary to address global challenges.

> Doing everything right to address climate change or counter organized crime in one country will not make enough of a difference if others do not act as well. The challenges we face are transnational in scope and trans-institutional in solution. We need coordinated transnational implementation. Government and corporate future strategy units are proliferating, but they have yet to sufficiently influence decisions on the scale and speed necessary to address the complex, integrated, and global nature of accelerating change. Intergovernmental organizations and public-private collaborations are also increasing, but they too have to become far more effective.

Underpinning these conclusions is the fact that, whilst there is positive progress in 18 of the 28 variables tracked in the State of the Future Index, the other 10 areas feature as "where we are losing or there is no progress"[50]. Areas of concern include growing unemployment, increasing fossil fuel and cement production emissions, declining freshwater resources, continuing deforestation, reduced biocapacity, a surge in terrorist incidents, growing income inequality (the share taken by the top 10%), and continued public sector corruption.

Even in areas where the statistical trends are in a positive direction, there is cause for concern. *Why isn't progress faster?* Even if the number of people living in abject poverty has declined, there are still huge numbers living in comparative misery and squalor – at risk from diseases that could easily be eradicated, if the world's resources were applied in different ways. The arms trade still thrives on the distribution of devastating weaponry to overseas buyers with poor human rights records and with scant processes to prevent the onward flow of these weapons to radical insurgent forces.

The perceived complacency of many mainstream politicians and business leaders in the face of these challenges generates contempt. Where they shrug their shoulders, saying "We're doing what we can", and then rush off to the next lusciously catered international gathering, this provides added impetus for the conspiracy theorists. They think to themselves: *These elites could be doing so much more. Evidently they don't really care.*

The fog of connections

If a "State of the Future" index had been calculated in, say, 1912, it would likely have shown the same mix of positive trends and negative trends as the one from 2017. Remarkable economic progress was taking place in the wake of electrification, the popularisation of the motor car, the manufacturing of synthetic chemicals, and assembly-line systems of mass production. Countries had put in place early welfare systems with basic pension plans. Public sector efforts in sanitation and vaccination were having noticeable effects on health. Growing trade interdependence between nations led many people to conclude that major wars could no longer be contemplated.

For example, in his 1910 book *The Great Illusion*[51], Norman Angell – a British journalist who was subsequently awarded the Nobel peace prize – argued that war between the great powers had become "an economic impossibility" because of "the delicate interdependence of international finance". Writing for Reuters one hundred years later, Anatole Kaletsky provides additional historical perspective[52]:

> A 1910 best-selling book, *The Great Illusion*, used economic arguments to demonstrate that territorial conquest had become unprofitable, and therefore global capitalism had removed the risk of major wars. This view… became so well established that, less than a year before the Great War broke out, the Economist reassured its readers with an editorial titled "War Becomes Impossible in Civilized World."
>
> "The powerful bonds of commercial interest between ourselves and Germany," the Economist insisted, "have been immensely strengthened in recent years… removing Germany from the list of our possible foes."

As late as spring 1914, Henry Noel Brailsford, a British member of the international commission reporting on the Balkan Wars, concurred[53]:

> In Europe the epoch of conquest is over… It is as certain as anything in politics that the frontiers of our national states are finally drawn. My own belief is that there will be no more war among the six powers.

Oops.

Similar over-confident predictions of ongoing stability, made by apparent experts, were heard ahead of other international crises, such as the financial crashes of 1929 and 2008. Here's an assurance made in a Wall Street investor conference call in August 2007 by Joe Cassano, AIG Chief Financial Officer:[54]

> It is hard for us, and without being flippant, to even see a scenario within any kind of realm of reason that would see us losing $1 in any of those [credit default swaps] transactions.

In view of subsequent enormous losses by AIG, Cassano's forecast was remarkably ill-judged.

What causes such forecasts to fail is:

- Connections that no-one fully understands (and innovations that no-one fully understands)
- Unfounded over-confidence: underestimates of the weaknesses in existing human psychology and the weaknesses in existing social institutions
- Systems that are pumped up and take on a life of their own, via runaway positive feedback cycles

- Sets of ideas that have been distorted from "hypothesis" through "ideology" to "faith" and "dogma".

It would be a brave – and foolhardy – forecaster who would maintain that the hugely complex massively interdependent systems of the present-day have no shocks and surprises left to deliver to us. The kind of systemic breakdown that happened in 1914 could well happen again, all too soon. But this time, the effect would likely be even more calamitous.

Two-edged crises

In the run-up to the 2020s, the world contains more opportunities than ever before, but also more risks than ever before. Both sets of possibilities need to be kept clearly in mind. To the extent that our political and other leaders lose sight of these major opportunities or major risks, that is a legitimate cause for outrage.

In my days at university in the 1970s and 1980s, lots of people were concerned with the risk of accidental nuclear war. Heated arguments took place over the relative merits of unilateral versus multilateral disarmament. Fortunately, the intervening decades have passed without these horrific arsenals of death being unleashed. But that's no reason for congratulation. As a 31-slide presentation by the Future of Life Institute documents[55], there have been dozens of "near-miss" situations where humanity came perilously close to the worst kind of accident. If military leaders had strictly followed their agreed defence protocols, massive retaliatory strikes would have been launched. And you and I probably wouldn't be here today. Thankfully, good human judgement prevailed in all these tense near-miss episodes. However, factors that increase the risks of nuclear war remain in place:

- An increasing number of countries have access to the requisite deadly technology – including the near-inscrutable "hermit kingdom" of North Korea

- Leaders whose grip on power depends on populist grandstanding may become carried away by their own dizzying rhetoric and/or depressed state of mind

- Due to confusion arising from rapidly changing local circumstances, some nuclear weapons may slip out of the supervision of national governments, into the control of radical groups who feel little moral restraint over using massive force

- It's not only the weapons themselves which are vulnerable to being stolen by dissident elements; the control systems that supervise these weapons are subject to being attacked as part of cyberwarfare, with unpredictable consequences.

Nuclear annihilation – with its effects compounded by a likely subsequent "nuclear winter" ice-age – is just one of the major threats to present-day civilisation. Biological weapons involving specially targeted viruses could prove just as devastating. And as I'll explore in more depth in the chapters ahead, other sorts of risk deserve urgent attention too:

1. Increasing social angst and mass protest in response to structural unemployment, lower wages, greater salary differentials, and difficulty in finding meaningful employment – with these changes arising in turn from factors such as workplace automation and dogmatic austerity spending cuts. Torrents of mass disaffection could dramatically eclipse the activities of the Tea Party and Occupy movements in terms of turning society upside down.

2. Intense corporate and governmental surveillance of everything that we do, via numerous sensors, cameras, and other eavesdropping devices, with these systems being vulnerable to misuse and hijacking for all kinds of undesirable purposes. Expect countermeasures from self-declared resistance fighters, and waves of change throughout society in the wake of a subsequent multi-pronged arms race.

3. Crises in healthcare funding, as people beset by chronic diseases demand fuller access to expensive treatments. Extended lifespans run the risk of being accompanied by an epidemic of dementia and a failure of budgets set aside for pensions. The resulting care costs may cripple national expenditure.

4. As more people around the world adopt features of the affluent lifestyles of Americans and Europeans, crises loom due to imminent shortages of fresh water, arable land, and rare elements. These crises could be worsened by increasingly adverse weather due to runaway global warming and by other tipping points in the biological systems in our environment.

5. The major banking failure of 2007-09 is unlikely to be the last. Financial innovations can have the advantage of making new forms of funding available to projects in need of investment, but they often also have the drawback of complicating the network of cause-effect monetary relationships beyond the comprehension and management of regulators. Add in software algorithms following rules that are beyond human understanding, and the stage is set for a financial meltdown that exceeds what has gone before.

6. It's not just banks and investment algorithms that can have adverse effects that are difficult to foresee. Ever-more powerful corporations likewise risk pushing society in unfavourable directions. Industrial policies which make sense for a given period of time – such as subsidies for the fossil fuel industry – can become stuck in a state of inertia, with a narrow pursuit of shareholder returns resulting in a grievous loss of planetary capital. The appropriate balance between government intervention in markets and laissez-faire libertarianism has proved hard to agree. If the biggest companies of all – such as Google and Apple – fall foul of some sudden major crisis, it may prove to be too late for the public as a whole to reassert sensible oversight. "Too big to fail" could take on a dreadful new meaning.

7. Just as markets can fail, so also can governments. Most countries evolved a set of checks and balances, with distributed power, to reduce the damage that could result if an autocrat were somehow elevated into a position of political leadership. However, recent trends have been towards national heads of government with increasing amounts of personal power. Some political leaders may acquire so much wealth they become the richest people in the world. As power tends to corrupt, absolute power tends to corrupt absolutely. That's far from being in the national interest.

8. The intergovernmental bodies set up after the second world war – the so-called Bretton Woods institutions such as the International Monetary Fund, the World Bank, and the United Nations – seem increasingly ill-suited to the complexities of twenty-first century life. Better methods of international cooperation are sorely needed, lest conflicts between diverse national interests spiral out of control.

9. Enhancements to human bodies and brains are at hand, but are highly controversial. Gene modifications and neural implants, to mention just two possibilities, might give some short-term benefits to the groups or nations that approve them, even before their longer term consequences have been understood. It could be like a repeat of the indiscriminate use of pesticides such as DDT or morning sickness drugs such as Thalidomide – each of which were subsequently deeply regretted. Biological modifications to human nature, even if motivated by desires for greater manifestation of human kindness and empathy, could have enormous adverse unpredictable side-effects.

The next nine chapters of this book address the above nine points in turn, as part of a set of wider discussions about the important opportunities that coexist with those existential risks. I will argue that:

- Failures of existing political leaders to comprehensively address these risks diminish their authority, making it more likely that maverick outsiders will seize power – regardless of the actual suitability of these outsiders for high office

- Although there are major risks ahead, this should not paralyse our thinking, or lead us to counterproductive attempts to stifle technological progress

- These forthcoming risks, seen in their larger context, can provide the right motivation for world-wide Apollo-scale endeavours to accelerate the beneficial development of technology, human nature, and the structure of society.

In short, we can transform our legitimate fear and outrage regarding present and future developments, from being a negative force that is sending politics on a downwards spiral, into a positive force to integrate and harness the best skills and insights from around the planet.

But for that to happen, we need to look squarely and soberly at the two-edged crises emerging in our midst. We need to identify the underlying drivers of change, and actively steer them in a radical technoprogressive direction.

Let's start that process by looking more closely at one fear that might be more fundamental than all those I listed above. It's fear of science.

Science and spirit

Whilst we humans have plenty of reasons to admire science, we are increasingly led to fear it as well.

Science deserves hearty applause for facilitating remarkable technological progress throughout recent history. With its comprehensive theoretical models of forces, materials, reactions, orbits, compounds, organisms, genetics, ecosystems, evolutionary pathways, and much more, science has done wonders to multiply our agricultural capacity, reduce childhood disease, enable speedy travel around the world, and create vast electronic systems for education and entertainment.

But despite these accomplishments, science is widely perceived to be a dehumanising force.

To be clear, it's rare for someone to say they are *flat-out opposed* to science. It's just that they fear science risks *overreach*. They fear that society is putting too much faith in science. At least some scientists are getting too self-assured.

As science grows more dominant, there may appear to be less room for some of the vital aspects of human experience. To the extent that scientists assert there's no such thing as a human soul, critics say they know in their own soul that these scientists are mistaken. To the extent that scientists deny the earth was mindfully designed, and assert instead that it emerged mindlessly from interstellar chaos, critics say these views engender chaos in the minds of upstanding men and women of religious faith. *Hence the fear.*

It's true that scientists have often overreached themselves. Consider Antoine Lavoisier, often heralded as the "father of modern chemistry", who enjoyed a reputation as a debunker of superstitious beliefs, such as water dowsing and remote viewing. Born in 1743, Lavoisier emerged as a leading critic of the populist idea that rocks could fall out of the heavens onto the earth. Meteorites, as we would now call them, were too closely tied up in Lavoisier's mind with prescientific fantasies of cloud-dwelling deities hurling thunderbolts at tiresome humans. When peasants in far-off fields reported that a glowing rock had dropped out of the sky at their feet, why, they had probably been drinking: their testimony was unreliable.

There was no room in Lavoisier's tidy scientific cosmology for rocks to exist in space. He declared at a meeting of the Académie Française des Sciences[56] that "Stones cannot fall from the sky, because there are no stones in the sky!" Luminary predecessors such as Aristotle and Newton had held similar views. Then in 1768 there were sufficient reputable spectators to a rock falling out of the sky at Luce, France, that a team involving Lavoisier took part in what was the world's first chemical analysis of such a rock. The chemists found a preponderance of iron pyrites, and concluded that it was simply a piece of normal sandstone that had been struck and dislodged by lightning[57]. Under the influence of such views, museums at Dresden, Vienna, Copenhagen, Bern, and Verone removed from their displays and discarded meteorites which had fallen in the sixteenth and seventeenth century – an act described by the writer Ernst Chladni as "enlightenment vandalism"[58].

Scientists themselves have reported their bitter regret at being carried away with particular projects. As they saw things afterwards, they had let their scientific enthusiasm override their better judgement. Many who were involved in the 1940s Manhattan Project to develop the first atomic bomb were subsequently horrified at the extent of human suffering caused, not only by the sheer blast of the weapons at Hiroshima and Nagasaki[59], but also by the unexpectedly high number of radiation victims[60].

Scientists are particularly unpopular with the administration of President Trump. Trump's cabinet regards with suspicion the views of the scientific establishment on matters such as climate change, environmental protection, and (in some cases) the safety of vaccinations. In July 2017, the Union of Concerned Scientists issued a report highlighting ways in which the Trump administration was sidelining science[61]:

> Since President Trump took office in January 2017, his administration (aided and abetted by Congress) has waged a war on science – undermining the role of science in public policy, giving industry undue influence on decision-making processes, creating a hostile environment for federal scientists, and reducing public access to scientific information.
>
> This pattern of anti-science actions threatens the health and safety of the American people, with the greatest impacts likely to fall on the nation's most vulnerable populations. The science community and the general public have responded to this threat with vigorous resistance, and we must continue to stand up for science if we are to prevent the worst potential consequences of the Trump administration's actions.

The report provides a historical perspective, before enumerating particular areas of concern:

Political interference in government science is not new. Previous administrations and their allies have engaged in many of the same kinds of attacks the report identifies. But under the Trump administration, these threats to the federal scientific enterprise have escalated markedly.

The report documents a long list of tactics being used by the Trump administration and Congress to diminish the role of science in our democracy:

- *Sidelining independent science advice.* The Trump administration has weakened federal advisory committees that provide scientific advice to the government.

- *Appointing conflicted individuals to scientific leadership positions.* President Trump has appointed to the highest positions in government individuals with little science background and with strong ties to the industries they are charged with regulating.

- *Leaving key science positions vacant.* President Trump has taken an unusually long time to fill many high-level science positions, signalling the low priority his administration places on science.

- *Revoking science-based safeguards.* Aided and abetted by Congress, President Trump has allowed politics to supersede science by signing an unprecedented 13 congressional resolutions rolling back science-based protections, including safe drinking water standards and safeguards to prevent worker exposure to harmful chemicals...

This evident disdain for science reflects the wider unease of many voters for the direction in which scientists appear to be headed – towards a world in which scientists increasingly tell people how to behave, restricting their freedom, whilst accumulating more funding and prestige for themselves. It's a world of perceived overreach, in which the magic of human individuality is curtailed. Science may be increasing the efficiency of human society, but at the cost, it is feared, of diminishing human spirit.

Even scientists are concerned about the status of science. They're concerned, not just about attacks on it from outsiders, but at structural problems with the way science is being carried out. In 2016, Vox researchers Julia Belluz, Brad Plumer, and Brian Resnick surveyed scientists from around the world, at numerous levels of seniority, about the status of scientific research. Here's how they described their research[62]:

In the past several years, many scientists have become afflicted with a serious case of doubt – doubt in the very institution of science.

As reporters covering medicine, psychology, climate change, and other areas of research, we wanted to understand this epidemic of doubt. So we sent scientists a survey asking this simple question: If you could change one thing about how science works today, what would it be and why?

We heard back from 270 scientists all over the world, including graduate students, senior professors, laboratory heads, and Fields Medallists. They told us that, in a variety of ways, their careers are being hijacked by perverse incentives. The result is bad science.

The scientific process, in its ideal form, is elegant: Ask a question, set up an objective test, and get an answer. Repeat. Science is rarely practiced to that ideal. But Copernicus believed in that ideal. So did the rocket scientists behind the moon landing.

But nowadays, our respondents told us, the process is riddled with conflict. Scientists say they're forced to prioritize self-preservation over pursuing the best questions and uncovering meaningful truths.

Based on the survey responses, the Vox researchers produced a daunting list of "the biggest challenges facing science":

1. Academia has a huge money problem
2. Too many studies are poorly designed
3. Replicating results is crucial – and rare
4. Peer review is broken
5. Too much science is locked behind paywalls
6. Science is poorly communicated
7. Life as a young academic is incredibly stressful

If science can no longer be trusted – if scientists themselves are doubtful about the value of their work – where should we turn for clarity?

Of course, various people have a vested interest in there being doubt and fear surrounding the findings of science:

- Various business leaders prefer to continue to make short-term profits, by sticking with industrial practices that scientists think will cause problems in the longer term and in the wider environment

- Various leaders of religious communities dislike the way that scientific findings challenge the doctrines of their faith

- Various government departments would prefer a larger share of public funding to come in their direction, with less being allocated to science-driven regulatory policy development.

The right response here is not *less* science but *better* science. Although strong evidence should be required before major changes are made to policy recommendations, good science is about *maintaining an open mind* to possible new phenomena and new explanations. And good science seeks to involve the public as a whole in understanding scientific issues – explaining the evidence both for and against different hypotheses, and highlighting the areas where significant doubt remains.

Thankfully, the survey covered in Vox covered, not just the set of the largest problems facing science, but also a comprehensive set of concrete recommendations to address these problems:

- Fixes for science's funding woes
- Fixes for poor study design
- Fixes for under-replication
- Fixes for peer review
- Fixes for closed science
- Fixes for better science communication
- Fixes to keep young scientists in science

None of these fixes are straightforward, but the encouraging news is that an increasing number of science professionals are aware of these issues and are working to improve the discipline. As fixes are implemented, the reputation of science will be set to rise again.

That still leaves the question of whether science should be seen as somehow opposed to the wellbeing of the human spirit. Transhumanists are emphatically opposed to any such conclusion. They share the sentiment expressed by biologist Richard Dawkins in his 1998 book *Unweaving the Rainbow*[63]:

> The feeling of awed wonder that science can give us is one of the highest experiences of which the human psyche is capable. It is a deep aesthetic passion to rank with the finest that music and poetry can deliver. It is truly one of the things that make life worth living.

As the book's publisher explains, the title of the book refers to a famous retort by the poet John Keats, concerning Newton's celebrated decomposition of white light into the colours of the rainbow. Was the beauty of the rainbow diminished by Newton's scientific experiment?

> Did Newton "unweave the rainbow" by reducing it to its prismatic colours, as Keats contended? Did he, in other words, diminish beauty? Far from it, says acclaimed scientist Richard Dawkins; Newton's unweaving is the key to much of modern astronomy and to the breathtaking poetry of modern cosmology. Mysteries don't lose their poetry because they are solved: the solution often is more beautiful than the puzzle, uncovering deeper mysteries.

Indeed, science can be an excellent ally to humanity, as we transcend the earlier period of our evolutionary history – a period in which blind faith often played a necessary role – into a period where constructive scepticism is the key to the richest of experiences. On this subject, I'll turn one more time to Dawkins and *Unweaving the Rainbow*:

> Not to grow up properly is to retain our 'caterpillar' quality from childhood (where it is a virtue) into adulthood (where it becomes a vice). In childhood our credulity serves us well. It helps us to pack, with extraordinary rapidity, our skulls full of the wisdom of our parents and our ancestors. But if we don't grow out of it in the fullness of time, our caterpillar nature makes us a sitting target for astrologers, mediums, gurus, evangelists and quacks.
>
> The genius of the human child, mental caterpillar extraordinary, is for soaking up information and ideas, not for criticizing them. If critical faculties later grow it will be in spite of, not because of, the inclinations of childhood. The blotting paper of the child's brain is the unpromising seedbed, the base upon which later the sceptical attitude, like a struggling mustard plant, may possibly grow. We need to replace the automatic credulity of childhood with the constructive scepticism of adult science.

Should we be content to leave citizens as "a sitting target for astrologers, mediums, gurus, evangelists and quacks"? (Nowadays any such list of the exploiters of scientific illiteracy would add in populist demagogues.) Or should we instead battle to prepare ourselves to take full collective advantage of the best that science can offer?

That's definitely a battle worth fighting. The "constructive scepticism of adult science" will play a vital role in addressing the major risks highlighted in each of the nine chapters that follow.

Evidence ahead

To help orient you on your way through the material ahead, look out for evidence that I will be offering from time to time in support of what I have labelled the four technoprogressive pillars. That is, look out for evidence of:

- The possibilities for extending and improving the technocratic application of empirical analysis and "the constructive scepticism of adult science"

- The merit of adopting inclusive, democratic approaches to the risks and opportunities ahead, and the dangers in relying on "hands off" libertarian approaches or elitist top-down prescriptions

- The relevance of the paradigm-busting ideas of transhumanism, setting out a motivational higher vision of what we all can achieve

- The urgency of accelerating serious analysis of the scenarios and options available to us: *now is no time for complacency*.

Let's move on to the looming crisis of work and purpose.

4. Work and purpose

The robots are coming. In the worst case, sometime later this century, they might run amok and kill us all. That's the Terminator scenario. It's not as absurd as you might think. After all, software, which is the animating power behind modern robots, has a history of going wrong. And super-complex software has a risk of going super-wrong.

We'll come back to the Terminator scenario in later chapters. For now, however, there's a shorter-term worry to consider. Instead of robots that might kill humans, we have to think about robots that might kill jobs. Robots may become so good at doing the kinds of work that we humans currently get paid to do, that our present jobs might disappear. The short label for this process is "technological unemployment".

Technological unemployment is a prospect which causes a lot of alarm. But the Transpolitica vision sees a larger opportunity in the rise of robots. Society should be able to welcome the disappearance of the need for people to undertake work that has often been tiresome, tedious, dangerous, or dispiriting. With the help of robots, we should all be able to spend much more of our time in activities that express and enhance our humanity.

The rise of the robots

Robots have been killing jobs, on noteworthy scale, since the first Industrial Revolution. Weaving machines were invented that could automate many of the tasks in the textile industry better than human weavers. Machines that drilled, hoed, rotated, or reaped dramatically changed the work of agricultural labourers. Assembly-line machinery transformed the work that needed to be done in factories. Word processors and spreadsheets – robots of a different kind – reduced the need for manual clerical staff. And that's just the start.

According to figures cited in a report from the United States Department of Agriculture[64], 41% of the nation's workforce was employed in agriculture in 1900. By 1930, this figure had fallen to 21.5%; by 1945, 16%; by 1970, 4%, and by 2000, only 1.9%. The report observes the profound transformation of rural America from "labour intensive" to "highly productive and mechanized":

Early 20th century agriculture was labour intensive, and it took place on a large number of small, diversified farms in rural areas where more than half of the U.S. population lived. These farms employed close to half of the U.S. workforce, along with 22 million work animals, and produced an average of five different commodities. The agricultural sector of the 21st century, on the other hand, is concentrated on a small number of large, specialized farms in rural areas where less than a fourth of the U.S. population lives. These highly productive and mechanized farms employ a tiny share of U.S. workers and use 5 million tractors in place of the horses and mules of earlier days.

The decline in use of "work animals", such as horses, deserves further attention. The total number of horses in the United States in 1900 was just over 21.5 million. This figure increased to a peak of 27.5 million in 1910, before declining to 16.7 million in 1935, 7.6 million in 1950, and just 3.1 million in 1960[65]. That's a population reduction *of nearly 90%* over fifty years.

Automation in transport and agriculture meant horses were needed in much smaller numbers than before. The equine population has subsequently increased again from that low point, on account of the growing use of horses in sport and leisure, but the figures remain far lower than at their 1910 peak. There are far fewer "jobs" for horses to do.

As for horses, so also for humans? Will new sorts of robot result in there being many fewer jobs for us humans to do?

A key difference between the two species is that humans are much more adaptable than horses. Human labourers who used to work on farms could move to cities and find new employment in factories, shops, restaurants, hairdressers, banks, and so on. What's more, humans have been able to use their brainpower to learn very different kinds of skills, including jobs that could hardly have been imagined in earlier generations. My grandparents in the 1930s wouldn't have been terribly surprised by a prediction that one of their grandchildren (that is, me) would spend part of his career as a mathematics teacher. But the concept of a software engineer, which I became afterwards, would have been alien to them. Mention of a neural network engineer (the profession of one of their great grandchildren) would have puzzled them even more.

This growth of new types of job is sometimes said to take the sting out of the encroachment by robots into the workforce. For example, consultants at Deloitte drew the following conclusions after studying census data in the UK from 1871 up to 2011[66]:

- Technology has created more jobs than it has destroyed in the last 144 years

- It has been saving us from dull, repetitive and dangerous work. Agriculture was the first major sector to experience this change. In 1871 it employed 6.6% of the workforce of England and Wales. Today that stands at 0.2%, a 95% decline

- Overall, technological innovation has resulted in fewer humans being deployed as sources of muscle power and more engaged in jobs involving the nursing and care of others. Just 1.1% of the workforce was employed in the caring professions during the 1871 census. By 2011, these professions employed almost a quarter of the England and Wales workforce

- Technology has boosted employment in knowledge-intensive sectors such as medicine, accounting and professional services

- Finally technology has lowered the cost of essentials, raising disposable incomes and creating new demand and jobs. In 1871, there was one hairdresser for every 1,793 English and Welsh citizens; now there is one for every 287.

The authors of this report, Ian Stewart, Debapratim De and Alex Cole, made these comments[67]:

> The dominant trend is of contracting employment in agriculture and manufacturing being more than offset by rapid growth in the caring, creative, technology and business services sectors. Machines will take on more repetitive and laborious tasks, but seem no closer to eliminating the need for human labour than at any time in the last 150 years.

But can this "dominant trend" really be projected forwards into the future? In this chapter, I'll argue that such a projection is unsound.

Extrapolating this trend requires there to exist skills where humans perform better than robots, artificial intelligence, and all other forms of automation. The extrapolation assumes the existence of "uniquely human talents" which can continue to give humans a competitive edge in the employment market place. In that case, so long as we humans are willing to be adaptable and to retrain, we'll keep one step ahead of the robots.

Consider traits such as creativity, compassion, emotional awareness, personal coaching, concept formation, "common sense", and intuition.

These human traits all *appear* to involve features beyond mechanical computation. And consider the kinds of ad-hoc skills needed by a professional such as a plumber, for whom each new plumbing repair task might involve an unpredictably different configuration of pipes, valves, cupboards, and household goods cluttering up these cupboards. What kind of robot could deal with all that variety?

However, impressions can be deceptive. Just because software, today, cannot perform a particular task, it does not mean the task will forever remain outside the reach of software. There has been a long history of tasks which initially appeared to be fundamentally beyond the capability of automation, but which were subsequently demonstrated as within the power of automation after all.

Automation accelerates

As recently as 2004, economists Frank Levy of MIT and Richard Murnane of Harvard confidently included the task of "driving a truck" in a list of occupations for which "computerization should have little effect on the percentage of the work force engaged in these tasks". This claim was part of an analysis in their book *The New Division of Labor: How computers are creating the next job market*[68]. This extract summarises part of their argument:

> [Consider] non-routine manual tasks: physical tasks that cannot be well-described as following a set of If-Then-Else rules, because they require optical recognition and fine motion control that have proven extremely difficult for computers to carry out. Examples include driving a truck, cleaning a building, and setting gems in engagement rings. Computers do not complement human effort in carrying out such tasks. As a result, computerization should have little effect on the percentage of the work force engaged in these tasks.

Since these words were written, the capabilities of self-driving vehicles have progressed enormously. In October 2016, a self-driven truck powered by software from Uber made its way along Interstate 25 in Colorado, to deliver 50,000 cans of Budweiser beer, in what was hailed as "the world's first autonomous truck delivery"[69]. Although this was a demonstration stunt rather than the launch of a regular line of business, few writers today would dare to defend the 2004 claim of Levy and Murnane that ongoing computerisation will have "little effect" on the profession of truck driving. The argument has changed from "if" to "when".

Much of this improvement is due to advances in computer hardware: faster processor clock-speeds, larger memory storage, and smarter, more numerous sensors. Even more significant is the enhancements in the software discipline known as "machine learning". Machine learning has in turn transformed fields such as optical recognition (computer vision). Remarkably, software is now often more reliable than humans in classifying particular kinds of picture[70]. As we'll see, that's only one of many dramatic examples of machine learning enabling software to catch up with human capabilities.

Machine learning turns on its head the basic idea of the first era of artificial intelligence. In that first era, the algorithms for calculation were supplied by human programmers. The software acted on these algorithms to transform a set of input data into a set of output data. These algorithms would include lots of detail about special cases, such as individual irregular verb conjugation and noun declension (for translating text from one language into another), or disambiguation rules for sounds commonly confused with each other (for speech recognition software).

In contrast, in the era of machine learning, the software is presented with matching sets of input and output data – such as text in two different languages – and in effect infers by itself the algorithms to turn the one into the other. Once these algorithms have been verified by their performance on a set of "training data", they can be applied to new data, where they frequently exceed the power of any algorithm provided by a human programmer.

As well as computer vision, machine learning has transformed tasks such as speech recognition, computer language translation, and email spam identification. Special examples of computer vision include traffic sign recognition, face recognition, lip reading, and emotion inference.

Machine learning powers ahead

Machine learning has existed, in various forms, almost as long as standard artificial intelligence. But it's only in the present decade that it has achieved significant results – aided by much more powerful computers, and larger datasets, than were previously available.

New software techniques have also helped. In what is called "deep learning", the learning system is broken down into multiple layers. Each layer aggregates or analyses information in lower layers, before its own output is processed in turn by higher layers. For example, groups of points in an image may be recognised as forming lines; groups of lines as forming noses, cheeks, chins, and so on; groups of facial features as forming faces; and groups of bodily features as forming individual people or animals, etc. In this example, the intermediate layers have all been described in terms that are familiar to human observers. However, in practice, the key features of the various intermediate layers can arise spontaneously and unpredictably, and often defy easy description.

The 2015 book *The Master Algorithm*[71], by University of Washington professor of computer science and engineering Pedro Domingos, provides a helpful survey of the impressive progress being made across the entire field of machine learning. The book is subtitled "How the quest for the ultimate learning machine will remake the world".

As Domingos sees things, there are currently five different "tribes" within the overall machine learning community. Each tribe has its origin in a different field of academic research, and also its own idea for the starting point of the (future) master algorithm:

- "Symbolists" have their origin in logic and philosophy; their core algorithm is "inverse deduction"
- "Connectionists" have their origin in neuroscience; their core algorithm is "back-propagation"
- "Evolutionaries" have their origin in evolutionary biology; their core algorithm is "genetic programming"
- "Bayesians" have their origin in statistics; their core algorithm is "probabilistic inference"
- "Analogizers" have their origin in psychology; their core algorithm is "kernel machines".

What's likely to happen over the next decade or two is that a single master algorithm will emerge that unifies all the above approaches – and, thereby, delivers great engineering power. Domingos suggests a comparison with the progress made by physics towards the unification of the fundamental forces of nature under a single theory.

Deep learning also powers the AlphaGo software of Google's DeepMind subsidiary, which in March 2016 out-performed the human Go champion 4-1 in a match held in Seoul, South Korea. This happened just over two years after the President of the International Computer Games Association, David Levy[72] told me, in an interview[73],

> I would guess that we are twenty years away from having a Go program that can play at a level equivalent to [chess world champions] Kasparov or Carlsen.

The actual progress was nearly ten times faster than Levy forecast.

Levy was by no means alone in such a prediction. Prior to AlphaGo, the best software for playing Go was *Crazy Stone*, written by independent AI researcher Rémi Coulom[74]. Asked in May 2014 when a machine could beat the best humans, in a level match, his answer was "maybe ten years"[75]. Professional Go players, aware of Coulom's prediction, expressed scepticism. Ten years was *too soon*, they thought. Here's some analysis by Wired journalist Alan Levinovitz[76] at that time:

> While programmers are virtually unanimous in saying computers will eventually top the humans, many in the Go community are skeptical. "The question of whether they'll get there is an open one," says Will Lockhart, director of the Go documentary *The Surrounding Game*. "Those who are familiar with just how strong professionals really are, they're not so sure."
>
> According to University of Sydney cognitive scientist and complex systems theorist Michael Harré, professional Go players behave in ways that are incredibly hard to predict. In a recent study, Harré analyzed Go players of various strengths, focusing on the predictability of their moves given a specific local configuration of stones. "The result was totally unexpected," he says. "Moves became steadily more predictable until players reached near-professional level. But at that point, moves started getting less predictable, and we don't know why…"
>
> This could mean that computer programs will eventually hit another wall.

But there was no wall. It didn't take an extra twenty years of effort, as Levy had suggested. It didn't even take the ten years forecast by Coulom. The goal was reached in just two years.

The significance of this result is more than simply that it was achieved faster than most experts had predicted. The significance is that it provides evidence of software with "artificial intuition"[77].

Top human players often choose a move in Go because "it feels right" to them. They cannot begin to calculate all possibilities, as games each generate their own complex patterns of black and white stones on the

19x19 board. But part of their minds tells top players that a particular arrangement of black and white stones "looks" strong (or weak). It is therefore said that these players have developed a deep intuition for picking good moves. Demis Hassabis, the CEO of DeepMind, explains[78]:

> "Good positions look good. It seems to follow some kind of aesthetic. That's why it has been such a fascinating game for thousands of years."

Similar principles were programmed into AlphaGo. By playing millions of games, the software developed its own principles for evaluating the strengths of different patterns of stones. These principles were embodied in the numerous layers of a deep neural network. The result, in effect, was artificial intuition.

This is not to claim that the software was conscious. Nor that it had any genuine feelings. Far from it. But it could make sense out of situations in which, previously, it was thought that deep human intuition would be needed. AlphaGo did this without calculating all possibilities – something that would in any case be impossible, given the vast number of possible games that could branch ahead from any given position. It did this by noticing key recurring patterns in the midst of overwhelming complexity.

80% job transformation?

As I mentioned, machine learning heralds a second era of artificial intelligence – one in which software plays a big part in determining the rules by which it operates. Software notices patterns and connections in the data surrounding it, and adjusts its algorithms in light of its observations. The result is software which is more adaptable, more responsive, and more flexible. In short, the software is more human. More accurately, the software displays characteristics which formerly were possessed only by humans.

Other developments amplify this pattern. Robots can pick up indications about human emotional states, and adjust their interaction style to match. They can display smiling faces, speak in calm tones, inject the right length of pauses into sentences, and even provide a reassuring touch or gentle squeeze to humans nearby. They can ingest large amounts of music, and create new music that listeners really enjoy. Before long, they'll be saying such interesting things to us, listening so attentively to our replies, and offering advice to us in exactly the right way, that we'll often prefer interacting with them to dealing with prickly human colleagues. For more on this topic, I recommend the 2017 book *Heart of the Machine* by Richard Yonck[79].

Evidently, there will be big implications for jobs – not just for truck drivers and taxi drivers, but for numerous other occupations. Robots have the potential to operate reliably, without getting tired, inebriated, distracted, or annoyed. They can communicate their learnings to each other, via "the Internet of Robots", with the result that they can all benefit from the new experiences and insights of any one of them. Add in the soft skills mentioned above to their powerful computational skills and robust mechanical strengths, and robots become very attractive as replacements for temperamental human employees. Employers concerned about costs and about quality are bound to consider hiring fewer humans and more robots.

This is a worldwide phenomenon. In May 2016, the South China Morning Post reported the following announcement from department head Xu Yulian, regarding factories in Kunshan, Jiangsu province[80]:

> The Foxconn factory has reduced its employee strength from 110,000 to 50,000, thanks to the introduction of robots. It has tasted success in reduction of labour costs. More companies are likely to follow suit.

On a smaller scale, but with wide implications for other companies in the near future, the Guardian reported from Japan in January 2017 that "Insurance firm Fukoku Mutual Life Insurance is making 34 employees redundant and replacing them with IBM's Watson Explorer AI"[81]:

> A future in which human workers are replaced by machines is about to become a reality at an insurance firm in Japan, where more than 30 employees are being laid off and replaced with an artificial intelligence system that can calculate payouts to policyholders.

> Fukoku Mutual Life Insurance believes it will increase productivity by 30% and see a return on its investment in less than two years. The firm said it would save about 140m yen (£1m) a year after the 200m yen (£1.4m) AI system is installed this month. Maintaining it will cost about 15m yen (£100k) a year.

> The move is unlikely to be welcomed, however, by 34 employees who will be made redundant by the end of March.

> The system is based on IBM's Watson Explorer, which, according to the tech firm, possesses "cognitive technology that can think like a human",

enabling it to "analyse and interpret all of your data, including unstructured text, images, audio and video".

Looking slightly further into the future, legendary Silicon Valley investor Vinod Khosla – co-founder of Sun Microsystems – went on record in 2012 with the following prediction[82]:

> By 2025, 80% of the functions doctors do will be done much better and much more cheaply by machines and algorithms.

Writing more recently – in September 2016 – Khosla offered some clarifying remarks[83]:

> Technology will reinvent healthcare as we know it. It is inevitable that, in the future, the majority of physicians' diagnostic, prescription and monitoring, which over time may approach 80% of total doctors'/internists' time spent on medicine, will be replaced by smart hardware, software, and testing. This is not to say 80% of physicians will be replaced, but rather 80% of what they currently do might be replaced so the roles doctors/internists play will likely be different and focused on the human aspects of medical practice such as empathy and ethical choices.

Medical doctors are just one of the set of occupations considered in the book *The Future of the Professions: How Technology Will Transform the Work of Human Experts* by father-and-son author pair Richard and Daniel Susskind. The authors review the likely evolution of work for lawyers, auditors, university lecturers, judges, accountants, architects, consultants, and even clergy, as well as doctors. In what may be the most comprehensive analysis of this subject to date, the authors highlight the likelihoods for major transformations ahead in all these professions – driven by cost pressures, and enabled by ever-more sophisticated automation[84]:

> In an Internet society, according to Richard Susskind and Daniel Susskind, we will neither need nor want doctors, teachers, accountants, architects, the clergy, consultants, lawyers, and many others, to work as they did in the 20th century.
>
> *The Future of the Professions* explains how 'increasingly capable systems' – from telepresence to artificial intelligence – will bring fundamental change in the way that the 'practical expertise' of specialists is made available in society.

The Susskinds share with Vinod Khosla the view that these professions will not disappear. But significant parts of what humans do at present, in these professions, will become automated. If Khosla is correct, that proportion may be as high as 80%. This scenario leaves 20% of present-day tasks to be handled by humans in the transformed circumstances of one or two decades in the future. But if only 20% of the effort is needed, human workforces could be reduced in size by a factor of five.

Limitations to retraining

Here's one response that is often heard to the threat of technological unemployment. Don't worry; humans will be able to retrain, moving to a new profession. That retraining may take some time, resulting, perhaps, in a temporary reduction in earnings. But with sufficient advance warning, people could be encouraged to acquire new skills in parallel with still working on their old job. That would minimise the disruption they will face.

However, note that machine learning is a *general purpose* utility. Any improvements to the mechanisms for machine learning are applicable, not just to a single occupation, but to multiple different occupations.

Therefore, as robots are becoming capable of doing key tasks for Profession A, the same breakthroughs mean that robots are also becoming capable of doing key tasks for Professions B, C, D, and E. Truck drivers who lose their jobs because of improvements in self-driving vehicles may find that, by the time they have retrained to a new profession, robots can do that profession better than them as well.

Computer vision, as already discussed, is one example of a general purpose skill. The same core skill that allows self-driving cars to reliably recognise objects crossing their paths will also allow workplace robots to reliably recognise objects passing through their environment.

The skill known as "common sense" falls into the same category. Common sense depends upon a large network of knowledge about real-world objects, including an understanding of humans and their motivations. Present-day chatbots, notoriously, display a low level of common sense. It's easy to catch them out. However, at least one leading researcher from the field of deep learning has predicted that software with common sense isn't that far away. As the Guardian reported[85],

> Computers will have developed "common sense" within a decade and we could be counting them among our friends not long afterwards, one of the world's leading AI scientists has predicted.

Professor Geoff Hinton, who was hired by Google two years ago to help develop intelligent operating systems, said that the company is on the brink of developing algorithms with the capacity for logic, natural conversation and even flirtation.

The researcher told the Guardian said that Google is working on a new type of algorithm designed to encode thoughts as sequences of numbers – something he described as "thought vectors".

Although the work is at an early stage, he said there is a plausible path from the current software to a more sophisticated version that would have something approaching human-like capacity for reasoning and logic. "Basically, they'll have common sense."

Geoff Hinton, by the way, has been involved in research into deep learning since the 1970s. Other experts in deep learning are less bold about predicting timescales for computers to manifest common sense. However, even partial acquisition of common sense will aid robots in many roles, including customer service, retail, entertainment, counselling, and the provision of therapy.

This stage-by-stage improvement process was good-humouredly acknowledged by Hinton in his interview with the Guardian:

Some aspects of communication are likely to prove more challenging, Hinton predicted. "Irony is going to be hard to get," he said. "You have to be master of the literal first. But then, Americans don't get irony either. Computers are going to reach the level of Americans before Brits."

Even though we cannot be sure of the timescales, we can make the following prediction: it's going to become increasingly hard for humans who are displaced from one job by automation, to quickly acquire new skills that will allow them to carry out a different job that has no short-term threat of *also being automated*.

Robots and humans in work partnership?

Here's a second response that is often raised to the threat of technological unemployment. When costs reduce for part of a task (due to automation), companies can provide their products and services more cheaply, reaching lower price points than before. With larger sales volumes, overall profits can end up higher (even if unit sales prices are lower). Companies can take advantage of these increased profits to hire a larger number of human employees. These humans won't be doing the same tasks as the robots, but will be spending more of their time on the 20% (say) of their original job specifications which cannot be automated. These humans could also get involved doing new types of task that add even more value. In short, automation that destroys some jobs could actually create more jobs overall.

As an example, consider the "hole in the wall" automatic teller machines (ATMs) which allow visitors to banks to withdraw money without having to interact with a human bank teller. ATMs have the splendid advantage of being available 24x7. Banks therefore no longer need to employ humans to perform the comparatively menial task of counting out cash and handing it over to customers. Does this mean that banks employ fewer humans?

Economist James Bessen stated in a 2015 EconTalk podcast that, even though around 400,000 ATMs have been installed throughout the USA since the 1990s, the number of human bank tellers has *increased* over that time period[86]:

> Not only have teller jobs increased, but they've been growing a bit faster than the labour force as a whole...

> The average bank branch in an urban area required about 21 tellers. That was cut because of the ATM machine to about 13 tellers. But that meant it was cheaper to operate a branch.

> Banks wanted... to increase the number of branch offices. And when it became cheaper to do so, demand for branch offices increased. And as a result, demand for bank tellers increased. And it increased enough to offset the labour-saving losses of jobs that would have otherwise occurred.

Bessen pointed out that a similar pattern applied during the 19th century to people employed as weavers:

> During the 19th century, if you look at the tasks of weavers, 98% of the work was automated; yet the number of weavers continued to grow. The reason was the greater degree of automation meant that the price of cotton cloth went down, and people started using more cloth. The demand was elastic...

> At the beginning of the 19th century, people had very few clothes. Clothing was dear. [People] had a couple of sets, maybe... [Later there was a] tremendous drop in the cost of cloth. And people found more and more things to do with it. They got more clothes..., draperies, carpets, rugs – all sorts of applications of textiles... Each time the price dropped,

the demand would kick in and it would increase more than enough to offset the labour-saving effect of the new technology.

Forbes writer John Tamny makes a related point[87]:

What is saved on labour redounds to increased capital availability for new ideas. Jobs aren't finite; rather they're the result of investment... In order for entrepreneurs to make big experimental leaps, they must first have the capital to do so. The profit-enhancing efficiencies that robots personify... foretell a massive surge of investment that will gift us with all sorts of new companies and technological advances that promise the invention of new kinds of work previously unimagined...

If they live up to their labour-saving billing, robots will generate massive profits that will lure even more investment into the companies and ideas of the future.

But observe that the examples noted by Bessen both only run so far. Eventually there's less need for human employment. In the case of fabrics:

Now, eventually we get to the 1920s, 1930s, and we see that all of a sudden demand doesn't increase so much any more. The demand for textiles gets saturated. And we see this beginning of a long, but very slow decline in relative employment and then ultimately around the 1970s, 1980s, decline in absolute employment in textiles. Driven almost all by technology at that point.

And in the case of banking, a reduction in the number of bank branches will cause a reduction in the number of bank tellers. The US Bureau of Labor Statistics makes the following forecast[88]:

Employment of tellers is projected to decline 8% from 2014 to 2024.

Historically, job growth for tellers was driven by the expansion of bank branches, where most tellers work. However, the number of bank branches has been in decline because of industry consolidation and technological change.

The rise of online and mobile banking allows customers to handle many transactions traditionally performed by tellers, such as depositing checks. As more people use these tools, fewer bank customers will visit the teller window. This will result in decreased demand for tellers. Some banks also are developing systems that allow customers to interact with tellers through webcams at ATMs. This technology will allow tellers to service a greater number of customers from one location, reducing the number of tellers needed for each bank.

The story of changing horse population conforms to the same two-stage pattern of tech-driven growth followed by tech-driven decline. I shared some of the statistics of horse numbers earlier in this chapter, but there's an important part of that story which deserves more emphasis.

A prediction that horses would in due course be made redundant by automation can be found as early as 1829, in a painting by British social commentator George Cruikshank. The picture has the title *The horses, 'going to the dogs*[89]. It shows a group of horses staring in disbelief at "A coach without horses!!!... the rummest go I ever saw!!!" Nearby, one dog asks another, "What do you think of this new invention?" The response: "Why, I think we shall have meat cheap enough". In other words, the new "fiery steed" would leave horses without work, and they would be turned into dogfood instead.

For the next eighty years, however, that appeared to be a *bad* prediction. The population of horses in the United States soared from 4.3 million in 1840 to 27.5 million in 1910 – growing at twice the rate of the human population. The railways, rather than diminishing job opportunities for horses, actually increased them. The rise in steamships had the same effect. An 1872 article in The Nation explained[90]:

> Our dependence on the horse has grown almost *pari passu* with our dependence on steam. We have opened up great lines of steam communications all over the country, but they have to be fed with goods and passengers by horses. We have covered the ocean with great steamers, but they can neither load nor discharge their cargoes without horses.

Throughout these same decades, there was lots of speculation that steam power would eventually extend beyond the railways and waterways into ordinary roads and fields. However, critics could point to seemingly major obstacles. As historian Robert J. Gordon has pointed out[91]:

> Disadvantages of steam engines within the narrow confines of cities included the ever-present danger of fires started by sparks, their acrid black smoke, their deafening noise, and their heavy weight, which cracked street pavements.

Horses, it could be argued, had unique skills that robots (automobiles) were incapable of matching. It's therefore little surprise that a famous photograph of the 1903 Easter Sunday parade on New York Fifth Avenue, taken by William H. Zerbe of the New York Tribune, shows a multitude of horse-drawn buggies[92]. If you peer carefully at the photograph, you can spot a solitary example of a new-fangled horseless carriage.

But step forward just ten years to a photograph of the 1913 Easter Sunday parade by George Grantham Bain[93], shot from almost the same location. This time, the numbers are reversed. The scene is awash with motor cars, with just one solitary horse in view. In the intervening ten years, Henry Ford's innovations in assembly line production had radically lowered the purchase costs of automobiles.

When circumstances are ready, changes that have been long envisioned yet also long delayed can take place surprisingly quickly. Pent-up demand finally has its answer. The 1829 forecast by George Cruikshank about the fate of horses did, *eventually*, prove prescient.

In the same way, human partnerships with robots in the workplace are likely to pass through two phases:

1. Initially, the combination results in productivity savings which allows business growth that in turn provides extra opportunities, overall, for the humans in the partnership

2. Subsequently, the remaining tasks that the humans were performing fall under the reach of improved robots, so that the opportunities for these humans in that workforce decline again.

As robots improve their general purpose skills, the second of these phases is likely to dominate the overall story. Humans, like horses before us, will find fewer jobs available to us.

Three possible futures for automation

It's time to take a different perspective on the main trend discussed in this chapter. Let's start with the observation that automation is likely to generate large amounts of additional profits. There are three views on what can be expected to happen to these profits:

1. The owners of the systems of automation will benefit the most, taking the profits for their own purposes, via increases in the salaries paid to managers and the dividends paid to shareholders

2. Employees will benefit as well, even if they are temporarily displaced from the workforce, because significant fractions of the profits will be invested in *business development* that creates new types of work

3. Employees will benefit as well, not via the creation of new types of work, but because significant fractions of the profits will be invested in *social development* that allows people to prosper even in the absence of paid employment.

The scenario that poses grave concern is that society's leaders will put most of their efforts (and most of their rhetoric) into the second of these options, in attempts to "bring back jobs" and "boost employment again", *but these efforts will fail.* The fruits of automation will, in that case, be taken by an increasingly small portion of society: the companies that own the most powerful automation systems and which can take fullest advantage of these systems. To all appearances, the first of the three outcomes listed above will come to pass. The result could be the starkest manifestation of inequality the world has seen in modern times. Without an adequate social safety network being in place – without sufficient effort having been put in advance into wise social development – such a state of inequality could prove explosive.

An analysis of the connection between technology and inequality is contained in a landmark 2014 article by David Rotman in MIT Technology Review[94]:

> The signs of the gap – really, a chasm – between the poor and the super-rich are hard to miss in Silicon Valley. On a bustling morning in downtown Palo Alto, the centre of today's technology boom, apparently homeless people and their meagre belongings occupy almost every available public bench. Twenty minutes away in San Jose, the largest city in the Valley, a camp of homeless people known as the Jungle – reputed to be the largest in the country – has taken root along a creek within walking distance of Adobe's headquarters and the gleaming, ultramodern city hall.

> The homeless are the most visible signs of poverty in the region. But the numbers back up first impressions. Median income in Silicon Valley reached $94,000 in 2013, far above the national median of around $53,000. Yet an estimated 31% of jobs pay $16 per hour or less, below what is needed to support a family in an area with notoriously expensive housing. The poverty rate in Santa Clara County, the heart of Silicon Valley, is around 19%, according to calculations that factor in the high cost of living.

> Even some of the area's biggest technology boosters are appalled. "You have people begging in the street on University Avenue [Palo Alto's main street]," says Vivek Wadhwa, a fellow at Stanford University's Rock Center for Corporate Governance and at Singularity University, an education

corporation in Moffett Field with ties to the elites in Silicon Valley. "It's like what you see in India," adds Wadhwa, who was born in Delhi. "Silicon Valley is a look at the future we're creating, and it's really disturbing."

Rotman goes on to quote legendary venture capitalist Steve Jurvetson, Managing Director at Draper Fisher Jurvetson. Jurvetson was an early investor in Hotmail and sits on the boards of SpaceX, Synthetic Genomics, and Tesla Motors:

"It just seems so obvious to me [that] technology is accelerating the rich-poor gap," says Steve Jurvetson… In many discussions with his peers in the high-tech community, he says, it has been "the elephant in the room, stomping around, banging off the walls."

Various factors behind the growing inequalities of "winner takes all" outcomes are detailed in the 2014 book *The Second Machine Age* by Erik Brynjolfsson and Andrew McAfee of MIT[95]:

- The digitization of more and more information, goods, and services, allowing the owners of powerful data analysis platforms to gain even more insight into improvement possibilities

- The vast improvements in telecommunications and transport – the best products can, therefore, be used in every market worldwide

- The increased importance of networks and standards – new capabilities and new ideas can be combined and recombined more quickly, by those who are well-positioned.

As a result, winning companies take a much larger share of rewards than in previous times. That's great news for the winners, but potentially bad news for everyone else.

This effect is also known as "the economics of superstars", using a term coined in 1981 by University of Chicago economist Sherwin Rosen[96]:

The phenomenon of Superstars, wherein relatively small numbers of people earn enormous amounts of money and dominate the activities in which they engage, seems to be increasingly important in the modern world.

However, just because there is strong market logic to the way in which technological superstars are able to command ever larger incomes, this does not mean that we should acquiesce in this fact. An "is" does not imply an "ought". An enlightened self-interest should cause a rethink within "the

1%" (and their supporters on lower incomes – who often aspire to being to reach these stellar salary levels themselves).

A plea for such a rethink was issued in 2014 by one of the wealthiest members of that 1%, Nick Hanauer. In an article in Politico[97], nominally addressing "fellow plutocrats", Hanauer introduced himself as follows:

> You probably don't know me, but like you I am one of those .01%ers, a proud and unapologetic capitalist. I have founded, co-founded and funded more than 30 companies across a range of industries – from itsy-bitsy ones like the night club I started in my 20s to giant ones like Amazon.com, for which I was the first nonfamily investor. Then I founded aQuantive, an Internet advertising company that was sold to Microsoft in 2007 for $6.4 billion. In cash. My friends and I own a bank. I tell you all this to demonstrate that in many ways I'm no different from you. Like you, I have a broad perspective on business and capitalism. And also like you, I have been rewarded obscenely for my success, with a life that the other 99.99% of Americans can't even imagine. Multiple homes, my own plane, etc., etc.

But Hanauer was not writing to boast. He was writing to warn. The title of his article made that clear: "The Pitchforks Are Coming… For Us Plutocrats". This extract conveys the flavour:

> The problem isn't that we have inequality. Some inequality is intrinsic to any high-functioning capitalist economy. The problem is that inequality is at historically high levels and getting worse every day. Our country is rapidly becoming less a capitalist society and more a feudal society. Unless our policies change dramatically, the middle class will disappear, and we will be back to late 18th-century France. Before the revolution.
>
> And so I have a message for my fellow filthy rich, for all of us who live in our gated bubble worlds: Wake up, people. It won't last.
>
> If we don't do something to fix the glaring inequities in this economy, the pitchforks are going to come for us. No society can sustain this kind of rising inequality. In fact, there is no example in human history where wealth accumulated like this and the pitchforks didn't eventually come out. You show me a highly unequal society, and I will show you a police state. Or an uprising.

As I said, there are two possible ways in which society's leaders can seek to avoid this outcome: the *business development* route that seeks to create more jobs that will pay good wages; and the *social development* route that seeks to create a better social safety network. Both routes need to be pursued, vigorously and intelligently. However, it is my judgement that, sooner or later, the business development route is going to run out of steam, as robot capabilities surpass those of humans in ever more areas. That's the reason to dramatically increase the priority of the social development route.

Two complementary initiatives are involved here:

1. Every citizen should be provided, from the community as a whole, with access to some kind of "citizen's income", allowing them to flourish as a core member of society

2. The costs of the standard elements of life – food, clothing, safety, housing, entertainment, education, healthcare, travel, and more – should be driven lower and lower.

Exactly what that involves is the subject matter of the rest of this book.

Citizen's income Qs & As

Examples of social development, funded by the rewards from automation, are indicated in the Forbes article by John Tamny that I mentioned earlier in this chapter[98]:

> In the world's poorest and most backward countries seemingly everyone works all day and every day. But in the U.S. and other economically advanced countries that have embraced the robot-equivalents of the past, kids are free to enjoy childhood, the elderly are able to enjoy retirement, plus mothers and fathers get to devote more of their time to watching their kids grow up. All of the latter is due to labour-saving advances throughout history that have showered us with staggering abundance for less and less in the way of labour inputs. Robots... signal more of this wondrous same.

Thanks to automation and the general prosperity arising from it, society has more money to cover, *if it chooses*, the costs when people:

*   Have retired from the workforce
*   Need to take a break from the workforce while ill
*   Work fewer hours, in order to be able to look after family members
*   Spend more time in education, training, or retraining
*   Have fallen on hard times, for whatever reason.

With greater automation, and associated greater general prosperity, these trends can be extended. Ideally, people will have the option to put fewer and fewer hours into paid employment:

- Fewer hours worked in an average week
- More weeks taken as holidays, away from work
- Longer periods of time in extended education
- More involvement in voluntary or recreational projects.

Instead of needing to earn money from paid work, people would have the option to receive a "citizen's income" from a share of society's overall wealth.

But any mention of "citizen's income" – or related terms such as "universal basic income" or "basic income guarantee" – spurs a host of questions and objections. I'll close this chapter by listing ten of these questions. I'll also suggest at least the beginnings of answers. These answers reinforce the idea that fuller automation is something that can be embraced and steered, rather than being fought against or feared.

Q1: Isn't the "money for nothing" aspect of citizen's income evidently absurd?

A: It's no more absurd than the "money for nothing" aspects that already provide basic pension payments to everyone (so long as they are old enough), basic educational funding to everyone, basic healthcare provisions, and standard tax exemptions on the first part of people's income (regardless of their overall wealth).

In any case, are these recipients really "doing nothing"? They are frequently making contributions to society, outside of the formal wage system.

Q2: Won't a citizen's income lead to lots of people squandering resources on indulgences and laziness?

A: Not necessarily. The trials of basic income schemes that have taken place around the world so far have suggested that, instead, people take advantage of the additional cash to pursue training, or to start or support new enterprises (in both the business and voluntary sectors).

Human tendencies to wastefulness, including drug abuse or overconsumption, aren't tied to people receiving "money for nothing". They stem instead from other social or psychological problems, which should reduce in the wake of the health-enhancing initiatives discussed in later chapters (as well as by the introduction of the citizen's income).

For more on this point – as well as many other key insights about a citizen's income – I recommend the 2017 book *Utopia for Realists: And How We Can Get There* by Dutch writer Rutger Bregman[99].

Q3: Won't any country that introduces such a citizen's income be flooded by waves of immigrants, who come to the country to receive that income?

A: Countries can impose conditions that need to be fulfilled before a citizen's income becomes payable. For example, it could be restricted to people who have been legally resident in the country for five years.

Q4: Where will the money come from, to provide sufficient citizen's income?

A: Part of the answer is that many of the basics of life ought to become less expensive, due to automation and general abundance. This means that the absolute quantity required for a basic income should reduce in real terms.

But it's true that any system of meaningful payments of citizen's income is going to require significant transfers of funds from the companies and individuals which are benefiting the most from the economy. This means increases in some combination of corporation tax, income tax, wealth tax, land tax, transaction tax, and/or equivalents such as a "citizen's dividend" scheme whereby the state takes an ownership stake in companies and receives dividends alongside all other shareholders.

Q5: Won't the companies and individuals who have to fund social development decide to move overseas, to avoid such taxes?

A: This depends on the fundamental motivation of these companies and individuals. To the extent that they are driven by short-term financial considerations, they may view these taxes as onerous, and fight hard to avoid them. Whether or not this would cause them to relocate overseas is another matter. There may be other economic benefits to staying put.

As it happens, many of the wealthiest people in the world have already committed to initiatives to transfer the bulk of their wealth into projects for social development. This includes the founders and senior managers of several of the world's leading technology companies. By the end of 2017, 173 participants had joined the "Giving Pledge" set up by Bill Gates and Warren Buffett[100]. These individuals see the benefits of well-managed social development. As other individuals and organisations come to appreciate the critical risks to social wellbeing from widespread technological unemployment, expect more motivations to switch from short-term financial concerns to longer-term social progress.

Key to this switch of motivation will be the demonstration of good answers to a number of other questions. Read on...

Q6: Why should hard-working individuals give up part of their income to support people who don't make the effort to enter the workforce? Isn't this akin to robbery?

A: This is a variant of the previous question. Successful businesses generally recognise that their prosperity is due, in no small part, to the support they have received from society as a whole. This support includes public infrastructure (roads and networks), the rule of law, employees who have received public education and public healthcare, and research and development from public universities and other state institutions.

For example, let's examine what made Apple's iPhone such a success. In an article to mark the tenth anniversary of Steve Job's launch of the iPhone, economics journalist Tim Harford raised the question of who should receive the credit for the wonder device[101]:

> We give credit to Steve Jobs and other leading figures in Apple – his early partner Steve Wozniak, his successor Tim Cook, his visionary designer Sir Jony Ive – but some of the most important actors in this story have been forgotten.
>
> Ask yourself: what actually makes an iPhone an iPhone? It's partly the cool design, the user interface, the attention to detail in the way the software works and the hardware feels. But underneath the charming surface of the iPhone are some critical elements that made it, and all the other smartphones, possible.

Citing research from Mariana Mazzucato, Professor in the Economics of Innovation at UCL, Harford proceeded to list 12 key technologies, each critical to the iPhone's success, which were each *strongly supported by government research*:

> 1) Tiny microprocessors, 2) memory chips, 3) solid state hard drives, 4) liquid crystal displays and 5) lithium-based batteries. That's the hardware.
>
> Then there are the networks and the software. So 6) Fast-Fourier-Transform algorithms – clever bits of maths that make it possible to swiftly turn analogue signals such as sound, visible light and radio waves into digital signals that a computer can handle.
>
> At 7) – and you might have heard of this one – the internet. A smartphone isn't a smartphone without the internet.

At 8) HTTP and HTML, the languages and protocols that turned the hard-to-use internet into the easy-to-access World Wide Web. 9) Cellular networks. Otherwise your smartphone not only isn't smart, it's not even a phone. 10) Global Positioning Systems or GPS. 11) The touchscreen. 12) Siri, the voice-activated artificial intelligence agent.

Harford offered this provocative conclusion:

The foundational figure in the development of the iPhone wasn't Steve Jobs. It was Uncle Sam [that is, the US government]... It was government funding and government risk-taking that made all these things possible.

You might reach a slightly different conclusion, in which more credit is given to Apple's leadership, and less is given to Uncle Sam. But it cannot be denied that *at least some* of the huge profits earned by Apple can be traced to significant prior government expenditure.

That's the argument for at least some of the fruits of business success to be shared with society as a whole.

And if society as a whole decides to fund social development projects that include providing a citizen's income, this ought (in principle) to be agreeable to taxpayers.

Q7: Can governments be trusted, to wisely redistribute cash from increased taxation into social development projects?

A: One reason individuals resist paying higher taxes is because they fear governments will make poor use of their tax receipts. That revenue might be misdirected to white elephant vanity projects, to undeserving "cronies" of politicians, to various sectors of the population in order to secure their votes, to overseas military adventures, and so on.

To the extent that politics needs to be fixed – the central theme of this book – this concern has a lot of validity. Before society can fully support the idea of a citizen's income, the reputation of government will need to improve.

This book argues that government can, indeed, regain the confidence of the electorate as a whole, by pursuing an integrative technoprogressive roadmap. But whilst major conflicts of opinion remain, sharply dividing people who feel ties to different sectors of society, any citizen's income proposal is likely to be hotly contested. To find our way through that minefield of conflicting opinion, we'll need the better methods of collaborative decision-making that are covered in later chapters.

Q8: Won't people feel deeply dissatisfied if they only receive a "basic" income? Don't they have desires to have enough money for at least some "luxury" goods? Mightn't this cause social alienation and discontent?

A: It's true that, even though most people nowadays have access to consumer goods and services beyond the dreams of just a couple of generations ago, we still feel strong pressures for "more, more, more…". If we could rest satisfied with the material comforts to which our predecessors yearned, we would be able to survive by working many fewer hours each week – perhaps just 15 hours per week, as foreseen by economist John Maynard Keynes nearly 90 years ago in his 1930 essay *Economic Possibilities for our Grandchildren*[102]. That was the essay in which Keynes introduced the term "technological unemployment":

> We are being afflicted with a new disease of which some readers may not yet have heard the name, but of which they will hear a great deal in the years to come – namely, *technological unemployment*. This means unemployment due to our discovery of means of economising the use of labour outrunning the pace at which we can find new uses for labour.

Keynes speculated that, one hundred years after the publication of his essay, society would be providing sufficient benefits to satisfy what he called the "absolute" needs of citizens. Once that happens, we ought to "prefer to devote our further energies to non-economic purposes". However, Keynes also recognised that we seem additionally to have strong "relative" needs whose "satisfaction lifts us above, makes us feel superior to, our fellows". This is the pressure to keep up with the Joneses, and even to surpass them. It's the pressure to maintain our personal sense of relative importance by acquiring and displaying trappings of accomplishment and success, like the latest model of car, consumer electronics item, fashionable clothes and jewellery, etc. So long as these relative needs remain "insatiable", as Keynes put it – and as long as advertising finds ways to stimulate our desires for consumption – citizens will be driven to work longer hours and obtain higher salaries. And no level of citizen's income is likely to prove sufficient.

One response here is to lament the culture of "conspicuous consumption" and the Protestant work ethic to which it is curiously intertwined. But there's good evidence that "status seeking" behaviour, such as the urge to wear distinctive decorative shells, long predates the rise of modern capitalism or Protestantism. Rather than condemning our desires for "relative" status, in Keynes' terms, we need to devise better ways to accommodate or refine the underlying aspects of our human nature. Rather than asking everyone to accept some kind of bland equality, we need to find ways to enable wide differentiation and experimentation, without such experiments costing huge amounts of money (beyond the levels of basic citizen's income). That brings us to the next question: the all-important question of human purpose.

Q9: Don't people have deeply personal reasons to work, beyond simply receiving income? Without ample work to be done, won't there still be a risk of social disintegration?

A: Work has often been viewed, not just as a means to earn income, but also as a means for self-fulfilment and for the development of interpersonal skills. Work, therefore, provides purpose as well as money. If there is nothing left for humans to do, that cannot be done better by robots, will humans lose their sense of purpose? Might they become vulnerable to joining wild rebellious schemes to obtain a sense of purpose by undermining the society which has left them feeling estranged?

The fear that people may become meaningless, in the face of the rise of robot automation, surely lies behind some of the attempts to avoid talking about this very topic. If human meaning is fundamentally connected to human employment, then anything that threatens the future of human employability is a threat to mental wellbeing. In that case, it becomes tempting to clutch at intellectual straws to try to dismiss the question of technological unemployment. That's why critics keep talking about, for example, "the Luddite fallacy", referring back to the wave of "Luddite" protests around the time of the first industrial revolution, and implying (with no good reason) that automation will continue to create more jobs than it destroys. Discussion earlier in this chapter has shown the weakness in that implication.

However, there's no need to tie human purpose so rigidly to human paid employment. Humans can find deep purpose (and plenty of reasons to work hard) in activities for which they receive no pay. Hobbies, exploration, creative pursuits, sports, puzzles, science, and mathematics are just some examples where human passion can come to the fore.

Note also that people can enjoy doing things, even if they are far from being the best in the world at doing them. Amateur players of sport or creators of art enjoy their endeavours, even though they recognise their capabilities are dwarfed by those of professional experts. As a personal example, I enjoy taking the time to solve Sudoku puzzles, even though I know computers can solve these puzzles much more quickly than me. It's the same with my stumbling activities on the golf course. My sense of accomplishment in occasionally propelling a golf ball close to the hole isn't demeaned by my realisation that other golf players can complete the same task in many fewer shots than me.

But there's an even bigger purpose awaiting human attention over the next few decades. It's the purpose of ensuring the successful transition of society from its present fraught state into a profoundly positive transhumanist future. The alternative to such evolution is to witness social chaos grow into a new dark age, with purpose and meaning hijacked by religious and regressive political radicals, as is already happening in many parts of the world. Steering towards the positive outcome, with humanity poised to venture into unimaginable riches of both inner and outer space, is a purpose which can absorb the passions of people around the planet. It's a veritable "hero's quest" for our time.

The pace of change

Q10: How urgent are these discussions? Isn't significant technological unemployment still many generations into the future?

A: The pace of change is, notoriously, hard to predict. Roy Amara, the past president of the Institute of the Future, observed that[103]:

> We tend to overestimate the effect of a technology in the short run and underestimate the effect in the long run.

That observation, known as Amara's Law, provides *two* reasons for caution about predicting future technological developments. Indeed, the history of forecasts contains grievous errors in both directions: forecasts that things would happen much more quickly than panned out in reality, and forecasts that things would happen much more slowly than reality.

Kevin Kelly, the co-founder and former executive editor of Wired, had this to say about progress, in an interview in March 2014[104]:

> If we were sent back with a time machine, even 20 years, and reported to people what we have right now and describe what we were going to get in this device in our pocket – we'd have this free encyclopaedia, and we'd have street maps to most of the cities of the world, and we'd have box

scores in real time and stock quotes and weather reports, PDFs for every manual in the world – we'd make this very, very, very long list of things that we would say we would have and we get on this device in our pocket, and then we would tell them that most of this content was free. You would simply be declared insane. They would say there is no economic model to make this. What is the economics of this? It doesn't make any sense, and it seems far-fetched and nearly impossible.

In other words, the last twenty years have seen astonishing progress, to an extent that would appear "insane" to people from the beginning of that time period. But Kelly then mentions a view that is sceptical about future progress:

There's a sense that all the big things have happened.

So many big things have happened in the last twenty years. Is there anything left to accomplish? Can science and technology really keep up the same frenetic pace?

Kelly's answer: We're by no means at the end of the set of major technological changes:

We're just at the beginning of the beginning of all these kind of changes.

And for a comparison of what will happen next, to what has happened in the recent past, Kelly predicts that

The next twenty years are going to make this last twenty years just pale.

I share Kelly's assessment. I base my views upon the positive feedback cycles which are in place:

- Technology magnifies our knowledge and intelligence, which in turn magnifies our technology
- Technology improves everyone's ability to access cutting-edge information, via free online encyclopaedias, massive open online courses, and open source software
- Critically, this information is available to vast numbers of bright students, entrepreneurs, hackers, and activists, throughout the emerging world as well as in countries with longer-established modern economies
- Technology improves the ability for smart networking between prospective partners – people in one corner of cyberspace can easily improve and extend ideas that arose elsewhere

- The set of pre-existing component solutions keeps accumulating through its own positive feedback cycles, serving as the basis for yet another round of technological breakthrough.

What's more, insight, tools, and techniques from one technology area can quickly transfer (often in innovative ways) into new technology areas. That's another factor which can result in unexpected acceleration, of the sort mentioned earlier in this chapter, with the examples of driverless cars and Go-playing computers.

It's true that some thoughtful critics take a different view, emphasising factors that can result in slow-downs of progress. As I'll review in later chapters, these critics make some good points. Ongoing technological progress is far from inevitable. Anyone who *insists* that we're on a predetermined path to complete automation is speaking from faith rather than from reason. But, equally, anyone who insists that automation *cannot* accelerate is likewise speaking from faith rather than from reason. Rather than taking either of these extreme ways, we ought to acknowledge a degree of uncertainty about future developments.

My own summary is that it is *prudent* to admit the *serious possibility* that technological unemployment:

- May soar in extent within as little as 20 years

- May already be having significant effects on the workforce, pushing increasing numbers of people into "precarious employment" or "involuntary underemployment" that is far from the kind of work they would prefer (though these effects admittedly remain difficult to disentangle from other factors such as globalisation and the weakening of collective bargaining)

- May cause deepening social unrest sooner rather than later, unless meaningful measures are taken to start introducing a citizen's income (or something broadly equivalent).

These possibilities add up to a powerful reason to consider, hard, how a citizen's income system could operate, and (at least as difficult a question) how it could be introduced. Since the introduction may require many years of experimentation and gradual roll-out, we had better start sooner rather than later.

I'll have more to say on these matters as this book unfolds. Before then, however, we need to broaden our perspective. The technologies that threaten technological unemployment also pose other threats, including the twin spectres of hyper-surveillance and infrastructure fragility. Alongside fearing for their jobs, people have good reasons to fear for their privacy, their sanity, and their security.

5. Surveillance and security

Connectivity has its advantages. Consider the needs of hard-pressed parents, who must periodically break away from other tasks to check how well their baby is sleeping. Remote baby monitors, plugged into domestic networks, can cut these parents some slack, by guaranteeing to alert them if their child wakes unexpectedly. Other systems, using small sensors in a "smart sock" worn by the baby, can provide additional assurance about the baby's heart rate and blood oxygen level. This can reduce anxiety about sudden cot death. The vendor's website explains[105], "More data, less worry: 83% of parents report having better sleep while using the Smart Sock on their baby".

What's not to like about this innovative use of connected technology? Alas, some baby monitors unwittingly provide the means for outsiders to spy on the children, and even to speak to them. Commissioner Julie Menin of the New York Department of Consumer Affairs issued a stark public warning in early 2016[106]:

> Video monitors are intended to give parents peace of mind when they are away from their children but the reality is quite terrifying – if they aren't secure, they can provide easy access for predators to watch and even speak to our children. There have been numerous reports by consumers, including those here in New York City, that these video monitors have subjected them to unwanted intrusions into the most private of spaces: their own homes. Internet-connected devices like video monitors provide convenience, but without proper safeguards, they pose serious privacy risks. We encourage parents to take steps to make sure their devices are secure and call on manufacturers to make security a top priority.

As we'll see in this chapter, the problems of insecure baby monitors are echoed in an avalanche of similar examples from the fields of smart cars and smart homes as well as smart healthcare. It turns out that connectivity is a two-edged sword.

The perils of connectivity

Let's reflect on the predicament experienced by more than 100 car owners in Austin, Texas, as a result of the actions of a disgruntled former employee of used car retail firm Texas Auto Center. As Wired reported[107],

More than 100 drivers in Austin, Texas found their cars disabled or the horns honking out of control, after an intruder ran amok in a web-based vehicle-immobilization system normally used to get the attention of consumers delinquent in their auto payments.

Police with Austin's High Tech Crime Unit on Wednesday arrested 20-year-old Omar Ramos-Lopez, a former Texas Auto Center employee who was laid off last month, and allegedly sought revenge by bricking the cars sold from the dealership's four Austin-area lots.

Texas Auto Center had included some innovative new technology in the cars they sold:

The dealership used a system called Webtech Plus as an alternative to repossessing vehicles that haven't been paid for. Operated by Cleveland-based Pay Technologies, the system lets car dealers install a small black box under vehicle dashboards that responds to commands issued through a central website, and relayed over a wireless pager network. The dealer can disable a car's ignition system, or trigger the horn to begin honking, as a reminder that a payment is due.

One attraction of the system is that it allows a greater number of customers to purchase cars, even when their credit history looks poor. Rather than extensive up-front tests of the credit-worthiness of a potential purchaser, the system takes advantage of the ability to immobilise a car if repayments should cease. However, as Wired recounts,

Texas Auto Center began fielding complaints from baffled customers the last week in February, many of whom wound up missing work, calling tow trucks or disconnecting their batteries to stop the honking. The troubles stopped five days later, when Texas Auto Center reset the Webtech Plus passwords for all its employee accounts... Then police obtained access logs from Pay Technologies, and traced the saboteur's IP address to Ramos-Lopez's AT&T internet service, according to a police affidavit filed in the case.

Omar Ramos-Lopez had lost his position at Texas Auto Center the previous month. Following good security practice, his own account on the Webtech Plus system had been disabled. However, it seems he gained access by using an account assigned to a different employee.

At first, the intruder targeted vehicles by searching on the names of specific customers. Then he discovered he could pull up a database of all 1,100 Auto Center customers whose cars were equipped with the device.

He started going down the list in alphabetical order, vandalizing the records, disabling the cars and setting off the horns.

His manager ruefully remarked, "Omar was pretty good with computers". That backhanded endorsement of the former employee's skills provided little comfort to all the drivers who had been deeply inconvenienced as a result of his actions.

In other cases, the risks from smart connected technologies move far beyond inconvenience and embarrassment to matters of life and death. Consider a possible side-effect of being fitted with one of the marvels of modern technology, namely an implantable heart pacemaker. Security researcher Barnaby Jack of IOActive gave a devastating demo at the Breakpoint conference in October 2012, showing how easy it was for an outsider to interfere with the system whereby a pacemaker can be wirelessly recalibrated. The result is summed up in this Computerworld headline, "Pacemaker hack can deliver deadly 830-volt jolt"[108]:

> The flaw lies with the programming of the wireless transmitters used to give instructions to pacemakers and implantable cardioverter-defibrillators (ICDs), which detect irregular heart contractions and deliver an electric shock to avert a heart attack.

> A successful attack using the flaw "could definitely result in fatalities," said Jack…

> In a video demonstration, Jack showed how he could remotely cause a pacemaker to suddenly deliver an 830-volt shock, which could be heard with a crisp audible pop.

This possibility had already been anticipated by Dr Jonathan Reiner, the cardiologist who looked after the former US Vice President Dick Cheney. Dr Reiner explained his concerns in a CBS 60 Minutes documentary[109]:

> In 2007, when Cheney needed his implanted defibrillator replaced, Dr. Reiner ordered the manufacturer to disable the wireless feature – fearing a terrorist could assassinate the vice president by sending a signal to the device, telling it to shock his heart into cardiac arrest.

Reiner commented:

> It seemed to me to be a bad idea for the vice president to have a device that maybe somebody on a rope line or in the next hotel room or downstairs might be able to hack into.

Before drawing some conclusions, let's review one more example, involving a surprise side-effect of attaching a new thermostat to a building. Modern thermostats exchange data with increasingly sophisticated systems that control heating, ventilation, and air conditioning. In turn, these systems can connect into corporate networks, which contain email archives and other confidential documents.

The Washington Chamber of Commerce discovered in 2011 that a thermostat in a townhouse they used was surreptitiously communicating with an Internet address somewhere in China[110]. All the careful precautions of the Chamber's IT department, including supervision of the computers and memory sticks used by employees, to guard against the possibility of such data seepage, was undone by this unexpected security vulnerability in what seemed to be an ordinary household object. Information that leaked from the Chamber potentially included sensitive material about US policy for trade with China, as well as other key IP (Intellectual Property).

It's not only thermostats that have much greater network connectivity these days. Toasters, fridges, washing machines, and even energy-efficient lightbulbs contain surprising amounts of software, as part of the implementation of the vision of "smart homes". And in each case, that software opens the potential for various forms of espionage and/or extortion. Former CIA Director David Petraeus openly rejoiced in that possibility, in remarks noted in a March 2012 Wired article, "We'll spy on you through your dishwasher"[111]:

> Items of interest will be located, identified, monitored, and remotely controlled through technologies such as RFID, sensor networks, tiny embedded servers, and energy harvesters – all connected to the next-generation internet using abundant, low-cost, and high-power computing.

Petraeus enthused:

> Transformational is an overused word, but I do believe it properly applies to these technologies, particularly to their effect on clandestine tradecraft.

Petraeus was right. But the scale of the transformation exceeds even what he had in mind:

- Security vulnerabilities that can be exploited by law enforcement and counter-espionage agencies can also be exploited by the enemies of these agencies – people who are animated by various criminal or political motivations or by personal vendettas

- These vulnerabilities allow not just the eavesdropping of conversations but also the manipulation *and sabotage* of connected systems

- Distributed denial-of-service (DDoS) attacks can be operated from large "botnets" consisting of compromised smart home devices[112]

- In addition to vulnerabilities due to bugs in the software, we are collectively opening ourselves to manipulation by unwittingly releasing huge amounts of data about ourselves – our preferences, our characteristic mood swings, our biases and prejudices, our idiosyncratic weaknesses, and so on.

Big Brother is watching

We are being monitored as never before. We've grown accustomed to CCTV cameras that allow security officials and property owners to keep an eye on goings-on. We're aware that online companies use cookies to keep track of our interactions with websites. Loyalty cards issued by retail stores make it easier for companies to understand our buying preferences. But that's just the beginning:

- Drones – unmanned aerial vehicles – frequently carry cameras that are small but powerful

- Reductions in costs of cameras, microphones, and other sensors mean that we are surrounded as never before by multitudes of hidden electronic eyes and ears

- Personal information which is collected by one organisation for one purpose can often be intercepted by other organisations and used for other purposes

- Information collected by sensors can be analysed and interpreted by increasingly powerful software; one example is software than can infer spoken words from observed lip movements more expertly than the best human lip readers[113]

- Other software is able to correlate information from multiple different web-browsing sessions, in order to pinpoint our personal characteristics – even when we thought we were protected by a veil of anonymity

- Our attempts at maintaining our own privacy can be undermined by what other people happen to say about us – online or offline.

Businesses naturally have an interest to improve their understanding of their customers and potential customers. The more they can find out about us, the more precisely they can target individuals:

- The customers who will be prepared to spend more money on "premium" offerings

- The time and place when specific customers will be most open to making purchases

- The indications of mood swings which let the business know that it's a good time to present a particular advertisement

- The kind of language, imagery, music, or fragrance that is most likely to appeal to given customers, at their moments of greatest openness to making large purchases.

What's good for a business, of course, isn't always good for a customer. Customers may well end up:

- Buying items they subsequently wish they had not bought

- Paying more for items than was necessary[114]

- Buying items with functionality and quality different in reality from what seemed to be promised

- Not being aware of the extent to which they've been misled or cajoled by subtle advertising, brand positioning, or other highly targeted sales techniques.

It's not just businesses that can take advantage of this kind of information. Others with a strong interest in accessing data about our personal preferences, prejudices, blind spots, and other weaknesses include:

- Politicians, who want us to vote for them – despite our interests often being significantly misaligned with those politicians

- Potential romantic partners – including ill-intentioned "gold diggers" and lotharios – who are searching around for hot buttons that can be used to progress a relationship

- Former romantic partners, filled with vengeful feelings, who wish us various types of harm

- Bored teenagers, self-absorbed trolls, or other ne'er-do-wells, who want to find ways to make fun of us, belittle us, blackmail us, or force us to act in ways we would never choose voluntarily

- Foreign intelligence agencies, industrial spies, terrorist organisations, aggressive religious sects, and so on, with their own reasons to want to manipulate us
- An international criminal fraternity, which is said to operate with a financial budget which is twice the size of all the world's military budgets added together[115]
- Police officers, security officials, or various self-appointed "public guardians", who are on the lookout for incriminating materials that will provide justification for harassing or arresting us.

In extreme cases, evidence of dissident ideas or unconventional personal orientation – including atheism, "apostasy", or variant sexuality or gender identification – could result in capital punishment. In less extreme cases, freedom of expression will be drastically curtailed.

In short, it's not just the CIA who will be spying on us through our dishwashers.

The Internet of Insecure Things

How bad could things become? Renowned management consultant Tom Peters foresees that a "catastrophic cyber disaster" is almost inevitable sometime in the next five to ten years. With rhetorical flourish, he tweeted that the only people who would deny this eventuality were "silicon-koolaid drinkers" who were "clueless, dangerous fools"[116].

Here, the term "silicon-koolaid drinker" is an alternative for what is more commonly termed "technolibertarian" – someone who believes that the tech-heavy products from Silicon Valley will inevitably have good social consequences, so long as regulators and politicians keep well out of the way. Peters predicts that any string of positive outcomes will, with probability[117] "waaaay above 95%", be rudely interrupted by a "megacybershitstorm" that includes the banking system going offline and the power grid going "kapooey". With consequent shutdown of TV networks, telecommunications, fridges, and traffic lights, the sorry result will be chaos throughout the social, political, and economic sectors.

Continuing his 15 January 2017 tweetstorm on the subject, Peters offers advice[118]: "If you are not reading deeply on cyber vulnerability, you are proactively endangering yourself, your family, your community, your country."

In his Twitter biography, Peters describes himself as a "professional agitator". It may be tempting, therefore, to dismiss his warnings as overblown theatrics. Never mind the sobering plausibility of his remarks that[119] "the more integrated a system is, the more vulnerable. We've literally become enslaved by Internet."

However, the general thrust of Peters' opinion is supported in an article that appeared a few days later, 27th January 2017. It was written by one of the world's most respected researchers on security, Bruce Schneier. Amongst other roles, Schneier is a fellow at the Berkman Klein Center for Internet & Society at Harvard University, and the Chief Technology Officer at Resilient, an IBM Company[120].

Schneier's article appeared in New York Magazine, with the ominous title "Click Here to Kill Everyone"[121]. It lists many different ways in which poor security aspects of connected software could bring havoc. As an example, here's what he says about "modern cars – those computers on wheels":

> The steering wheel no longer turns the axles, nor does the accelerator pedal change the speed. Every move you make in a car is processed by a computer, which does the actual controlling. A central computer controls the dashboard. There's another in the radio. The engine has 20 or so computers. These are all networked, and increasingly autonomous.
>
> Now, let's start listing the security threats. We don't want car navigation systems to be used for mass surveillance, or the microphone for mass eavesdropping. We might want it to be used to determine a car's location in the event of a 911 call, and possibly to collect information about highway congestion. We don't want people to hack their own cars to bypass emissions-control limitations. We don't want manufacturers or dealers to be able to do that, either, as Volkswagen did for years. We can imagine wanting to give police the ability to remotely and safely disable a moving car; that would make high-speed chases a thing of the past. But we definitely don't want hackers to be able to do that. We definitely don't want them disabling the brakes in every car without warning, at speed. As we make the transition from driver-controlled cars to cars with various driver-assist capabilities to fully driverless cars, we don't want any of those critical components subverted. We don't want someone to be able to accidentally crash your car, let alone do it on purpose. And equally, we don't want them to be able to manipulate the navigation software to change your route, or the door-lock controls to prevent you from opening the door. I could go on.

In conclusion:

That's a lot of different security requirements, and the effects of getting them wrong range from illegal surveillance to extortion by ransomware to mass death.

Schneier points out a number of reasons why we all need to take these security vulnerabilities more seriously. First, the complexity of the software that connects smart sensors and smart devices creates "a large attack surface":

More complexity means more people involved, more parts, more interactions, more mistakes in the design and development process, more of everything where hidden insecurities can be found... A complex system means a large attack surface. The defender has to secure the entire attack surface. The attacker just has to find one vulnerability – one unsecured avenue for attack – and gets to choose how and when to attack. It's simply not a fair battle."

Second, "Most software is poorly written and insecure":

Well-written software, like the kind found in airplane avionics, is both expensive and time-consuming to produce. We don't want that. For the most part, poorly written software has been good enough. We'd all rather live with buggy software than pay the prices good software would require. We don't mind if our games crash regularly, or our business applications act weird once in a while. Because software has been largely benign, it hasn't mattered. This has permeated the industry at all levels. At universities, we don't teach how to code well. Companies don't reward quality code in the same way they reward fast and cheap. And we consumers don't demand it.

But poorly written software is riddled with bugs, sometimes as many as one per 1,000 lines of code. Some of them are inherent in the complexity of the software, but most are programming mistakes. Not all bugs are vulnerabilities, but some are.

Third, "Connecting everything to each other via the internet will expose new vulnerabilities" arising from unexpected interactions:

The more we network things together, the more vulnerabilities on one thing will affect other things... Vulnerabilities like these are particularly hard to fix, because no one system might actually be at fault. It might be the insecure interaction of two individually secure systems.

Fourth, "Everybody has to stop the best attackers in the world":

One of the most powerful properties of the internet is that it allows things to scale. This is true for our ability to access data or control systems or do any of the cool things we use the internet for, but it's also true for attacks. In general, fewer attackers can do more damage because of better technology. It's not just that these modern attackers are more efficient, it's that the internet allows attacks to scale to a degree impossible without computers and networks.

This is fundamentally different from what we're used to. When securing my home against burglars, I am only worried about the burglars who live close enough to my home to consider robbing me. The internet is different. When I think about the security of my network, I have to be concerned about the best attacker possible, because he's the one who's going to create the attack tool that everyone else will use.

Taking control of surveillance and security

What steps should we be taking, in the face of so many challenges to the security and wellbeing of our connected infrastructure?

Schneier makes three broad recommendations – each of which makes good sense to me. First, we should be resisting the trend toward ever-greater connectivity. Just because two networks *can* be connected together is no reason to make that connection:

> My guess is that we will soon reach a high-water mark of computerization and connectivity, and that afterward we will make conscious decisions about what and how we decide to interconnect. But we're still in the honeymoon phase of connectivity. Governments and corporations are punch-drunk on our data, and the rush to connect everything is driven by an even greater desire for power and market share. One of the presentations released by Edward Snowden contained the NSA mantra: "Collect it all." A similar mantra for the internet today might be: "Connect it all."…
>
> Large, centralized systems are not inevitable. The technical elites are pushing us in that direction, but they really don't have any good supporting arguments other than the profits of their ever-growing multinational corporations. But this will change. It will change not only because of security concerns, it will also change because of political concerns. We're starting to chafe under the worldview of everything producing data about us and what we do, and that data being available to both governments and corporations. Surveillance capitalism won't be the business model of the internet forever. We need to change the fabric of

the internet so that evil governments don't have the tools to create a horrific totalitarian state.

Second, Schneier advocates an improved conversation between technologists and politicians:

> The historical divide between Washington and Silicon Valley – the mistrust of governments by tech companies and the mistrust of tech companies by governments – is dangerous.

> We have to fix this. Getting IoT security right depends on the two sides working together and, even more important, having people who are experts in each working on both.

In practical terms, this advice breaks down into a set of individual recommendations:

> We need technologists to get involved in policy, and we need policy-makers to get involved in technology. We need people who are experts in making both technology and technological policy. We need technologists on congressional staffs, inside federal agencies, working for NGOs, and as part of the press. We need to create a viable career path for public-interest technologists, much as there already is one for public-interest attorneys. We need courses, and degree programs in colleges, for people interested in careers in public-interest technology. We need fellowships in organizations that need these people. We need technology companies to offer sabbaticals for technologists wanting to go down this path… We need a viable career path that ensures that even though people in this field won't make as much as they would in a high-tech start-up, they will have viable careers. The security of our computerized and networked future – meaning the security of ourselves, families, homes, businesses, and communities – depends on it.

In short: "We need more public-interest technologists". Indeed.

The third of Schneier's broad recommendations is arguably the most important, but is the most controversial of the three:

> *Regulation* might be a dirty word in today's political climate, but security is the exception to our small-government bias. And as the threats posed by computers become greater and more catastrophic, regulation will be inevitable. So now's the time to start thinking about it…

> I know [regulation is] a sullied concept in today's world, but I don't see any other possible solution. It's going to be especially difficult on the internet, where its permissionless nature is one of the best things about it and the underpinning of its most world-changing innovations. But I don't

see how that can continue when the internet can affect the world in a direct and physical manner.

Schneier offers the following rebuttal to those critics who would advocate, instead, a free-market solution to security, in which consumers will learn over time not to purchase equipment that has security holes:

> Markets alone can't solve our security problems. Markets are motivated by profit and short-term goals at the expense of society. They can't solve collective-action problems. They won't be able to deal with economic externalities, like the vulnerabilities in DVRs [Digital Video Recorders] that resulted in Twitter going offline [as a result of a massive denial of service attack that utilised DVRs in homes throughout the country]. And we need a counterbalancing force to corporate power.

The limit of the abilities of free markets to address economic externalities is one of the prime concerns of technoprogressives. I'll review this further in Chapter 9, "Markets and fundamentalists". For now, I'll simply state that the risks of infrastructure catastrophe are far too high for us to put our complete reliance on any theoretical arguments that free markets will always find good solutions. As Schneier says, "Now's the time to start thinking".

Small thinking won't save the Internet

If you're still unconvinced about the grave risks posed to our collective security by flaws in the networks that connect more and more aspects of our lives, you should take the time to read the 2015 book *Future Crimes*[122] by Marc Goodman. Goodman's background includes the Los Angeles Police Department, Interpol, NATO, NASA, and much more[123]. The book carries the subtitle "Everything is connected, everyone is vulnerable, and what we can do about it." Singularity 1on1 podcast interviewer Nikola Danaylov describes *Future Crimes* as "the scariest book I have ever read in my life"[124]. That's a sentiment I can endorse. The book has a panoply of "Oh my god" moments.

Here's Goodman's overall assessment of the situation:

> Computers run the world. They run our airports, our airplanes, our cars, our hospitals, our stock markets and our power grids and these computers too are shockingly vulnerable to attack. Though we're racing forward at break neck speed to connect all the objects in our physical world – the tools we need to run our society – to the Internet, we still fundamentally

do not have the trustworthy computing required to make it so. We've wired the world, but failed to secure it.

Indeed it has become plainly clear that we can no longer neglect the security, public policy, legal, ethical, and social implications of the rapidly emerging technological tools we are developing. We are morally responsible for our inventions and though our technological advances are proceeding at an exponential pace, our institutions of governance remain decidedly linear. There is a fundamental mismatch between the world we are building and our ability to protect it. Though we have yet to suffer the sort of game-changing calamitous cyber-attack of which many have warned, why wait until then to prepare?

The summary I've just quoted comes from an urgent plea by Goodman for society to create "a Manhattan project for cyber security"[125]. Goodman asserts, "Grand thinking created the Internet. Small thinking won't save it."

The creation of this kind of large-scale concerted project is one of a string of recommendations at the end of Goodman's book. These include applying to security design more of the principles of the discipline of human-centred design, adopting encryption by default, removing reliance on people remembering and using passwords, reducing the amount of unneeded "data pollution" emitted from our digital systems, and creating a cyber CDC (centre for disease control) analogous to the health CDCs that already exist to address problems of the spread of medical pandemics. These all form parts of the envisioned Manhattan project for cyber security.

I'd like to highlight several of Goodman's recommendations for special attention. The joint effect of these recommendations would be to change the culture under which software is created, so that security gains a much higher priority. Goodman highlights Facebook as an example of a company where the culture needed to change:

Facebook's software developers have long lived by the mantra "Move fast and break things." The saying, which was emblazoned on the walls across the company's headquarters, reflected Facebook's hacker ethos, which dictated that even if new software tools or features were not perfect, speed of code creation was key, even if it caused problems or security issues along the way. According to [Mark] Zuckerberg, "If you never break anything, you're probably not moving fast enough."

Facebook is not alone in its software-coding practices. Either openly or behind closed doors, the majority of the software industry operates under a variation of the motto "Just ship it" or "Done is better than perfect."

Many coders knowingly ship software that they admit "sucks" but let it go, hoping, perhaps, to do better next time. These attitudes are emblematic of everything that is wrong with software coding and represent perhaps the largest single threat against computer security today.

The general public would be deeply surprised at just how much of the technology around us barely works, cobbled together by so-called duct-tape programming, always just a few keystrokes away from a system crash… Most computer programmers are overwhelmed, short on time and money. They too just want to go home and see their kids, and as a result what we get is buggy, incomplete, security-hole-ridden software and incidents such as Heartbleed or massive hacks against Target, Sony, and Home Depot.

Changing this culture will require changes in incentives – otherwise developers will continue to follow practices that they know to be dangerous:

In order to turn this ship around, incentives will need to be aligned to ensure the badly needed emphasis on secure computing actually occurs. For example, today when hackers find a vulnerability in a software program, they can either sell it on the black market to Crime, Inc. for a significant profit or report it to a vendor for next to nothing while facing the threat of prosecution. Thus they make the rather obvious choice. Though this is beginning to change and some companies have established "bug bounty programs," few offer cash rewards, and among those that do, the amounts are far less than those available in the digital underground. That needs to change. Creating well-funded security vulnerability reporting systems that pay hackers for bringing major flaws to vendors' attention would help minimize the damage these software companies themselves created when they rushed insecure and buggy code out the door onto an unsuspecting public.

This change in incentive for members of the general public who find bugs needs to be matched with a change in incentive for the companies that write the software in the first place. Almost all software is currently shipped with licence agreements that remove any obligation of responsibility from the vendor. If the user experiences financial loss as a result of a defect in the software, the user has no legal recourse to sue the software vendor. Goodman explains:

We can make a change by holding those in the software industry… accountable for their actions. Absent this demand from the public, in the battle between profitability and security, profit will win every time. We need to help companies understand it is in their long-term interest to write more secure code and that there will be consequences for failing to do so. As things stand today, the engineers, coders, and companies that create today's technologies have near-zero personal and professional responsibility for the consequences of their actions...

The fact of the matter is that when you click on those lengthy terms of service without reading them, you agree that you are using a company's software or Internet service "as is," and all liability for any damages lands on you. These firms use language such as "you will hold harmless and indemnify us and our affiliates, officers, agents, and employees from any claim, suit, or action arising from or related to the use of the Services" and "we do not guarantee that our product will always be safe, secure, or error-free."

The software industry stands resolutely opposed to any changes in the assignment of legal culpability for defects. Goodman reviews their arguments, and finds them wanting:

The software industry is vehemently against any such change. It claims that allowing liability lawsuits would have catastrophic effects on its profitability and would bankrupt it. It also asserts that the complexity of software interactions is so great that it would be impossible to fairly adjudicate blame in case of injury. Both arguments fall short. We've been here before, particularly with the automobile industry, whose products through the 1960s had a terrible safety record. Through consumer advocacy and congressional action, the National Traffic and Motor Vehicle Safety Act was passed in 1966, allowing the government to enforce industry safety regulations. Doing so resulted in one of the largest achievements in public health of the twentieth century. Automobile deaths dropped precipitously, saving tens of thousands of lives.

Just as strong political support was needed in the 1960s to enforce a change of culture in the automobile industry, regarding its attitude towards safety, strong political support will be needed over the next few years to change the culture in the software industry, regarding its attitude towards security and privacy. And for that to happen, it's all the more imperative that we fix politics quickly.

Controlling military AI

I'll draw this chapter towards a close by reviewing two ways in which the problems of insecure, unsafe software could be even more significant than what's already been covered. The first of these is when the software is connected to military armaments.

In May 2009, an Oerlikon MK5 anti-aircraft system was part of the equipment used by 5,000 South African troops in a large-scale military training exercise. On that morning, the controlling software suffered what a subsequent enquiry would call a "glitch". Writing in the Daily Mail, Gavin Knight recounted what happened[126]:

> The MK5 anti-aircraft system, with two huge 35mm cannons, is essentially a vast robotic weapon, controlled by a computer.
>
> While it's one thing when your laptop freezes up, it's quite another when it is controlling an auto-loading magazine containing 500 high-explosive rounds...
>
> "There was nowhere to hide," one witness stated in a report. "The rogue gun began firing wildly, spraying high explosive shells at a rate of 550 a minute, swinging around through 360 degrees like a high-pressure hose."
>
> By the time the robot has emptied its magazine, nine soldiers lie dead. Another 14 are seriously injured.

A number of organisations have spoken out against any trend towards weapons systems have increased autonomy. They perceive major risks if decisions are taken by software, rather than by human deliberation, on matters such as when to open fire. *Imagine if that software goes wrong.*

Here's a statement of the problem from a group called "Campaign to stop killer robots"[127]:

> Over the past decade, the expanded use of unmanned armed vehicles has dramatically changed warfare, bringing new humanitarian and legal challenges. Now rapid advances in technology are resulting in efforts to develop fully autonomous weapons. These robotic weapons would be able to choose and fire on targets on their own, without any human intervention. This capability would pose a fundamental challenge to the protection of civilians and to compliance with international human rights and humanitarian law.

As the statement goes on to emphasise, this is no abstract concern:

> Several nations with high-tech militaries, particularly the United States, China, Israel, South Korea, Russia, and the United Kingdom are moving toward systems that would give greater combat autonomy to machines. If one or more chooses to deploy fully autonomous weapons, a large step beyond remote-controlled armed drones, others may feel compelled to

abandon policies of restraint, leading to a robotic arms race. Agreement is needed now to establish controls on these weapons before investments, technological momentum, and new military doctrine make it difficult to change course.

Allowing life or death decisions to be made by machines crosses a fundamental moral line. Autonomous robots would lack human judgment and the ability to understand context. These qualities are necessary to make complex ethical choices on a dynamic battlefield, to distinguish adequately between soldiers and civilians, and to evaluate the proportionality of an attack. As a result, fully autonomous weapons would not meet the requirements of the laws of war.

Other commentators suggest that, on the contrary, autonomous systems could prove safer than ones under the control of humans – especially if these humans are tired, emotional, rushed, or fearful[128]. However, this depends on how well the software is written: whether it contains bugs, whether the developers have correctly foreseen the various circumstances in which it might be used, whether it can be hacked by outsiders, and so on. If any "AI arms race" takes place, with lots of new solutions being hurried into place in order to pre-empt enemies from gaining an overwhelming first-strike advantage, corners may be cut in the full analysis and testing of solutions. For this reason, an appeal made by the Future of Life Institute (FLI) has considerable merit:[129]

> Autonomous weapons select and engage targets without human intervention. They might include, for example, armed quadcopters that can search for and eliminate people meeting certain pre-defined criteria... Artificial Intelligence (AI) technology has reached a point where the deployment of such systems is – practically if not legally – feasible within years, not decades, and the stakes are high: autonomous weapons have been described as the third revolution in warfare, after gunpowder and nuclear arms.

> Many arguments have been made for and against autonomous weapons, for example that replacing human soldiers by machines is good by reducing casualties for the owner but bad by thereby lowering the threshold for going to battle. The key question for humanity today is whether to start a global AI arms race or to prevent it from starting.

The FLI statement goes on to spell out the consequences of a military AI arms race:

If any major military power pushes ahead with AI weapon development, a global arms race is virtually inevitable, and the endpoint of this technological trajectory is obvious: autonomous weapons will become the Kalashnikovs of tomorrow. Unlike nuclear weapons, they require no costly or hard-to-obtain raw materials, so they will become ubiquitous and cheap for all significant military powers to mass-produce. It will only be a matter of time until they appear on the black market and in the hands of terrorists, dictators wishing to better control their populace, warlords wishing to perpetrate ethnic cleansing, etc. Autonomous weapons are ideal for tasks such as assassinations, destabilizing nations, subduing populations and selectively killing a particular ethnic group. We therefore believe that a military AI arms race would not be beneficial for humanity. There are many ways in which AI can make battlefields safer for humans, especially civilians, without creating new tools for killing people.

Just as most chemists and biologists have no interest in building chemical or biological weapons, most AI researchers have no interest in building AI weapons – and do not want others to tarnish their field by doing so, potentially creating a major public backlash against AI that curtails its future societal benefits. Indeed, chemists and biologists have broadly supported international agreements that have successfully prohibited chemical and biological weapons, just as most physicists supported the treaties banning space-based nuclear weapons and blinding laser weapons.

The FLI conclude:

In summary, we believe that AI has great potential to benefit humanity in many ways, and that the goal of the field should be to do so. Starting a military AI arms race is a bad idea, and should be prevented by a ban on offensive autonomous weapons beyond meaningful human control.

The problem, of course, is that individual countries will be fearful about adopting any such ban, if they suspect that other countries will surreptitiously develop measures to sidestep that ban. Without a comprehensive shared agreement about a desirable future state of the planet, any such ban will face real difficulty.

Controlling superintelligent AI

When software controls powerful military armaments, few people will say we should disregard any risk of that software having bugs. Instead, the overwhelming majority will say there's a clear need for that software to be thoroughly reviewed and thoroughly tested. For such software, safety is paramount.

But what about software with a very different mission? For example, is there any risk from software with the mission to calculate the optimal stock market investment strategy for a company? How about calculating the optimal set of marketing messages to boost the revenues for that company? What could go wrong if there are bugs in such software? In some circumstances, a lot more than you might initially think. These problems can arise if the software possesses elements of so-called "general intelligence" or "superintelligence".

Imagine if that software:

- Contains monitoring functionality, so as to learn as much as possible about relevant features of the world, in order to carry out its optimisation task more accurately

- Is able to improve its own calibration and algorithms, in the light of what it observes and calculates

- Has the ability to act directly in the world – that is, *autonomously* – in order not to miss time-critical opportunities

- Contains some defensive measures, so as to anticipate and prevent possible attacks on its performance by agents hostile to it (or to the company on whose behalf it operates)

- Embodies state-of-the-art capabilities in general reasoning.

None of these assumptions appear especially far-fetched. But adding them all together yields the possibility of the emergence of genuinely novel behaviour – similar to the way that the DeepMind software AlphaGo (discussed in the previous chapter) produced types of moves in the game of Go that human experts had previously not contemplated. And since the software may take evasive action against operations intended to interfere with its performance, the possibility arises that the software may prove difficult to control. For example:

- To guard against the possibility that the programme might be shut down, the software could take its own decision to tunnel a copy of itself out to a safe location

- To guard against the possibility that such copies would be intercepted and rendered inoperative, the programme could take steps to keep the copying process secret, and to disguise its intentions

- To forestall other possible attacks on itself, the software might devise innovative new defensive strategies that the programmers had not foreseen – strategies potentially outside the imagination even of science fiction writers.

By freeing itself from human control, the software magnifies the problems that would result from any error it contains – whether errors in implementation or errors in specification. Human operators may believe they possess an "off switch" for use in the event of software malfunction, but the software would continue to operate, despite the off switch being pressed. The software might resume execution from a new location, perhaps after a time delay to throw human antagonists off track.

Note that the above line of thinking makes *no assumption* that the software has somehow become conscious or has "woken up". The assumption is simply that the software has been assigned an objective, which it then pursues, doggedly and without distraction, using all the resources available to it. To carry out its assigned task at higher levels of performance, it may take steps to obtain even more resources – including resources that human society would strongly prefer to be used for quite different purposes.

Some critics might object that any software smart enough to carry out the above steps would also be smart enough to know that its actions would run counter to the true intentions of its human programmers. Nevertheless, the software is governed by its own hard-wired objectives – its "prime directive", so to speak – not by what it subsequently deduces about human intentions. Any information it acquires about human intentions becomes input to the calculations of the software, but needn't cause that software to alter its fundamental goal.

For this reason, it's especially important that these fundamental goals are set wisely. Otherwise, it would be like a more sophisticated but equally tragic version of the ancient fable of King Midas, who bitterly regretted making a wish that everything he touched would turn into gold.

As an example, the stock market value of the company owning the software may shoot upwards, in fulfilment of the software's prime directive, but that might be accomplished by a vast series of "zombie financial trades" (or whatever) that add no real value to the human economy. Alternatively, humans may find themselves cleverly pressurised by super-smart personalised advertising to purchase huge quantities of items they don't actually need – items that end up severely damaging their health. Or the software may figure out by itself that it can make more money for its parent company by devising and selling new kinds of weaponry, triggering great financial results but also horrific military conflicts and terrorist attacks. In the worst case, it's as in the title of the article mentioned above by Bruce Schneier, "Click Here to Kill Everyone"[130].

Raising awareness of the threat landscape

The positive news about existential risks posed by malfunctioning superintelligence is that a number of clear and accessible books on this subject have been published in the last few years. These include:

- *Life 3.0: Being Human in the Age of Artificial Intelligence*, by Max Tegmark[131] of the FLI (mentioned earlier)
- *Our Final Invention: Artificial Intelligence and the End of the Human Era*, by James Barrat[132]
- *Surviving AI: The promise and peril of artificial intelligence*, by Calum Chace[133]
- *The Technological Singularity*, by Murray Shanahan[134]
- *Superintelligence: Paths, Dangers, Strategies*, by Nick Bostrom[135].

The negative news, however, is that the analysis in such books indicates that there are no easy answers to taming these existential risks. Whatever ideas may have occurred to you, while reading the previous section, have likely already been analysed by the existential risk community, and found wanting.

Two underlying problems are particularly hard:

- *The control problem* – how to ensure that humans retain the ability to intervene, by an "off switch" or otherwise, if software starts taking action that threatens human wellbeing
- *The value alignment problem* – how to set the prime directives of the software, so that, even if it is no longer under the control of human overseers, it continues to pursue objectives that serve humanity rather than diminishing it.

Without going too far afield, I'll briefly share some considerations:

- This is not a question of robots becoming evil, but rather of robots pursuing objectives that turn out to be misaligned with those of humanity as a whole

- There's no inherent reason why an entity with greater powers in calculating will automatically become more empathetic towards human beings; on the contrary, raw intelligence and emotional empathy are independent; artificial superintelligence may simply decide that it doesn't care about human flourishing

- Powerful software, with a rich understanding of human psychology, will likely be able to devise ways to make humans do things that are aligned with the objectives of the software

- All attempts throughout history to write down an agreed set of "ultimate human values" – such as we might try to implant deep inside AI software – have run into matters of profound disagreement when moving beyond statements of principle to matters of detail.

I agree with this assessment by Professor Stuart Russell of UC Berkeley in an interview by Edge[136]:

> Is there some mistake in my thinking that has led me to the conclusion that the control problem is serious and difficult? I'm always asking myself if I'm making a mistake.
>
> I go through the arguments that people make for not paying any attention to this issue and none of them hold water. They fail in such straightforward ways that it seems like the arguments are coming from a defensive reaction, not from taking the question seriously and thinking hard about it, but not wanting to consider it at all. Obviously, it's a threat.

Russell gives this analogy about the timescales required for conceptual breakthroughs, such as those still needed before artificial intelligence can progress beyond its current state to reach parity with all aspects of human intelligence:

> We can look back at the history of nuclear physics, where very famous nuclear physicists were simply in denial about the possibility that nuclear physics could lead to nuclear weapons.
>
> The idea of a nuclear weapon was around since at least 1914 when H.G. Wells wrote *The World Set Free*, which included what he called atomic

bombs. He didn't quite get the physics right. He imagined bombs that would explode for weeks on end. They would liberate an enormous amount of energy – not all at once, but over a long period; they would lay waste gradually to a whole city. The principle was there. There were famous physicists like Frederick Soddy who understood the risk and agitated to think about it ahead of time, but then there were other physicists like Ernst Rutherford who simply denied that it was possible that this could ever happen. He denied it was possible up until the night before Leó Szilárd invented the nuclear chain reaction.

Russell, incidentally, is the co-author of one of the most influential textbooks on AI[137]. And the 1933 contribution of Leó Szilárd, a Hungarian physicist who had come to London as a refugee, was to conceive a mechanism that had not previously occurred to physicists, namely a nuclear chain reaction based on a cascade of neutrons. The neutron had only been properly understood in the previous year (1932)[138]. Szilárd's breakthrough idea occurred only one day after Ernst Rutherford publicly declared that[139]:

Anyone who looks for a source of power in the transformation of the atoms is talking moonshine.

The comparison with nuclear power is a good one in other ways too. Nuclear power, used wisely and under secure control, can provide huge amounts of positive energy to society. It could also cause the destruction of all human life. It's the same with superintelligence, which likewise could have either very bad or very good consequences. The comparison extends further:

- The good consequences won't arise automatically; safety considerations need to be anticipated plenty of time in advance, lest the bad consequences completely overshadow the good

- Many of the consequences of nuclear weapons were conceived only dimly (if at all) ahead of time – including the extent of deaths from radioactive fallout, the devastation inflicted on electronic circuitry by the electromagnetic pulse emitted by the explosion, and the deadly "nuclear winter" cooling of the earth's temperature caused by massive clouds of soot in the stratosphere; in the same way, fast-improving artificial general intelligence is likely to have its own set of unexpected unwelcome consequences

- People from all walks of life, including politicians, feel deeply uncomfortable about thinking through these issues. It's hard to "think the unthinkable", in the phrase of nuclear weapons strategist Herman Kahn[140]. People find it more reassuring to focus on smaller, current, more local issues, than on the potential larger risks of the future. But to avoid such lines of thinking is to make future disaster more likely.

The pace of progress with nuclear weaponry was driven, of course, by an arms race – a *literal* arms race. The pace of progress with artificial intelligence, to the point when an abrupt "intelligence explosion" could occur, is being driven by a competitive arms race of a different kind. The corporations who develop and deploy improved artificial intelligence have the largest valuations on the planet – nowadays exceeding the valuations of energy companies, finance companies, retail companies, and so on. The perceived advantages of more powerful artificial intelligence are immense.

Vladimir Putin, President of Russia, acknowledged this point in remarks in September 2017[141]:

> Artificial intelligence is the future, not only for Russia, but for all humankind. It comes with colossal opportunities, but also threats that are difficult to predict. Whoever becomes the leader in this sphere will become the ruler of the world.

Towards truly beneficial AI

In early January 2017, many of the world's leading politicians and business people gathered in Davos, Switzerland, for the annual meeting of the World Economic Forum[142]. At almost the same time, another meeting was taking place in Asilomar, California, that will probably have greater long-term significance. The Asilomar event was organised by the Future of Life Institute[143], and had the title "Beneficial AI 2017"[144]. AI researchers from academia and industry spent five days in workshops with thought leaders from the fields of economics, law, ethics, and philosophy. The goals of the workshop were:

- To gain a better understanding of the opportunities and challenges related to the future of AI
- To clarify the steps that can be taken to ensure that AI technology is beneficial.

An important output from the event was the publication of the "Asilomar AI principles"[145]. This set of agreed principles was introduced as follows:

Artificial intelligence has already provided beneficial tools that are used every day by people around the world. Its continued development, guided by the following principles, will offer amazing opportunities to help and empower people in the decades and centuries ahead.

The 23 principles are split into three groups: "Research Issues", "Ethics and Values", and "Longer-term Issues". As an example, here's Principle #2 from the list, "Research Funding":

Investments in AI should be accompanied by funding for research on ensuring its beneficial use, including thorny questions in computer science, economics, law, ethics, and social studies, such as:

- How can we make future AI systems highly robust, so that they do what we want without malfunctioning or getting hacked?

- How can we grow our prosperity through automation while maintaining people's resources and purpose?

- How can we update our legal systems to be more fair and efficient, to keep pace with AI, and to manage the risks associated with AI?

- What set of values should AI be aligned with, and what legal and ethical status should it have?

And here are the principles covering "Longer-term Issues":

19) *Capability Caution*: There being no consensus, we should avoid strong assumptions regarding upper limits on future AI capabilities.

20) *Importance*: Advanced AI could represent a profound change in the history of life on Earth, and should be planned for and managed with commensurate care and resources.

21) *Risks*: Risks posed by AI systems, especially catastrophic or existential risks, must be subject to planning and mitigation efforts commensurate with their expected impact.

22) *Recursive Self-Improvement*: AI systems designed to recursively self-improve or self-replicate in a manner that could lead to rapidly increasing quality or quantity must be subject to strict safety and control measures.

23) *Common Good*: Superintelligence should only be developed in the service of widely shared ethical ideals, and for the benefit of all humanity rather than one state or organization.

The event also reviewed the progress that had been made by researchers worldwide in the two years since a similar (but smaller) conference had been held, in Puerto Rico[146], by several of the same participants. You can view videos of these reports on the Asilomar conference website. Whilst there is doubtless a great deal of hard work ahead, the path has been mapped out for significant research to take place. The research is funded in part by charitable donations from successful business leaders like Elon Musk and Jaan Tallinn. It also takes place inside the corporations where AI is being developed and put to lots of real-world use – companies such as Amazon, Apple, Facebook, Google, IBM, and Microsoft – companies who are coordinating their efforts via the recently created body, "Partnership on AI to benefit people and society"[147].

Despite these encouraging signs of progress, four points of concern deserve to be noted:

1. The underlying problems being researched remain truly challenging

2. These international collaborations are noticeably short of official participation from companies from China – a country where an increasing amount of AI research and development is happening[148]

3. Whilst the active support from leading software companies is welcome, it can't be overlooked that these companies have commercial objectives as well as humanitarian ones

4. Conversations between these researchers and politicians are still at an early stage; an unhealthy political climate could jeopardise the spirit of cooperation that has accompanied the efforts so far.

The same comments apply to the entire range of issues and opportunities covered in this chapter – issues about all the potential downsides and upsides of increased connectivity, increased surveillance, and increased "intelligence in the cloud". These issues demand large thinking, rather than small tweaks to existing systems. They demand central involvement by people other than those with financial motivation. They require politicians to become much more fully informed about the full set of possibilities ahead.

A technoprogressive roadmap raises the priority of attending to all the above issues. It's a roadmap that envisions a healthy *partnership* between humans and technology, rather than a domination of humans by technology. It sees the possibility that the growing power of AI can be used to help design and oversee the system for safe adoption of AI that is even more powerful. To keep AI safe we can take advantage of AI itself, as it explores and verifies options for next generation software. But we'll need to keep our hands on the steering wheel throughout.

6. Health and recovery

On the face of things, the field of healthcare poses a stern challenge to the technoprogressive vision that I am championing. In countries all around the world, costs of healthcare are rocketing. Chronic diseases such as diabetes, heart disease, and dementia are consuming huge resources. National budgets are facing crises under the resulting strains and stresses.

To give one example, Simon Stevens, the CEO of Britain's NHS (National Health Service), has spoken out on several occasions about the growing financial burden of chronic diseases. Here are his comments in an NHS England news article entitled "Get serious about obesity *or bankrupt the NHS*"[149]:

> Obesity is the new smoking, and it represents a slow-motion car crash in terms of avoidable illness and rising health care costs. If as a nation we keep piling on the pounds around the waistline, we'll be piling on the pounds in terms of future taxes needed just to keep the NHS afloat.

Speakers in support of a campaign by the British Pharmacological Society emphasised the risks of runaway expenditure on medicinal drugs[150]:

> The NHS drugs bill is spiralling out of control and will bankrupt the service unless urgent action is taken, experts say. It jumped more than £1 billion between 2014/15 and 2015/16, to nearly £17 billion. This means the cost of providing medicines is the second biggest NHS expenditure after staff salaries...

> The problem is partly due to an aging population, which has more health problems and a wider range of medication to treat them. However, drug wastage is also to blame. Up to 40% of patients prescribed drugs long term do not take them, wasting the equivalent of £350 million a year...

> Sir Munir Pirmohamed, the society vice president, said: "We cannot carry on like this. We urgently need to reduce drug wastage and optimise the drugs patients are on to ensure they get the right drugs, and the correct number of drugs, so that they are not being over-medicated."

> Simon Maxwell, chairman and professor of clinical pharmacology at Edinburgh University, added: "This will bankrupt the NHS and is not sustainable."

In January 2018, stirred to action by a series of fraught experiences in their hospitals over the ongoing winter period, a group of highly experienced healthcare professionals wrote a public letter to Theresa May, the British Prime Minister[151]:

> We are writing to you as Consultants in Emergency Medicine, Fellows of the Royal College of Emergency Medicine and as Clinical Leads (Consultants in charge) of our Emergency Departments, representing 68 Acute Hospitals across England and Wales...
>
> We feel compelled to speak out in support of our hardworking and dedicated nursing, medical and allied health professional colleagues and for the very serious concerns we have for the safety of our patients.
>
> This current level of safety compromise is at times intolerable, despite the best efforts of staff.
>
> The cause of this "intolerable" level of compromise in safety?
>
> The facts remain... that the NHS is severely and chronically underfunded. We have insufficient hospital and community beds and staff of all disciplines especially at the front door to cope with our aging population's health needs...
>
> Some of our own personal experiences range from:
>
> - Over 120 patients a day managed in corridors, some dying prematurely
>
> - An average of 10-12 hours from decision to admit a patient until they are transferred to a bed
>
> - Over 50 patients at a time waiting beds in the Emergency Department
>
> - Patients sleeping in clinics as makeshift wards.
>
> Simon Stevens, the CEO of the NHS, has made this grim forecast[152]:
>
> 2018, which happens to be the 70th anniversary of the NHS, is poised to be the toughest financial year.

Meanwhile, in the United States, debt arising from medical fees is the number one cause for people to become bankrupt[153].

Technology is not enough

In principle, technology ought to be reversing these expenditure trends. Innovative technology has the potential to automate aspects of medical treatment, to provide timely early warnings of ill health, and to deliver targeted new therapies that are more effective than previous treatments. However, rather than being a part of the solution, it seems, worryingly, that technology is part of the growing healthcare budget problem:

- Technological solutions are intended to reduce costs, but often fail to deliver the expected benefits – due to poor usability, data incompatibilities, and difficulties in integrating different systems (these problems are well documented in physician Robert Wachter's excellent 2015 book *The Digital Doctor: Hope, Hype, and Harm at the Dawn of Medicine's Computer Age*[154])

- Projects to develop new health information systems often end up being cancelled because of escalating implementation problems – witness the recent headlines "NHS pulls the plug on its 11bn IT system"[155] and "Oh dear, is this another costly IT failure?"[156]

- New drugs have the benefit of preventing people from dying from conditions which would formerly have proved fatal, but often leave the patients dependent for years or even decades on expensive aftercare treatments

- Diagnostic tests that indicate potential medical problems often result in costly follow-up investigations, especially in the "false positive" cases where it turns out that nothing was actually amiss

- New drugs are frequently more expensive than previous ones; pharmaceutical companies justify their high prices by pointing to the large costs they incur over lengthy testing cycles.

As an example of prices of medical treatment for diseases such as cancer rising, steeply, rather than falling, consider the points noted in the May 2016 National Daily Press article "Cancer becomes one of the most expensive and riskiest diseases to treat"[157]:

> A new study shows that cancer drugs have become significantly more expensive compared to the drugs used 15 years ago.
>
> It's no secret that treating cancer is no walk in the park and it could leave someone's bank account in the red. Treating cancer today with drugs has been found to be costlier than treating the disease with drugs several years ago.
>
> Researchers have showed that the cost for a month of treatment with the latest cancer drugs from 2014 cost six times more than cancer drugs from 2000. That is even after adjusting the prices for inflation.
>
> To put that into more understandable figures, the researchers said that the cancer drugs from 2000 had an average cost of $1,869 per month. The cancer drugs from 2014 cost $11,325 which is nearly $10,000 more.

A similar stark hike in costs applies for insulin, pushing access beyond the means of large numbers of patients. This is described by Gary Stoller, writing in the Connecticut Health-Team[158]:

> The high cost of insulin, which has risen by triple-digit percentages in the last five years, is endangering the lives of many diabetics who can't afford the price tag, say Connecticut physicians who treat diabetics.
>
> The doctors say that the out-of-pocket costs for insulin, ranging from $25 to upwards of $600 a month, depending on insurance coverage, are forcing many of their low-income patients to choose between treatment and paying their bills...
>
> A study by Philip Clarke, a professor of health economics at the University of Melbourne in Australia, reported that the price of insulin has tripled from 2002-2013.

Exponential problems

The growing costs of healthcare fly in opposition to a techno-optimistic assumption which is often heard, namely that prices for medical treatment will inevitably fall over time. This assumption sees medical costs as being bound, in due course, to follow the pattern trail-blazed by consumer electronics product categories. Digital cameras, autonomous flying drones, data storage devices, flat screen TVs, 3D printers, smartphones, and computers of all sorts: their prices have all plunged lower, sometimes by several orders of magnitude, over the last few decades. Some medical diagnostic services have followed suit, including – remarkably – DNA sequencing, which experienced a 10,000-fold reduction in the cost of sequencing an entire human genome, from $10M in 2007 to just $1,000 in 2016[159]. These cost reductions have arisen from wave after wave of innovations in manufacturing, engineering, and information processing.

But this trend of dramatic cost reductions exists alongside other trends which point in an opposite direction. One of these negative trends has been dubbed "Eroom's Law", in a pointed reversal of the name "Moore's Law". Famously, Moore's Law describes the tendency of computer hardware to *halve in cost* in real terms, roughly once every eighteen months, whilst still delivering the same raw processing power. In essence, Moore's Law celebrates repeated innovations in how many transistors can be packed together productively on a single semiconductor integrated circuit. By contrast, Eroom's Law describes the tendency of pharmaceutical research to *double in cost* in real terms, roughly every nine years, whilst bringing the same number of new drugs to the market. In essence, Eroom's Law highlights increasing complications with the research, development, and testing of new medical compounds. Whereas computer integrated circuits are becoming exponentially more efficient, pharmaceutical development is becoming exponentially *less* efficient.

The two laws both apply over a period of at least fifty years. Moore's Law takes 1959 as its origin point: the date of the first practical integrated circuit. Eroom's Law is dated back to 1950.

Eroom's Law was first described in a 2012 article in Nature, entitled "Diagnosing the decline in pharmaceutical R&D efficiency"[160]:

> The past 60 years have seen huge advances in many of the scientific, technological and managerial factors that should tend to raise the efficiency of commercial drug research and development (R&D). Yet the number of new drugs approved per billion US dollars spent on R&D has halved roughly every 9 years since 1950, falling around 80-fold in inflation-adjusted terms.

The authors of the article were Jack Scannell, Alex Blanckley, Helen Boldon, and Brian Warrington – four UK-based pharmaceutical industry analysts.

The Nature article continues:

> There have been many proposed solutions to the problem of declining R&D efficiency. However, their apparent lack of impact so far and the contrast between improving inputs and declining output in terms of the number of new drugs make it sensible to ask whether the underlying problems have been correctly diagnosed. Here, we discuss four factors that we consider to be primary causes, which we call the 'better than the Beatles' problem; the 'cautious regulator' problem; the 'throw money at it' tendency; and the 'basic research–brute force' bias...

To summarise the four factors discussed by Scannell and his colleagues:

- *Better than the Beatles*: Most new drugs turn out to provide poorer, or similar, levels of treatment than existing drugs; those that do perform better often only provide a few extra months of life to patients; unlike in pop music, novelty by itself is no reason to replace one drug by another

- *Cautious regulators:* Regulators have, understandably, grown cautious about the risks of bad side-effects from new drugs (consider the problems with Thalidomide and Vioxx) – side-effects that can be considerably worse than the problem the drug is intended to address; as a result, increasingly lengthy testing processes take place prior to drugs being approved

- *Throw money at it:* Businesses are set up to keep chasing ideas that haven't yet lived up to their promise but which might, with further effort, reach some breakthrough threshold – this is sometimes called "throwing good money after bad"; this effect is compounded by cultures of secrecy in which different drugs companies rarely share with each other detailed information about failures of particular research ideas (hence they repeat each other's missteps)

- *Basic research brute force bias:* Innovative ideas which sound good at a theoretical level often run into major obstacles during the messy process of real-life development and testing, in which multiple different biological subsystems coexist and interfere with each other.

In short, although many of the underlying technical tools may be improving exponentially (in line with Moore's Law), the problems they have to solve are also exponentially hard.

For example, studies of actuarial data of people's ages at death repeatedly show that an individual's mortality doubles roughly every eight years (from around the age of thirty five onwards). The observation is known as Gompertz Law, after the British actuary Benjamin Gompertz who first noticed it, in 1825[161]. Recent data from the UK's Office of National Statistics confirms this trend[162]:

- If a man in the UK is aged 35, he has only a 1/1000 chance of dying in the next year

- Once he has reached the age of 60, this probability has risen tenfold, to 1/100

- By 85, there has been another tenfold increase in his mortality: he now has 1/10 chance of dying during the next twelve months.

One interpretation of Gompertz Law is that there's a doubling roughly every eight years in the number of biological subsystems that lose their youthful vitality and start malfunctioning. Colloquially, we can say that, the older we get, more and more things go wrong with our bodies. It's like a game of whack-a-mole in which the pesky moles appear at ever faster rate. Therefore, it's no surprise that doctors have to work harder and harder to give us extra years of healthy life.

Steering technology for better healthcare

Despite negative trends such as Eroom's Law, I believe technology does have the potential to leapfrog over the exponential complexities of both human biological interactions and healthcare industry dynamics. However, this outcome will require *active steering* of technological capability.

First, a great deal more attention needs to be given to questions of the *design* of medical solutions, so that they are easy and compelling to use, by both patients and medical professionals. Designers of healthcare tech products and systems need to put a much higher priority on ease of use, simplifying usage patterns, and on redesigning the overall flow of activity. They also need to recognise and deal with the multiple complexities of the world of medicine. Smartphones – to mention the industry where I worked for the best part of two decades – only became widely adopted once high-quality applications were easier to develop, find, install, and use. It will be the same with many potential improvements in healthcare.

Second, we need to reconsider the design of what we might call *the medical industrial complex*. In some parts of the world (such as the USA), healthcare interactions seem to be deliberately kept complicated in order to protect high profit margins. Lack of transparency prevents formulation and observation of meaningful metrics, therefore standard competitive market dynamics fail to operate. As a result, prices remain high. In further complications, doctors over-test patients, because lawyers can make lots of money by suing doctors for medical malpractice.

For some incisive analysis of how complexity in healthcare systems keeps costs unnecessarily high, I strongly recommend the 2008 book *The Innovator's Prescription: A disruptive solution for health care*, by Harvard Business School professor Clayton Christensen and co-authors[163].

Third, as a special case of raising the priority of considering human psychology, we need to become collectively smarter at finding ways to steer each other away from the *unhealthy behaviours* which lie at the heart of so many healthcare problems. The last few decades have seen impressive progress regarding smoking, and a reduction of drink-driving, but issues with poor diet and exercise are proving much more stubborn.

As with the previous point, one complication is that steps which are best for the long-term health of the population often clash with the steps that are best for the short-term profitability of business corporations. Medicines that have proven prophylactic (preventive) powers are often unprofitable – therefore they receive little advertising.

Once society cuts back on the current obsession with maximising GDP each year, and instead puts a higher priority on increasing human flourishing – with positive health being a key component of flourishing – we should see a much greater focus on enabling cost-effective *prevention* of disease rather than cost-ineffective long-term *treatment* of disease.

Fourth, some fundamental new ideas need to be given more attention. Rather than "more of the same" incremental improvements, healthcare stands to be transformed by the disruptive application of *breakthrough next-generation technologies* that are on the point (if society shepherds them wisely) of coming of age: nanotechnology, stem cell therapies, genetic engineering, 3D printing, and machine learning analysis of large datasets.

Fifth, even more than a set of new tools, a new *attitude* is required – something that can be called a "paradigm shift", in which new factors are seen as important to healthcare, that were previously little studied. To be specific, *the importance of cellular aging* needs to be recognised and addressed, as an underlying factor which exacerbates a huge number of other healthcare issues. What's particularly significant is that the next-generation technologies mentioned a moment ago can be deployed to reverse and repair cellular aging, and thereby alleviate the entire set of aging-related diseases. I'll have more to say about this paradigm shift later in this chapter.

Finally, because many of these next-generation technologies are still some way from being able to deliver large commercial profits to companies who deploy them, society needs to find other ways to ensure that *sufficient funding* is available to develop these technologies. It won't suffice to rely on financial venture capitalists who are looking for a relatively fast return on their investments. Instead, society must decide to provide longer-term, more patient investment – akin to the centralised government funding in the early days of projects such as the Internet and the GPS network of global positioning satellites. These are investments which we cannot leave it to market forces to organise. Market forces lack the necessary degree of far-sightedness. Technoprogressive interventions will be required.

Tackling root causes

Some of history's most important healthcare initiatives involved tackling root causes which had, until that time, been only poorly understood.

For example, consider the dramatic decrease in childhood mortality in the United States and Western Europe in the late nineteenth and early twentieth century. Infant mortality at the beginning of that period has been estimated at 100-350 per 1000 live births[164]. By 1950 that figure had dropped to below 50 deaths per 1000. KS Lee of the University of Chicago has argued that the leading cause of this remarkable improvement was a wide-ranging programme to ensure all milk was pasteurised[165]:

> Systematic review of historical data suggests that cleaning the market milk supply was the single most important contributor to this decline in both diarrheal and overall infant mortality, and that this development played a far more important role than family income, other sanitary measures, or medical intervention.

Political scientists Jacob Hacker and Paul Pierson, in Chapter 2 of their 2016 book *American Amnesia: Business, Government, and the Forgotten Roots of Our Prosperity*[166], point out that the connection between untreated milk and high infant mortality was discovered almost by accident:

> In the late nineteenth century, public health experts noticed that fewer infants died during wartime sieges – even as everyone around them was at greater risk. The reason was that their mothers were more likely to breast-feed them. Breast milk was not contaminated by bacteria; cow's milk and water were.

Hacker and Pierson go on to comment:

> Growing understanding of infection and disease, coupled with increased education and income, helped change private behaviour and motivate philanthropic campaigns. But only government authorities with the power to restructure markets and compel behaviour could translate this knowledge into sustained social progress.

> Though taken for granted today, making milk safe and cleaning up water supplies were herculean efforts, involving massive investments of public dollars and new laws mandating that farmers, milk distributors, and other

private actors change their behaviour. No city required milk pasteurisation at the beginning of the twentieth century. By the early 1920s, virtually all the larger cities did, and many offered "milk stations" where poorer residents could buy clean milk. Infant mortality plummeted.

An earlier set of observations, made by Austrian physician Ignaz Semmelweis in the 1840s, had laid important groundwork for understanding the critical role of hygiene in preventing disease. Alas, his theories found little respect at the time. Semmelweis became severely depressed, and was confined to a mental institution where he was beaten by guards and confined in a straitjacket. He died within two weeks of entering the institute, aged only 47[167]. He did not live to see his insights vindicated.

In 1846, the young Semmelweis had been appointed as a medical assistant in the maternity department of Vienna's General Hospital. The hospital had two maternity clinics, and townspeople already knew that the mortality rate at one of these clinics (10% and upwards) was considerably higher than at the second (4%). Large numbers of women in the first clinic were dying from puerperal fever (childbed fever) after giving birth. Semmelweis put a lot of effort into trying to understand this variance. He finally observed that medical students working at the first clinic frequently also performed autopsies on cadavers, before visiting the maternity ward and examining women there; no such students worked in the second ward. It was a keen piece of empirical observation.

Based on his observations, Semmelweis surmised that some kind of microscopic material from dead bodies, carried on the hands of trainee doctors, was the cause of the high mortality rate in the first clinic. He introduced a system of rigorous hand-washing, using chlorinated lime. This process removed the odour of dead bodies from doctors' hands, in a way not accomplished by conventional washing with soap and water. The death rate plummeted, reaching zero within one year.

From our modern standpoint, we are inclined to say "Of course!" We find ourselves astonished at the prior lack of thorough hand-washing. However, all this took place several decades before Louis Pasteur popularized the germ theory of disease. At that time, it was commonly thought that diseases were spread by "bad air" (miasma). Accordingly, lacking any awareness of germs, the medical orthodoxy of the time resisted the advice of Semmelweis that rigorous hand-washing be introduced.

From the viewpoint of the medical establishment at the time, the ideas of Semmelweis were seen as being too all-encompassing: too far-reaching, and too disruptive. Semmelweis boldly claimed that one single cause – poor cleanliness – was responsible for a large proportion of hospital illnesses. That flew in the face of prevailing medical doctrine, which held that each individual case of illness had its own unique causes, and therefore needed its own tailored investigation and treatment. Blaming everything on poor hygiene was too singular an idea.

The practice of painstaking hand-washing was also something that, it seems, offended at least some doctors. These doctors were affronted by the idea that their normal gentlemanly levels of personal hygiene might somehow be substandard. They could not accept that they, personally, were responsible for the deaths of the patients they examined.

Semmelweis lost his position at Vienna's General Hospital in 1848, the year of many revolutions throughout Europe. The head of the department was politically conservative, and increasingly distrusted Semmelweis, some of whose brothers were actively involved in the movement for Hungarian independence from Austria. This political difference exacerbated an already fraught personality conflict. Semmelweis left the hospital and was replaced in his role by Carl Braun. Remarkably, Braun undid much of the progress in the clinic. Braun later published a textbook that listed thirty different causes of childbed fever. The mechanism identified by Semmelweis, poisoning from microscopic material from corpses, featured as lowly number 28 on the list[168], with little prominence. Maternal death rates rose again in the clinic, as focus on proper hygiene was replaced by a predilection for improved ventilation systems – a predilection that fitted the prevailing miasma ("bad air") paradigm for the cause of many diseases.

Therefore even at the hospital where the breakthrough insight had occurred, the heavy weight of orthodox tradition resulted in numerous women subsequently dying needless deaths. Similar dismal patterns were followed throughout Europe, until such time as independent evidence in favour of the germ theory of disease had accumulated, through the work of (among others) John Snow, Joseph Lister, and Louis Pasteur. By 1880s, thorough antiseptic washing had become standard practice, and the miasma paradigm had been overturned by the germ theory one.

To summarise this sad tale of the rejection of the insights of Semmelweis: faulty thinking by establishment doctors perpetuated poor hygiene and therefore caused an avalanche of unnecessary harm. This harm arose in part from lack of knowledge (ignorance of the germ theory of disease). It was also due in part to the overhang of prior habits and prior styles of thinking.

As for poor hygiene, so also for other root causes of disease. The tobacco industry fought long and hard to obscure the statistical connection between smoking and cancer. Their goal was to sow doubt in the minds of consumers. "More doctors smoke Camels than any other cigarette", proclaimed a 1940s advertising slogan[169]. If doctors smoked them, they must be good for your health, was the implication. Once again, the obstacle to identifying and addressing the root cause involved inertia. In this case, the enormous profits of the tobacco firms provided the inertia.

As for smoking, so also for poor diet. Many companies imply that their sugary, addictive, high-carbohydrate food products are, somehow, good for us. Genuinely useful health advice is frequently drowned out by waves of marketing from well-funded corporations who have unhealthy products to sell. Worse, there appear to be sharp divisions even between different medical experts as to what kind of diet is actually good for us. Some writers recommend a vegan diet (usually augmented with some mineral supplements), whereas others swear by a "paleo" diet with plenty of meat. Other controversies rage over different kinds of fat, different kinds of cholesterol, different kinds of sweetener, different kinds of wine, and so on. Given these ambiguities, it's no surprise that inventive advertising material is able to suggest all kinds of health benefits from products that are actually more likely to harm us than to benefit us.

Despite these controversies, we should keep one core idea in mind: identifying and tackling root causes of ill health should in principle result in major gains. We just need to be sure that:

- We have indeed identified the root causes correctly

- We have found effective behavioural changes or other therapies to alleviate these root causes

- We are able to provide support to help people make the necessary behaviour changes, in the face of social or psychological inertia to the contrary.

The abolition of aging

It's time to mention the single most important root cause of ill health. It's aging. Aging kills more people than smoking. It kills more people than obesity or air pollution. It kills *far* more people than industrial accidents, terrorism, warfare, and violent crime.

To be more precise, the causes of more than two thirds of all deaths are diseases whose severity and occurrence increase with age. These diseases include senile dementia (such as Alzheimer's), motor neuron disease, most cancers, respiratory diseases, heart diseases, stroke, asthma, diabetes, and sarcopenia (muscle degeneration). Collectively, these diseases are sometimes called non-communicable diseases (NCDs), since, as far as we know, they aren't spread by infection. Progress in curing NCDs has been nothing like as comprehensive as for infectious diseases. That fact, alone, suggests that a new approach is needed.

As it happens, one thing that NCDs have in common is that their prevalence – and their deadliness – increases as people become older. The older people are, the more likely they are to develop any given NCD, and, once they have acquired an NCD, the more likely they are to die from it.

There are two broad approaches regarding this relationship between aging and non-communicable diseases:

1. In the first approach – the approach of mainstream medicine today – each of these diseases is viewed as having its own particular cause and its own course of development. Each disease therefore needs its own investigation and its own treatment. In this approach, aging is seen as an especially hard issue, which should be left to the end of the queue for research dollars, since it falls at the end of life, and appears intractable

2. In the second approach, aging is seen as an underlying common cause and exacerbating agent of all sorts of disease (including NCDs). Addressing aging can be expected to reduce both the occurrence and the severity of these diseases.

The second approach may be compared to the Copernican revolution, in which the centre of the solar system was recognised as the sun, rather than (as previously widely believed) the earth. This second approach puts aging at the centre of analysis, rather than individual aging-related diseases. This approach depends upon the following assumptions:

- The term "aging" covers a number of objective underlying biological conditions which are themselves treatable
- Treating these conditions has the side-effect of reducing the impact of NCDs
- The underlying conditions are sufficiently common between different NCDs; for example, treatments which reduce the likelihood of certain types of cancer can also reduce the likelihood of certain types of senile dementia.

Having studied this matter carefully over the course of more than ten years, I've become a strong supporter of this second approach. I see good reasons to accept the three assumptions listed just above. To share my findings, I've written a 400 page book[170] arguing that the abolition of aging could well be feasible by around the year 2040. Here are its opening words:

> Within our collective grasp dwells the remarkable possibility of the abolition of biological aging.
>
> It's a big "if", but *if* we decide as a species to make this project a priority, there's around a 50% chance that practical rejuvenation therapies resulting in the comprehensive reversal of aging will be widely available as early as 2040.
>
> People everywhere, on the application of these treatments, will, if they wish, stop becoming biologically older. Instead, again if they wish, they'll start to become biologically younger, in both body and mind, as rejuvenation therapies take hold. In short, everyone will have the option to become ageless...

For more details of a seven-fold classification of biological damage that collectively constitute aging – and for proposed engineering interventions to repair and reverse that damage – please refer to the book *Ending Aging* by the Chief Science Officer of SENS, Aubrey de Grey[171].

From my experience, it often takes considerable time to change someone's mind on the credibility and/or the desirability of the abolition of aging. Powerful forces of inertia need first to be overcome. I don't expect that a few short paragraphs in this chapter will suffice. But I'll point out five changes that can collectively accelerate progress in this field:

1. The above-mentioned "Copernican revolution" paradigm shift, switching the roles of disease and aging, in which addressing aging becomes the key to solutions to numerous diseases

2. Ever greater numbers of medical practitioners having ever better tools with which to conduct their research and development, at low cost but high capability, including big data analytics and deep machine learning (artificial intelligence)

3. Improved ability to re-engineer biological entities with atomic precision, that is, at the nanoscale; this includes techniques such as stem cell therapies and genetic re-engineering

4. The transformational power of profoundly increased public interest in the field; as this interest accumulates, it can alter the political and investment landscape, and increase the number of people who put at least some of their time into supporting the project

5. The impact of fast increasing investments in new approaches to curing the diseases of aging – investments by huge corporations like Google (Calico) and Microsoft, as well as by private individuals, as covered in the recent book *Juvenescence* by multi-millionaire investment fund manager Jim Mellon[172].

Each of these changes is a revolution of its own kind. Together, suitably integrated, they can add up to the biggest transformation of human history. In turn, that transformation will play a vital part in the Transpolitica roadmap towards profoundly enhanced health.

The longevity dividend

I've used the term "paradigm shift" to refer to the adoption of the programme to abolish aging. A paradigm is a set of ideas and concepts that mutually reinforce and support each other. Here are some aspects of the existing, mainstream paradigm, which can be called "accepting aging":

- The transition from "older" to "elderly" is a natural part of human life; whilst we should respect the elderly, we should also expect them to become increasingly frail

- Elderly people experience a growing range of comorbidities, with multiple medical issues overlapping and complicating each other

- As a result, medical costs inevitably rise for elderly people, with society increasingly being unable to fully meet these costs

- Previous hopes for progress in curing diseases such as dementia seem to have proven unfounded

- Elderly people, when afflicted by drawn-out age-related diseases, experience a poor quality of life
- Society needs a rational, humane approach to dividing up its limited healthcare resources
- Elderly people have already lived the best years of their lives, including peak productivity and peak creativity
- It's selfish and irresponsible for any one elderly person to try to hold onto an unfair amount of social resources
- The appropriate course of action for elderly people is to treat them with dignity and respect, whilst accepting as inevitable a downward spiral in their vigour and health.

But the "abolishing aging" paradigm sees things differently:

- There's no fundamental reason why diseases such as dementia cannot be solved

- The tendency towards increased comorbidities with greater age can be reversed, by the regular application of forthcoming new medical treatments

- These treatments will undo the cellular and molecular damage that naturally arises as a side-effect of normal metabolism, and will periodically rejuvenate all aspects of the body to a more youthful state

- With renewed vigour, there's no reason for people to lose their creativity or their zest for life as they age; on the contrary, they can continue to develop new skills, to have new experiences, to share their expertise more fully, and to contribute in new ways to society

- Treatments that delay or even reverse aging will *save* huge amounts of money, rather than imposing extra costs on society.

The last point is known as the principle of *the longevity dividend*. This concept was introduced in a 2006 article in The Scientist, "In pursuit of the Longevity Dividend"[173]. The article was written by a quartet of deeply experienced researchers from various fields of aging: S. Jay Olshansky, professor of epidemiology and biostatistics at the University of Illinois, Chicago; Daniel Perry, executive director for the Alliance for Aging Research in Washington, DC; Richard A. Miller, professor of pathology at

University of Michigan, Ann Arbor; and Robert N. Butler, president and CEO of the International Longevity Center in New York.

The article urged that

A concerted effort to slow aging [should] begin immediately – because it will save and extend lives, improve health, and create wealth.

The last of these reasons deserves highlighting: this effort to slow aging will *create wealth*.

The authors of the article are optimistic about the prospects for the science of aging:

In recent decades biogerontologists have gained significant insight into the causes of aging. They've revolutionized our understanding of the biology of life and death. They've dispelled long-held misconceptions about aging and its effects, and offered for the first time a real scientific foundation for the feasibility of extending and improving life.

The idea that age-related illnesses are independently influenced by genes and/or behavioural risk factors has been dispelled by evidence that genetic and dietary interventions can retard nearly all late-life diseases in parallel. Several lines of evidence in models ranging from simple eukaryotes to mammals suggest that our own bodies may well have "switches" that influence how quickly we age. These switches are not set in stone; they are potentially adjustable...

The belief that aging is an immutable process, programmed by evolution, is now known to be wrong. In recent decades, our knowledge of how, why, and when aging processes take place has progressed so much that many scientists now believe that this line of research, if sufficiently promoted, could benefit people alive today. Indeed, the science of aging has the potential to do what no drug, surgical procedure, or behaviour modification can do—extend our years of youthful vigour and simultaneously postpone all the costly, disabling, and lethal conditions expressed at later ages.

As a result, they see many benefits ahead – including "enormous economic benefits":

In addition to the obvious health benefits, enormous economic benefits would accrue from the extension of healthy life. By extending the time in the lifespan when higher levels of physical and mental capacity are expressed, people would remain in the labour force longer, personal income and savings would increase, age-entitlement programs would face less pressure from shifting demographics, and there is reason to believe that national economies would flourish. The science of aging has the potential to produce what we refer to as a "Longevity Dividend" in the form of social, economic, and health bonuses both for individuals and entire populations—a dividend that would begin with generations currently alive and continue for all that follow.

They go on to list a number of ways in which the extension of healthy life creates wealth for individuals and the nations in which they live:

- Healthy older individuals accumulate more savings and investments than those beset by illness.

- They tend to remain productively engaged in society.

- They spark economic booms in so-called mature markets, including financial services, travel, hospitality, and intergenerational transfers to younger generations.

- Improved health status also leads to less absenteeism from school and work and is associated with better education and higher income.

In their 2005 review article "The Value of Health and Longevity"[174], University of Chicago economists Kevin Murphy and Robert Topel, carry out a calculation of the historical gains from extended longevity. It's a lengthy calculation: the article fills sixty pages of A4. Their conclusions can be read from the abstract:

The historical gains from increased longevity have been enormous. Over the 20th century, cumulative gains in life expectancy were worth over $1.2 million per person for both men and women. Between 1970 and 2000 increased longevity added about $3.2 trillion per year to national wealth... Reduced mortality from heart disease alone has increased the value of life by about $1.5 trillion per year since 1970.

Murphy and Topel look forward to continuing gains from further healthcare improvements:

The potential gains from future innovations in health care are also extremely large. Even a modest 1% reduction in cancer mortality would be worth nearly $500 billion.

Investing in rejuvenation

It's one thing to calculate the possible financial upside from a project, such as extending healthy longevity. But what about the costs of this project? Might the costs exceed the benefits? I claim that's very unlikely.

Here's the overall assessment of Kevin Murphy and Robert Topel, whose research I mentioned in the previous section:

> Between 1970 and 2000 increased longevity yielded a "gross" social value of $95 trillion, while the capitalized value of medical expenditures grew by $34 trillion, leaving a net gain of $61 trillion... Overall, rising medical expenditures absorb only 36% of the value of increased longevity.

They point out the implications of their analysis for setting the level of future investment in healthcare innovation:

> An analysis of the social value of improvements in health is a first step toward evaluating the social returns to medical research and health-augmenting innovations. Improvements in health and longevity are partially determined by society's stock of medical knowledge, for which basic medical research is a key input. The U.S. invests over $50 billion annually in medical research, of which about 40% is federally funded, accounting for 25% of government research and development outlays. The $27 billion federal expenditure for health related research in FY 2003, the vast majority of which is for the National Institutes of Health, represented a real dollar doubling over 1993 outlays. Are these expenditures warranted?

> Our analysis suggests that the returns to basic research may be quite large, so that substantially greater expenditures may be worthwhile. By way of example, take our estimate that a 1% reduction in cancer mortality would be worth about $500 billion. Then a "war on cancer" that would spend an additional $100 billion (over some period) on cancer research and treatment would be worthwhile if it has a 1-in-5 chance of reducing mortality by 1%, and a 4-in-5 chance of doing nothing at all.

Note the mention of probabilities. Investment can make sense, even if the probability of success is relatively low. This principle is already well understood by venture capitalists, who are prepared to accept low probabilities that a given company will succeed in its market goals, provided the extent of such a success (if it occurs) is large enough. A 5% chance of an eventual multi-billion dollar capitalisation of a company could support a significant investment – if, for example, the eventual valuation would exceed its present one by a factor of 100 or more.

This kind of consideration is familiar to anyone contemplating insurance policies. Disasters that have only a tiny probability of occurrence may nevertheless be well worth insuring against.

If only tiny probabilities deserve our attention, when the impact of occurrence is sufficiently huge, how much more attention should we give a possibility that has (as I believe) around a 50% probability of happening, with the financial consequences of that occurrence being in the trillions of dollars? That's the scenario if the rejuveneering programme would succeed in even a modest scale, compared to its overall ambitions.

Happily, there are at least five potential sources for the funding that could accelerate rejuvenation therapies and therefore accelerate the realisation of the longevity dividend.

First, consider all the funding that, today, is targeted at individual diseases, in comparison to funding that targets the underlying mechanisms of aging. Of the 30 billion dollar annual budget for medical research[175] overseen by the US NIH (National Institute for Health), currently around 2.5 billion is targeted at aging, with the other 27.5 billion spread around numerous individual diseases. This present division of funding (which has echoes in other healthcare budgets worldwide) fits the mainstream "disease first" approach to improving healthcare. However, if aging is given a larger share of the overall budget – rising, perhaps, to 20% over the next ten years, rather than its present figure of around 8% – then many diseases could become less prevalent, and less severe, despite the reduction in research funding specifically linked to them.

A second way to achieve greater progress in this field is by an increase in the proportion of discretionary time from people around the world that is spent on researching rejuvenation therapies. A small tweak in percentages is all that is required, on individual bases, to add up to a large increment across the entire population. For example, if just one person in a thousand devotes as little as four more hours per week to useful rejuvenation research – and four less hours to other leisure-time activities, such as watching light entertainment on TV – the total number of person hours spent on the subject in a country could rocket upwards. Such is the potential power of "citizen scientists" – who may be self-taught, taking advantage of the superb online training courses that are increasingly widespread. Of course, much of this effort could have little absolute significance, if it has low quality, if it merely revisits what other people have already done, or if the people involved have limited access to experimental equipment. Nevertheless, if suitable frameworks and processes are put in place to support "collaborative rejuveneering", including educational and mentoring activities, the overall benefit could, in due course, be substantial.

Third, rather than giving more of their *time*, individuals around the world can donate more of their *personal funds* to rejuvenation research initiatives. Rather than, say, donating on a regular basis to the college where they spent their formative years, or to their local church group, they can redirect at least some of these funds to philanthropic organisations in the anti-aging field (one important example is the SENS Research Foundation[176]). They can view these investments as a kind of parallel to contributions they make to pensions and health insurance schemes: the more people who pitch in with donations, the less the likelihood that family members, neighbours, and other acquaintances will suffer from aging-related diseases. With a dramatic change in public mood, along the lines discussed in this chapter, we could see a growing momentum of this kind of funding, similar to the way that other charitable campaigns have hit their own tipping points (for example, the ice bucket challenge of a few years back in support of motor neuron disease).

Fourth, businesses (both large and small) may choose to invest in the field, seeing the potential to benefit financially from a share of the longevity dividend. After all, if these therapies really will generate more wealth for society – by increased positive economic activity, and by decreased drawn-out sick-care – there ought in principle to be some way for the companies providing these therapies to receive a portion of that additional wealth. If that kind of benefit-sharing can be engineered, it will allow more of the remarkable entrepreneurial power of the business world to assist the rejuveneering cause.

Fifth, we come to the subject of *additional public funds* (rather than the *reallocation* of existing public healthcare funds, as in the first paragraph above). Public funds can often bridge a gap that business funds cannot handle – a gap that requires greater patience, and where the benefits apply to society as a whole rather than being easily redirected to particular commercial suppliers. One example of this pattern is American funding, to the tune of $12 billion dollars in 1940s value, of the Marshall Plan for the rebuilding of Western Europe after the devastation of the Second World War. Britain's public funding of the creation of the National Health Service also fits this pattern.

As one more example of massive public funding, consider Europe's investment in CERN, the European Organization for Nuclear Research, with its astonishing large hadron collider. This multi-billion euro investment, over many decades, was not undertaken with any simple thoughts of short-term economic benefit. Instead, politicians supported CERN out of a general view that it would contribute fundamental insight about nature – and, perhaps, create positive economic benefits in ways that could not be directly anticipated. The CERN project to detect the Higgs boson is, by itself, thought to have consumed[177] around $13.25 billion. As a long-time fan of fundamental physics, I have a warm space in my heart for the activities at CERN – and I admire the fact that the World Wide Web arose from work done at CERN by Tim Berners-Lee around 1989-1991. However, I believe there's a case for various public activities such as CERN (to give just one example) being relatively deprioritised, over the next few decades, in favour of more public research funding being applied instead to rejuvenation.

In conclusion, there are several sources of significant extra effort that can be applied to the rejuvenation project, with the expectation that at least some of that effort will result in very large economic benefits.

Becoming better than well

The abolition of aging is only one of a number of related "super health" initiatives that technology is making possible.

The short summary is that we cannot simply say "we'll all be living longer and healthier, but everything else will be basically the same as before". The same engines of technological progress that will enable the abolition of aging will, in parallel, enable other profound changes in human nature. These changes will result in humans who not only live longer but are much smarter, much stronger, and much more capable. New sensory experiences could become possible – such as seeing ultraviolet or sensing magnetic fields. New depths of emotional experience and heightened consciousness beckon, as do abilities to temporarily alter aspects of our body. Examples of morphological experimentation include the acquisition of gills that would enable us to swim underwater, fish-like, and wings that would enable us to fly through the air, bird-like. We might switch our genders. Going further, we humans could become cyborgs, enmeshing our original physical bodies in mechanical prosthetics, silicon add-ons for enhanced memory and calculation, and numerous other "wearable" and "embedded" computers.

Consider the ancient human trait of giving birth to children. That, too, is something which technology can change – not only by making caesarean deliveries much more common, but by altogether doing away with the requirement for the baby to develop in a womb inside a mother's body. The technology of ectogenesis would allow a fertilised zygote to develop for nine months in an external, synthetic womb, where it would receive all the nutrients and nourishment required for proper growth. This technology will extend and unify two capabilities that already exist outside of the womb: in-vitro fertilisation at the very beginning of life, and the protection of babies in hospital incubators when they are born premature. The technique will provide opportunities for aspiring parents who, for whatever reason, find themselves unable (or unwilling) to have children by the "natural" route.

The thought of ectogenesis – originally described by JBS Haldane[178] in 1924 – brings its own share of apprehension, fuelled by its depiction in Aldous Huxley's 1932 novel *Brave New World*. In that novel, the concept of motherhood is held up to ridicule, as is that of live birth, as being fit only for savages. In that dystopia, children belong only to the state, not to families – and "everyone belongs to everyone else". This is a future free from love or other deep feelings. However, there's no inherent reason why ectogenesis would have to evolve in such a direction.

Huxley's *Brave New World* forecast wide future use, not only of ectogenesis, but also of eugenics – the control of attributes which will be present in any given child in the next generation. In the novel, this included the deliberate creation of "lower castes" (such as "epsilons") with reduced mental capacities, consisting of people suited to menial tasks. It's no surprise that eugenics has a dreadful reputation – particularly due to its association with ideas of racial superiority and inferiority, and with the zeal of the Nazis to prevent various types of people from having children. Nevertheless, the core concept of eugenics can, *in principle*, be used in ways that everyone benefits:

- Rather than children being designed as "dumbed down" (like the epsilons in *Brave New World*), genetic precursors for positive features could be selectively accentuated, including creativity, sociability, generosity, open-mindedness, musicality, and persistence

- It's not just new generations that can be enhanced in this way, but existing people from earlier generations (including you and me), who could have our genetic makeup incrementally upgraded, helping us to overcome some of our innate negative dispositions.

These radical changes won't just impact individuals. As transhumanists point out, the human species as a whole stands poised to undergo a new, accelerated phase of evolution, in which intelligent life remoulds itself by conscious, thoughtful redesign[179]. That redesign can fix the worst bugs that we have inherited from our biological evolution and from our history – bugs such as cognitive blind spots, systematic biases and prejudices, flawed rationality, and perverse incentive schemes. In short, we need to contemplate, not only the abolition of aging but also the abolition of stupidity and the abolition of avarice. Rather than looking forward to "humans with longer healthspans", what we're really talking about is the advent of "better than well" super-humans, namely a step-up from present-day humanity that could be every bit as significant as the prehistoric step-up from ape to human.

It's one thing to note the possibility of this kind of radical evolution of humans, from Humanity v1.0 (so to speak) to a Humanity+ state[180]. It is, of course, quite another thing to decide that any such evolution is desirable. Mere possibility does not imply desirability. Figuring out which upgrades to pursue, and which to decline or to forbid, is one of the most pressing political tasks of the next decade. We'll return to this question in the pages ahead. First, however, we need to consider something that could upturn the whole framework in which this discussion has been taking place. The question of the level of health of individual humans may be rapidly superseded by the question of the health of the planet as a whole.

7. Energy and emissions

What's the point of extending our potential lifespans (as discussed in the previous chapter), if the planet upon which we are living suffers an ecological collapse? Who cares about extra medicines that could undo the damage of cellular aging, if we're unable to undo the damage we're collectively inflicting on our environment, via greenhouse gas emissions and other chemical distortions? Why bother about reducing the build-up of trauma within our biological bodies, if the trauma in our atmosphere, our oceans, and our countryside grows inexorably?

The structure of the argument in this chapter mirrors that of its predecessor. That chapter started by lamenting society's apparent inability to reduce the escalating costs of healthcare. This chapter starts by lamenting our apparent collective inability to reduce the escalating risks of runaway global warming. In both cases, the answer to the lament *should* be straightforward. A techno-optimist would say, *don't worry: better technology will take care of things*. In both cases, my response is: *It's more complicated than that*. Better technology will only work its magic if society actively steers technological development in the right direction. And that will probably be a lot harder than it sounds.

Note: to avoid undue complications, I'll exclude from the following discussion several other potential environmental disasters that loom in our future, such as fresh water depletion, soil erosion, and the distortion of the phosphorus and nitrogen biogeochemical cycles[181]. I'll restrict my focus to global warming. The themes that emerge from analysing global warming will illustrate the wider point, which is the need for new politics to emerge as an active partner to new technology. It's only the combination of new technology and new politics that will provide the means for us to avoid these environmental disasters.

The potential of green technology

From one point of view, it's absurd that there's any risk of greenhouse gas emissions pushing the planet into any danger territory. Instead of making such heavy use of carbon-based fuels, such as oil, gas, and coal, we should be transitioning rapidly to greener, cleaner energy sources. After all, it is frequently remarked that the earth receives from the sun enough energy in a single hour to meet all human needs for energy for a whole year. This assertion can be traced back to calculations made for the year 2001[182]: in that year, the total energy used by humans was 425 exajoules, whereas 430 exajoules of energy from the sun is absorbed every hour by Earth's atmosphere, oceans and land masses.

As long ago as 1986, German physicist Gerhard Knies estimated that human energy needs for an entire year could be met by the solar energy striking the earth's deserts in a period of just six hours[183]. A more recent calculation on the Land Art Generator Initiative website[184] concludes that an area the size of Spain would be sufficient, if covered by solar panels, to meet the energy needs of the whole human population. That calculation makes the modest assumptions that:

- The sun shines on average for only eight hours a day, and only for 250 days in the year (the other 30% of days are treated as non-sunny)

- Solar panels are only 20% efficient

- The global human needs for energy will expand by around 44% from the date the calculation was made (2009) to the date when it is considered sufficiently many solar panels could be in place (2030).

In case someone objects that Spain is already heavily populated, and its land cannot easily be covered with solar panels, the author of the calculation points out that the Sahara Desert in North Africa is eighteen times as large as the needed area. That includes large portions that are presently uninhabited.

Alongside solar power, other sources of non-carbon energy also have huge potential, to meet the energy needs of humanity, without resulting in any side effects of greenhouse gases. This includes energy from waves, wind (both onshore and offshore), geothermal, and various nuclear sources.

Accordingly, techno-optimists assert that it's only a matter of time before society converts more fully to energy sources that avoid any emissions of greenhouse gases. If that conversion happens to proceed slowly, techno-optimists anticipate that a different kind of technology could be deployed as an interim measure, namely "carbon capture" mechanisms to extract greenhouse gases from the atmosphere. Finally, as a fall-back option, geoengineering technologies could be deployed to artificially lower the temperature of the planet, by (for example) adding sulphur particles high in the atmosphere, counteracting the effects of greenhouse gases. Overall, there are plenty of potential technological solutions to consider.

Indeed, we can observe some encouraging signs. Total worldwide solar power installation has been growing exponentially for 25 years, doubling in capacity every 25.2 months on average. Global installation of 105 MW in 1992 grew to 422 MW in 1997, 2.069 GW in 2002, 9.183 GW in 2007, 100.5 GW in 2012, and reached 401.5 GW by the end of 2017[185]. That's equivalent to an average of a 39.1% increase each year.

One reason for this growth in capacity is the decreasing cost of the photovoltaic modules used. According to what has been called Swanson's Law[186] – which is an example of a "practice makes perfect" law of how greater experience leads to greater productivity – these modules drop 20% in price each time the cumulative amount of installation doubles. At present rates, that's equivalent to a halving of costs every 8-10 years. The decline in costs of these modules contributes in turn to the reduced fees for electricity that consumers need to pay. The median PPA (Power Purchase Agreement) prices in the United States fell by nearly 75% between 2009 and 2015, down to $40 per MWh (40 cents per kWh)[187]. Elsewhere in the world, PPA prices are even lower. In a report published in November 2016, Bloomberg New Energy Finance highlighted news from Chile, Mexico, and Dubai[188]:

> In solar, there have been some spectacularly low electricity prices agreed in recent auctions around the world – most recently, just $29.10 per MWh for a project in Chile, breaking the records established earlier in the year first in Mexico, then in Dubai.

Even before that report had been released, the $29.10 figure had already been surpassed by another bid in Dubai, by the Abu Dhabi Water and Electricity Authority, of just $24.2 per MWh[189].

India is another country that is trailblazing record breakthroughs with installations of solar power. The Kamuthi Solar Power Project in Tamil Nadu, southern India, which has been operational since November 2016, was heralded as the world's largest solar farm[190]. Extending over an area of ten square km, the farm contains 2.5 million solar modules. Perhaps the most remarkable aspect of the farm was that it was constructed in just eight months.

I've concentrated in the last few paragraphs on progress with solar power. Similar statistics could be quoted, almost as impressive, for wind and wave power. For example, following an energy auction in Spain in May 2017, nearly 3GW of wind-powered energy will be made available at the PPA of just €43 per MWh, which was reported to be the lowest price so far for onshore wind in Europe[191].

But is this progress fast enough? And if need be, could it be accelerated?

Technology is not enough (again)

April 30th 2017 saw the nation of Germany reach a new highpoint in the production of renewable energy. For several hours that day, 85% of the electricity generated in Germany came from renewable energy sources: solar, onshore wind, offshore wind, hydroelectric, and biomass[192].

That day featured breezy weather in the north of Germany (good for wind power generation) and sunny weather across most of the country (good for solar power). However, Patrick Graichen of Agora Energiewende Initiative commented that, as Germany's Energiewende (energy transition) initiative continues apace, it would become "completely normal" by 2030 for renewable energy to provide such a large proportion of the country's electricity.

At the time of writing, the highest corresponding figure for the United Kingdom is 61.7%, as measured at 1pm on 26th May 2017[193]. At that time, solar made up 22.9%, wind 11.2%, nuclear 22.0%, biomass 5.4%, and hydro 0.2%.

Other countries have figures that are even more striking – especially where there are large networks of hydroelectric generators. Iceland, Norway, Albania, and Paraguay have 100% of their electricity coming from renewable sources most of the year round[194].

These statistics suggest that it won't be long until the majority of energy avoids any emission of greenhouse gases.

However, there's a lot more to humanity's usage of energy than simply our usage of electricity. Aside from being accessed as electricity, energy is consumed when oil, coal, and gas are used for transport, heating, and other industrial purposes.

Taking figures from the IEA (International Energy Agency) report "Key world energy statistics" published in September 2016)[195], and looking at the last year (2014) for which complete data is included:

- The total amount of electricity generated in the year is 23,816 TWh, which equates to 85.7 exajoules

- The total energy consumed in the year is expressed as the equivalent of 13,699 million tonnes of oil (Mtoe), which equates to 574 exajoules

- Electricity therefore amounts to *only 15%* of total world energy usage.

Reducing the amount of greenhouse gas emissions to a sustainable level accordingly requires, not only increasing the proportion of electricity which is generated from renewable sources, but also converting transport systems, heating systems, and so on, to use electricity instead of carbon-based energy sources. This task is complicated by the fact that a growing population with ever larger aspirations for energy-rich lifestyles means that the increase of demand for energy may grow faster than can be accommodated by renewable sources.

In principle, the conversion of transport, heating, and industrial processes to electricity can be facilitated by means of:

- Improved electrical storage systems (that is, batteries)

- Improved electrical transmission systems (such as smart grids).

However, a great deal of inertia stands in the way of this wider transformation. The "Renewables Global Futures Report"[196] published in April 2017 by REN21 (the Renewable Energy Policy Network for the 21st Century) provides insight into the difficulties that threaten to impede this conversion. The publication distils information from interviews with 114 acknowledged experts on energy matters from a variety of think tanks, industry associations, government departments, NGOs, and universities worldwide. One question the experts faced was to forecast the likely percentage of all energy in 2050 that would be generated from renewable sources – as compared to the baseline figure of 19% from 2015. The experts picked the range of 51-60% as being most likely: that range was selected by 23% of the experts. Another 28% forecast renewables as generating various amounts less than 50%. 15% chose 61-70%, 12% chose

71-80%, and 14% chose 81%-90%. Only 8% of the experts were optimistic enough to predict renewables providing more than 90% by 2050.

Specific transition difficulties highlighted in interviews with the energy experts in the REN21 report included:

- The immaturity of systems to cope with large amounts of variable production (associated with cloud cover or lack of wind)
- Consumer resistance to lifestyle changes such as switching from private car-ownership to public transport and car sharing
- Political reluctance to endorse changes to energy distribution infrastructure
- Concerted opposition from vested interests within existing energy companies – companies that presently make huge profits
- Questions over business models: how energy companies might continue to earn profits, as renewables reach lower price points
- Unresolved public controversy over the possible role of specific energy sources such as nuclear power
- Lack of a sense of urgency to drive needed changes.

Unreliable politics

On the last of these points, opinions differ on how quickly changes *ought* to be taking place towards energy policies that are more sustainable. These opinions vary widely in their assumptions about:

1. The speed at which greenhouse gas emissions are pushing our planet towards deeply undesirable consequences
2. The risk of any acceleration in changes in global climate (rather than simply a slow continuation of present trends)
3. The potential for human society to make adaptations to increased global temperatures
4. The potential for human society to switch more quickly to environmentally sustainable policies, in the event that it becomes more widely recognised that such policies are needed
5. How much uncertainty it is reasonable to accept in answers to the previous questions.

If you have confidence in the capability of technology to dramatically transform human circumstances, you will likely provide optimistic answers to the third and fourth questions. You'll probably be comfortable with considerable uncertainty in answers to the first two questions, since you think technology will be able to provide the solutions needed, even if climate destabilisation accelerates.

I'm unable to share that happy spirit of optimism. That's because I see deep fragility in our political systems. Our global society often proves unable to take the steps that would be in our collective best interest. Powerful vested interests distort conversations, casting doubt, and playing on primeval fears and instincts. These vested interests include not only the large corporations that are currently making huge profits from carbon-based energy, but also the countries which owe their geopolitical influence in part to their large oil and gas reserves.

As a comparison, apologists for the tobacco industry sewed doubts over many decades about the links between smoking and chronic disease[197]. Huge armies of online bots (and their willing human helpers) obscured the presence of Russian troops in the Ukraine in 2014-15[198]. The so-called popular press in the United Kingdom, under the control of a small number of ultra-wealthy backers, seized countless opportunities to portray immigrants to the country in detrimental light, stoking an upsurge of xenophobia[199]. We voters prefer reassuring falsehoods to inconvenient truths. Our politicians prefer to reassure us in our chosen falsehoods than to confront us with the full gravity of the situation. Collectively, we applaud occasional rhetoric that gives lip-service to sustainability, before rushing away again to whatever new seven-day wonder distracts us from taking any real action. *Climate change? That's something the next set of politicians and business leaders can take seriously.*

Politicians wax and wane in the level of their support for switching to non-carbon energy sources. In May 2006, David Cameron, leader of the Conservative Party which was at that time the opposition in the UK Parliament, coined the phrase "Vote blue, go green"[200], claiming that his Conservative Party (the "blues") would deliver the best green policies. But by November 2013, after he had been Prime Minister for more than three years, he was apparently telling his ministerial team to "get rid of all this green crap"[201]. More recently, the government of his successor as Prime Minister, Theresa May, has been reported as seeking, behind the scenes[202],

> To weaken rules and regulations set out by the EU for energy efficiency and renewable energy governance… Specifically, the UK provided a series of 'amendments' it recommends be made to EU regulations that only

serve to reduce key renewable energy and energy efficiency targets proposed by the European Commission, make them non-binding and give Member States a lot more leeway to wiggle, or even scrap them altogether.

One measure of the lack of seriousness of international politicians about the threats from carbon-based energy is the size of the subsidies that are in place for various energy sources. No less an organisation than the International Money Fund calculated in 2015 the world's energy subsidies as follows[203]:

Post-tax energy subsidies are dramatically higher than previously estimated: $4.9 trillion (6.5% of global GDP) in 2013, and projected to reach $5.3 trillion (6.5% of global GDP) in 2015…

The fiscal, environmental, and welfare impacts of energy subsidy reform are potentially enormous. Eliminating post-tax subsidies in 2015 could raise government revenue by $2.9 trillion (3.6% of global GDP), cut global CO_2 emissions by more than 20%, and cut pre-mature air pollution deaths by more than half. After allowing for the higher energy costs faced by consumers, this action would raise global economic welfare by $1.8 trillion (2.2% of global GDP).

As the report makes clear, the vast majority of these subsidies apply to coal, oil, and gas. I'll return shortly to an important aspect of how these huge figures were calculated – a consideration about negative externalities not being priced into the costs charged to customers. First, here's how the Guardian's environment editor Damian Carrington summarised the IMF findings[204]:

Fossil fuel companies are benefitting from global subsidies of $5.3tn (£3.4tn) a year, equivalent to $10 million a minute every day, according to a startling new estimate by the International Monetary Fund.

The IMF calls the revelation "shocking" and says the figure is an "extremely robust" estimate of the true cost of fossil fuels. The $5.3tn subsidy estimated for 2015 is greater than the total health spending of all the world's governments.

The vast sum is largely due to polluters not paying the costs imposed on governments by the burning of coal, oil and gas. These include the harm caused to local populations by air pollution as well as to people across the globe affected by the floods, droughts and storms being driven by climate change.

Carrington goes on to quote Nicholas Stern, climate economist at the London School of Economics:

This very important analysis shatters the myth that fossil fuels are cheap by showing just how huge their real costs are. There is no justification for these enormous subsidies for fossil fuels, which distort markets and damages economies, particularly in poorer countries.

By way of comparison, also in 2015, David Cameron's governments took steps to axe wind farm subsidies, with the stated rationale "to stop turbines covering beautiful countryside". As reported in the Daily Telegraph, Chris Grayling of the Conservative government had only a lukewarm commitment to sustainable energy policy[205]:

This Government are committed to renewable energy, but I am afraid that my idea of renewable energy does not involve covering some of the most beautiful parts of the United Kingdom and the highlands of Scotland with wind farms… I am still befuddled by the way in which the SNP [the leading party in the devolved administration in Scotland] appears to want more wind farms in some of the most beautiful parts of the United Kingdom, which I want to cherish and protect for future generations.

If government ministers were truly serious about "cherishing and protecting" the landscape "for future generations", they would hardly cut back subsidies for renewable energy, at the same time as vast subsidies continue in place for carbon-based energy. Evidently, their minds are somewhere else.

A disappointing decade

I've been researching and writing about climate change for more than ten years. Over that period of time, I've seen plenty of evidence of systemic inertia – factors which, in aggregate, allow only modest changes in the make-up of our energy usage.

As an example of this slow progress, let me refer to notes I published in my personal blog after attending a BusinessWeek "European Leadership Event" in November 2009[206]. "Energy and sustainability" was one of the key themes of that event.

Mark Williams, Downstream Director of Royal Dutch Shell, kicked off the discussion with a number of sober predictions:

- Almost certainly, the total energy needs of the world will double by 2050

- It seemed to Williams highly unlikely that this vast energy requirement can be met by non-fossil fuels

- We need to prepare for a scenario in which at least 70% of the world's energy needs in 2050 will still be met by fossil fuels

- In other words, "we have to come to grips with carbon"

- Even as we continue to rely on fossil fuels, we have to "decarbonise" the system

- There's no reasonable alternative to developing and deploying technology for widespread CCS (Carbon Capture and Storage)

- It's already possible to store CO_2 underground, safely, "for geological amounts of time"

- It's true that there is public concern over the prospect of leaks of stored CO_2, and over failures in warning systems to detect leaks, but "governments will have to take the lead in public education".

Eight years later, as I write these words, precious little progress has taken place on systems for CCS. Consider a report issued in May 2016 by the International Centre for Climate Governance[207]. Tellingly, the report is entitled "Advances *and slowdowns* in Carbon Capture and Storage technology development" (my emphasis added). Here's an extract from the introduction to the report:

> Carbon capture and storage (CCS) technology, after having been hailed as a promising mitigation option around a decade ago, is undergoing a gruelling path to stay on top of the expectations... Despite potential benefits, CCS development and deployment have proceeded at a far slower rate that what was expected, and CCS is struggling to emerge as a sound low-carbon choice for governments and investors.

Later pages in the report provided more details of the reasons for slow progress. Withdrawal of government support for specific trials is one factor:

> Some planned projects may not be completed due to changes in the political or economic context, as is the case for two planned projects in UK, the Peterhead Project by Shell in Scotland and the White Rose site in North Yorkshire, whose fates are on hold after the UK government in November 2015 withdrew its £1bn CCS Commercialisation Programme as part of a spending review. Dozens of CCS projects across the world have been dismissed or postponed due to investment shortages and

government U-turns, such as the FutureGen CCS-equipped coal plant in Illinois, from which the US government pulled out in early 2015.

Moving on from the discussion of CCS, Mark Williams in the BusinessWeek "Energy and sustainability" event next made the point that, thus far, it has taken any new source of energy at least 25 years to achieve 1% of global energy delivery. That point should be kept in mind, he said, to avoid anyone becoming "too optimistic about new energy sources".

In response, people around the table asked whether the equivalent of a wartime situation might provide a different kind of reaction from both markets and governments.

Williams answered: "Don't underestimate the tyranny of the installed base". Alternative energy sources have to face very significant issues with storage and transport: "electricity is not easily stored".

Drawing on my experience in the mobile phone industry, I offered the meeting a techno-optimistic counter:

- Consider the fact that, 25 years ago, there were virtually no mobile phones in use. Over that timescale, enormous infrastructure has been put in place around the planet, and nowadays more than half of the world's population use mobile phones. Countless technical difficulties were solved en route

- Key to this build-out has been the fact that many companies were prepared to make huge financial investments, anticipating even larger financial paybacks as people use mobile technology

- If energy pricing is set properly (including full consideration for "negative externalities"), won't companies find sufficient incentives to invest heavily in sustainable energy sources, and develop solutions – roughly similar to what happened for the mobile industry?

- As a specific example, what about the prospects for gigantic harvesting of solar energy from a scheme such as the Desertec scheme proposed for a huge area in the Sahara desert?

Williams gave this response:

- The investment needed for new energy sources (at the scale required) dwarfs the investment even of the mobile telephony industry

- New energy sources have too much ground to catch up. For example, every year, China installs as many additional coal-based energy generators as the entire existing UK installed base of such generators.

The Desertec scheme to which I referred had been designed as a practical embodiment of the analysis made back in 1986 by German physicist Gerhard Knies – analysis mentioned near the start of this chapter. In 2009, I had a lot of optimism about the potential of Desertec.

I had learned about Desertec from a refreshingly matter-of-fact book *Sustainable energy without the hot air*[208] written by David JC MacKay, physics professor at Cambridge University. MacKay was subsequently appointed Chief Scientific Advisor at the UK's Department of Energy and Climate Change.

MacKay said he sought to avoid being labelled as "pro-wind" or "pro-nuclear", declaring instead that he wished to be known as "pro-arithmetic"[209]. Whatever solutions are contemplated, he said, must meet the test of adding up. He disagreed with those who say that "if everyone does a little, it will add up to a lot". Instead, he said, if everyone does a little, it will add up to a little. That's because of the scale of the total amount of energy used by an entire country.

The overall conclusion of MacKay's book was as follows:

We have a clear conclusion: the non-solar renewables may be "huge," but they are not huge enough. To complete a plan that adds up, we must rely on one or more forms of solar power. Or use nuclear power. Or both.

Eight years later, I believe MacKay's verdict still holds good. But so are his observations about the necessary scale. Any viable solar power solutions need to consider collecting energy from sunnier climates, and then transporting huge amounts of that energy to sun-deprived countries like the UK. MacKay put it like this:

What area is required in the North Sahara to supply everyone in Europe and North Africa with an average European's power consumption? Taking the population of Europe and North Africa to be 1 billion, the area required drops to 340 000 km^2, which corresponds to a square 600 km by 600 km. This area is equal to one Germany, to 1.4 United Kingdoms, or to 16 Waleses.

The UK's share of this 16-Wales area would be one Wales: a 145 km by 145 km square in the Sahara would provide all the UK's current primary energy consumption.

But how is Desertec doing, eight years later? Their website makes for dismal reading, with a marked slowdown in the number of news stories about progress at the company[210]. Five press releases in 2008 were followed by six in 2009, six in 2010, seven in 2011, eight in 2012, six in 2013, four in 2014, but then only one each in 2015 and 2016, and two in 2017.

It's as Mark Williams of Royal Dutch Shell predicted: large-scale new energy initiatives face formidable obstacles.

Might such obstacles be overcome simply by progress in technology itself, aided by visionary business entrepreneurs such as Elon Musk? Might we move beyond a disappointing decade to an exhilarating decade (or two)?

My considered assessment is that such an outcome is possible, but is by no means assured. Current improvement initiatives may run out of steam. It's dangerous to extrapolate curves of exponential improvement into the future, without a clear understanding of where the funding will come from, to accelerate the required core research in next generation greentech.

However, if the global political landscape could be tilted more decisively in favour of this transition (as opposed to politicians just offering occasional lip service in support of green energy), that could make all the difference.

The countdown to climate catastrophe

One of the main reasons why large-scale real-world action has made such slow progress, over the last decade, is the extent of scepticism regarding the future impacts of climate change. In some cases, the scepticism is made explicit. In many other cases, it remains implicit.

Scepticism about global warming often lurks in the back of someone's mind, even as that same person makes occasional professions of belief in the reality of human-induced climate change. When put on the spot, in a calm moment, that person might acknowledge that it's significant that such a large proportion of scientists speak out about the dangers of global warming. But away from that moment of clarity of thought, they act as if they don't really believe what they have just said. And they can convince themselves there are reasons to justify their inaction:

1. Scientists appear to disagree on various aspects of their predictions about the future, such as timescales
2. The recent "pause" (or "hiatus") in rise in global temperatures, although subsequently explained away by climate scientists, was not predicted in advance; this calls into question the models used by these scientists, and makes it plausible that there may well be other shortcomings in these models
3. Factors such as different types of cloud cover, deep ocean currents, alternative greenhouse gases (apart from CO2), and sunspot variability, may complicate calculations
4. Systematic efforts to impose a tax on carbon-based fuels could only work if some global coordination of national governments took place, of a sort that would spark fear in the hearts of many freedom-loving individuals
5. Rather than accepting significant economic drawbacks in the short-term for uncertain long-time environmental benefit, it would be preferable to leave matters until better technological solutions have been developed in the coming decades
6. Humans have proven themselves to be masters of adaptation in the past, and will likely prove themselves to be masters of adaptation in the future, even if global temperatures change.

My own judgement is that all these reasons for inaction are flawed. If we continue to prevaricate and delay, we risk a countdown to a climate catastrophe:

- Uncertainty about the details of timing of significant climate change shouldn't be allowed to magically turn into denial of any possibility that such changes will take place

- We cannot be certain, but it does seem likely that increases in global temperature will cause increases of all sorts of extreme weather events, including droughts, floods, severe storms, and periods of both dramatic cold and dramatic heat

- Once again, we cannot be certain, but there are risks that local tipping points might be reached, that will precipitate rapid transitions from one weather regime to another, as adverse positive feedback cycles are triggered (involving, for example, long-buried methane gases being exposed by the melting of Siberian tundra);

these tipping points could be reached by mid-century, that is, before the time when current efforts to reverse temperature growth are likely to have become effective

- Hostile weather is one of the factors that increase the likelihood of people wanting to migrate from one part of the world (with adverse weather) to another (with better weather); among other bad consequences, extreme weather damages agriculture

- Hostile weather also increases the risks of local conflicts, as different groups fight over access to reduced natural resources; in turn, these local standoffs have the potential to spiral towards global conflict

- An international situation of conflict and suspicion is one that will make it even harder to apply sensible global policies to address climate change

- Humans have, indeed, often triumphed in the face of adversity; however, examples such as the outbreak of world war one and the seizure and abuse of power by dangerous populist politicians show that humans are also capable of stumbling from adversity into disaster.

In subsequent chapters, I'll argue that global coordination, over matters such as setting a carbon tax, needn't involve any kind of oppressive global government. Better examples to bear in mind are the existing methods to coordinate international airplane flights. In other words, there's no reason for people to allow their deep suspicion of "international government" to ride roughshod over evaluating risks from runaway climate change.

In the meantime, as inaction prevails, data from the National Oceanic and Atmospheric Administration revealed in May 2017 that the amount of CO_2 in the atmosphere reached another all-time record in: 409.65 parts per million (ppm). Climate Central science writer Brian Kahn offered this commentary[211]:

> With May in the books, it's official: carbon dioxide set an all-time monthly record. It's a sobering annual reminder that humans are pushing the climate into a state unseen in millions of years...
>
> The reading from May is well above the 407.7 ppm reading from May 2016. And it's far above the 317.5 ppm on record for May 1958, the first May measurement on record for Mauna Loa, the gold standard for carbon

dioxide measurements. Prior to the Industrial Revolution, carbon dioxide stood at roughly 280 ppm.

The problem isn't just that this figure has reached a high unprecedented throughout the entire geological timespan in which humans have walked the earth. The problem is compounded by the swift pace at which this figure is now increasing, year by year. As Kahn explains:

> The new carbon dioxide high water mark follows a report released last week showing that last year the world saw its second-biggest annual leap in carbon dioxide in the atmosphere. It's second only to 2015, a year in which El Niño helped boost levels. Both years saw jumps that were roughly double the increase seen in 1979 when the National Oceanic and Atmospheric Administration started keeping the index.

Kahn spells out the likely consequences:

> The rise in carbon dioxide is tipping the climate into a volatile state, one in which Arctic sea ice is scraping the bottom of the barrel, oceans are rising and causing flooding even on sunny days, and the earth has warmed 1.8°F above pre-industrial levels. As carbon dioxide levels continue to increase, those impacts will only become more pronounced.

> There's a finite amount of climate pollution that humans can emit before we blow past the world's main climate goal of 2°C. If emissions continue on their current trajectory, we'll create an atmosphere unseen on this planet in 50 million years. Back then, the earth was 18°F warmer and the Arctic was more like the tropics with palms on the shores and crocodiles prowling the shallows.

But we don't need to wait decades until we observe horrific consequences of the increased CO2 in our atmosphere. Records for extremes in weather are being breached on a regular basis. Consider this news story from Weather Underground from June 2017[212]:

> The last week of May 2017 and first week of June brought one the most extraordinary heatwaves in world history to Asia, the Middle East and Europe. The mercury shot up to an astonishing 53.5°C (128.3°F) at Turbat, Pakistan on May 28, making it Earth's hottest temperature ever recorded in the month of May—and one of Earth's top-five hottest reliably-measured temperatures on record, for any month. Both Pakistan and Oman tied their all-time national heat records for any month during the heat wave, and all-time national heat records for the month of May were set in Iran, Norway and Austria…

An intense heat wave caused by downslope winds from the Laotian mountains towards the Vietnamese coast affected the area around Vietnam's capital of Hanoi in early June, particularly between June 2 - 4. The central observatory of Lang on June 3 recorded 41.5°C (106.7°F), destroying its previous all-time record of 40.4°C, set in 1971. On June 4, the district of Ha Dong (which hosts an international weather station representative of Hanoi) recorded 42.5°C (108.5°F), by far the highest temperature ever recorded in the Hanoi area... In the central area of Hanoi, near Hoan Kiem Lake, the humidity is usually higher than its surroundings, and the combination of temperatures as high as 41°C (105.8°F) with humidity values near 50% made the heat index an unbearable 55°C (131°F).

The biggest risk of all is that increased heat could trigger a comparatively sudden phase change in the earth's climate, pushing up the global average temperature by several degrees in less than a decade. Similar changes have taken place in the past. For example, around 11,500 years ago, in a transition known as "the end of the Younger Dryas", temperatures rose by 10°C within a single decade. This abrupt jump in temperature has become known from study of ice cores extracted from Greenland, and has been verified from data from lake sediments elsewhere in Europe[213]. Much further back in geological history, an episode some 251 million years ago, at the end of the Permian era, has become known as "the great dying", since 95% of all marine species and 70% of all terrestrial vertebrate species suffered extinction at that time. (As such, this considerably exceeds the extinctions experienced by dinosaurs and others 65 million years ago.) A front-running explanation (but not the only contender) for the cause of this calamity is a sudden increase of temperature, of around 6°C. Michael Benton and Richard Twitchett of the University of Bath describe the hypothesis as follows[214]:

> The assumption is that initial global warming at the [end of the Permian], triggered by the huge Siberian eruptions, melted frozen gas hydrate bodies, and massive volumes of methane rich in ^{12}C rose to the surface of the oceans in huge bubbles. This vast input of methane into the atmosphere caused more warming, which could have melted further gas hydrate reservoirs. The process continued in a positive feedback spiral that has been termed the 'runaway greenhouse' phenomenon. Some sort of threshold was probably reached, which was beyond where the natural systems that normally reduce carbon dioxide levels could operate

effectively. The system spiralled out of control, leading to the biggest crash in the history of life. Life came close to complete annihilation.

It's a different kind of example, but I'm reminded of the celebrity status acquired for a couple of months in 1980 by the caretaker of a lodge just below the timberline of Mount St Helens in Washington State. Harry R. Truman (not to be confused with Harry S. Truman, the former US president) had lived in that lodge for 54 years. Throughout March to May, Mount St Helens showed signs of a possible volcanic eruption. Nearby residents were urged to evacuate their homes, out of caution. Truman would hear nothing of it. A flurry of small earthquakes did nothing to damp his self-reliance. He refused to pack his belongings and move. His scepticism was supported by comments by Don Mullineaux of the US Geologic Survey, who said there was no evidence that the tremors were volcanic in origin. Mullineaux offered some reassurance: "The best guess is that it [an eruption] would not happen without some warning, such as venting"[215].

When I saw Truman on TV news reports, transmitted all the way from Washington State to the United Kingdom, I felt a surge of admiration for his bravado and folk-hero status. It seemed heart-warming that someone was standing up to the authorities.

However, that bravado was misplaced. On the morning of 18th May, Mount St Helens suffered the most destructive eruption in the recorded history of the United States. Almost immediately, Truman's lodge was buried under 150 feet of volcanic debris, from a landslide that had hurtled downhill at around 110-155 miles per hour. More than fifty people were killed, in most cases presumably instantly, including journalists, photographers, and volcanologists, as well as Truman himself[216]. Critically, there were no other warning signs such as the vents that some had anticipated. And there was no time to adapt to the explosion.

If the climate tilts into a new mode, generating unprecedented weather as a result, we probably will have at least some notice. We won't be caught out quite so suddenly as Harry R. Truman. But the forces unleashed will likely be ones for which we have no answer. Even a sudden wartime mentality will do us little good. Our long decades of prevarications and delays will have pushed us over the edge. We need that intense wartime mentality ahead of the transition, not after it.

A proper price for externalities

I don't claim any certainty regarding timescales for climate catastrophe. There are too many unknowns involved. Politicians, along with other members of society, can find, if they wish, plenty of reasons to delay action.

To break out of this impasse, society needs more than a foreboding of potential climate disaster. We need a positive vision of a credible roadmap of steps that can avoid that disaster. It has to become clear how the technological solutions which we can foresee, will actually be developed and deployed, rather than continuing to suffer slow take-up.

The missing ingredient is economics. Let's revisit the International Centre for Climate Governance report on CCS (Carbon Capture and Storage)[217]. The authors have no hesitation in identifying the root cause of delays with CCS projects:

> The economic case is the Achilles' heel of CCS. Without predictable government support, emission limits or a strong carbon price, private investors and utilities are reluctant to build new CCS-equipped plants or retrofit the existing ones. At the same time, governments cannot entirely finance projects whose financial viability, especially in the power sector (where the majority of greenhouse gases are produced), is unclear. But without new investment, deployment and testing, it is unlikely to achieve the progress needed to reduce costs and increase efficiency.

That analysis also indicates the solution: "a strong carbon price". Whenever companies are responsible for emitting greenhouse gases, they should pay a price large enough to cover the costs of undoing the associated damage. When this pricing mechanism is in place, it will be economically advantageous for companies to invest in CCS systems. This mechanism will also increase pressure on all aspects of society to:

- Transition transport systems, heating systems, and industrial systems, etc, from carbon-based energy to renewable energy

- Invest in technologies to enable such transitions to take place.

It is the *lack* of such a pricing mechanism that explains the huge subsidies for carbon-based energy quantified in the IMF report "How Large Are Global Energy Subsidies?" mentioned earlier in this chapter. The report sets out the concept in a section entitled "Pigouvian taxation"[218] (where the adjective 'Pigouvian' refers to the economist Arthur Pigou who first developed the notion of economic externalities):

When the consumption of a good by a firm or household generates an external cost to society, then efficient pricing requires that consumers face a price that reflects this cost. In the absence of a well-functioning market for internalizing this cost in the consumer price, efficiency requires the imposition of a Pigouvian tax equal to the external cost generated by additional consumption. This issue is especially pertinent for energy consumption since the consumption of fossil fuels generates a range of external costs including:

- *Outdoor air pollution from fine particulates* that result from fossil fuel combustion (either produced directly or indirectly from atmospheric reactions of other emissions), the main environmental damage of which is elevated risks of mortality for populations exposed to the pollution.

- *Broader externalities associated with the use of road fuels in vehicles,* such as traffic congestion and accidents...

- *CO_2 emissions* resulting from fuel combustion, which, along with other greenhouse gases accumulating in the atmosphere, can pose very serious risks for the future stability of the global climate system.

Let's note a couple of related examples, in which people have to pay a fee (or a tax) in order to carry out an activity which has a socially detrimental side-effect. Both examples involve driving cars, and both apply in London.

The first example is the "congestion charge", currently £11.50 per day, which drivers need to pay if their cars pass through designated areas of central London between 7am and 6pm, on any weekday[219]. Similar schemes apply in other cities around the world. The rationale for the charge is to reduce the number of drivers in these congested areas, thereby reducing damage to the neighbourhoods involved.

The basic theory of congestion charging was explained in testimony in 2003 to the Joint Economic Committee by Douglas Holtz-Eakin, Director of the Congressional Budget Office[220]:

As commuters in most large urban areas can affirm, highway congestion has become a serious problem that carries high costs in terms of time. The Texas Transportation Institute has estimated that rush-hour travellers in major metropolitan areas spent 3.6 billion hours in traffic jams in 2000 – at a cost of about $67.5 billion...

One policy response to the problem of congestion is to use the mechanism that works so well throughout the market economy: pricing. Congestion is considered an external cost (or "externality") by economists. A motorist on a busy highway not only incurs a cost of delay but also imposes that cost on other motorists. Because individual motorists make the decision to drive on a certain road at a certain time solely on the basis of the costs they incur (not the costs they impose on others), each motorist tends to overuse the road...

It is impractical to estimate and assign to each motorist the cost of his or her congestion. That difficulty has led policy analysts to approach the congestion problem from a different angle. In that approach, congestion is considered to arise from the mispricing of a good – namely, highway capacity at a specific place and time. The quantity supplied (measured in lane-miles) is less than the quantity demanded at what is essentially a price of zero.

Holtz-Eakin continued his testimony with a specific proposal:

If a good or service is provided free of charge, people tend to demand more of it – and use it more wastefully – than they would if they had to pay a price that reflected its cost. Hence, congestion pricing is premised on a basic economic concept: charge a price in order to allocate a scarce resource to its most valuable use, as evidenced by users' willingness to pay for the resource.

Introducing congestion pricing on a crowded highway – that is, charging tolls that are higher during peak times of the day and lower during off-peak ones – has two economic effects. First, it dampens demand for the highway during the most congested periods by inducing some motorists to alter their travel plans. Some drivers will be able to modify their schedules so they use the road at less busy times. Others will find alternative routes or switch to public transit. Second, continued demand in the face of appropriate congestion pricing serves as a signal for additional investment in road capacity.

For a second example of a Pigouvian tax, consider the vehicle pollution tax introduced by mayor Sadiq Khan in London from October 2017. Political editor Rowena Mason of the Guardian newspaper describes the scheme as follows[221]:

Older, more polluting cars will have to pay a £10 charge to drive in central London from 23 October, the city's mayor has said.

Confirming he would press ahead with the fee, known as the T-charge, Sadiq Khan said: "It's staggering that we live in a city where the air is so toxic that many of our children are growing up with lung problems. If we don't make drastic changes now we won't be protecting the health of our families in the future..."

The announcement came after fresh warnings this week about the poor quality of London's air...

The levy is expected to affect up to 10,000 of the oldest, most polluting vehicles every week day, as it will apply to motorists who own vehicles that do not meet Euro 4 standards – typically those diesel and petrol vehicles registered before 2006.

It will operate on top of, and during the same times, as the congestion charge, meaning it will cost £21.50 a day to drive a pre-Euro 4 vehicle in centre London between 7am and 6pm Monday to Friday.

Just as the T-charge for vehicle pollution extends the congestion charge for inflicting damage on roads and neighbourhoods, a "carbon tax" charge would, in effect, extend the idea further. All processes that allow CO_2 to be emitted into the atmosphere would be subject to an additional fee.

Ideally, the carbon tax would be set to increase, year-by-year, gradually applying increasing pressure on all parts of society to transition to cleaner energy sources.

Another useful comparison is with the tax that governments levy on cigarettes. In part, the tax helps to deter people from smoking. And in part, the revenues raised help to offset the additional costs incurred by the health services in treating people with diseases that smoking has induced or exacerbated. As with the health of individuals, so also with the health of the planet. Right?

What Milton Friedman would do

Concepts such as pollution tax and carbon tax have a long heritage. Doyen of libertarian economics, Milton Friedman, spoke positively about the idea as long ago as 1979. He was replying to a question posed by television interviewer, Phil Donahue: "Is there a case for the government to do something about pollution?" Here's Friedman's reply[222]:

Yes, there's a case for the government to do something. There's always a case for the government to do something about it... when what two people do affects a third party... There is a case for the government protecting third parties, protecting people who have not voluntarily agreed to enter... But the question is: what's the best way to do it? And the best way to do it is not to have bureaucrats in Washington write rules and regulations saying a car has to carry this that or the other. The way to do it is to impose a tax on the cost of the pollutants emitted by a car and make an incentive for car manufacturers and for consumers to keep down the amount of pollution.

A video recording of this exchange was played for the audience at an event in October 2014 at the University of Chicago. The forum was entitled "What Would Milton Friedman Do About Climate Change?" Michael Greenstein, the Milton Friedman Professor of Economics at the University of Chicago, offered this commentary:

> What's happening when we turn on the lights, when the power is derived from a coal plant, or when we drive our car, is that carbon dioxide is emitted into the air, and that's sprinkling around damages in Bangladesh, London, Houston.

> And those costs are real, and they're not being reflected in the costs of that electricity or the tank of gas. Emitting carbon dioxide into the atmosphere does allow you to produce electricity more cheaply, but there's a whole other set of people who are being punished or penalized. It's a poor idea of economics.

Another professor attending, Steve Cicala from the Harris School of Public Policy, was even blunter:

> It is theft. That's a loaded term, but if anyone can come up with a better term for taking something from people without their consent and without compensating them, I'm happy to use that term.

These are strong words, from the successors to Milton Friedman. The present situation, lacking carbon taxes, is "a poor idea of economics". It is "theft". Greenstone commented further:

> The price system isn't working in the energy sector right now exactly because carbon is priced at zero.

> The problem isn't the U.S. has no carbon policy, but that it has a poor carbon policy, namely, that it's fine to pollute. By introducing a price on carbon, the government could create a market for free enterprise solutions.

> It would be very hard for companies to raise money for innovation when there's no market for it. And this is a case where the government can set the market and then get out of the way and let the private sector figure out what's the best way to get to low carbon energy.

Here, I'm following the analysis of Forbes energy and environment contributor Jeff McMahon. As McMahon points out, there's considerable controversy about the appropriate role of government in intervening in market mechanisms[223]:

> Whenever government gets involved in externalities caused by a market, some people object to government intervention, but Cicala said the government would not be intervening in a market:
>
> "People say isn't it the case that with regulation you're intervening in this market? It's not the case. There is no market," he said. "The intervention of the government is to create a market and then get out of the way and let the market figure out the efficient allocation. The problem is there is no market for carbon"...
>
> One audience member challenged the economists at this point, saying Friedman would not be so cavalier about a tax when there is uncertainty about its optimum level and likely effects.
>
> "There is uncertainty," Cicala replied. "There is no question. Name me another policy where there was no uncertainty."
>
> The uncertainty, Cicala said, "should have us terrified" – not terrified of the effects of a price on carbon, but terrified of the effects of increased carbon concentrations in the atmosphere and ocean.

That exchange of views serves as a handy reminder of issues still bedevilling any implementation of carbon tax:

- There is controversy about the level to set the carbon price – and on how the effects may fall disproportionately on some of the poorer members of society

- There is controversy, at a more ideological level, about the idea of governments interfering with free markets – this controversy is connected with a deep distrust of the competence and motivation of governments

- There is difficulty in coordinating carbon pricing around the world, to avoid companies in one country being excessively penalised, as compared to the effects on their competitors in other countries.

I don't deny that these are hard issues. However, these issues are no harder in principle than the technological problems which scientists and engineers are collectively solving, in order to create renewable energy solutions. The economics and political angles aren't inherently more difficult than the technical ones. If society as a whole is willing to prioritise putting in the effort to solve these issues, we should be able to find a way forwards.

The next two chapters continue this discussion, by looking harder at the relation between governments and markets. I'll start by looking at the prospects for a different kind of collapse – not in the sphere of climate, but in the sphere of finance. Subsequent chapters will revisit the all-important question of international cooperation.

8. Exuberance and scarcity

Let's set aside for the time being the subject of the previous chapter, namely the threat of an environmental meltdown triggered by reckless human activity. Instead, to start this chapter, let's consider a different kind of meltdown, in which financial systems cease working around the world.

In such a scenario, ordinary citizens might try to withdraw cash from bank teller machines, sometime in the next few years, only to find they've all stopped working. The funds in savings accounts may be significantly reduced overnight. Payment requests using credit cards may be declined, causing chaos in shops and restaurants. In an atmosphere of profound uncertainty, corporations will avoid taking risks. Business contracts will be cancelled, with growing numbers of employees being made redundant. Supermarket shelves will become bare. Populist politicians and newspapers will be quick to blame bankers, businessmen, overseas cabals, the so-called "elites", reds-under-the-bed, or whoever. Tempers everywhere will flare. Soon, people will be trying to take matters into their own hands. The few "survivalists" who have been able to hoard scarce resources will find their stashes under attack. It won't be long until law and order breaks down.

That's a possible disturbing future which has echoes in many past upheavals. History bears witness to a long series of financial crashes, each ugly in their own way. Simpler times saw simpler kinds of crashes, but the effects were still often catastrophic for the individuals involved.

In this chapter, I'll explore the likely effect on future financial stability from the trend that underpins all the others discussed in this book, namely the acceleration of technological innovation. Should that acceleration make us more apprehensive about forthcoming financial crises? Or will it instead diminish the importance of money? Indeed, if economics is the study of the allocation of scarce resources, and accelerating technology delivers a sustainable abundance of all the basic necessities of life, where will that leave economics? Will the displacement of scarcity by abundance transform the so-called "dismal science" (economics) into an *unnecessary* science?

To give my answer in advance: that's not going to happen any time soon, contrary to the apparent expectation of various techno-utopians. Technological innovation, by itself, isn't going to free society from the risk of financial meltdowns. Instead, we're going to need better politics: technoprogressive politics.

Lost fortunes over the centuries

One example from each of the last four centuries will set the scene for the question of: *what next?*

The South Sea Bubble investment craze of 1720 saw thousands of investors losing huge chunks of their personal fortunes. One notable victim was Sir Isaac Newton, who lost the equivalent of £3M in today's money[224]. These investors were misled by the lure of apparent quick profits from a company (the South Sea Company) with monopoly rights in what we would now call South America. What was unclear to most investors is the fact that South America was under Spanish dominion at the time, so any monopoly granted by UK authorities was essentially valueless. In the wake of that bubble bursting, the rate of suicides in London soared 40% higher than normal[225]; many other people from all walks of life were left destitute. Newton is said to have lamented[226], "I can calculate the movement of stars, but not the madness of men."

The Panic of 1857 has been described as the first worldwide economic crisis[227]. Over-excited investment in railway stocks in the American Midwest was one of the causes. The Ohio Life insurance company invested $3M of its overall holding of $4.8M in railways, and was forced to shut down in August 1857 as railway share prices plummeted. The panic spread quickly from Cleveland and New Orleans to New York, and from there across the Atlantic in turn to Liverpool, Glasgow, London, Paris, Amsterdam, Leipzig, Hamburg, Copenhagen, and Vienna. For neither the first nor last time, banking regulations underwent a wave of reform in the wake of the crisis[228].

The Great Depression that followed the Wall Street Crash of 1929 lasted the best part of a decade. The resulting scale of human misery is captured in epic literature such as John Steinbeck's *The Grapes of Wrath* and *Of Mice and Men*. Industrial production in the United States fell nearly 50%; car manufacturing declined by two thirds, and steel factories operated at only around 6% of their capacity. Unemployment rose above 25%, whereas in other decades, before and since, it hardly ever exceeded 10%[229]. Similar jumps in unemployment rates (from below 10% to 25% or higher) were experienced by other countries too, as geographically diverse as Australia, Germany, and Britain.

In more recent times, the collapse of the US subprime mortgage market in 2007 triggered multiple banking failures around the world. These came as a nasty surprise, for politicians and other leaders who had convinced themselves that previous problems of "the boom and bust cycle" had somehow been solved by modern financial policies. For a terrifying few months in 2008, until cooler heads prevailed, it looked as if numerous major companies would be declared bankrupt. Hank Paulson, US Treasury Secretary during that time, starts his book *On the Brink: Inside the Race to Stop the Collapse of the Global Financial System*[230] of his account of the crash with the words "The pace of events during the financial crisis of 2008 was truly breathtaking." Later in his book, Paulson utters a cry for divine assistance, lest a truly huge injection of government bail-out funds not be made available to bolster the economy:

> "We need to buy hundreds of billions of assets", I said. I knew better than to utter the word trillion. That would have caused cardiac arrest. "We need an announcement tonight to calm the market, and legislation next week," I said. What would happen if we didn't get the authorities we sought, I was asked. "May God help us all," I replied.

In crises such as the four I've mentioned – and in the potentially worse crises of the not-too-distant future – wealth that was thought to be safely invested can lose significant parts of its value. Real estate prices can plummet, far below the value of mortgage loans secured on these houses. Bank balances can be reduced by a so-called "haircut", as happened in Cyprus in March 2013, when depositors with over €100,000 in their accounts were forced to lose either 40% or 60% (depending on the bank) of their savings, as part of a national debt restructuring[231]. And it's not just the rich who will suffer. Pension pots may evaporate. Schools and hospitals may be closed down. Rubbish may sit uncollected on street corners, attracting vermin. Diseases could ricochet through communities. On a local scale, mafia-like gangs might emerge, to try to impose some order. On a national scale, the route would be open to demagogues.

Financial meltdowns are, in part, the unhappy outcome of technological innovation going wrong (after a period of seemingly going splendidly well). The technology in this case can be called "fintech". Fintech is admired by investors, bankers, and other financiers for its promise of improved wealth management and superior monetary rewards. Throughout history, the pattern has repeated: new waves of investment have moved from cautious optimism to rational enthusiasm to "irrational exuberance" (the last phrase being coined by Alan Greenspan[232]). By the time the meltdown occurs, the exuberance turns sour, as an apparent abundance of ready money morphs unexpectedly into a scarcity.

As in the case of the environmental meltdown previously discussed, the cause of these financial crashes involves human activity which can be identified, in retrospect, as reckless. But prior to the meltdown, that same activity was frequently lauded as being smart, street-savvy, and exemplary. What was thought, or *imagined*, to be sustainable, turned out to be unsustainable.

Overconfidence over the centuries

What makes these financial crashes more ominous is their degree of apparent unexpectedness. "You've never had it so good", optimists tell the general public. "We're now in the period of the great moderation". "From now on, house prices will always rise, and never fall." And in the phrase adopted by economists Carmen Reinhart and Kenneth Rogoff for the title of their 2009 book chronicling what they describe as "Eight centuries of financial folly": *This time is different*[233]. Optimism, optimism, optimism.

In their book, Reinhart and Rogoff reproduce an image of an advertisement placed in New York's *Saturday Evening Post* by a long-forgotten company called Standard Statistics. The advert is dated the 14th of September 1929, and itself refers to the circumstances of a previous notorious financial crash – the 1720 failure of the Mississippi Company, which turned many people in France from millionaires to paupers[234]. The advert starts off as follows[235]:

Famous wrong guesses in history

When all Europe guessed wrong

The date: Oct. 3, 1719. The scene: *Hotel de Nevers*, Paris. A wild mob: fighting to be heard.

"Fifty shares!" "I'll take two hundred!" "Five hundred!" "A thousand here!" "Ten thousand!"

Shrill cries of women. Hoarse shouts of men. Speculators all – exchanging their gold and jewels or a lifetime's meagre savings for magic shares in

John Law's Mississippi Company. Shares that were to make them rich overnight.

Then the bubble burst. Down went the shares. Facing utter ruin, the frenzied populace tried to "sell". Panic-stricken mobs stormed the *Banque Royale*. No use! The bank's coffers were empty. John Law had fled. The great Mississippi Company and its promise of wealth had become but a wretched memory.

Following this prelude, the advert switches to the present day (1929). It oozes optimism about modern "facilities for obtaining the facts":

Today, you need not guess.

History sometimes repeats itself – but not invariably. In 1719 there was practically no way of finding out the facts about the Mississippi venture. How different the position of the investor in 1929!

Today, it is inexcusable to buy a "bubble" – inexcusable because unnecessary. For now every investor – whether his capital consists of a few thousand or mounts into the millions – has at his disposal facilities for obtaining the facts. Facts which – as far as is humanly possible – eliminate the hazards of speculation and substitute in their place sound principles of investment.

Just one month later, the Wall Street crash erupted. So much for the "sound principles of investment" touted by Standard Statistics.

Another overconfident prediction of the flourishing of the stock market is more famous. Leading economist Irving Fisher of Yale University commented in the New York Times on 5th September 1929, in response to some initial declines in the Dow Jones Industrial Average[236]:

There may be a recession in stock prices, but not anything in the nature of a crash.

Emboldened as the index rose again, Fisher offered further thoughts in the same newspaper on 17th October 1929:

Stock prices have reached what looks like a permanently high plateau. I do not feel there will be soon if ever a 50 or 60 point break from present levels, such as bears have predicted. I expect to see the stock market a good deal higher within a few months.

Twelve days later came "Black Tuesday". Desperate efforts by investors to sell their shares resulted in a volume of stocks sold in a single day that would not be matched for nearly forty years.

Even at this stage, the market was capable of rallying. On 10th November, Fisher again spoke confidently:

> The end of the decline of the Stock Market will probably not be long, only a few more days at most.

In year-end remarks, Andrew Mellon, Secretary to the Treasury (and hence a predecessor of Hank Paulson) shared this sunny disposition:

> I see nothing in the present situation that is either menacing or warrants pessimism... I have every confidence that there will be a revival of activity in the spring; and that during this coming year the country will make steady progress.

The US President of the time, Herbert Hoover, concurred[237]:

> I am convinced that through these measures we have re-established confidence. Wages should remain stable. A very large degree of industrial unemployment and suffering which would otherwise have occurred has been prevented. Agricultural prices have reflected the returning confidence.

But the worst part of the fall still lay ahead. In 1931 and the first half of 1932, the index slid, and slid, and slid, bottoming on 8th July 1932 at a figure just 11% of the valuation on 3rd September 1929. 89% of the value of stocks had been lost. It would take the Dow index until 1954 to match that previous peak.

That history of unwarranted overconfidence did nothing to prevent similar hubris in the run-up to subsequent crashes. Any sceptics who dared to urge caution were criticised as being unhelpful doom-mongers who were holding on to outdated concepts, or who failed to see the bigger picture. The discipline of macroeconomics would, it was affirmed, ensure the ongoing stability of the economic landscape. Here's an assertion made by Economics Nobel Prize laureate Robert Lucas of the University of Chicago, in his 2003 presidential address to the American Economic Association[238]:

> Macroeconomics was born as a distinct field in the 1940's, as a part of the intellectual response to the Great Depression. The term then referred to the body of knowledge and expertise that we hoped would prevent the recurrence of that economic disaster. My thesis in this lecture is that macroeconomics in this original sense has succeeded: Its central problem of depression prevention has been solved, for all practical purposes...

This kind of confidence about the practical capabilities of macroeconomics had evaporated by late 2008. With the global financial system in evident crisis, no less an observer than Queen Elizabeth II of the United Kingdom asked a collection of economists, on the occasion in November 2008 of the opening of a new building at the London School of Economics, why no-one had predicted the credit crunch in advance. A few months later, a group of economists, led by LSE professor Tim Besley, a member of the Bank of England monetary policy committee, sent a three-page letter to the Queen with some answers. According to a report in the Observer newspaper[239], themes covered in the letter included:

- A "feelgood factor", encouraged by the low cost of borrowing, which "masked how out-of-kilter the world economy had become beneath the surface"

- A "psychology of denial" that "gripped the financial and political world in the run-up to the crisis"

- Over-trust in "financial wizards" who "managed to convince themselves and the world's politicians that they had found clever ways to spread risk throughout financial markets".

The Observer quoted the following summary from the letter:

In summary, the failure to foresee the timing, extent and severity of the crisis and to head it off, while it had many causes, was principally a failure of the collective imagination of many bright people, both in this country and internationally, to understand the risks to the system as a whole.

Backing up this analysis in an essay in the Financial Times in December 2008, Chris Giles pointedly noted[240]:

Britain's nasty recession was not foreseen by Mervyn King, Bank of England governor. In May, he insisted: "It's quite possible that at some point we may get an odd quarter or two of negative growth. But recession is not the central projection at all."

International organisations, the great new hope of world leaders to provide an early warning of future problems, are just as fallible. The International Monetary Fund's spring 2007 forecast gushed at the success of the world economy. "Overall risks to the outlook seem less threatening than six months ago," its World Economic Outlook purred, in prose overseen by Simon Johnson, its then chief economist.

Alan Greenspan, chair of the US Federal Reserve from 1987 until 2006, confessed in an exchange at a congressional hearing in October 2008 that he had made a mistake in his handling of the financial regulatory environment in the long run-up to the subsequent crash[241]:

> I have found a flaw. I don't know how significant or permanent it is. But I have been very distressed by that fact…
>
> I made a mistake in presuming that the self-interests of organisations, specifically banks and others, were such that they were best capable of protecting their own shareholders and their equity in the firms.

To establish a comprehensively better political framework, it will be critical to understand more clearly this relationship between the self-interest of organisations and the overall wellbeing of the economy.

From slow change to fast change

Mervyn King, the governor of the Bank of England mentioned in the Financial Times review article quoted above, retired from the governorship in July 2013, and has subsequently published his own extensive reflections on the role of banking in economic wellbeing, in his 2016 book *The End of Alchemy: Money, Banking and the Future of the Global Economy*[242].

King summarises some of his observations via two laws of financial crises, which he attributes to the late Rudiger Dornbusch of MIT[243]:

> It is always surprising how many bricks can be piled one on top of another without their collapsing. This truth is embodied in the first law of financial crises: an unsustainable position can continue for far longer than you would believe possible. That was true for the duration of the Great Stability [the period starting in the mid-1980s which saw reduced volatility of business cycle fluctuations]. What happened in 2008 illustrated the second law of financial crises: when an unsustainable position ends it happens faster than you could imagine.

In other words: financial systems can continue for a long time in a state of intrinsic instability, whilst casual observers just notice the outwards signs of stability, and draw the wrong conclusions about likely future developments. It's similar to the wrong conclusions drawn by people like Harry R. Truman, mentioned in the previous chapter, who lived for 54 years on the slopes of dormant volcano Mount St Helens, with mistaken confidence that he had no need to relocate.

The two stages of financial system evolution covered by these two laws bring to mind a famous dialogue between two characters in Ernest Hemingway's 1926 novel *The Sun Also Rises*[244]:

> "How did you go bankrupt?" Bill asked.
>
> "Two ways," Mike said. "Gradually and then suddenly."

Hemingway's dialogue has in turn featured in several recent analyses about disruptions caused by exponential change. As a new technology platform evolves via positive feedback loops, it often passes through a slow, disappointing phase – when its performance remains stubbornly below that of earlier, competing platforms – before reaching a fast, decisive phase. Here's commentary from futurist Ira Wolfe in Forbes[245]:

> While written over 90 years ago, those words – "gradually and then suddenly" – could be headline news today about once-admired companies that fell from riches to rags. Exponential change doesn't care how long you've been in business. Just ask former employees and executives of Blockbuster, Borders and Kodak. Putting your head in the sand and hoping the future won't happen is a leadership tactic that may leave your career or your company on life support.
>
> Our world is changing at an extraordinary rate. More than ever, resting on your laurels can be catastrophic. Unlimited opportunity exists for leaders who leverage the power of disruptive change. Every leader should be asking his team: "What's going to bankrupt our business in the next two years?"

Swiss futurist Gerd Leonhard makes a similar point, in the opening chapter of his 2016 book *Technology vs. Humanity: The coming clash between man and machine*[246]:

> For me, this line from Ernest Hemingway's *The Sun Also Rises* describes the nature of exponential change perfectly: "How did you go bankrupt?" "Two ways. Gradually, then suddenly."
>
> When thinking about creating our future it is essential to understand these twin memes of exponentiality and 'gradually then suddenly', and both are key messages in this book. Increasingly, we will see the humble beginnings of a huge opportunity or threat. And then, all of a sudden, it is either gone and forgotten or it is here, now, and much bigger than imagined.
>
> Think of solar energy, digital currencies and the blockchain, or autonomous vehicles: All took a long time to play out, but all of a sudden, they are here and they are roaring. History tells us that those who adapt

too slowly or fail to foresee the pivot points will suffer the consequences...

I tend to think that markets will not self-regulate and deal with these issues by means of some 'invisible hand'. Rather, traditional profit-and-growth-driven open markets will only escalate the challenges of humanity versus technology...

Economics commentator John Mauldin brings the discussion back to the perils of financial collapse[247]:

"How did you go bankrupt?" asked Hemingway's protagonist. "Gradually," was the answer, "and then all at once." European governments are going bankrupt gradually, and then we will have that infamous *Bang!* moment when it seems to happen all at once. Bond markets will rebel, interest rates will skyrocket, and governments will be unable to meet their obligations...

While each country's crisis may seemingly have a different cause, the problems stem largely from the inability of governments to pay for promised retirement and health benefits while meeting all the other obligations of government. Whether that inability is due to demographic problems, fiscal irresponsibility, unduly high tax burdens, sclerotic labor laws, or a lack of growth due to bureaucratic restraints, the results will be the same. Debts are going to have to be "rationalized" (an economic euphemism for default), and promises are going to have to be painfully adjusted. The adjustments will not seem fair and will give rise to a great deal of societal *Sturm und Drang* [storm and stress], but at the end of the process I believe the world will be much better off. Going through the coming period is, however, going to be challenging.

As you can see, Mauldin takes an optimistic view on the final outcome of the economic transformation: "at the end of the process... the world will be much better off". To me, however, this places too much confidence on the capabilities of society's institutions and global leaders.

Yes, each previous economic collapse was, in the end, finally followed by a larger upturn. But the problems en route were gargantuan. Especially if coupled with other crises happening in parallel, from other fields – such as those covered in other chapters of this book – the result next time could prove beyond human ability to manage. That's why we need to carefully think through the potential scenarios well in advance, without allowing ourselves to get caught up in the cognitive biases noted by the letter sent to

Queen Elizabeth II: a "feelgood factor", a "psychology of denial", or over-trust in "financial wizards".

Financial clouds gathering again

It's not possible to provide any strict forecast of a timescale for a new financial crash. It may lie a decade or more into the future; alternatively, affairs could unravel within the next few years. Despite this uncertainty, we should notice at least seven factors which make it plausible that significant problems lie ahead:

1. Long-developing tensions in the Eurozone suggest that more banks will fail; eminent analysts as diverse as Mervyn King (former governor of the Bank of England) and Yanis Varoufakis (former Greek Finance Minister) believe that the Eurozone suffers from deep design flaws

2. Many financiers still have a strong desire to "innovate" complex new methods for making money, embracing a similar set of risks to those "weapons of mass financial destruction"[248] (Mortgage-Backed Securities, Collateralized Debt Obligations, and so on) whose hidden interconnections greatly multiplied the effects of the 2008 crisis

3. Some governments – such as in the United States – are winding back the regulations put in place after the 2008 crisis, thereby further increasing the risk margins for new financial misadventures

4. Actions that could be taken by individual countries to improve the overall sustainability of the global financial system are likely to put these countries at a short-term competitive disadvantage, compared to other countries where no such regulatory change happens; comprehensive solutions will probably require international coordination of a degree that is difficult to obtain (except in times when crisis has already struck – by which time it will be too late)

5. A metric which has been persuasively correlated to the onset of past financial crises, namely the ratio of private debt (money owed by individuals and businesses) to GDP (the overall size of the economy), remains alarmingly high in many countries; the consequence is that larger proportions of income therefore need to be allocated to servicing interest payments, depressing the level of

economic activity unless further loans are obtained, in turn pushing matters further into unsustainability (see the writing of economist Steve Keen for trenchant analysis of this topic[249])

6. As one particularly important example of the previous point: the levels of indebtedness in China are unprecedented; in other words, the economy in China may be dangerously unstable

7. The field of the study of macroeconomics remains in a troubled state of wide disagreement and controversy, with little sign of any consensus emerging.

That's not all. Additional complications include the availability of new technological solutions, such as financial trading driven by superfast artificial intelligence, and new coordination mechanisms involving blockchain distributed ledgers. In both cases, there are large potential upsides *and downsides* from unforeseen interactions. Consider the so-called "Flash Crash" of 6th May 2010, which is generally thought[250] to be caused by "a toxic interaction of high-frequency and algorithmic trading systems". Consider also that cryptocurrencies like bitcoin and ether, based on blockchain technology, are by no means immune from overconfidence, scams, crashes, and chaos[251].

How widespread can we expect the effects of future financial crises? As human societies become increasingly interconnected, localised monetary problems risk being spread contagiously to wider regions. This interconnectedness has two aspects: objective and subjective. The objective connections are when money invested in one financial asset is split up and reinvested in multiple secondary financial assets, often via complicated intermediaries or "shadow banking" mechanisms, whose details are often deliberately opaque (in part, to try to circumvent the attention of financial regulators). The subjective connections involve the spread of sentiment and mood – referred to by John Maynard Keynes as "animal spirits".

Given the speed at which social media propagates sentiment nowadays, it would be prudent to anticipate problems that are global rather than local in scale. Animal spirits have never before been so animated.

Economic maximisation is not enough

Mention of "animal spirits" is a reminder that individual investors often behave irrationally. Stated more correctly, people often act in ways different from the axiom of "economic maximisation" from which many of the theories in mainstream economics are derived.

One indication of a flaw in this assumption can be found from the psychology experiment known as the ultimatum game.[252] This experiment involves two participants. The first is given $100, and is told to choose a portion of this bounty to pass to the second. For example, the bounty could be split 50:50, 60:40, 70:30, or any other combination. The second participant has the choice to accept or reject the offer. Whether or not the first gets to keep the remainder of the $100 depends on whether or not the second accepts the offer. Mainstream economics would suggest the former should offer something like $5 to the second, since the second participant will choose to gain $5 over the option to gain nothing at all. That would appear to be the economically rational thing to do. However, in such cases, the second participant frequently opts to receive nothing at all, thereby punishing the first for perceived unfairness. In this case, both participants go home empty-handed from the experiment. Anticipating this outcome, the first participant is in practice more likely to split the money in a ratio much closer to 50:50.

George Cooper, author of the 2016 book *Fixing Economics: The story of how the dismal science was broken – and how it could be rebuilt*[253], notes that the behaviour in this experiment fits the theory that evolution has led humans to seek, not *maximisation*, but *competitive advantage*:

> When we were evolving on the plains of Africa into the tribal, social animals that we are, was it more important that we were able to run fast or that we could run faster than our neighbour? My guess is that when a lion was looking for lunch, the most important thing was not to run fast; it was to run faster than the person next to you. That is to say, it was the ability to *compete successfully* that ensured survival.

Cooper comments as follows on the ultimatum game:

> Neoclassical economists, working to an optimising paradigm, have puzzled over why the second player tends to reject small offers and why the first player typically makes offers that appear overly generous. Viewed from a competitive rather than an optimising paradigm, this behaviour looks much less odd.
>
> The second player will reject an offer in which the split of the money is especially uneven, because this result will give the first player a substantial competitive advantage. The first player instinctively understands this

psychology and therefore offers to split the money more evenly. The first player's motivation is to make an offer that retains only as much relative advantage as the second player will tolerate.

The ultimatum game is also an example of the importance of the concept of *fairness* in human decisions. Our own wellbeing depends on maintaining good relationships within our community. If that community is striven apart by lack of fairness, most members of that community will suffer as a result (even though a small number may benefit – for a time).

Writing towards the end of a long and distinguished academic career, Professor Albert Rees of Princeton University lamented that mainstream economics theories pay far too little attention to the concept of fairness[254]:

> The neoclassical theory of wage determination, which I taught for 30 years and have tried to explain in my textbook [published 20 years earlier], has nothing to say about fairness. In this theory, wages are determined by a demand schedule based on marginal productivity and a supply schedule based on the utility function of workers... The wages of worker B do not enter the utility function of worker A.

> Beginning in the mid-1970s, I began to find myself in a series of roles in which I have participated in setting or controlling wages and salaries. These included sitting on three wage stabilization bodies during the Nixon and Ford administrations, as a director of two corporations, as a provost of a private university, as a president of a foundation, and as a trustee of a liberal arts college. In one of the corporations I serve as chairman of the compensation committee.

> In none of these roles did I find the theory that I taught so long to be the slightest help. The factors involved in setting wages and salaries in the real world seemed to be very different from those specified in the neoclassical theory. The one factor that seemed to be of overwhelming importance in all these situations was fairness.

The first criticism of the prevailing "economic maximisation" theory of human activity, therefore, is that economic decisions frequently include motivations other than individuals gaining as large as possible an individual economic benefit. We are motivated, additionally, by concerns about fairness, and about competitive relationships. We want to better our situation, but not at the cost of damaging a set of relationships that are important to us. Mathematical descriptions of economies in which everyone acts to maximise their economic value are, accordingly, deficient. Ignoring human variety is one reason why mainstream economic theories underestimate the risks of financial crises.

A second criticism has been developed in the blossoming field of behavioural economics[255]. We often behave in ways that are clearly divergent from the goals we say we are trying to fulfil (whether that's maximisation, competitive advantage, long-term security, or whatever). That's because we are victims of numerous cognitive biases: we rely too heavily on the familiar, our estimates are skewed by whatever numbers we have heard recently (these estimates act as so-called "anchors"), our memories are nothing like as reliable as we tend to think, we are overly attached to "sunk costs", and so on.

A third criticism is that people often cannot tell which actions are the best ones, in order to pursue whatever economic goal we are actually trying to follow. Even if we could overcome all the flaws in our reasoning processes enumerated by the discipline of behavioural economics, we lack sufficient knowledge to make reliable decisions. In some cases, that's because information is deliberately hidden from us, by vendors who would like to sell us a so-called "lemon" – an item which turns out to be defective. For example, a vendor may be trying to sell us a second-hand car without its key flaws being noticed. But in other cases, there's a more fundamental problem: the future is *fundamentally unknowable*. In these cases, we are especially vulnerable to subjective factors influencing our decisions.

Animal spirits

Radical uncertainty – to use a phrase highlighted by John Maynard Keynes – isn't just that there's a spectrum of possibilities, to which we could in principle assign different probabilities based on our prior experiences. It's a circumstance in which the only probabilities that can be meaningfully assigned are extremely vague ones. Financial Times writer John Kay addresses this topic as follows[256]:

> "By uncertain knowledge," wrote Keynes in 1921, "I do not mean merely to distinguish what is known for certain from what is only probable. The sense in which I am using the term is that in which the prospect of a European war is uncertain… There is no scientific basis to form any calculable probability whatever. We simply do not know."

> While the long-term future of interest rates or copper prices, about which Keynes also speculated, might be approached probabilistically, questions

about the social system 50 years hence are too open-ended, and the outcomes too varied and insufficiently specific, to be described in probabilistic terms.

If you had described your smartphone to [Milton] Friedman in 1976 he would not have understood what you were talking about, far less been able to speculate intelligently on the probability that it would be invented or bought. These are the "black swans" Nassim Taleb has described. The reader who once asked me which black swans were most likely to materialise in the next five years could not have missed the point more comprehensively.

There is a world of difference between low-probability events drawn from the tail of a known statistical distribution and extreme events that happen but had not previously been imagined. And it is usually the latter that give rise to crises – and opportunities.

In the case of the second hand car salesman, we can draw on prior experience (and on records of other people's experience) to realize in advance that there's a reasonable chance of the car having more defects than are obvious to a cursory inspection. But in the case of a brand new event, different in nature from what has ever occurred before, how are we to estimate different probabilities?

For example, should households spend more money in the present, anticipating a positive upturn of the economy? Should companies take risks by hiring many new employees, anticipating a positive market response to their new product offerings? Or should they instead prepare for downturns, thereby holding onto their money and resources? The notion of radical uncertainty says that, in at least some occasions, there are no objective grounds to estimate the likelihoods of various outcomes. Circumstances are too novel. In the words of former US Defence Secretary Donald Rumsfeld, the existence of "unknown unknowns" will undermine any attempts at rational calculation of these probabilities.

In such circumstances, we may search for comparisons with past historical episodes: this economic situation is *a bit* similar to what happened in the past, we might reason to ourselves – but, goodness, there are lots of differences too. Or, we tell ourselves, this modern day upstart politician has some similarities to Benito Mussolini, so maybe things will develop similarly to the Europe of the 1920s and 1930s – but, again, so many things are different nowadays, so all bets are off.

In these cases, what determines the economic choices that people actually make? Objective evaluations are supplemented by subjective sentiment – also known as "animal spirits". These include feelings about confidence, about fairness, about trust, and about the desirability or undesirability of various visions of the future.

How the economy performs, in such circumstances, depends critically on public sentiment. It also depends on people's assessments of *other people's sentiments*. If you think that other people are going to lose their confidence in the ability of a bank to let them withdraw their savings, it's rational for you to join the "bank run", so that you have the chance to withdraw your own savings from that bank before it, indeed, runs out of money. You'd better claim your place in the queue before the queue grows too long. Again, it's not rational to invest money in a new business venture, if you think that potential clients will all be tightening their financial belts in a period of foreboding – so you tighten your belt too.

It's part of the job of leading bankers to avoid the onset of a public mood of despondency. From time to time, they make bold public statements of confidence, trying to propel the economy towards a positive spiral of investment and enterprise, and away from the negative spiral of belt-tightening known as "the paradox of thrift": the more that people save, fearing an economic downturn ahead, the fewer goods and services are purchased, meaning that people end up *less* well off, despite their savings.

Some of the statements quoted earlier in this chapter as examples of unwarranted overconfidence, from various central bankers and finance officials, can be reinterpreted more charitably as these spokespeople trying to create self-fulfilling prophecies. If authority figures speak boldly of a forthcoming economic upturn, it can change public sentiment, increasing the likelihood of that upturn taking place.

I'm sympathetic to what these spokespeople were trying to do. Changing the public narrative about the future is important to securing a better future. In the absence of a compelling vision of steps that can be taken towards a positive restructuring of society, a dark weight of pessimism can drive people back into their shells. The best response to the risk of financial crashes, therefore, is to spell out a credible model of the future global economy in which there will be ample provision for everyone to flourish. That's my task in the closing portion of this chapter.

Note in passing that there are two risks with any public statements that are intended to change public sentiment from apprehension to confidence:

1. The statements need to be consistent with the underlying objective situation; for example, no amount of positive animal spirit, by itself, can overcome an unsustainable level of private indebtedness (it will just delay the inevitable future crash)

2. In order to boost public confidence, spokespeople may need first to convince themselves that the future is rosy, thereby predisposing themselves to pay insufficient attention to underlying risks. That's an argument for increased transparency, and for the avoidance of groupthink.

A technoprogressive future for money

A technoprogressive account of the future of money starts with the recognition that money is a technology – a powerful, sophisticated technology. Like other technologies, money is a mechanism that:

- Allows humans to do things that would not otherwise be possible (or to do these things more fully)
- Has experienced many innovations in its operation over the years – consider developments such as paper money, cheques, insurance contracts, limited liability companies, mutual investment funds, deposit insurance guarantees, and cryptocurrencies
- Can interact with other technologies in multiple ways (some hard to anticipate in advance)
- Can have both good and bad societal impact.

The final point just noted deserves underscoring. Money and its related institutions, such as banking and investment mechanisms, have enabled profound advances in the human condition.

It's not just that money enables a more efficient sharing of produce than simple barter mechanisms. It's that money enables and encourages people to become involved in enterprises which would otherwise scarcely have been possible. If you need extra resources to start a project, you can obtain investment from far-distant sources, rather than just trying to rely on good will from family and friends. Financial risks can be spread out in ways that make them more tractable. Rather than a single business person being liable for all the downside if, say, a ship carrying lots of cargo is sunk by an unseasonable storm – and the person in question therefore being deterred from commencing the project in the first place – insurance can provide the incentive to take the plunge.

Indeed, the Industrial Revolution would probably not have taken place, or would have proceeded much more slowly, in the absence of financial innovations such as joint stock companies. The Economist magazine suggested[257] in 1926 that the unknown person who had devised the idea of the limited liability company deserved "a place of honour with Watt [the steam engine trailblazer], Stephenson [the railways innovator] and other pioneers of the industrial revolution".

In other words, business development initiatives have been facilitated by a growing network of commercial banks and other financial intermediaries. These banks have, in turn, been facilitated by central banks that were prepared to act, with government backing, as the "lender of last resort".

Will Rogers, the American humourist (1879-1935), is said to have quipped[258] that "There have been three great inventions since the beginning of time: fire, the wheel and central banking". Many a true word is said in jest (albeit in exaggeration). The institutions of central banking – such as the Federal Reserve in the United States and the Bank of England in the United Kingdom – have provided significant extra stability to financial systems, compared to before their introduction. These institutions intervene from time to time to loan funds to commercial banks, to prevent the failure of these banks.

But there are plenty of dissenting views. The New Testament in the Bible warns us that "The love of money is the root of all evil"[259]. Many religions have declared it sinful to charge interest ("usury") on loans. Contemporary critics use lots of choice insults to describe bankers. Celebrity chef Mario Batali of the Food Network opined, in a 2011 Time Magazine Person of the Year debate, that bankers had the same moral standing as Stalin and Hitler[260]:

> [The institution with] the largest effect on the whole planet without us really paying attention... is the entire banking industry and their disregard for the people that they're supposed to be working for... The ways the bankers have... toppled the way money is distributed and taken most of it into their hands is as good as Stalin or Hitler and the evil guys.

An area of particular controversy is the ability of banks to create money out of nothing – by so-called "fiat". This money has no direct backing from any material "gold standard" or other tangible set of goods. Nor does it correspond to money loaned to the bank by investors. Instead, a bank simply adds extra credit into the balance of a borrower. The borrower is expected in due course to repay that loan, thereby cancelling out the fiat creation. In the meantime, the bank earns interest from the loan.

Fiat money creation takes place at two levels: from commercial banks to business investors (as well as to private households); and from central banks to commercial banks. In both cases, the extra money has the potential to distort the economy: with more money chasing the same quantity of real-world goods, prices rise, resulting in inflation, which in turn diminishes the values of savings.

To some critics, fiat money creation seems an absurd state of affairs. These critics have in the back of their mind the idea that money is some kind of substitute for a fixed scarce commodity, like gold bars.

My own view is that there is nothing fundamentally wrong with these money-creation mechanisms. Banning these mechanisms completely would be akin to governments banning the creation of all new cryptocurrencies – an unwarranted intrusion on economic liberty. Money is much more than a streamlined version of barter.

Nevertheless, money creation has its drawbacks as well as its benefits. As mentioned, too much money creation can result in inflation, or a declining public respect for a currency. And as reviewed earlier, too much private debt can be a prelude to a horrific financial downturn.

Moreover, the very perception that a central bank will be ready to loan new money to troubled commercial banks, with government backing, encourages a "moral hazard" in which banks act unduly recklessly. These banks see themselves as "too big to fail". For these reasons, it's important that frameworks are agreed that put limits on money creation.

In turn, these frameworks are part of a vital wider review process that seeks to strike an appropriate balance between the envisioned benefits and the potential risks of financial technology.

Fintech therefore should be treated similarly to other major technological innovations such as artificial intelligence:

- These technologies need to be actively steered, so that their usage is highly likely to be beneficial

- Reassuring words from industry insiders should be viewed sceptically

- A strong safety culture needs to be developed

- Ongoing toleration of unstable situations should be challenged as thoroughly irresponsible

- Scenarios should be drawn up, with initiatives to address the accumulation of underlying toxic problems such as the extent of private indebtedness – similar to the initiatives to address the accumulation in the atmosphere of greenhouse gases.

Discussions along such lines have already been taking place, in multiple forums, such as the International Monetary Forum, the World Bank, and the Basel Committee on Banking Supervision. Progress has not been encouraging. Obstacles include the following:

- Proposals for "debt forgiveness" are controversial: critics believe any such forgiveness will act as an encouragement for a repetition of financially irresponsible borrowing

- Any ideas on reforming the Eurozone are deeply politically contentious

- Participants in these discussions are frequently constrained by powerful system inertia – as vividly chronicled in the riveting disclosures by former Greek Finance Minister Yanis Varoufakis about his numerous dialogues with leading financial professionals[261]

- Participants clash on their different theories of economics.

To move beyond this impasse, a stronger vision is needed. That's the vision of the profound social transformations which lie ahead – both the profoundly bad transformations which a new financial crisis could trigger (as outlined earlier in this chapter), and the profoundly good transformation of technoprogressive transhumanism. Contemplation of both these transformations should concentrate minds more effectively than before.

Investing for sustainable abundance

The world is not short of energy. It receives ample energy from the sun. The only challenge is to capture, store, and transmit that energy effectively.

In the same way, the world is not short of money. Paradoxically, one of the causes of the current slowdown in economic growth is the so-called "global savings glut". Individual savers in countries as diverse as China and Germany have saved significant portions of their income – being fearful of future developments in which they will need to rely on these savings (especially in circumstances lacking a public welfare network). These savers are persisting in keeping their money in long-term storage, such as in US government bonds, despite receiving only low interest rates.

Writing in Slate in September 2016, Daniel Gross assessed this situation[262]:

> A defining (and frustrating) aspect of our era is that there's too much money – both ready cash and cheap or free borrowing capacity – in the hands of the wrong people. And there is a widespread shortage of ideas about what to do with capital. Strange as it seems… money in the 21st century simply doesn't know what to do with itself.

> The concept of the saving glut – and its mirror image, the ideas deficit – helps explain the extraordinary circumstances that have come to define our financial era. In a world awash in money, investors struggle to find returns and often settle for nothing. Rather than invest and spend, companies stockpile hundreds of billions of dollars on their balance sheets, where it is guaranteed to net no return. Governments that could borrow essentially for free practise austerity. The savings glut is self-reinforcing: When you don't think you can find a good return, you're less likely to invest, which lowers returns even more.

Gross goes on to point out the international dimension:

> We've seen an almost entirely new and unpredicted phenomenon – negative rates. In a global economy that is growing modestly, many investors are so desperate for safety that they purchase government bonds that offer interest rates below zero. This inversion – paying for the privilege of lending money – flies in the face of intelligent capital. And yet it has spread. First seen in Japan, negative rates are now evident – even prevalent – in Germany, Italy, and other European countries. Last summer, some $13 trillion in assets around the world had negative yields. The yield on Germany's 10-year bonds is negative 29 percent.

Think about it. Around the world, tens of thousands of people are tasked with managing capital—at central banks, insurance companies, pension funds, sovereign wealth funds, hedge funds. These people are motivated partially or wholly by the pursuit of money, and many of them get paid based on the returns they deliver. And a large percentage of them are content to have their capital essentially do nothing – or worse than nothing.

As with energy, the issue with money isn't one of absolute scarcity. It's with the distribution and application of that money.

The Transpolitica roadmap envisions a series of major investments into technologies that each has enormous potential to improve the human experience. These technology areas were listed in the opening chapter of this book. Here's a reprise:

- The next-generation *greentech* which can provide an abundance of clean energy, from the likes of sun, wind, wave, and geothermal

- The nature-enhancing *synthetic biotech* which can provide an abundance of healthy food and drink

- The atomically-precise *nanotech* which can provide an abundance of all sorts of material goods, including low-cost 3D-printed housing

- The restorative and preventive *rejuvenation tech* which can provide an abundance of affordable healthcare, with people able to become "better than well" and even, if they choose, youthful again

- The brain-boosting *cognotech* which can provide an abundance of all-round intelligence: emotional, rational, social, spiritual, and more

- The labour-saving *automation tech* which can provide us with an abundance of time for creativity

- The world-transforming *geotech* which can address the threats of natural disasters such as tsunamis and supervolcanoes

- The world-transcending *space tech* which will allow us to explore and find purpose in the vast terrains of both outer and inner space

- The resource-enhancing *fintech* which can empower society to make best use of our collective energies, without risk of economic chaos

- The bridge-building *collabtech* which can enable us to cooperate better, in pursuit of our technological and social progress

- The sorely-needed *politech* which will improve our political processes – leveraging elements of the other technologies listed above.

Just as the "New Deal" infrastructure investments of President FD Roosevelt helped to lift the United States out of its deep depression in the 1930s, so can these Transpolitica investments help steer society out of its present state of deep risk. These investment projects will increasingly be seen as worthy recipients of the funds currently locked into the savings glut.

Three other types of abundance need to be mentioned. First, *ingenuity abundance*. The world is *not* suffering from any scarcity of ingenuity. Far from it: with a global population in the billions, and with levels of overall education and access to information that are unprecedented, humanity has more than enough ingenuity available to solve its global problems. The problem, once again, is one of collaboration and interaction. The solution involves a number of the technology areas listed above – specifically, collabtech, politech, and (last but not least) the fintech improvements which can ensure that suitable financial resources are made available to the innovators with the greatest potential.

That brings us to the topic of *information abundance*. Sadly, this is an area where major problems exist. Many of the most important pieces of information are kept secret. This includes the deliberations of ratings agencies, as they decide to award unduly high credit assignments to various investment schemes[263]. It also includes the calculations of auditors, such as Arthur Anderson, who gave a green light to the nefarious financial practices of high-flying corporation Enron. It includes the meetings of many of the key bodies in the Eurozone. Behind closed doors, vested interests are often able to overcome the cold light of logic. Ratings agencies, auditors, and politicians are by no means as independent as they publicly attest. They are motivated by the appeal of repeat business, or their personal political career.

Achieving an *abundance of transparency* is, therefore, one of the cornerstones of the overall set of reforms proposed in this book. Without such transparency, three problems persist:

- Hidden motivations are able to distort conclusions, away from the general good

- The latent insight of the world's abundance of ingenuity has no means to suggest better solutions for the problems being discussed

- Lacking visibility, many outsiders jump to conclusions about imagined behind-the-scenes conspiracies with motivations that are even more perverse than what's actually happening; these conspiracy theories stoke fake news and cloud public discussion.

Constancy amidst change

If the technologies listed above undergo the kinds of investment and development envisaged – enabled by a new spirit of transparency – wide changes will be taking place throughout society over the next couple of decades. To the extent that the overall governance of these changes is wise, these developments will be hugely positive for humanity.

But for clarity, I expect that various key aspects of society will continue in existence. By no means will everything change.

First, I expect that economies will continue to grow. I don't accept the arguments that the future of humanity necessarily involves accepting zero-growth, or even a decline in the economy. Instead, there's plenty of scope for what can be called green growth – that is, sustainable growth. Nevertheless, I look forward to changes in the way such growth is measured and targeted. Rather than metrics focussing on raw economic output – such as GDP (gross domestic product), we need to shift to metrics focussing on human flourishing. I'll pick up that discussion in Chapter 12, "Humans and superhumans".

Second, I expect that money will continue to exist. Just because more and more goods will become available at prices that are lower and lower – becoming essentially free – it does not mean that *all* goods will be abundant. At the same time as costs diminish for one generation of goods, new generations of goods are created, including totally new kinds of goods, which are, at least initially, relatively scarce in quantity. These goods will *not* be free, and it will be the choice of individual members of society whether or not to purchase them.

It may be the case that, in due course, all human experiences can be simulated in virtual reality, as vividly and compelling as in physical reality. Once the basic energy costs of running the computational infrastructure is covered, then each new experience inside the simulation may be zero cost. At that time, perhaps all vestiges of scarcity will vanish. In such worlds, everybody can experience the most desirable locations. Decisions about who gets to live in highly prized beachfront villas will become a thing of the past. But before we reach these circumstances, sometime later this century, there are very many real-world tasks to handle. And these real-world tasks will require the continued existence of money.

Third, building on the previous point, there will continue to be a positive role for financial innovation and financial intermediation. A technoprogressive society includes bankers and financiers. Nevertheless, their operation will differ markedly from at present. The finance sector needs to form a smaller part of the economy, and increased financial activity should cease to be goal in its own right. That's the case made by Financial Times columnist John Kay in his 2015 book *Other People's Money: The Real Business of Finance*, which is described as follows by the publisher[264]:

> The finance sector of Western economies is too large and attracts too many of the smartest college graduates. Financialization over the past three decades has created a structure that lacks resilience and supports absurd volumes of trading. The finance sector devotes too little attention to the search for new investment opportunities and the stewardship of existing ones and far too much to secondary-market dealing in existing assets. Regulation has contributed more to the problems than the solutions. Why? What is finance for?

> John Kay... believes in good banks and effective asset managers, but good banks and effective asset managers are not what he sees.

The conclusions offered by Kay seem completely correct to me:

> We do need some of the things that Citigroup and Goldman Sachs do, but we do not need Citigroup and Goldman to do them. And many of the things done by Citigroup and Goldman do not need to be done at all.

> The finance sector needs to be reminded of its primary purpose: to manage other people's money for the benefit of businesses and households. It is an aberration when some of the finest mathematical and scientific minds are tasked with devising algorithms for the sole purpose of exploiting the weakness of other algorithms for computerized trading in securities. To travel further down that road leads to ruin.

To recap, a technoprogressive future involves positive roles for economic growth, for money, and for the financial sector. Importantly, in all three cases, these roles will be significantly evolved from at present. This evolution is a necessary prerequisite to society reaching sustainable abundance. *This evolution is the most important task for fintech to address.*

The next questions to ask are: what about the future role of the profit motive, free markets, and for capitalism as a whole? Are these features of social life needed to propel humanity further forwards? Or are they constraints and distractions that need to be dismantled?

In the next chapter, I'll outline what I see as an integrative response to these questions. The answer is neither to champion capitalism nor to abolish it, but to transcend it.

9. Markets and fundamentalists

Transhumanists look at the human condition and proclaim: *humanity deserves better*. By taking advantage of the best insights and energies of present-day humanity, we can elevate humanity to a comprehensively better state. We can, and should, comprehensively improve our physical vitality, our mental acuity, our emotional wellbeing, and, yes, our economic relationships. In all these aspects, we can reach strikingly higher levels than at any time in human history (or prehistory).

This proclamation alarms a series of different kinds of critics.

First, it alarms *religious fundamentalists*, who believe that humanity is already the end point of divine creation. Any apparent flaws in the human condition – such as the physical blind spot in our eyes, our many cognitive biases, and our destructive tendencies towards tribalism and xenophobia – must be self-inflicted (they say), being the result of human sinfulness, in past or present-day generations. Or perhaps these flaws form part of some vast inscrutable divine plan, beyond human comprehension.

In response, transhumanists view these flaws as being, instead, unhappy consequences of our evolutionary heritage. Natural selection was limited in its foresight. Because of the incremental nature of biological evolution, there were many engineering solutions that lay outside its grasp. Because of the resulting shortcomings in human body and mind, the social structures that grew up over history had their own shortcomings, in turn causing further problems in the human experience. Transhumanists accept that there are many aspects of humanity that are "very good" – to use the description of the first humans placed into the divine mind by the authors of the opening chapter of the biblical book of *Genesis*[265]. But there are many other aspects of the human condition that are capable of radical improvement, via *intelligent design* that can be carried out by far-sighted twenty-first century human engineers. When these improvements are in place, humans will become very good indeed.

Second, transhumanism alarms a group of critics who can be described as *humanist fundamentalists*. These critics abhor the transhumanist idea that technology can profoundly *augment human consciousness and human character*. Transhumanists anticipate humans reaching systematically better decisions, with the help of advanced computer algorithms, artificial intelligence, and enhanced mental states accessed via (among other means) increasingly smart drugs. Humanist critics fear that any solutions based on digital technology will be cold, unimaginative, and blinkered. A world that maximises efficiency, they warn, will be an inhuman one. These critics prefer the random whimsy and creative variability of the present-day human mind. Therefore they oppose the transhumanist project to use technology to improve the human mind. It won't actually be an improvement, they say.

In response, transhumanists point out that digital technology can improve our creativity as well as our rationality. Rather than being limited to measures such as efficiency and productivity, new technology can augment our emotional responsiveness and spiritual capacity. As well as making us smarter, technology can make us kinder and more sensitive. Rather than dehumanising us, technology, used wisely, can humanise us more fully. Instead of most humans spending most of their lives in an impoverished mental state, the humans of the future can inhabit much higher planes of consciousness. But if we stick with our unaided mental capacity – as humanist fundamentalists would prefer – our quirkiness and (to use a candid term) stupidity will likely be the death of us. *Humanity deserves better!*

Third, consider a group of critics that I will call *cultural fundamentalists*. To them, when it comes to determining human capabilities, nurture is far more important than nature. If we want to improve human experience, we should prioritise changing human culture (the environment in which humans are nurtured). Let's restrain advertising messages that encourage destructive consumerist tendencies. Let's ensure popular soap operas have characters that demonstrate positive behaviour. Let's avoid situations in which different people live side by side but receive very different rewards for roughly similar amounts of work, thereby stirring up feelings of alienation and resentment. Let's improve lifelong education. Let's arrange for everyone to be able to meet regularly with trained counsellors to talk through their underlying personal struggles, and to receive fulsome personal affirmation. Above all, let's *not* focus on individual biological differences. To such critics, transhumanist interest in genetic influences on behaviour and personality is a retrograde step. Any idea of choosing the genetic makeup of your baby – or of editing your own genome – harks back to the discredited ideology of eugenics. These critics, therefore, regard transhumanists as being perhaps just one or two steps removed on a slippery slope from the dreadful biological experiments of the Nazi era.

In response, transhumanists say we have to consider *both* nurture and nature. It would be perverse to rule out improving our biological selves, via enhanced nutrition, dietary supplements, medicinal compounds, detox programmes, or (an extension of the same line of interventions) genetic reprogramming. Just because some past genetic experiments have been moral scandals, there's no necessity to group all future genetic experiments under the same heading. After all, various past experiments to improve human culture went horribly wrong too – but that's no reason to give up on the "improve culture" pathway. Similarly, there's no good reason to give up on the "improve biology" pathway. It is by taking fully into account both the biological and cultural influences on human capabilities, that we will have the best opportunity to improve human experience. *That's what humanity deserves.*

To recap, transhumanists alarm religious fundamentalists, humanist fundamentalists, and cultural fundamentalists – but in all three cases, the alarm is misplaced. In the remainder of this chapter, I want to consider a fourth group of critics: *market fundamentalists*. I'll also be considering the mirror image of that group, who can be called *anti-market* fundamentalists.

Conflicting views on markets

Market fundamentalists believe that free markets are absolutely the best way to decide the allocation of resources.

For example, what price should a taxi company charge to transport passengers a given distance? A free market solution will allow the price to be adjusted according to supply and demand. If there are more people wanting to hire a taxi at a given time than there are drivers available, the price should be raised, using a "surge" multiplier (as in the practice of Uber). The higher price will encourage a greater number of part-time drivers to make themselves available to pick up passengers. And if some potential passengers have less of a need to take a taxi service at this precise time, they can cancel (or defer) their transport plans, in view of the higher prices. Supply and demand will both change, rationally, in line with the dynamically adjusted price.

Likewise, how many units should a manufacturer produce of, say, a new model of car with some smart new driver-assist features? In an open society, with freedom of choice for consumers and vendors alike, there's no formula that can reliably predict the right sales figure ahead of time. Manufactures need to monitor the purchases actually made by consumers, and to adjust production accordingly. No one can be sure whether consumers will tend to prefer to spend their money, instead, on cars from a different manufacturer, or on overseas holiday vacations, or on Kickstarter investments. The choice belongs to them: it's not something that should be dictated in advance by any government officials.

To boost sales of their new model, should the manufacturer reduce the retail price of the car? Again, that's a decision under their own control, and shouldn't be determined by any state planners of the economy. Out of the myriad individual free choices of the buyers and sellers of different goods and services, companies that are responsive to changing consumer needs will do well. In turn, consumers will benefit.

What about similar questions for the introduction of a new medical drug? Who should determine the price at which that drug will be sold? If there's a free market, pharmaceutical companies that are responsive to changing patient needs will do well. If one company sets the price of the drug too high, another could introduce a competing product that is less expensive. In this system, there's no need for any state planners of healthcare to determine the prices in advance.

Market fundamentalists resist attempts to override the operation of free markets. They maintain that planned economies have never performed as well as countries where decisions remain in the hands of buyers and sellers.

In response, transhumanists say: *we can do better*. The free market no more represents an ultimate pinnacle of design than does the makeup of the human body, the composition of our DNA, or the output of evolution by natural selection. None of these features of the human species should be put onto a pedestal and worshipped. Resource allocation should be determined by the combined operation of *several* different social institutions – not by the free market *alone*. These institutions should steer the operation of the free market, for significantly better outcomes.

More accurately, *some* transhumanists say that we can do better. Unlike in the three previous cases, the transhumanist community is divided when it comes to free markets. Recall the distinction made in Chapter 1, between techno*libertarian* and techno*progressive*. Both sides of this transhumanist divide see the tremendous transformational potential of technology. Both look forward avidly to the development and deployment of technology to overcome the limitations of the human condition. But whereas technoprogressives see important limitations within the operation of the free market, technolibertarians take a different view. Free markets don't need to be *steered*, they say. Instead, free markets just need to be *protected* – protected against distortions that can arise from government interference, from monopolies (when free choice vanishes), and from "crony capitalism" – which is a particular type of government interference, since legislators in this case unduly favour the businesses of their "cronies".

To round out this picture, one other position should be mentioned. Anti-market fundamentalists see the market system as having a pre-eminently *bad* effect on the human condition. The various flaws with free markets – flaws which I'll be exploring throughout this chapter – are so severe, say these critics, that the most important reform to pursue is to *dismantle* the free market system. That reform should take a higher priority than any development of new technologies – AI, genetic engineering, stem cell therapies, neuro-enhancers, and so on. Indeed, if these new technologies are deployed whilst the current free market system remains in place, it will, say these critics, make it all the more likely that these technologies will be used to oppress rather than liberate.

In contrast, technoprogressives look forward to *wiser management* of the market system, rather than dismantling it. As I'll argue, key to this wise management is the reform and protection of a number of other social institutions that sit alongside markets – a free press, free judiciary, independent regulators, and, yes, independent politicians.

Collusion and cartels

To proceed, let's consider one of the ways in which free markets can fail.

In *The Wealth of Nations*, published in 1776, Adam Smith observed the dangers of collusion between tradespeople[266]:

> People of the same trade seldom meet together, even for merriment and diversion, but the conversation ends in a conspiracy against the public, or in some contrivance to raise prices.

For example, if all pharmaceutical companies were to hold a closed-door meeting, and decide on a threshold minimum price for a particular type of drug, in order to keep their revenues high, this would violate the principle of a free market. In the absence of competition driving companies to reduce their prices, patients would have to pay more for medicines.

Let's look at an actual historical case of collusion: the Phoebus cartel of manufacturers of lightbulbs, created in 1924. Markus Krajewski, a professor from Basel, analysed this cartel in a 2014 article for IEEE Spectrum[267]:

The Great Lightbulb Conspiracy

On 23 December 1924, a group of leading international businessmen gathered in Geneva for a meeting that would alter the world for decades to come. Present were top representatives from all the major lightbulb manufacturers, including Germany's Osram, the Netherlands' Philips, France's Compagnie des Lampes, and the United States' General Electric.

As revellers hung Christmas lights elsewhere in the city, the group founded the Phoebus cartel, a supervisory body that would carve up the worldwide incandescent lightbulb market, with each national and regional zone assigned its own manufacturers and production quotas. It was the first cartel in history to enjoy a truly global reach.

Key to the collusion was an agreement to reduce lightbulb lifetimes:

The cartel's grip on the lightbulb market lasted only into the 1930s. Its far more enduring legacy was to engineer a shorter lifespan for the incandescent lightbulb. By early 1925, this became codified at 1,000 hours for a pear-shaped household bulb, a marked reduction from the 1,500 to 2,000 hours that had previously been common. Cartel members rationalized this approach as a trade-off: Their lightbulbs were of a higher quality, more efficient, and brighter burning than other bulbs. They also cost a lot more. Indeed, all evidence points to the cartel's being motivated by profits and increased sales, not by what was best for the consumer. In carefully crafting a lightbulb with a relatively short lifespan, the cartel thus hatched the industrial strategy now known as planned obsolescence.

Krajewski describes the extensive activity undertaken by the Phoebus cartel to reduce lightbulb lifespan *and to keep it low* – despite that lower lifespan being detrimental for consumers of lightbulbs:

How exactly did the cartel pull off this engineering feat? It wasn't just a matter of making an inferior or sloppy product; anybody could have done that. But to create one that reliably failed after an agreed-upon 1,000 hours took some doing over a number of years. The household lightbulb in 1924 was already technologically sophisticated: The light yield was considerable; the burning time was easily 2,500 hours or more. By striving for something less, the cartel would systematically reverse decades of progress…

The cartel took its business of shortening the lifetime of bulbs every bit as seriously as earlier researchers had approached their job of lengthening it. Each factory bound by the cartel agreement… had to regularly send samples of its bulbs to a central testing laboratory in Switzerland. There, the bulbs were thoroughly vetted against cartel standards. If any factory submitted bulbs lasting longer or shorter than the regulated lifespan for its type, the factory was obliged to pay a fine.

From the manufacturers' point of view, the collusion was a commercial success:

Of course, given the collective ingenuity of the cartel's engineers and scientists, it should have been possible to design a lightbulb that was both bright and long-lived. But such a product would have interfered with members' desire to sell more bulbs. And sell more bulbs they did, at least initially. In fiscal year 1926–27, for instance, the cartel sold 335.7 million lightbulbs worldwide; four years later, sales had climbed to 420.8 million. What's more, despite the fact that the actual costs of manufacturing were dropping, the cartel maintained more or less stable prices and therefore higher profit margins. From its inception until the end of 1930, the cartel retained its overwhelming share of a growing market.

For a more recent example, consider the exorbitant "roaming" prices charged by mobile network operators to owners of phone handsets when travelling abroad. In February 2007, BEUC, a group representing the rights of consumers throughout Europe, complained that roaming charges were excessively high. Alain Bazot, president of UFC Que Choisir, the French equivalent of the UK Which magazine, decried the rationales offered by mobile operators for the high prices[268]:

Mobile phone operators are twisting the truth; from the beginning they have organised collusion on a massive scale throughout Europe. The time has come to put an end to this, and build a Europe of telecommunications.

How should society respond to the possibilities of cartels and market collusion? The technoprogressive answer is to argue for *thoughtful regulation of markets*. Independent regulators should be empowered to fine companies when they are discovered to have colluded. In other words, collusion should be legally prohibited.

A different answer, which comes from the libertarian perspective, is to look to new competitors to undermine any collusion. For example, if existing pharmaceutical companies conspire (directly or indirectly) to set drug prices high, that's no problem, since it creates an opportunity for a competitor to bring a product to market at a lower price, thereby bringing rewards both to themselves and to patients. The companies that collude will lose out, due to market forces.

This last answer, however, relies on it being possible for new companies to enter the market. In practice, there are often high barriers to entry. Drugs are protected by patents, with high licensing costs. Likewise, mobile network operators require enormous investment on infrastructure, such as masts and backhaul. In short, competition isn't always as feasible as it might sound in theory. That's why society needs to keep a close eye on potential collusion, to be ready to legislate against it.

The abuse of market power

Cartels pose one challenge to free markets: several companies collude to keep prices high, quality low, and/or innovation constrained.

Monopolies take this situation one stage further: a single company obtains such a dominant position in the market that, in effect, it is able to dictate terms to its customers. Once again, what poses a problem is if there is too large a hurdle for new competitors to be able to enter the market.

Consider the hurdle facing manufacturers of web browsers for PCs in 1998. At that time, the Microsoft Windows operating system was pre-installed on the vast majority of PCs. Microsoft supported a community of software vendors that sold a wide range of different applications for use on PCs – applications that worked in the Windows environment. The web browser was a particular kind of application. As alternatives to Microsoft's own Internet Explorer browser, users could in principle choose to install the Netscape Navigator browser or browser software from the Norwegian company Opera. That looked like a free market in web browsers. But that was a misleading impression.

Microsoft had already taken the strategic decision to expand its dominance of the PC operating system market into a dominance of the web browser market. It foresaw, rightly, as things turned out, that the web browser would grow in relative importance in the years ahead. Accordingly, it pursued measures to tie Internet Explorer more closely to Windows – measures that would put competing products such as Netscape and Opera at a disadvantage. Windows would run more slowly unless Internet Explorer was used, claimed Microsoft. The two pieces of software – the web browser and the operating system – worked best as an integrated whole. For their own good, users should be deterred from using any other browser. In this way, Microsoft sought to tilt the competitive landscape.

A similar pattern appeared to hold in other types of PC application as well. Microsoft was alleged to provide "backdoor" application programming interfaces (APIs) for use by applications written by its in-house teams (applications such as Word and Excel), which were not available to other vendors.

In the wake of widespread complaints by applications developers against Microsoft's actions, the US Department of Justice took Microsoft to court. Having heard evidence and cross-examined witnesses between November 1998 and June 1999, Judge Thomas Penfield Jackson issued his findings[269]:

> Microsoft enjoys so much power in the market for Intel-compatible PC operating systems that if it wished to exercise this power solely in terms of price, it could charge a price for Windows substantially above that which could be charged in a competitive market. Moreover, it could do so for a significant period of time without losing an unacceptable amount of business to competitors. In other words, Microsoft enjoys monopoly power in the relevant market.

> Viewed together, three main facts indicate that Microsoft enjoys monopoly power. First, Microsoft's share of the market for Intel-compatible PC operating systems is extremely large and stable. Second, Microsoft's dominant market share is protected by a high barrier to entry. Third, and largely as a result of that barrier, Microsoft's customers lack a commercially viable alternative to Windows...

The problem wasn't that Microsoft had monopoly power in the operating system market. The problem was in what the company did with that power to distort adjacent markets, namely the market for applications.

On that matter, the final conclusion of the judge's findings was damning:

> To the detriment of consumers..., Microsoft... engaged in a concerted series of actions designed to protect the applications barrier to entry, and

hence its monopoly power, from a variety of middleware threats, including Netscape's Web browser and Sun's implementation of Java. Many of these actions have harmed consumers in ways that are immediate and easily discernible. They have also caused less direct, but nevertheless serious and far-reaching, consumer harm by distorting competition...

Microsoft has retarded, and perhaps altogether extinguished, the process by which these two middleware technologies could have facilitated the introduction of competition into an important market.

Most harmful of all is the message that Microsoft's actions have conveyed to every enterprise with the potential to innovate in the computer industry. Through its conduct toward Netscape, IBM, Compaq, Intel, and others, Microsoft has demonstrated that it will use its prodigious market power and immense profits to harm any firm that insists on pursuing initiatives that could intensify competition against one of Microsoft's core products. Microsoft's past success in hurting such companies and stifling innovation deters investment in technologies and businesses that exhibit the potential to threaten Microsoft. The ultimate result is that some innovations that would truly benefit consumers never occur for the sole reason that they do not coincide with Microsoft's self-interest.

The very last word in that 207 page court judgement is significant: "self-interest". The ability of a free market to convert the self-interest of large numbers of participants into positive results for the community as a whole is noted in a justly famous quotation from *The Wealth of Nations*:

It is not from the benevolence of the butcher, the brewer, or the baker that we expect our dinner, but from their regard to their own interest.

However, when competitors are unable to step in to offer lower prices or better quality, the coincidence of individual self-interest and general wellbeing breaks down. Things can only improve again if society steps in to restore the practical possibility of competition.

To finish the web browser case history: after several rounds of additional legal wrangling, Microsoft agreed to enable users to install other web browsers. That decision enabled many waves of innovation by new browsers such as Mozilla Firefox and Google Chrome. The spur of honest competition also led to increased rates of improvement in Microsoft's browser software – Internet Explorer and, more recently, Microsoft Edge.

I picked this web browser example since it was observed closely from the industry where I spent many years working as an executive: mobile computing and smartphones. But numerous other examples could also be given, of companies with monopoly power abusing their position to the detriment of consumers. I'll mention just one of them, from further back in history.

Standard Oil, which produced, refined, and transported oil from 1870 onwards, can be compared to Microsoft, in that it initially gained a position of market dominance through a feisty combination of technical and business innovation. In both examples, it's what happened next that is less admirable – requiring state intervention on behalf of wider market interests.

By 1890, Standard Oil controlled nearly 90% of the oil business in the United States. Having obtained a near-monopoly, it then colluded with key customers, such as the railways, in ways that unfairly enhanced its own position. The US Department of Justice brought a legal suit against the company, claiming as follows[270]:

> The general result of the investigation has been to disclose the existence of numerous and flagrant discriminations by the railroads in behalf of the Standard Oil Co. and its affiliated corporations. With comparatively few exceptions… the Standard has been the sole beneficiary of such discriminations. In almost every section of the country that company has been found to enjoy some unfair advantages over its competitors, and some of these discriminations affect enormous areas…

> The evidence is, in fact, absolutely conclusive that the Standard Oil Co. charges altogether excessive prices where it meets no competition, and particularly where there is little likelihood of competitors entering the field, and that, on the other hand, where competition is active, it frequently cuts prices to a point which leaves even the Standard little or no profit, and which more often leaves no profit to the competitor, whose costs are ordinarily somewhat higher.

The conclusion of that court case was that Standard Oil was split up into 33 separate companies, helping to restore a competitive marketplace.

When competition needs to be curtailed

To recap: one significant issue with free markets is that they can evolve in ways that reduce competitiveness and therefore undermine their own rationale. With fewer companies actively competing against each other, the genuine needs of consumers can be left unmet.

A different kind of issue is that competition can often result in a "race to the bottom" with highly undesirable side-effects. This is a case, not of too little competition, but of too much competition.

To illustrate this, let's go yet further back into history. Imagine you were the owner of a cotton mill in the north of England, in the 1830s. Many of the work tasks in the mill could be carried out by children as young as nine. The small stature of young children meant, indeed, that they were often *more* capable than full-grown adults to work in confined spaces. Since children need only be paid around one quarter of an adult's wage, what should you as the owner do?

Bear in mind that the children in such factories typically experienced appalling work conditions. The public had grown aware of these practices, in part due to campaigners such as Richard Oastler, whose letter on the subject of "Yorkshire slavery" had generated considerable discussion on its appearance in 1830 in the Leeds Mercury. Controversially, the letter compared the miserable situation of children working in factories to that of slaves working in the "colonies" (the West Indies)[271]:

> Let truth speak out, appalling as the statement may appear. The fact is true. Thousands of our fellow-creatures and fellow-subjects, both male and female, the miserable inhabitants of a Yorkshire town... are this very moment existing in a state of slavery, more horrid than are the victims of that hellish system 'colonial slavery'.
>
> The very streets which receive the droppings [pamphlets] of an 'Anti-Slavery Society' are every morning wet by the tears of innocent victims at the accursed shrine of avarice, who are compelled (not by the cart-whip of the negro slave-driver) but by the dread of the equally appalling thong or strap of the over-looker, to hasten, half-dressed, but not half-fed, to those magazines of British infantile slavery – the worsted mills in the town and neighbourhood of Bradford!
>
> Thousands of little children, both male and female, but principally female, from seven to fourteen years of age, are daily compelled to labour from six o'clock in the morning to seven in the evening, with only – Britons, blush while you read it! – with only thirty minutes allowed for eating and recreation...

Oastler subsequently gave evidence to a Parliamentary Select Committee[272]:

On one occasion… I was in the company of a West India slave master and three Bradford spinners; they brought the two systems into fair comparison, and the spinners were obliged to be silent when the slave-owner said, "well, I have always thought myself disgraced by being the owner of black slaves, but we never, in the West Indies thought it was possible for any human being to be so cruel as to require a child of 9 years old to work 12½ hours a day; and that, you acknowledge, is your regular practice."

I have seen little boys and girls of 10 years old, one I have in my eye particularly now, whose forehead has been cut open by the thong; whose cheeks and lips have been laid open, and whose back has been almost covered with black stripes; and the only crime that that little boy, who was 10 years and 3 months old, had committed, was that he retched three cardings, which are three pieces of woollen yarn, about three inches long. The same boy told me that he had been frequently knocked down with the billy-roller, and that on one occasion, he had been hung up by a rope round the body, and almost frightened to death; but I am sure it is unnecessary for me to say anything more upon the bodily sufferings that these poor creatures are subject to. I have seen their bodies almost broken down, so that they could not walk without assistance, when they have been 17 or 18 years of age.

You might think that, if you were an enlightened person owning a cotton mill in the 1830s, you would avoid hiring any young children, and subjecting them to such a harsh regime. That would be the humanitarian course of action. But in that case, your operating costs would be significantly increased. Compared with other mills, your products would be more expensive. Your business might cease to be economically viable.

This dilemma was expressed in a famous pamphlet entitled "The curse of the factory system" written in 1836 by factory owner John Fielden[273]:

Here, then, is the "curse" of our factory-system; as improvements in machinery have gone on, the "avarice of masters" has prompted many to exact more labour from their hands than they were fitted by nature to perform, and those who have wished for the hours of labour to be less for all ages than the legislature would even yet sanction, have had no alternative but to conform more or less to the prevailing practice, or abandon the trade altogether.

Fielden knew what he was talking about. As a child, he had laboured in a factory himself. His own father had been a mill owner before him, and had put him to work in the family factory from the age of ten:

I well remember being set to work in my father's mill when I was little more than ten years old; my associates, too, in the labour and in recreation are fresh in my memory. Only a few of them are now alive; some dying very young, others living to become men and women; but many of those who lived have died off before they had attained the age of fifty years, having the appearance of being much older, a premature appearance of age which I verily believe was caused by the nature of the employment in which they had been brought up... I shall never forget the fatigue I often felt before the day ended, and the anxiety of us all to be relieved from the unvarying and irksome toil we had gone through...

Fielden highlighted the moral dilemma facing the managers and owners of the factories:

Most of the masters are obliged to admit the excessive hours of labour imposed on children, and the ministers have done it in the most solemn manner; but they cannot interfere with the labour, the "free labour"... because that is against sound principle!

Without laws being put in place – *and enforced by independent inspectors* – any factory owner who listened to the "solemn" preaching of ministers of religion (or to the prompts of their own conscience), and reduced their employment of young children, would, as Fielden remarked, risk having to "abandon the trade altogether", being out-competed by other factories.

Given this bind, many factory owners came up with rationalisations for why the prevailing state of "freedom" – freedom for them to employ young children in highly arduous conditions – was actually good for the children involved. The adversity built their character. Their employment took good advantage of their youthful nimbleness and agility. The children were able to contribute some much-needed money to their families. Parents actually pushed their children to work in factories, for the sake of the family finances. Although demanding, the work was no different in principle from arduous activities that children had undertaken on farms in times past. Perhaps most surprising from a modern viewpoint, the preacher John Wesley, who founded the Methodist movement within Christianity, was an admirer of child employment, on account of it "teaching the virtues of labour and discipline and preventing youthful vice"[274].

A comprehensive solution to the issue of young children working long hours therefore depended upon a number of factors: changes in the law, provision of inspectors to ensure adherence to the law, and reforms in education so that useful schooling became available, free of charge, to the children concerned. These institutional changes could not have arisen simply by the operation of any free market by itself. It required a different kind of social coordination. Namely, it required politics.

Restrictions on economic freedom

Laws limiting the employment of children are just one example of a restriction on economic freedom that is, nowadays, widely accepted. These laws intrude on the operation of the free market for employment. Even if a child would voluntarily accept arduous working conditions over long hours – and has the support of his or her family, in their quest for more income – society prohibits employers from engaging them in this way.

For a different kind of example, consider legal restrictions on misleading advertising. From one point of view, such restrictions are unnecessary. A free market would allow advertisers to make any kind of bogus claims they liked about their products. Consumers will *eventually* find out if a company is disreputable, and will avoid them. So there's actually no need for regulators to control advertising, right? Wrong!

The problem is indicated by the word "eventually". Considerable harm can take place, due to people believing the incorrect advertising, before the company becomes generally known as being untrustworthy. In the meantime, people can lose lots of money, or their health may suffer. Sometimes they may even die.

What's more, in the absence of binding legal penalties, the people behind flawed companies could go on to create brand new companies, with no obvious connection to the previous ones – and could therefore delude or defraud another set of consumers.

Indeed, laws exist against companies deceiving customers by adopting product names or packaging similar to that of reliable brands from other companies. That kind of "freedom to imitate" is not permitted. Likewise, companies are prevented from claiming to conform to safety standards or hygiene standards that they do not in fact observe. Again, the motivation is to protect consumers from potentially significant harm.

Potential harm is particularly high in the fields of food and medicine. Companies that store, transport, or sell food or drugs are obliged to respect various rules and regulations. In other words, companies who operate in these areas are required to accept some limitations on their freedom of action. A number of constraints on the freedom of these markets date back to the 1906 Pure Food and Drugs Act in the United States. This Act was introduced following public uproar when grossly unhygienic conditions in the meatpacking industry in Chicago were detailed in the novel *The Jungle* written by Upton Sinclair – a novel that sold a million copies in its first year of publication alone[275]. Theodore Roosevelt, the US President at the time, was moved to take action. It would be a poor society that left it to ordinary citizens to notice when outbreaks of food poisoning occurred, and to adjust their buying habits accordingly, switching from one meat distributor to another. Although "free", that kind of free market would involve a needless amount of disease and death. Instead, just as a network of inspectors kept an eye on employment conditions for children, another network of inspectors would keep an eye on hygiene conditions in the food industry.

Restrictions on the free market for food were paralleled by restrictions on the free market for medicines. These restrictions were intended to curtail the liberty of itinerant conmen and hucksters who peddled various miracle cures to gullible townspeople. One example in the mid nineteenth century was William Avery Rockefeller. Rockefeller would arrive in towns and gain attention through his skills as a firearms marksman. With a consequent aura of authority, Rockefeller would proceed to sell people a compound he said was a cure for cancer. In reality the compound was a mixture of a laxative and oil. Having made some sales, he would scarper from the town, never to return[276]. This Rockefeller, as it happens, was the father of JD Rockefeller, who put his inherited skills of quick wittedness to the different task of creating the company Standard Oil mentioned earlier in this chapter.

Rockefeller senior was by no means alone in the business of misleading consumers about the contents of medicinal compounds. Many so-called "patent medicines" contained addictive substances, whose details, however, weren't revealed to purchasers. The investigative journalist Samuel Hopkins Adams published an excoriating series of articles in 1905 entitled "The Great American Fraud". The series started with the following lament[277]:

> Gullible America will spend this year some seventy-five millions of dollars in the purchase of patent medicines. In consideration of this sum it will swallow huge quantities of alcohol, an appalling amount of opiates and narcotics, a wide assortment of varied drugs ranging from powerful and dangerous heart depressants to insidious liver stimulants; and far in excess

of all other ingredients, undiluted fraud. For fraud, exploited by the skilfulest of advertising bunco men, is the basis of the trade.

Adams continued with a vision of a better future:

> Should the newspapers, the magazines, and the medical journals refuse their pages to this class of advertisements, the patent medicine business in five years would be as scandalously historic as the South Sea Bubble, and the nation would be the richer not only in lives and money, but in drunkards and drug-fiends saved.

The evidence assembled by Adams provided further impetus for the 1906 Pure Food and Drugs Act. That Act set out its intent clearly[278]:

> An Act for preventing the manufacture, sale, or transportation of adulterated or misbranded or poisonous or deleterious foods, drugs, medicines, and liquors, and for regulating traffic therein…

This Act is one of many that, over time, imposed restrictions on economic activities. Companies were restricted from mislabelling products, omitting key ingredients from the label, or replacing standard ingredients with ineffective lower quality substitutes. Newspapers were restricted from carrying various kinds of misleading advertisements. Later, car manufacturers were restricted from manufacturing cars that fell short of given safety standards, or which emitted excess amounts of pollutants. As car safety improved, the numbers of deaths and injuries from traffic accidents plummeted.

In all these cases, companies were prohibited from following what would have been in their own short-term self-interest. Society took the decision that there was a better way to organise matters, than to allow every company to carry out whatever measures it fancied. Self-interested attempts to bribe officials, to cheat standards inspections, or to use monopoly power to crush competitors in adjacent market spaces – all of these have been recognised as lying outside the set of "acceptable pursuit of self-interest" that is covered in the above-quoted extract from Adam Smith:

> It is not from the benevolence of the butcher, the brewer, or the baker that we expect our dinner, but from their regard to their own interest.

Determining boundaries and externalities

Where should the boundary fall, between the permitted and the impermissible? What is the method to tell whether a particular item of food or medicine is suitable to be freely bought and sold, as opposed to needing regulation? What safety regulations should employers be obliged to observe, in their treatment of employees or contractors? Which new technologies need careful monitoring (such as hazardous new biochemicals), and which can have all details freely published on the open Internet?

The answer to all these questions is: *it's complicated*. We would be wrong to expect simple guidelines to provide all the answers. We would also be wrong to say that all restrictions should be abolished.

One possible guideline would be: anything that is agreed between well-informed, consenting adults, is fully permissible. The government has no business interfering in any such case. If someone is aware of the content of a new psychoactive substance, say, or the details of an innovative new medical treatment – and if they assert that they understand and accept the risks involved – then the government should have nothing more to say.

I have a lot of sympathy for this suggestion. However, this argument assumes that no third parties will be involved – in short, that there will be no significant *externalities*. But imagine if the treatment drives the recipient mad, and an innocent bystander is attacked and killed while the person has lost their mind. Imagine if the treatment unexpectedly interferes with other medicines which the person is already taking, for a different condition, and that substantially larger medical costs result. Or imagine if the treatment involves some waste product which is itself hazardous to the environment, impacting the lives of others in the neighbourhood (or further afield, in the case of air-borne pollutants), who gave no consent to the matter.

I raise these objections, not as a counsel of despair. Instead, what's necessary is to be aware of the potential rich complications arising from economic interactions. These are matters that require continuing ongoing review, from multiple perspectives. Something that is judged as too risky today may be assessed as less risky at a future date – or vice versa – as more information has been gathered, and new methods of analysis developed.

One thing that can cause a revision of a previous assessment is an updated understanding of the externalities of an economic interaction.

Recall that an externality is a side-effect on people other than the buyer and seller in a relationship. Externalities can be either positive or negative. If someone pays a tutor to teach them to play the drums, there's an effect on any neighbours who are disturbed by the sound of drumming coming through the walls. In this case, the externality is negative. If a company purchases medical vaccinations for its employees, to reduce their likelihood of becoming ill with the flu, others in the community benefit too, since there will be fewer ill people in that neighbourhood, from whom they might catch flu. In this case, the externality is positive. Another positive example is when a company purchases on-the-job training for an employee, who is then able to pass on some of the skills learned to family members and acquaintances. Again, if a company pays employees to carry out fundamental research, which is published openly, people in other companies benefit from that research too, even though they did not pay for it. As for other negative examples, recall the discussions in previous chapters about damage to the environment – including damage to roads infrastructure and damage to the atmosphere.

It's far from easy to agree the magnitudes of externalities, and to decide what kind of policies, regulations, or taxes to introduce in consequence. A report produced in 2013 by Trucost on behalf of the TEEB for Business Coalition, "Natural Capital at Risk", sought to quantify what it described as "The 100 top externalities of business"[279]. ("TEEB" stands for "The Economics of Ecosystems and Biodiversity"[280].) The report starts as follows:

> This report... finds that the world's 100 biggest risks are costing the economy around $4.7 trillion per year in terms of the environmental and social costs of lost ecosystem services and pollution...
>
> [The report] demonstrates that some business activities do not generate sufficient profit to cover their natural resource use and pollution costs.

Examples from the top ten externalities around the world, according to the report, include:

- Impact on water supplies from *rice farming in Southern Asia* (natural capital cost $123.7B per annum)
- Greenhouse gas emissions from *cement manufacturing in Eastern Asia* ($139.9B)
- Impact on water supplies from *wheat farming in Southern Asia* ($214.4B)
- Greenhouse gas emissions from *iron and steel mills in Eastern Asia* ($216.1B)

- Impact on land use from *cattle ranching and farming in South America* ($312.1B)

- Greenhouse gas emissions from *coal power generation in Eastern Asia* ($361.0B).

Here's what is particularly striking. For all the industries covered, if their total impacts on natural capital are taken into account, they all incur costs greater than the profits they make. From one point of view, therefore, these industries ought to be shut down. Less drastically, their methods of operation ought to change quickly. It's similar to what we would say when confronted by a factory that demonstrates a profit in its financial accounts, but which is being allowed to pump its effluent into a freshwater lake, storing up problems for disease in the people who depend on water from that lake. We would say that the factory should be forced to spend some of its profits cleaning up its waste. Once that has happened, the company may be less profitable than before, and might even record a financial loss. That would be something of great interest to potential investors (among others).

But as I said, these calculations are far from easy. It can be argued that the industries mentioned have many positive externalities as well as the negative ones just reviewed. By providing short-term economic benefits to their employees, these industries enable families to send their children to better education, allowing them to envision and achieve a better future in the longer term. And more bluntly, if these industries were shut down, many people would starve, in the absence of rapid adaptation measures.

If externalities have effects that are difficult to estimate, should we therefore stop trying to perform such calculations? Should we simply trust that all the positive and negative effects will somehow cancel each other out? Should we, in other words, leave it to the operation of a free market to determine resource allocation after all? That is the course recommended, it would appear, by free market fundamentalists.

My response is that, just because a field of activity is hard, that's no reason to give up on the field. Each sector of science and technology was incredibly hard, as it was being developed. Likewise, each area of regulatory oversight of the economy – each set of taxes or safety standards imposed or revised – needs careful attention by an extended community of reviewers.

The good news is that we humans have brains as well as mouths. We don't just emit waste products: we also produce ideas. By drawing on technological solutions that can orchestrate the input of large numbers of human thinkers, we can keep improving our collective understanding of the best regulatory frameworks and institutions. We can collectively decide which constraints are needed on the activity of the free market, so that we benefit from its good consequences without suffering unnecessarily from its bad consequences. *That is the technoprogressive vision.*

The dangers of absolutism

I started this chapter by discussing a number of different types of people, each of which I described as one-or-other sort of fundamentalist. I used the word "fundamentalist" with some care. It applies when someone allows one belief or insight to dominate all other aspects of their thinking. For example, cultural fundamentalists move beyond the viewpoint that "culture is important" to "culture is *all*-important". Similarly, free market fundamentalists move beyond the viewpoint that "market regulations *frequently* produce more harm than good" to "market regulations will *inevitably* produce more harm than good". In this way, they transition beyond "free market advocates" to "free market fundamentalists".

The human tendency towards fundamentalism is a dangerous flaw in our psyche. It reflects an age-old longing for certainty and simplicity in the face of a complex, hostile world. The positive trajectory of the human species over the decades ahead depends in large measure on us being able to tame our tendencies towards fundamentalism.

I echo the view offered by Nobel prize-winning physicist Max Born – someone who had to flee for his life in 1933 as the Nazis consolidated their grip on power in Germany[281]:

> I believe that ideas such as absolute certitude, absolute exactness, final truth, etc are figments of the imagination which should not be admissible in any field of science.

Born, who developed the use of probabilities within quantum physics, urged adoption of probabilistic rather than absolutist thinking in wider fields of life:

> This loosening of thinking seems to me to be the greatest blessing which modern science has given to us. For the belief in a single truth and in being the possessor thereof is the root cause of all evil in the world.

It's a great pity when arguments are presented in overly extreme versions – when a fundamentalist spirit magnifies an advocate's position excessively. That creates unnecessary divisions, and prevents the rest of an argument from being given the attention it deserves.

When regulations cripple innovation

One piece of analysis that does deserve more attention – despite it often being wrapped up in over-extreme rhetoric – is the evidence offered by free market advocates about glaring flaws in existing regulatory systems.

In his 2011 book *Pharmocracy*[282], Bill Faloon, co-founder and director of the Life Extension Foundation, has marshalled more than 300 pages of arguments about "the corruption and ineptitude" of the American FDA (Food and Drugs Administration). The book carries the striking subtitle "How Corrupt Deals and Misguided Medical Regulations Are Bankrupting America – And What to Do about It".

Faloon's objection to the operation of the FDA is that it results in medicines costing *much* more than is necessary. The FDA has moved far beyond the core mandate envisaged in legislation such as the 1906 Pure Food and Drugs Act.

Near the start of his book, Faloon reviews the example of the drug AndroGel[283]:

> An increasingly popular prescription drug in the United States is a testosterone ointment called AndroGel. Last time we checked, pharmacy chains sell a one-month supply for $348. Many men who try it will continue it each month for the rest of their lives.
>
> The cost of the active ingredient in AndroGel is around $4. It costs a few more dollars to put it into ointment form under good manufacturing practices. So for less than $15 retail, consumers could purchase the same amount of testosterone as is in AndroGel – if it were not for FDA over-regulation.
>
> Even though transdermal testosterone delivery technology has been known for decades, and the patent for bioidentical testosterone expired a long time ago, the FDA only allows a chosen few pharmaceutical companies to sell it. When a compounding pharmacy tries to develop more efficient ways to make testosterone creams, FDA inspectors use existing regulations to stop them. The regulations mandate that individually compounded drugs be made from scratch. If a pharmacy tries

to produce larger quantities in bulk, it is no longer classified as "compounded" according to FDA regulations and is therefore illegal.

The conclusion is a whopping 23-fold market failure:

In this Orwellian tragedy, the annual cost of regulated AndroGel comes to $4,176 whereas the same amount of topical testosterone in an unregulated environment would drop to only $180 a year.

Regulated testosterone thus costs *23 times more* than free-market testosterone… Is it any wonder why medical insurance premiums are increasing so sharply?

In effect, the FDA is preventing a competitive marketplace from operating. It grants permissions to only "a chosen few pharmaceutical companies". From one point of view, the constraints are sensible: companies need to demonstrate they meet various safety standards. But Faloon sees this instead as "institutionalised corruption":

Institutionalized corruption artificially inflates the cost of virtually every health care service.

Going back to the AndroGel example, we estimate that more than 80 million American men could benefit by restoring their testosterone levels to youthful ranges. If these men are forced to use only FDA-approved testosterone drugs, the excess cost to the United States will be $319 billion *each* year for this *one* drug.

It used to be just a few years ago that when the entire federal deficit reached $300 billion, the public and some politicians complained. Yet the overpayment Americans are stuck with for this *one* class of drug (AndroGel and others) because of FDA over-regulation may exceed previous federal deficits unless the law is amended.

When one considers there are thousands of medically related products and services that are artificially inflated by senseless regulations, it becomes clear that radical change is required to avoid an economic meltdown…

Consumers have to band together to demand Congress introduce emergency legislation that repeals the absurd over-regulation of medicine that exists today.

Why do regulations exist, asks Faloon. He sees good reasons and bad reasons, but the bad seem to be dominant:

Americans have been deceived by those who associate regulations with beneficial outcomes. As it relates to medical progress, the opposite has occurred.

Few understand that the underlying purpose of any given regulation is to provide a government-protected advantage to the group favouring that regulation. It's not about how a regulation will protect the public, but instead a matter of "how can it financially benefit a special interest."

Here's another example that Faloon highlights:

An oft-cited example is a petition the drug maker Wyeth filed with the FDA asking that a natural human form of oestrogen called estriol be banned. The female hormone drugs Wyeth is selling (Premarin and PremPro) had been shown to inflict all kinds of lethal side effects. Instead of spending money on research to come up with safer forms of oestrogen... it was much cheaper to persuade political hacks at the FDA to outlaw the competition (i.e., bioidentical estriol hormone compounds).

Pharmaceutical companies have spent enormous amounts of money persuading the FDA to reclassify nutrients like pyridoxamine into prescription drugs so they can monopolize them for their own economic benefit. If it were not for aggressive letter-writing campaigns by consumers to Congress, *all* dietary supplements would be expensive prescription drugs by now.

These are serious allegations – and there are many more in later chapters of Faloon's book. The book contains ample references, for readers to check the background details. If even a small portion of the case stories are true, it's a matter for genuine concern.

Pharmocracy also contains a series of positive recommendations to improve matters. Here's the first:

Our proposal is quite simple. Change the laws to allow good manufacturing practice (GMP)-certified manufacturing facilities to produce generic prescription drugs that do not undergo the excessive regulatory hurdles that force consumers to pay egregiously inflated prices.

To alert consumers when they are getting a generic that is not as heavily regulated as it is currently, the law would mandate that the label of these less-regulated generic drugs clearly state:

"This is not an FDA-approved manufactured generic drug and may be ineffective and potentially dangerous. This drug is not manufactured under the same standards required for an FDA-approved generic drug. Purchase this drug at your own risk."

By allowing the sale of these less costly generics, consumers will have a choice as to which companies they choose to trust.

It's noteworthy that Faloon recommends an ongoing role for regulatory oversight:

> A concern critics raise about this free-market solution is safety. Who will protect consumers from poorly made generic drugs, they ask?
>
> The manufacturers of these drugs would be subject to the same regulation as GMP-certified dietary supplement makers. FDA inspectors will visit facilities, take sample products, and assay them to ensure the potency of active ingredients, dissolution, etc. Laboratories that fail to make products which meet the label's claims would face civil and criminal penalties from the government.

Faloon also makes a good point about safety concerns. Although there are risks to loosening the regulatory regime, there are also many large risks in maintaining the current regulatory regime:

> No matter how many facts show that free-market generic drugs will be safe, there are alarmists who believe that even if one person might suffer a serious adverse event because of a lower-cost generic drug, the law should not be amended to allow the sale of these less-regulated products.
>
> What few understand is that enabling lower-cost drugs to be sold might reduce the number of poorly made drugs. The reason is that prescription drug counterfeiting is a major issue today. Drugs are counterfeited because they are so expensive. Yet in the free-market environment we espouse, a month's supply of a popular cholesterol-lowering drug like simvastatin would sell for less than $3.00. It is difficult to imagine anyone profiting by counterfeiting it. So amending the law to enable these super-low-cost drugs to be sold might reduce the counterfeiting that exists right now.
>
> Another reason these less-regulated generics will do far more good than harm is that people who need them to live will be able to afford them. The media has reported on heart-wrenching stories of destitute people who are unable to pay for their prescription drugs. They either do without, or take a less-than-optimal dose. The availability of these free-market generics will enable virtually anyone to be able to afford their medications out of pocket.

As you can see, Faloon writes in the style of an advocate, rather than a fundamentalist. His proposals deserve full consideration. Lined up against any such reforms, however, is the logic of powerful entrenched industry pursuing its own self-interest:

> It is critical to understand the magnitude of control that pharmaceutical and other special interests exert in Washington. The tragic result is that

corrupt legislation is enacted that garners outlandish profits to those with political connections, while driving up healthcare costs to levels that are unaffordable by governmental and private entities.

The [2003] Medicare Prescription Drug Act is an egregious example of how Congress can be corrupted into passing laws that pour hundreds of billions of dollars in profits into Big Pharma, while hastening the financial collapse of our healthcare system... This 1,000-page bill, written by pharmaceutical lobbyists, provided $395 billion of taxpayer subsidies over a ten-year period for the purchase of prescription drugs at full retail prices.

Faloon explains the self-interest of the pharmaceutical companies:

Just imagine you owned a business (like a pharmaceutical company) in which you sold a product for $100 that cost you only $5 to make. You are protected against competition by federal agencies that destroy those who make less expensive options (like alternative therapies) available. Your only problem is that consumers cannot afford your overpriced product.

Most industries respond to these kinds of issues by initiating more efficient business practices and cutting prices. What if, instead of lowering prices, you influenced the federal government to use tax dollars to buy your overpriced product? That's exactly what the pharmaceutical industry accomplished when they snuck through the Medicare Prescription Drug Act, with more drug lobbyists in the halls of Congress that night than elected officials.

The operations of these lobbyists raise a whole pile of questions:

The insidious way this law was passed provides an intriguing window into how pharmaceutical influence causes Americans to overpay for prescription drugs and then plunders tax dollars to subsidize some of those who cannot afford the artificially inflated prices.

The Medicare Prescription Drug Act was passed at 3:00am, long after most people in Washington had gone to sleep. Most members of Congress initially refused to vote for the bill, arguing it was too expensive and provided a windfall to the drug companies. The drug lobbyists went into overdrive, going as far as to threaten to support opposing candidates in future elections if certain members of Congress did not vote for the bill.

For neither the first nor the last time, industry lobbyists rode roughshod over ethical concerns:

Despite there being no surplus federal revenue available to fund the Medicare Prescription Drug Act, pharmaceutical lobbying prevailed over ethical consciousness as Congress narrowly enacted this bill.

To add insult to injury, within two weeks of the bill's passage, Medicare released data showing the true projected cost of the bill would be $534 billion, instead of the $395 billion Congress was misled into believing.

In sworn testimony before Congress, it was revealed this $534 billion cost projection was intentionally withheld from Congress on orders from a Medicare official who went to work for a high-powered Washington, DC, lobbying firm ten days after the bill was signed into law.

Lobbyists from the pharmaceutical industry have their counterparts in several other industries. In each case, the lobbyists exist to advance the self-interest of the industry in question. The self-interest is cloaked in expressions of grander purpose – safety, protection, community, and so on – but we would be naïve to ignore the underlying self-interest.

Lobbyists for the pharmaceutical industry operate alongside those for the oil industry (whose effects were discussed in Chapter 7), the military industrial complex (including arms traders), existing transport companies (who are concerned about the impact from Uber), newspapers (who are concerned about restrictions on their freedom of speech), information technology, and many more. The wealthier an industry is, the more it can afford to spend in numerous clever schemes to subvert the processes of regulation. The more power an industry has at a given time, the more it stands to lose in future upheavals, and the greater its interest, therefore, in influencing the course of any such upheavals.

Given the enormous power possessed by incumbent industries, it may seem a hopeless cause to imagine that positive change can happen. Won't these industries move heaven and earth to maintain a stranglehold on product innovation and revenue flow?

Overcoming vested interests

Vested interests are powerful, but they are not *all*-powerful. Technoprogressives can point to many examples of disruptive forces overcoming the resistance put up against change by incumbent industries.

For example, the tobacco industry used to sponsor lots of research that *appeared* to be independent, and which threw doubt over evidence linking smoking to cancer. Correlation does not imply causation, the industry pointed out: just because smokers get cancer more often, it doesn't follow that smoking is the cause of their cancer. And in any case, the industry proclaimed, people should be allowed the freedom to smoke, if that's what they want to do. As such, the tobacco industry cloaked itself in the banner of personal liberty. Clever marketing linked the notion of smoking with sex appeal and smouldering glamour – witness famous photographs of the likes of Hollywood stars Lauren Bacall and Humphrey Bogart. High-placed friends of the tobacco industry offered their support. Politicians benefited from tax dollars levied on tobacco. Numerous people found profitable employment inside the industry. Tobacco companies sponsored sports events, games shows, and even cartoons. Health concerns were therefore brushed aside… but only for so long.

In due course, at the culmination of what has been called a "hundred-year cigarette war"[284], public health influences succeeded in winding back the power of the tobacco industry. Whereas over 50% of men in England were smokers in 1974, the figure fell to 16.9% by September 2016[285]. Similar reductions have taken place globally.

The process by which the power of the tobacco industry was clipped can serve as a model for progress in other areas of life. Scientific evidence was presented in ways that were clearer and more convincing. It was no longer credible to deny that tobacco damaged human tissue and dramatically increased health risks. Public figures previously associated with the industry changed their allegiance, and were emboldened to speak out against it. The longer term social costs of the industry became more widely understood. The underhand methods of the industry were exposed to greater public scrutiny, strengthening the appetite for stronger legislation. New political administrations had fewer personal ties to the industry[286]. The industry found they had fewer friends in high places. The power of the many – the taxpayers who needed to pay extra to fund public healthcare costs, as well as family members who saw their loved ones spiralling downwards under addiction to tobacco – eventually prevailed over vested interests.

Part of the decline of power of tobacco, unexpectedly, may be the rise of other consumer habits that demanded a higher share of people's discretionary income: habits such as electronic gaming and smartphones. These new habits don't just compete with smoking on grounds of cost; they also provide alternative means of personal buzz and stimulation[287]. However, the impact of this new competition to cigarettes likely depended on the background change in social attitudes towards tobacco – changes that arose due to action by health advocates and public-minded politicians.

The public campaign against the negative externalities of the tobacco industry was far from being *fully* successful. Blogger Pepe Lepew ruefully noted that, in many ways, "Big Tobacco got away with the Crime of the Century"[288]:

> Tobacco executive lost their jobs for lying to Congress, were investigated for perjury, but avoided an indictment. Big Tobacco was convicted by a federal judge of... racketeering, and that conviction was upheld by an appeals court, but no executives went to jail, nor was the industry even forced to pay penalties. A huge civil settlement with the states has simply turned into a windfall for state government.

> Big Tobacco murdered people for decades. And murder is not too strong of a word for it. They knew since the early 1950s, maybe even earlier, that they had a product that was addicting people and was killing people. And they continued to sell it and market it, and then they marketed it to kids. And they covered up and lied. For decades. It's amazing to me that not one person has ever spent a day in jail for it. And people are rotting in prison in Texas and Florida for selling pot.

Executives in other industries did not get away so lightly. Andrew Fastow, CFO (Chief Financial Officer) of the energy trading company Enron, received from CFO Magazine in 2000 their "Excellence Award for Capital Structure Management"[289]. This award reflected what seemed to be an excellent execution of innovative financial policies. As noted in the award citation, "How Enron financed its amazing transformation from pipelines to piping hot":

> When Andrew S. Fastow, the 37-year-old CFO of Enron Corp., boasts that "our story is one of a kind," he's not kidding. In just 14 years, Enron has grown from a heavily regulated domestic natural-gas pipeline business to a fully integrated global energy company with thriving activities in natural gas, electricity, infrastructure development, marketing and trading, energy financing, and risk management. And much of that growth has been fuelled by unique financing techniques pioneered by Fastow...

> When energy stock analysts look for paradigm companies to vaunt, they point resolutely in the direction of Houston-based Enron, with $31 billion in revenues last year. And when they seek to explain how Enron has remade itself so completely, they point to "remarkably innovative financing"...

> Fastow reduced the balance-sheet debt, maintained the credit rating, and reduced the cost of capital while simultaneously growing the balance sheet.

> In just the last two years, Enron has nearly doubled its total assets from $16 billion to $30 billion – without shareholder dilution and without a drop in the company's credit rating.

Enron was an upstart that grew to be the world's largest energy trading firm. It was audited by the venerable firm Arthur Andersen – one of the world's top five accountancy firms – and received a clean bill of health. Andersen accountants apparently viewed Enron's methods of "structuring financial instruments to be on the cutting edge"[290]. Politicians of both leading parties in the United States were on friendly terms with the executives of Enron. While Governor of Texas, George W. Bush made a phone call to Tom Ridge, governor of Pennsylvania at the time (1997) at the request of Kenneth Lay, Enron's Chairman. According to an article in the New York Times[291], the purpose of the phone call was "to vouch for Enron, which was trying to break into that state's electricity markets". The same article reported that Lay played golf with President Bill Clinton. As the New York Times reported, Enron had spread huge amounts of funding in the direction of politicians[292]:

> Like many Fortune 100 companies, Enron, a Houston energy-trading company, spread largess all over Washington. Although it gave more money to Republicans, it gave plenty to Democrats...
>
> Enron has written campaign checks to three-fourths of the senators, and nearly half of the members of the House.

However, the power and influence that Enron possessed was insufficient to save it, once diligent reporters started querying how the finances of the company actually worked. In due course, the legal system took action. Andrew Fastow, Enron's CFO, went from being "CFO of the year" to being charged with 98 counts of crimes such as fraud, conspiracy, insider trading, and money laundering. He went on to serve a six-year prison sentence. Kenneth Lay was found guilty of 10 counts of security fraud. He died of a heart attack shortly prior to his sentencing. The auditing company Arthur Andersen that had, shamefully, failed to properly investigate questionable activities at their client Enron, went out of business as their mistakes became public knowledge due to the legal process.

Consider also the fact that 29 senior bankers in Iceland have received significant jail sentences for negligence and fraud in connection with the 2008 financial crash. Their power and privilege could not fend off the consequences of their reckless activities[293]. Although an admittedly rare case

– bankers in most other countries have, so far, escaped imprisonment for their collective misdeeds in the run-up to the crash – this demonstrates the principle that vested interests can (at least in some cases) have their power overturned by the actions of public institutions.

One last example deserves mention: the institutions of the nation of South Korea have recently imprisoned, not only the incumbent president of the country, Park Geun-hye, but also the leader of the most powerful company in the country – namely Samsung's Lee Jae-yong, who also happened to be the country's third richest man[294].

Beyond economic fundamentalism

Whereas market fundamentalists believe that free markets are absolutely the best way to decide the allocation of resources, *anti*-market fundamentalists believe that such markets inevitably have deeply deplorable side-effects.

Here are the kinds of things anti-market fundamentalists highlight. Free markets emphasise personal greed, as in the brazen Gordon Gecko mantra "Greed is good" from the 1987 film *Wall Street*. Free markets encourage competitive behaviour, as opposed to collaborative behaviour. Free markets support the disturbing logic of "price gouging", when prices of scarce goods (such as bottled water) are spiked high during times of humanitarian crisis. Free markets inspire companies to create products with built-in obsolescence, so that consumers are obliged to keep repurchasing the item. Free markets lead to a "sickness industry" rather than a "health industry", since there are more profits to be made when sick people keep on repurchasing medicines, than when they take one-time treatments that will make them completely better. And so on.

However, in this chapter I've argued that there is no *necessity* for free markets to lead to any of these behaviours. Yes, these *tendencies* exist, but such tendencies can be countered by other institutions that co-exist in any healthy society – institutions such as a free press, regulations, legal redress, and parliamentary review.

Anti-market fundamentalists argue, in response, that these institutions will inevitably fall under the spell of an economy's most powerful forces. The press will be governed by millionaire press barons. Regulators will be subject to financial pressures that favour vested interests. Judges and politicians will be dependent on support from the strongest businesses; they may growl on occasion, but they won't actually bite. In the end, money will triumph every time. Accordingly, true progress can be expected only if society's sources of finance are tightly controlled – or (in a slightly different version of this vision) if the "forces of production" are placed under the control of true representatives of the people. Society can experience only superficial improvements until such time as capitalism is overthrown.

In response to that response, I highlight once more the examples of vested interests being overcome, not via any dramatic social upheaval, but via the measured evolution and application of institutions and processes. I also highlight the fact that many of the world's richest people are ready to deploy the bulk of their personal wealth in service of non-financial goals – people including Rockefeller and Carnegie in the last century, and Bill Gates and Mark Zuckerberg in the present century. The motivation to accumulate wealth may be powerful, but the motivation to serve humanity can be every bit as powerful. I understand that legislators and journalists may, on occasion, sell out to the highest bidder, producing all kinds of rationalisation to justify their actions; but I see plenty of other occasions where they hold fast to their principles.

What's less clear is the *pace* at which positive institutional change can take place. Even if legislators, journalists, politicians, and business leaders honestly wish to rise above the pressures of the economic environment in which they all exist, they might find these pressures to be suffocating. In that case, what may make the biggest difference is the extent of support they receive from the population as a whole. Will they be cheered on, in their efforts to speak truth to power and to tame the excesses of establishment forces? Or will the populace instead display hostility to their efforts (or perhaps just as bad, apathy)?

It's time to look more closely at democracy itself – both its strengths and its weaknesses. Will the voice of the people empower positive social change, or instead drag us all down into a populist madness?

10. Democracy and inclusion

I'll start this chapter by repeating a set of questions from midway through the previous chapter:

> Where should the boundary fall, between the permitted and the impermissible? What is the method to tell whether a particular item of food or medicine is suitable to be freely bought and sold, as opposed to needing regulation? What safety regulations should employers be obliged to observe, in their treatment of employees or contractors? Which new technologies need careful monitoring (such as hazardous new biochemicals), and which can have all details freely published on the open Internet?

My basic answer to all these questions was: *it's complicated, but we can work out the answers step by step.* I now want to pose a follow-up set of questions:

- *Who is it* that should decide where the boundary should fall, between the permitted and the impermissible?

- *Who is it* that should decide which health and safety regulations should be introduced?

- *Who is it* that should decide which technologies need careful monitoring?

Should these decisions be taken by civil servants, by academics, by judges, by elected politicians, or by someone else?

There's a gist of an answer in what I said later in the previous chapter:

> Each area of regulatory oversight of the economy – each set of taxes or safety standards imposed or revised – needs careful attention by *an extended community of reviewers…*

> By drawing on technological solutions that can orchestrate the input of *large numbers of human thinkers*, we can keep improving our collective understanding of the best regulatory frameworks and institutions. *We can collectively decide* which constraints are needed on the activity of the free market, so that we benefit from its good consequences without suffering unnecessarily from its bad consequences.

But how will this work in practice? How do we prevent the bad effects of "group think" or (worse) "mob rule"? If there's "an extended community of reviewers" involved, won't that be far too cumbersome and slow in its deliberations?

Just as important, how do we avoid decisions being overly influenced by self-proclaimed experts who, in reality, have expertise in only a narrow domain, or whose expertise is out-of-date or otherwise ill-founded? And how do we guard against decision-makers being systematically misled by clever misinformation that builds a "false consciousness"?

Technoprogressive decision-making

Here is my answer to the questions I've just raised. The decision-making process should embody a set of *technoprogressive decision-making principles*. As I list them here, there are seventeen such principles (I'll provide more justification for these principles as the chapter unfolds):

1. *Transparency:* Decisions should be subject to open review, rather than taking place secretly behind closed doors; reasons for and against decisions should be made public, throughout the decision-making process, so they can be scrutinised and improved

2. *Accessibility:* Details of the decision process should be communicated in ways so that the key points can be understood by as wide a group of people as possible; this will allow input into the decision by people with multiple perspectives and backgrounds

3. *Disclosure:* Assumptions behind decisions should be stated clearly, so they can be subject to further debate; potential conflicts of interest – for example if someone with ties to a particular company is part of a standards-setting exercise that would impact the company's products – should, likewise, be stated upfront

4. *Accountability:* People who are found to have deliberately miscommunicated points relevant to a decision – for example, suppressing important evidence, or distorting a competing argument – should be liable to public shaming, or tougher sanctions, and may have privileges withdrawn as a consequence

5. *Deliberation:* In the terminology of Unanimous.AI CEO Louis Rosenberg[295], the decision should express the "convergent opinion" rather than the "average opinion"; decision-makers should work as a "swarm" that dynamically exchanges opinions and adjusts ideas, rather than as a "crowd" that merely votes on an

answer; in this way, the outcome is "the opinion the group can best agree upon"

6. *Open-mindedness:* All assumptions and opinions should be open to questioning: none should be placed into an untouchable category of "infallible foundation" or "sacrosanct authority" by saying, for example, "this was our manifesto commitment, so we have to do it", or by saying "this is the express will of the people, so we cannot reopen this question"

7. *Constructiveness:* Whilst the previous principle, open-mindedness, encourages questioning of existing proposals, questions and objections should be raised in ways that enable new alternative assumptions to be considered in place of the ones being criticised

8. *Creativity:* The facilitators of the discussion should be ready to remind participants of the ways in which deep-rooted cognitive biases act to stifle creativity and hinder rationality; for example, the facilitators should prevent new ideas from being hastily dismissed by critics as "self-evidently mad" or "clearly impossible", without the critics providing a good reason for their opposition

9. *Autonomy:* Each decision should be judged on its own merit, with each decision-maker expressing their own independent views, rather than any system of horse-trading or party politics applying, in which individuals would act against their own consciences in order to follow some kind of "three line whip" or "party line"

10. *Data-driven:* To guide them in their deliberations, decision-makers should seek out relevant data, and verify it, rather than giving undue credence to anecdote, supposition, or ideology

11. *Experimentation:* In any case where significant uncertainty exists, rather than relying on pre-existing philosophical commitments, an incremental experimental approach should be preferred, in order to generate useful data that can guide the decision process

12. *Agility:* To avoid the perils of drawn-out "analysis by paralysis", hard decisions should be broken down into smaller chunks, with each chunk being addressed in a separate "sprint" (to borrow a term from the methodology of software development); for each sprint, the goal is to gain a better understanding of the overall landscape in which the decision needs to be taken; breaking a

decision into sprints assists in preventing decisions from dragging on interminably with no progress

13. *Reversibility:* Wherever possible, a reversible approach should be preferred, especially in areas of major uncertainty, so that policies can be undone if it becomes clear they are mistaken

14. *Adaptability:* The system should applaud and support decision-makers who openly change their mind in the light of improved understanding; decision-makers should feel no undue pressure to stick with a previous opinion just in order to "keep face" or to demonstrate "party loyalty" through thick and thin

15. *Leanness:* Decisions should focus on questions that matter most, rather than dictating matters where individual differences can easily be tolerated; by the way, "lean", like "agile", is another term borrowed from modern thinking about manufacturing: lean development seeks to avoid "waste", such as excess bureaucracy

16. *Tech-embracing:* Technology that assists with the decision process should be embraced – including wikis (or similar) that map out the landscape of a decision, automated logic-checkers, modelling systems that explore outcomes in simulated worlds, and other aspects of collabtech; importantly, discussion participants should be supported in learning how to excel in use of this technology

17. *Independent facilitation:* The outcome of decisions should not depend on the choice of which people coordinate the process; these people should be *enablers* rather than *dictators* of the solution; *coaches* rather than *front-runners.*

Two underlying points deserve emphasis. These decisions about social institutions should be taken *by everyone* (that is, no-one is excluded from the process); and they should be taken *by no-one in particular* (that is, the process gives no special status to any individual decision-maker). These two points can be restated: the decisions should follow the processes of *democracy*, and they should follow the processes of *the scientific method*.

There's a forest of details lurking behind that simple restatement. I've already discussed in Chapter 3 of this book how present-day practice of the scientific method is experiencing a significant set of problems. The question of how to facilitate good science, as opposed to bad science (or "pseudoscience"), is more complicated than people might imagine – but solutions are at hand. As I'll explore in this chapter, similar questions apply to democracy.

But before that, you may be thinking that the above seventeen principles set the bar impractically high. How is society going to be able to organise itself to observe all these principles? Isn't it going to require a great deal of effort? Given the urgency of the challenges facing society, do we have the time available to us, to follow all these principles?

Here's my response. First, there are billions of capable people on the planet. Provided we can find suitable ways of dividing up the tasks of decision-making, we have enough human brainpower available to follow all the principles proposed.

Second, many of the tasks can be aided by technological automation. That is, our human brainpower can be supported by artificial brainpower.

Third, if our political decisions continue to follow processes with lower quality, we should not be surprised if bad outcomes arise – with key decisions being bungled, and with hatred growing between groups holding different political opinions. We owe it to ourselves to do better!

Finally, we don't need to get there in a single step. Following the principle of agility (item number 12 in the list), we can make incremental improvements towards the envisaged process. (That same principle of agility predicts, incidentally, that the statement of seventeen principles will evolve over time, as we gain better insight through experience and reflection.)

The roadmap of incremental improvements in our decision-making processes starts with our current situation. Let's be clear about what in our current practice of democracy should be preserved, and which features are ripe for transformation and improvement.

When democracy goes wrong

Democracies can make horrific mistakes.

In March 1933, fourteen different parties contested a general election in Germany, for the 647 seats of the Reichstag parliament. Nearly 89% of the electorate cast votes[296]. Third place in the election was taken by the German communist party (KPD), who won 81 seats, with a popular vote of 12.3%. Second place went to the Social Democratic Party (SPD), who won 120 seats with a popular vote of 18.25%. The winners of the election were the

NSDAP, that is, the Nazi Party, with 288 seats and a popular vote of 43.9%. Although not an absolute majority, this figure of 43.9% was the largest share gained by any party in any vote in the history of the German Weimar Republic (1919-1933)[297].

In August of the following year, the German President Paul von Hindenburg died. Already in the role of Chancellor, Adolf Hitler, leader of the Nazi Party, jumped at the opportunity to combine both roles. A national plebiscite took place, requesting democratic approval for this move. The question put to the electors was as follows[298]:

> The office of the President of the Reich is unified with the office of the Chancellor. Consequently all former powers of the President of the Reich are demised to the Führer and Chancellor of the Reich Adolf Hitler. He himself nominates his substitute.
>
> Do you, German man and German woman, approve of this regulation provided by this Law?

The plebiscite was passed, with 88.1% voting in favour, 9.9% against, and 2% spoilt ballots. Turnout was impressively high: 95.7%. In this way, Adolf Hitler's rise to absolute power in Germany received a fulsome democratic mandate. This was evidently the will of the people. *Or was it?*

It can reasonably be objected that neither the March 1933 election nor the August 1934 plebiscite were "free and fair". In turbulent times, voters felt intimidated. Thus the website FactMyth adjudicates as "myth" the claim that Hitler was elected President in a democratic election[299]:

> Although Hitler and his Nazi party rose to power in "a democracy" (in a representative mixed-republic), they rose to power via corruption. So even loosely speaking, it is hard to consider Hitler and the Nazis "democratically elected". Yes, the Nazis were voted in, but it is hard to call the two general elections of 1932 "democratic" given the events surrounding the Machtergreifung (the Nazi seizure of power)…
>
> Perhaps it is best phrased as, "Hitler and the Nazi party seized power in a democratic system."

Nevertheless, this was an example of when extreme politics took advantage of a democratic system and drove the government of a country in a direction that turned out to be deeply regrettable. This is far from being the only example.

Consider what happened in Venezuela after Hugo Chávez won the democratic vote to become President of the country in December 1998.

Chávez received 56.4% of the popular vote on that occasion[300]. He went on to win a number of additional democratic votes in the years that followed. However, the same time period saw a marked reduction in regard for basic human rights. A report by Human Rights Watch in 2013 gave this bleak assessment[301]:

> Hugo Chávez's presidency (1999-2013) was characterized by a dramatic concentration of power and open disregard for basic human rights guarantees.
>
> After enacting a new constitution with ample human rights protections in 1999 – and surviving a short-lived coup d'état in 2002 – Chávez and his followers moved to concentrate power. They seized control of the Supreme Court and undercut the ability of journalists, human rights defenders, and other Venezuelans to exercise fundamental rights.
>
> By his second full term in office, the concentration of power and erosion of human rights protections had given the government free rein to intimidate, censor, and prosecute Venezuelans who criticized the president or thwarted his political agenda. In recent years, the president and his followers used these powers in a wide range of prominent cases, whose damaging impact was felt by entire sectors of Venezuelan society…

Or consider what happened – or what *might* have happened – following the first round of the democratic elections in Algeria in 1991. These were the country's first multi-party elections after it had gained independence in 1962[302]. As such, expectations were high. What happened next is described by human rights activist Hicham Yezza writing in Open Democracy[303]:

> After months of bitter and virulent campaigning, results of round one of Algeria's first multi-party legislative elections had confirmed the wildest hopes, and worst fears, of millions of Algerians: the Islamic Salvation Front (FIS) had secured a resounding victory, trouncing the mighty dinosaurs of the, hitherto-unmovable, National Liberation Front (FLN) and securing 188 of a possible 232 parliamentary seats at the first time of asking, with plenty more expected to fall into its orbit at the second round scheduled two weeks later.
>
> But there would be no second round…
>
> Instead, the president announced the dissolution of parliament:
>
> Three days later, a five-man unelected leadership, the Haut Comité d'État, was installed as an interim de-facto presidency of the country…

> The move was presented by many within the democratic and secular movement as a necessary last ditch attempt to "save the republic" from an imminent Islamist takeover.

The country could not be trusted to the Islamic Salvation Front with their "totalitarian designs", the argument ran. Sadly, the country was plunged into a decade-long civil war. Yezza comments,

> What followed was a dark decade of untold tragedy and suffering. Tens of thousands, mostly civilians, perished in the all-out war for supremacy and survival between government forces and armed Islamists, with the bulk of the population maintaining a precarious balance in between. Hundreds of thousands were displaced or exiled, tens of thousands kidnapped or "disappeared", not to mention tens of billions of dollars of losses that brought the country to the brink of ruin.

Would things have proceeded more smoothly if the Islamists had been allowed to take power? That's far from clear.

Depending on your own political sensibilities, you might disagree with my particular choices of examples. However, I doubt you will deny that there are circumstances in which democracy can go wrong. Evidently, the mere fact that a democratic election endorses a party is no guarantee that the party will steer the country in a positive direction.

Reasons why the democratic process can result in bad outcomes include:

- Elections not being "free and fair": opposition candidates being prevented from being able to stand, not having equal rights to publicity, or having their free speech curtailed

- The electorate being bribed – either explicitly, via payments of cash, or via policy promises tailored to different groups – in order to cast votes differently from the national interest

- Politicians making pledges that they have no intention of keeping, deceiving electors in the process

- Politicians engineering short-term feel-good factors, to win favour with voters ahead of an election, instead of taking more painful measures necessary for longer-term progress

- Electors not being offered a meaningful choice – or being in constituencies where a vote for their preferred candidate would amount to a wasted vote due to a "first past the post" election system

- Electors acting on feelings of revenge or alienation, casting "protest votes" in favour of politicians who seem to empathise with their predicaments but who lack any credible programme to improve matters

- Electors taking decisions based on a very flimsy or distorted understanding of the key issues at stake

- Minority viewpoints being trampled and silenced – either before or after an election – under the claim that the majority has already won the argument.

None of these problems negates the core importance of democracy. I'll review in a moment why it's vital to make democracy work, despite the above difficulties.

But first, it's useful to compare the operation of democracy to the operation of free economic markets (as addressed in the previous chapter). Both systems are key parts of a healthy society. However, neither can operate entirely by themselves. Without the support of vigorous social institutions, including a free press and an independent judiciary, both systems can go wrong – badly wrong. Just as cartels and monopolies can form within a free market and then act against the common interest, transitioning from a phase of innovation and service to one of stagnation and dominance, so also can the internal dynamics of democracy become unhinged. Just as a society needs more than free markets to ensure that free markets continue to have a positive outcome, so also a society needs more than democratic voting to ensure that democratic voting continues to have a positive outcome.

Why democracy matters

Democracy is far more than the idea that decisions should be put to a vote.

Theodore Parker, American reformer and abolitionist, used this phrase in a speech at an anti-slavery convention in Boston in 1850[304]:

Democracy... is a government of all the people, by all the people, for all the people.

This idea was cemented into public consciousness due to its incorporation by Abraham Lincoln in his 1863 Gettysburg Address[305]. Democracy owes its authority to the extent that it operates with the effective collective approval of "all the people" and in service to "all the people".

Critically, this means that when politicians stray too far from serving the community as a whole, the community should have the power to remove them from office.

Veteran UK politician Tony Benn expressed it well in remarks in his farewell speech to the House of Commons in 2001, more than fifty years after first being elected a Member of Parliament[306]:

> In the course of my life I have developed five little democratic questions. If one meets a powerful person – Adolf Hitler, Joe Stalin or Bill Gates – ask them five questions: "What power have you got? Where did you get it from? In whose interests do you exercise it? To whom are you accountable? And how can we get rid of you?" If you cannot get rid of the people who govern you, you do not live in a democratic system.

Benn developed the theme further[307]:

> Only democracy gives us that right [to ask these questions]. That is why no one with power likes democracy. And that is why every generation must struggle to win it and keep it – including you and me, here and now.

This power to "get rid" of our present political leadership depends in turn on a number of prerequisites:

- Journalists who can write about what our politicians are actually doing, rather than what these politicians say they are doing

- Media who can distribute the findings of journalists, without fear of being shut down by wrathful authorities

- The availability of a set of candidates for alternative political leadership, who can offer a meaningfully different approach

- The actual mechanism of a democratic vote, free from intimidation and distortion

- A set of independent institutions that oversee and protect the above processes.

The complication, of course, is that once new politicians have benefited from these processes in their own rise to power, they can become threatened by the continued actions of these institutions. They can transition from being apparent champions of freedom to apparent suppressors of freedom. This can involve:

- Criticisms of the press as purveyors of "fake news"; the press becomes pilloried as an alleged enemy-of-the-state within the state

- Tinkering with electoral boundaries, in a process known as gerrymandering, to make it more likely that voters clump in ways that disproportionately support the party currently in power

- Side-lining of potential up-and-coming rivals, perhaps by handing them difficult "poisoned chalice" responsibilities

- Denigration of the judiciary and other bodies as being "non-elected" and therefore "opposed to the will of the people".

It's as stated in the chilling observation from Lord Acton[308] that I quoted in Chapter 1:

> Power tends to corrupt. Absolute power corrupts absolutely.

Defence of democracy therefore requires stout defence of these broader practices and institutions. It requires, ideally, the adoption of the seventeen principles that I set out at the beginning of this chapter.

Whether or not these principles are adopted will mainly depend on whether society as a whole wants to adopt them – whether analysts see them as desirable, voters demand them, independent organisations start to embody them, and politicians take action to promote them.

Better voters for a better future

A democracy fit for a better future requires, not just better processes, but also better voters, better politicians, and better political parties.

That may seem a lot to request. However, it comes down to requesting *progress*. Human life has progressed in many ways over the past centuries. Why can't it also progress in the sphere of democracy?

Shortcomings in how voters take decisions have long been highlighted as a fundamental issue for democracy. A saying attributed (probably incorrectly)[309] to Winston Churchill puts it like this:

> The best argument against democracy is a five-minute conversation with the average voter.

Analysts sometimes wonder about a possible threshold that would need to be passed, before someone would receive the right to vote. Professor Jason Brennan of Georgetown University has advocated a system called "epistocracy"[310] – meaning "the rule of the knowers". I don't endorse his proposals, but it's worth taking some time to consider them.

Brennan starts with an observation:

> In spreading power among the many – as in a democracy – individual votes no longer matter, and so most voters remain ignorant, biased and misinformed.

Because most voters think their vote probably won't make any real difference to the outcome, they don't put much effort into fully researching the options.

Brennan then sets out an alternative:

> Consider an alternative political system called *epistocracy*. Epistocracies retain the *same* institutions as representative democracies, including imposing liberal constitutional limits on power, bills of rights, checks and balances, elected representatives and judicial review. But while democracies give every citizen an equal right to vote, epistocracies apportion political power, by law, according to *knowledge* or *competence*.

Here's the motivation for this alternative system:

> The idea here is not that knowledgeable people deserve to rule – of course they don't – but that the rest of us deserve not to be subjected to incompetently made political decisions. Political decisions are high stakes, and democracies entrust some of these high-stakes decisions to the ignorant and incompetent. Democracies tend to pass laws and policies that appeal to the median voter, yet the median voter would fail Econ, History, Sociology, and Poli Sci 101. Empirical work generally shows that voters would support different policies if they were better informed.

Brennan recognises that most voters are well-intentioned – but that fact is, by itself, insufficient to extend the same voting privileges to everyone:

> Voters tend to mean well, but voting well takes more than a kind heart. It requires tremendous social scientific knowledge: knowledge that most citizens lack. Most voters know nothing, but some know a great deal, and some know *less* than nothing. The goal of liberal republican epistocracy is to protect against democracy's downsides, by reducing the power of the least-informed voters, or increasing the power of better-informed ones.

How might an epistocracy be implemented? Brennan offers a number of suggestions:

> There are many ways of instituting epistocracy, some of which would work better than others. For instance, an epistocracy might deny citizens the franchise unless they can pass a test of basic political knowledge. They might give every citizen one vote, but grant additional votes to citizens who pass certain tests or obtain certain credentials. They might pass all laws through normal democratic means, but then permit bands of experts to veto badly designed legislation. For instance, a board of economic advisors might have the right to veto rent-control laws, just as the Supreme Court can veto laws that violate the Constitution...

Is such a system inherently discriminatory? After all, it fails to regard everyone as equal (from the point of voting rights). However, Brennan raises an interesting counter:

> We could... view the franchise as no more significant than a plumbing or medical licence. The US government denies me such licences, but I don't regard that as expressing I'm inferior, all things considered, to others.

CNN writer LZ Granderson offered a similar proposal in his 2011 article "Don't let ignorant people vote"[311]:

> If I were to ask you to ingest an unknown medicine from someone who knew nothing about the medical field, you probably wouldn't do it. And I doubt many of us would feel comfortable as a shareholder in a company that asked people who knew nothing about business to hire its next CEO?
>
> Yet we all know people who gleefully admit they know nothing about politics, don't have time to find out what the current issues are or even know how the government works, but go out and vote. Want to know why it seems Washington is run by a bunch of idiots? Blame this hiccup in our political system for starters. What's a solution? Weed out some of the ignorant by making people who want to vote first pass a test modelled on the one given to those who want to become citizens.

Granderson clarifies that by the word "ignorant" he is not implying the meaning "stupid":

> Before getting all bent out of shape by my assertion that you or someone you love is ignorant, please know I am not referring to the dictionary's first definition of the word, which typically means an uneducated or unsophisticated person. I am operating with the second usage, defined as a lack of knowledge in a specific area.

No one is omniscient; we're all ignorant about something.

I know close to nothing about the inner workings of my car, and so I come to my mechanic, ignorant – but not stupid. As this relates to voting, if people don't know much about current government and politics, they too are ignorant, not necessarily stupid. The difference is that naively paying too much for repairs on a car is not nearly as damaging to foreign policy as a bunch of ignorant voters hitting the polls.

Granderson accepts that his proposal can be viewed as "elitist":

Am I advocating for some sort of elitism?

You betcha.

One of the more counterproductive by-products of having our political system hijacked by campaigns obsessed with ignorant voters is that the word "elite" has been saddled with terrible PR. True, one boilerplate definition essentially means "rich snobs" but another – and the one more central to my point – means the best or most skilled in a group. We don't seem to have a problem understanding the importance of having elite athletes on our favourite sports team, but some of us have been trained to have a gag reflex at the very mention of the country's elite thinkers running the country.

However, in that final sentence, Granderson conflates two different roles:

- The role of actually running the country – including civil servants, judges, and elected politicians
- The role of choosing the people who run the country.

Saying that we are comfortable with having elites in the former role is a far cry from saying that we should be comfortable with only elites being allowed to fill the second (voting) role.

I fully support the idea of preferring competence for key leadership roles. However, we should shy away from suggestions to restrict voting rights.

I share the criticism of Brennan's notion of epistocracy made by George Mason University professor of law, Ilya Somin[312]:

There is a substantial likelihood that real-world governments cannot be trusted to implement epistocracy in any kind of unbiased way. Instead of limiting the franchise to the knowledgeable, they are likely to structure tests, lotteries, or other similar mechanisms, in ways that over-represent supporters of the party in power and exclude opponents.

Professor Lisa Hill of the University of Adelaide raises further concerns about restricting voting rights[313]:

> Brennan's notion that democracy exists to generate "correct" decisions is based on a fundamental misunderstanding of its history. Democracy emerged as a reaction to aristocracy and other hierarchical, elite-based forms of rule. It was, and continues to be, as a struggle for political equality, for the right of people to participate – irrespective of social standing or levels of political competence – as the necessary condition for the enjoyment of liberty...

> Campaigners for suffrage rights in the early and late-modern period did not argue that the disenfranchised knew best: what they fought for was a voice, an equal share in power so that everyone could enjoy their liberty and rights. Thomas Paine made no mention of truth or wisdom when he called for equal representation; instead he demanded a universal release from political slavery and the right to bear rights. There was no mention of epistemic considerations when Susan B. Anthony demanded voting rights for women in 1872. Who knew best or worst was beside the point; voting meant liberty, equality, rights, representation, power-sharing and the capacity to confer or withhold consent. It meant protection from wrongful imprisonment, exploitation and being taxed without being consulted about how the money was spent. Similarly when Lyndon B. Johnson defended the voting rights of all African-Americans he spoke only of equality, 'liberty' and 'government by the consent of the governed'.

A similar point can be found in the literature of the Chartist movement, which campaigned in the United Kingdom in from the 1830s to the 1850s for an extension of voting rights. Here's a message from 1838 from Chartist supporter Joseph Rayner Stephens[314]:

> The question of universal suffrage is a knife and fork question after all. The question of universal suffrage is a bread and cheese question after all... By universal suffrage ... I mean that every working man in the land has a right to have a good coat upon his back, a good roof for the shelter of his household, a good dinner upon his table, ... and as much wages as will keep him in plenty and in the enjoyment of all the pleasures of life which a reasonable man can desire.

In other words, without the right to a vote, the right to economic rewards also becomes vulnerable.

Nevertheless, the problem of voter incompetence is a pressing one. Professor Hill has a lot of sympathy for the problems with democracy pointed out by Brennan:

> For philosopher Jason Brennan, the "rise of Trump" – a candidate "seemingly as ill-informed as he is uninterested in policy" – "should challenge our faith in democracy". Similarly, the Brexit vote delivered by an electorate imperfectly aware of its implications should prompt us to "put aside the childish and magical theory that democracy is intrinsically just". As he sees it "most voters are ignorant of both basic political facts and the background social scientific theories needed to evaluate the facts". Further "they process what little information they have in highly biased and irrational ways" and vote "largely on whim".

So what can be done? To my mind, the best solution to incompetent voters is to increase their competence level, not *by mandate and restriction*, but *by education and communication*. This fits the technoprogressive vision that personal improvement is something that can – and must – be available for everyone.

An important part of improving the level of understanding and engagement by voters will be the growth of what can be called the "technoprogressive knowledge base": a set of information websites that are widely recognised as providing objective, accessible guides to key questions of politics, economics, society, and changing technology. These guides can follow the general pattern already established by crowd-sourced encyclopaedias like Wikipedia and fact-checking sites like Snopes. Over time, these new guides should reach increasingly high levels of public approval, for their impartiality, reliability, convenience, engagingness, and user-friendliness. Developing and improving this technoprogressive knowledge base will be one of the key tasks of the months and years ahead.

Better politicians for a better future

When we consider issues of incompetence and lack of knowledge – especially lack of awareness of the large disruptions that will potentially arise in the wake of rapidly advancing technology – it's not just incompetent voters that we need to worry about. We also need to worry about incompetent politicians.

The abovementioned technoprogressive knowledge base that will keep the electorate much better informed about fundamental questions will also be a major benefit to politicians. That's an important ingredient of raising the knowledge and performance of our elected representatives.

Regularly hearing intelligent, well-informed questions and suggestions from electors will also help to transform the attitudes displayed by politicians. They'll put less effort into deliberately dumbing down their slogans or appealing to perceived lowest common denominators. Instead, the conversation will rise to a higher calibre.

Three other factors will play critical roles as well:

1. As early transhumanist technologies become more widely available, politicians, like the rest of us, will be able to take advantage of what I called in Chapter 1 "concentration systems" – nootropic drugs, improved nutrition, more productive sleep, smart meditation helmets, personal feedback from wearable AI assistants, and so on – in order to concentrate more effectively on key decisions, free from adverse tiredness, distraction, bias, or prejudice

2. Politicians should be supported by an increasingly competent set of technocratic assistants, whose recommendations are driven by expertise rather than by a sense of party loyalty, personal favours, or financial ties

3. Politicians should be able to express their own independent opinions on a wider range of matters, free from restrictions imposed by the present party-based system of politics.

Let's dig deeper into these last two points. The present-day situation is that politicians often find their freedom of expression constrained in practical terms by people who hold financial purse strings, and by the whips or other officials in their chosen political parties who have the power to make or break careers.

The distorting effect of large financial donors on the political process has frequently been highlighted. Harvard Professor Lawrence Lessig has campaigned hard for greater attention to this matter. For example, he gave a TED talk in October 2015 on the subject, with the title "Our democracy no longer represents the people"[315]. Instead of representing the people as a whole, he argued, the US democracy represents the financially powerful. He quoted the saying of notorious nineteenth century American politician William Magear ("Boss") Tweed:

"I don't care who does the electing, as long as I get to do the nominating."

Things are little better today, Lessig argued. It's not a particular individual (such as Boss Tweed) that's doing the nominating, but the tiny minority of Americans who make substantial donations to political campaigns:

> We take it for granted in the United States, that campaigns will be privately funded. But we need to recognize funding is its own contest, funding is its own Primary. We have the voting system, where people vote, but in the first stage to that there is a Money Primary that determines which candidates are allowed to run in those voting elections.

Lessig points out that Americans tend to be critical of recent changes to the democratic process in Hong Kong, in which candidates for democratic election nowadays first have to be approved by a nominating committee that consists of just 1200 people. This change sparked a series of student protests throughout Hong Kong. Lessig comments:

> There's a two-step process. The first step was nomination, and then the second step was an election. And the nominating committee would be comprised of about 1200 people, which means out of 7 million people, that is 0.02% of Hong Kong...
>
> So 0.02% get to pick the candidates, that the rest of Hong Kong gets to vote among. And the protest was because the fear was this filter would be a biased filter. The claim was that 0.02% would be dominated by a pro-Beijing business and political elite. So 99.98% would be excluded from this critical first step with the consequence, obviously, of producing a democracy responsive to China only.

But Lessig asks: are things really better in the United States? Instead of needing to attend (as in Hong Kong) to the special views of the pro-Beijing elite, politicians in the United States need to put disproportionate effort into understanding and supporting the special views of the financial elite, in what is a time-consuming process:

> Now, that Money Primary takes time. Members of Congress and candidates for Congress spend anywhere between 30% and 70% of their time... dialling for dollars. Calling people all across the country to get the money they need to run their campaigns, or to get their party back into power.
>
> B. F. Skinner gave us this wonderful image of the Skinner Box where any stupid animal could learn which buttons it needed to push for its sustenance. This is the picture of the life of the modern American Congress person who comes to learn which buttons he or she needs to

push to get the sustenance he or she needs to make his or her campaign successful. This is their life, and it has an effect.

The process isn't just time-consuming; it fundamentally alters the candidates' opinions on numerous topics, as they revise their professed opinions to fall into line with the views of the largest potential funders:

> Each of them, as they [solicit funds], develop a "sixth sense": a constant awareness of how what they do might affect their ability to raise money. They become, in the words of "X Files", "shape shifters", as they constantly adjust their views in light of what they know will help them to raise money.

Evidence of the undue influence of the economic elites can be found in a 2014 analysis by political scientists Martin Gilens of Princeton and Benjamin Page of Northwestern University[316]. New Yorker writer John Cassidy summarises this analysis as follows[317]:

> The issue is what happens when some income groups, particularly the rich, support or oppose certain things, and other groups in society don't share their views...

> This is what the data shows: when the economic elites support a given policy change, it has about a one-in-two chance of being enacted. (The exact estimated probability is forty-five per cent.) When the elites oppose a given measure, its chances of becoming law are less than one in five...

> The study suggests that, on many issues, the rich exercise an effective veto. If they are against something, it is unlikely to happen. This is obviously inconsistent with the median-voter theorem – which holds that policy outcomes reflect the preferences of voters who represent the ideological centre.

There are two aspects to controlling the adverse impact of finance on politics:

1. Impose strict limits on how much money can be spent in any particular campaign

2. Reduce the barriers to participation by candidate politicians.

The second point is similar to how it has become much easier, in recent decades, for people to start their own businesses. The requisite tools and services are available online at low cost (and are often free of charge).

As a society, we need to keep examining what are the forces that exclude or deter capable people from advancing in political circles. As we understand these obstacles more clearly, we should look to a combination of new technology, new processes, and new culture, to address them. The result will be an improvement in what I called in Chapter 1 "encouragement systems":

> Systems to encourage greater positive participation in the political and regulatory processes by people who have a lot to contribute, but who are currently feeling pressure to participate instead in different fields of activity.

Note: for some inspiring examples of campaigns to reduce the effect of finance on politics in America – as well as some warnings about setbacks (among *many* other important topics) – I strongly recommend the 2017 book *Daring Democracy: Igniting Power, Meaning, and Connection for the America We Want* by Frances Moore Lappé and Adam Eichen[318].

Beyond the stranglehold of political parties

It's not just the economic elite who exert huge influence on the thinking and decisions of politicians. The political party system is another factor that constrains what politicians do.

In many countries, including the US and the UK, it's hard for new parties to achieve any significant parliamentary breakthrough. First-past-the-post voting systems discriminate against newcomers and against parties whose support is more distributed than localised. This fact leads aspiring politicians to cluster around the mainstream parties where, however, they are frequently limited in the opinions they can champion.

In order to gain re-election, most politicians are dependent on support from a nationwide political party. These parties have "brand recognition" in the eyes of voters that tends to far exceed the reputation of individual political candidates. The parties also assist with publicity, with funding, and with a flow of volunteers to assist candidates. Politicians who fail to toe the party line risk losing all this support. It's no wonder that the party system self-perpetuates.

For a higher calibre of political discussion, there needs to be more politicians who feel empowered to speak honestly and openly, without regard to the dictates of party leadership.

One way this can happen is when politicians develop an independent power base, outside of traditional parties. For instance, a politician might become known as a strong supporter of pro-environmental policies, or as a strong critic of immigration. Some recent examples of politicians breaking the previous mould include Donald Trump and Bernie Sanders in the US and Jeremy Corbyn in the UK. Each of them rose into national political prominence despite resistance from the existing leadership of mainstream parties. This highlights that significant change can arise outside of the political party system, before being incorporated into it.

I look forward to candidates emerging in a similar way as recognised representatives of a technoprogressive political initiative. These leaders will amplify increasing public interest in technoprogressive ideals, such as:

- A vision of society centred on increased human flourishing and enhanced human consciousness, rather than on economic growth

- More focus on enabling next-generation greentech, to expedite a transformation to clean energy and sustainable living

- Promoting new methods of manufacturing that take advantage of nanotech and synthetic biotech to reduce to near-zero cost all the key goods and services needed for a positive, fulfilling lifestyle

- Championing labour-saving automation tech which can provide everyone with an abundance of time for creativity and self-education – so long as changes are planned and delivered in the overall social contract

- Accelerating the development and adoption of the restorative and preventive rejuvenation tech which can provide an abundance of affordable healthcare, enabling citizens to become "better than well" and even, if we choose, youthful again

- Support for freer access to brain-boosting cognotech which can provide an abundance of all-round intelligence: emotional, rational, social, spiritual, and more

- Putting rationality and the scientific method at the forefront of political decisions, rather than ideology or party loyalty.

As these ideals grow in public support outside of existing mainstream parties, people in these parties will in due course become bolder in speaking in favour of these ideals too.

But I envision some key differences between the rise of technoprogressive leaders and the other breakthrough populist politicians mentioned previously:

- In the technoprogressive case, it is the ideas that have greater importance than the personalities and characteristics of individual representatives

- The technoprogressive cause should beware "us vs. them" polemics and divisiveness, as it seeks to build bridges of common underlying interest with people from multiple different perspectives

- Technoprogressive principles include openness to revising policies in the light of new information and improved understanding; the overall goal of increasing human flourishing and human consciousness rises above short-term commitments to particular policy initiatives.

Better elections for a better future

Countries in which a first past the post "winner takes all" electoral system applies – such as the United Kingdom and the United States – make it harder for creative new political ideas to gain wide traction. If a new political party is created to champion these ideas, the new party may receive smatterings of support from throughout the country, without winning any seats in parliament. Support may be too geographically diffuse for it to be sufficiently concentrated in any one constituency that the new party comes top in that local poll. As a result, the party will end up under-represented.

These dynamics give preference to the political parties that are already well established. They are biased against newer or smaller parties.

As mentioned above, it's possible for outside ideas to become adopted by older parties – hence the examples of Donald Trump, Bernie Sanders, and Jeremy Corbyn. I expect that, in the same way, various technoprogressive ideas will become increasingly adopted by existing political parties. But one thing that would accelerate this progress of political innovation is the adoption of a voting system of proportional representation.

Such systems are already in wide use around the world. Data from the Electoral Knowledge Network, which documents the electoral systems of 235 countries, confirms that proportional representation is used in 92 countries to elect the members of the main legislative assembly[319]. This includes nearly every country in Europe. Of the different systems covered, first past the post was the second most widely used: 63 countries – most being former colonies of Britain. Zeroing in on the 35 democracies where the population is at least two million and where the country received a 2012 Freedom House Average Freedom Ranking[320] of 1 or 2, the FairVote organisation lists 22 countries as using proportional representation, and only 6 as using winner-takes-all systems[321].

The Electoral Reform Society summarises the case for adopting proportional representation for parliamentary elections in the UK[322]:

> The way we elect our MPs is bad for voters, bad for governance and bad for democracy...
>
> With the system we use, First Past the Post, one party can get millions of votes and one MP, whilst another can get ten times as many MPs on a few hundred thousand votes...
>
> We need reform so that every vote counts – and where public opinion is properly represented in Parliament. The system we use to elect our MPs has a real impact on life in Britain – it's time we made sure seats matched votes.

The considerations raised by the Electoral Reform Society include:

Voters ignored

Voters are tired of being told that the party they support 'can't win here'. Half the votes cast in 2015 didn't help elect an MP to Westminster – the highest proportion in a recent election. This made it the most disproportionate in British history, people's votes simply didn't translate into seats.

Some 15 million people's votes had no impact on the result. We saw the same in 2010, when 53% of votes didn't elect anyone.

MPs – and governments – elected by a minority

MPs can be elected to Parliament even though the vast majority of voters don't want them. In 2015 one MP was elected with just a quarter of the vote. That means someone opposed by 75% of the local electorate can get to speak on their behalf in Parliament –a disaster for democracy...

Safe Seats

Because of the way we elect our MPs in some 'safe seats' the odds are firmly stacked against any voters looking for change.

Safe seats are the 21st Century's rotten boroughs. The average constituency last changed hands between parties in the 1960s, with some super safe seats having remained firmly in one-party control since the time of Queen Victoria.

An oft-raised objection to proportional representation is that it leads to the need for messy coalitions and lukewarm compromises. It's much preferable, say critics, to have the strength and stability of single-party governments. However, the outcome of the 2017 general election has undermined this argument. And 2017 is by no means the only time when the first-past-the-post system resulted in a government lacking parliamentary strength.

As it happens, proportional representation *is* already used within the United Kingdom, to select members of the London Assembly, and for the devolved administrations in Scotland, Wales, and Northern Ireland. In none of these cases have there been objections about the need for coalitions, or complaints about extremist parties gaining too much power. In none of these examples does a campaign exist to revert to first-past-the-post.

Accordingly, Transpolitica supports the case for wider adoption of proportional representation. This change will be an important step forward towards better politics. Not only will voters feel more engaged, but politicians will have to improve their skills in the vital art of collaboration – needed for coalition governments to work. Last but not least, it will enable acceleration of the adoption of key new political ideas.

Could we dispense with politicians?

A somewhat different proposal for improving our political system also deserves attention. This is the proposal to dispense altogether with the role of career politicians. Political decisions, in this proposal, should be taken by groups of citizens selected at random, in the same way that juries selected at random determine guilt or innocence at criminal trials.

Just as legal juries have a temporary existence – no one is a "professional jury member" – so also would political juries have a strictly limited timespan. This prevents any jury members from growing attached to their position of apparent power and responsibility. It avoids the growth of systems of self-preservation, misinformation, bribery, and so forth.

This idea – variously known as "sortition", "allotment", and "demarchy" – has venerable roots. Ancient Athens, often viewed as the starting point of democracy, made extensive use of sortition. A governing council that oversaw the operation of a larger assembly, and which could take direct action in times of crisis or war, was made up of 500 members, who were selected by lot from the wider community (these council members needed to be at least 30 years old; women, slaves, and foreigners were excluded). Service on the council was for one year only; people could serve on the council two times in total, but not in consecutive years[323].

Witness Aristotle's negative assessment (the word "oligarchic") of the use of elections to decide political leaders[324]:

> It is accepted as democratic when public offices are allocated by lot, and as oligarchic when they are filled by election.

Here, the word "oligarchic" implies that it would only be a small subset of citizens who could aspire to win a democratic election. This process, therefore, would not be "government by all" but "government by the few".

Instead, Aristotle advocated that:

> The appointment to all offices, or to all but those which require experience and skill, should be made by lot.

In his 2017 book *The End of Politicians: Time for a Real Democracy*[325], Brett Hennig argues for a revival of these ideals of sortition. The introduction of his book culminates with the following battle cry:

> The tantalising possibility that we can govern ourselves has presented itself – we no longer need politicians to do it for us. It is time for the end of politicians and for us to become the next wave in the ongoing struggle to demand real democracy, now.

Hennig's website devoted to sortition urges us to "Do democracy differently"[326]:

> Our politicians are constrained. By the media, by corporate and institutional backers, by factions within their own parties, but most of all by their desire to win the next election. Every decision is made with one eye on the ratings, the media, and what donors and campaign focus groups say.

> But what can be done? How can democracy be freed so it is responsive to the needs and concerns of the people it is meant to serve? Can democracy be *of the people, by the people, for the people*?

Yes, it can. Decision-making assemblies full of randomly selected ordinary people already exist and are becoming more and more common. They are comprised of people just like you and me: a representative sample of people deliberating together, free from the constraints of today's politicians. And they work; they come to legitimate decisions that people trust.

Let's make democracy serve the people, with a democracy using sortition.

Hennig describes how sortition could operate[327]:

Sortition is the use of random selection to populate assemblies or fill political positions. An assembly that uses sortition would be composed of people just like you and me: it would be a representative random sample of people, making decisions in an informed, fair and deliberative setting.

Perhaps it… uses networked, facilitated small table deliberation to make decisions. Each table discusses proposals, with a facilitator making sure no one dominates and everyone gets his or her say, and a note-taker typing comments and decisions into a computer. A "theme team" can see what every table is discussing and summarises the output, which is then presented to the entire assembly, who have individual voting keypads to prioritise results. In this way the assembly can come to large group decisions.

Stratified random sampling ensures that participants accurately reflect the community they are drawn from, unlike open meetings where often only socially privileged or more vocal people attend and dominate discussions. Stratified random sampling ensures that half the participants are women and half men, with proportional representation for the young and old, and across all geographical areas and educational levels.

If this assembly formed a legislative parliament, then every year a part of the assembly (say, one fifth) would be replaced with people randomly selected from the electoral roll, ensuring the assembly remained representative of the general populace. These representatives would be paid as politicians are paid now, and would serve one single term in office of five years.

I share with Henning the strong conviction that we need to do better than the present-day political system. I also agree that changes over the last few decades in both technology and culture enable a better politics:

- The availability of pervasive communications mechanisms which bypass hierarchies of command, enabling "leadership" initiatives to spring up from a network as a whole, rather than having to be initiated top-down

- The growth in importance of "immaterial goods", such as digitised information and algorithms, which can be shared freely, and which can in some cases "go viral", circumventing attempts by authority figures to control discussions

- The rise of a "participatory culture", in which contributions to online resources arise, not just from centrally appointed experts, but from all sectors of society; in this way, Wikipedia has grown to become a profoundly useful repository of information; likewise, the cumulative weight of online reviews of restaurants, resorts, books, music, and so forth, provide a helpful balance to any one-sided narratives that owners of these goods would prefer to circulate.

Indeed, Hennig suggests that the model of collaborative generation of the content of Wikipedia could be adopted for definition and evolution of the laws and regulations that govern society:

> The laws that govern us are precisely the kind of immaterial product that are, in theory, perfectly suited to production through a modern peer-to-peer, deliberative and open network. Could all the laws that bind us be placed on a wiki – perhaps called WikiPolicy, WikiLaws or WikiGovernment – along with a history of the changes made to them? What would happen if everyone and anyone could propose, discuss and deliberate on suggested changes?

This proposal has much in common with the concept of "technoprogressive knowledge base" that I mentioned earlier in this chapter:

> A set of information websites that are widely recognised as providing objective, accessible guides to key questions of politics, economics, society, and changing technology.

However, there's a significant jump from the collaborative creation of a knowledge base to the collaborative agreement on laws and regulations. The pages of a knowledge base can fluctuate back-and-forth under the influence of "edit wars". Imagine if the legality of some action likewise varied according to which group of people had most recently edited a webpage. Instead, there has to be a more formal process of "sign-off" or "approval" or "going live", which gives legal force to a set of proposals. Could this sign-off task be left in the hands of a randomly selected team of jury participants? I see three problems with the idea.

The first problem is that of potential structural bias within the jury. Significant steps would need to be taken to ensure a fair representation of all relevant backgrounds and viewpoints.

A second problem is when members of the jury are disinterested in the matters placed before them for resolution. They may go through the motions of being involved in discussions, but lack the enthusiasm or aptitude to engage deeply.

The third problem extends the second problem. Many of the decisions of modern politics are, frankly, complicated. They can be compared with the details of convoluted trials of financial fraud for which many observers are querying the practicality of leaving the decisions to a jury. Consider comments made after the recent 20-month long trial in the Glasgow High Court of Edwin and Lorraine McLaren. During this extended period, an initial jury of 15 members had dwindled in number to just 12, the bare minimum required by law. A BBC news account of the trial summarised some of the concerns[328]:

> Law lecturer Andrew Tickell… said fraud cases were complex and difficult to follow.
>
> In the case of Edwin McLaren, the indictment carried 29 separate charges and it was the Crown's job to prove every one.
>
> This required a large number of witnesses and mountains of documents.
>
> The Glasgow Caledonian University law lecturer said: "If the Crown is going to bring forward a mega case then it really has to bring forward quite substantial evidence to buttress that claim.
>
> "Juries have to decide on the guilt in the cases and so have to sit through many months of evidence. That has real challenges for them and challenges for the justice system as a whole.
>
> "Certainly in terms of very serious cases involving complicated financial concepts and instruments that the ordinary person might not be familiar with then you might well ask 'is it right for 15 ordinary members of the public to spend a year of their life trying to get on top of these questions?'
>
> "Is this most cost effective, and effective generally, way of delivering justice in these cases?"

As the BBC news report explained, the alternative to a random group of citizens forming a jury is that the evidence is weighed and the decision is reached by a group of identified experts:

> Mr Tickell put forward the alternative of an expert bench of judges who know the area and are able to identify fraud when they see it.
>
> But he said: "On the other hand, some people would say having a jury of your peers deciding your fate in the most serious of cases, with massive prison sentences at the end of the line if you are convicted, that's a matter of principle.
>
> "We apply that in murder cases, in very serious fraud cases some people would argue we should maintain that safeguard as well."
>
> He added: "I would imagine the Scottish government and a range of politicians may look at this case and say 'is this value for money'?
>
> "Is it the best way to deliver justice? I'm not sure on either of those two tests we are delivering that in Scotland today."

Note that the definition of democracy given by Aristotle, which I quoted earlier, excludes from random selection "offices... which require experience and skill":

> The appointment to all offices, or to all but those which require experience and skill, should be made by lot.

Indeed, the ancient Athenians selected their council members by lot from the general citizenry, but they were much more selective when choosing their military generals and financial managers.

For the foreseeable future, therefore, I expect the role of career politicians to continue to be essential within society. They will be drawn from the subset of the overall population that has the skills and aptitude necessary to coordinate overall political decision-making. They will remain subject to the regular approval – or disapproval – of voters. But compared to the present, they should be initiating new policy ideas less often, and responding more often to the policy suggestions that arise from the kind of increased public consultation that new technology facilitates. Moreover, they will be fighting battles against groups of perceived political enemies less often, and forging positive links more often across previous party boundaries.

In these changes, politicians will be responding to an electorate that is increasingly informed and increasingly engaged. The growth of the technoprogressive knowledge base will help to counter the excess influence of present vested interests, such as media magnates, evangelists for religious or ideological standpoints, lobbyists supporting corporations and industries, and agents of influence promoting the agendas of overseas governments.

To be clear, these developments are unlikely to take place so long as large segments of the population feel they are excluded or ignored by the perceived leadership of society. Public institutions – in both the economic and political spheres – need to be visibly "inclusive" rather than "extractive", to use the terminology advanced by political scientists Daron Acemoğlu and James Robinson in their landmark 2012 book *Why Nations Fail: The Origins of Power, Prosperity, and Poverty*[329]. I'll conclude this chapter with a brief exploration of this distinction between inclusive and extractive.

Why nations fail

Acemoğlu and Robinson address the following question in their book *Why Nations Fail*:

> Why are some nations rich and others poor, divided by wealth and poverty, health and sickness, food and famine?

It's a deeply important question. In the course of over 500 pages, the authors provide numerous examples, drawn from throughout many centuries, of countries that had the potential to use technology to improve the collective wellbeing, but which *turned aside from that possibility*. What led to such actions? What distinguishes situations where a country is able to embrace the positive transformational potential of new technology, compared to those in which a country proceeds backwards?

The publisher's description of the book by Acemoğlu and Robinson continues, by listing some of the ideas that other scholars have given in response to such questions:

> Is it culture, the weather, geography? Perhaps ignorance of what the right policies are?
>
> Simply, no. None of these factors is either definitive or destiny. Otherwise, how to explain why Botswana has become one of the fastest growing countries in the world, while other African nations, such as Zimbabwe, the Congo, and Sierra Leone, are mired in poverty and violence?

Daron Acemoglu and James Robinson conclusively show that it is man-made political and economic institutions that underlie economic success (or lack of it).

Korea, to take just one of their fascinating examples, is a remarkably homogeneous nation, yet the people of North Korea are among the poorest on earth while their brothers and sisters in South Korea are among the richest. The south forged a society that created incentives, rewarded innovation, and allowed everyone to participate in economic opportunities. The economic success thus spurred was sustained because the government became accountable and responsive to citizens and the great mass of people. Sadly, the people of the north have endured decades of famine, political repression, and very different economic institutions – with no end in sight. The differences between the Koreas are due to the politics that created these completely different institutional trajectories.

Other examples cover the difference between the USA and Mexico, more broadly the difference between North and South America, the difference between West and East Europe, and the difference between Japan and China.

The authors provide the following description of different kinds of institutions[330]:

Extractive economic institutions: Lack of law and order. Insecure property rights; entry barriers and regulations preventing functioning of markets and creating a non-level playing field.

Extractive political institutions: In the limit, "absolutism". Political institutions concentrating power in the hands of a few, without constraints, checks or balances or "rule of law".

Inclusive economic institutions: Secure property rights, law and order, markets and state support (public services and regulation) for markets; open to relatively free entry of new businesses; uphold contracts; access to education and opportunity for the great majority of citizens.

Inclusive political institutions: Political institutions allowing broad participation – *pluralism* – and placing constraints and checks on politicians; rule of law (closely related to pluralism). Also some degree of *political centralisation* for the states to be able to effectively enforce law and order.

The authors point out the ways in which inclusive institutions support sustained economic growth:

- By encouraging investment (because of well-enforced property rights)

- By harnessing the power of markets (better allocation of resources, entry of more efficient firms, access to finance for starting businesses etc)

- By generating broad-based participation (education, free entry, broad-based property rights).

Critically, inclusive political institutions, in which power is distributed amongst a plurality of different interests, support the social disruption that typically accompanies new waves of technology. In the famous phrase of Joseph Schumpeter, this disruption is called "creative destruction"[331]:

> Creative destruction refers to the incessant product and process innovation mechanism by which new production units replace outdated ones. This restructuring process permeates major aspects of macroeconomic performance, not only long-run growth but also economic fluctuations, structural adjustment and the functioning of factor markets. Over the long run, the process of creative destruction accounts for over 50% of productivity growth.

As Acemoğlu and Robinson point out, creative destruction is likely to reduce the grasp on power and influence by people associated with existing industries. Given a choice, these individuals will usually prefer to stick with the status quo, since they fare well from it, even though the country as a whole would do better once the creative destruction has taken place. That's why inclusive economic institutions need the active support of inclusive political institutions.

Here are a just a few examples of once-powerful empires that decided to resist innovations that enabled economic progress elsewhere:

- The empires of Austria-Hungary and Russia resisted the adoption of railways

- The Ottoman empire restricted the adoption of printing presses based on movable type

- The Chinese empire turned back from contact with overseas countries, dismantling its fleet of huge sailing ships.

Much of the book *Why Nations Fail* is uncomfortable reading. Again and again, political and economic leaders took actions that discriminated horribly against groups of people they were exploiting. But the book also contains positive examples of the gradual adoption of more inclusive institutions. Just as there's a "vicious cycle" in which extractive institutions tend to perpetuate themselves, there's also a "virtual cycle" in which inclusive institutions can, over time, become strengthened and expanded. This includes, in the United Kingdom, the "Glorious Revolution" of 1688 which helped to set the scene for the Industrial Revolution that gathered pace in the following century. It also includes the Meiji restoration of nineteenth century Japan, and democratic progress in Botswana in southern Africa. To be clear, the authors emphasise that there's no inevitability about either cycle – the vicious one towards greater extraction, or the virtual one towards greater inclusion.

The analysis in *Why Nations Fail* provides wide support for four of the core viewpoints I've been advancing in this book, namely that

1. Politics exerts a powerful influence on whether or not technological innovations are developed and adopted

2. The mechanisms of politics are themselves a form of "technology" which can be improved (or, alas, in some cases worsened) as a result of the attention of innovators, entrepreneurs, and engineers

3. Societal progress isn't anything that can be taken for granted; it's something that requires persistent clear thinking and hard work

4. Society is unlikely to be able to make significant progress, unless that progress is accessible (via inclusive institutions) to all members of that society; hence the fundamental importance of open markets and meaningful democracy.

Why Nations Fail also provides numerous examples of how the prosperity in one country was impacted – sometimes positively, but often negatively – by actions taken by other countries. The roadmap to a healthier society therefore involves not only the politics of your own nation, but the politics of the other nations (and blocs of nations) in the world. In the next chapter, I'll set out a technoprogressive vision for enhancing, not just the politics of single countries, but the overall politics of international relations.

11. Nations and supernations

I started this book by covering two reasons why politics urgently needs to be improved:

1. Bad politics *is obstructing the development and application of important solutions to human problems*; via both incompetence and malice, it hinders or forbids what actually deserves to be enabled and encouraged; conversely, it accelerates what actually deserves to be restricted

2. Bad politics *is creating problems of its own*; via misguided overzealous pursuits of half-truths, it increases the likelihood of social alienation, group conflict, and national catastrophe.

As I'll argue in this chapter, the problems and opportunities of local politics are mirrored and magnified by the problems and opportunities of international politics:

1. Bad international politics, via both incompetence and malice, is preventing the adoption of optimal regulatory policies which, in order to be fully effective, would need worldwide endorsement

2. Bad international politics is creating problems of its own; via misguided overzealous cross-border pursuits of half-truths, it increases the likelihood of global schism, military conflict, and planetary catastrophe.

In each case – the local and the international – the basic solution is the same: harness technology more wisely and more profoundly than before. To improve politics, what's needed is a compelling integrative vision setting out the progressive application of enhanced technologies of abundance and enhanced technologies of collaboration.

Improving local politics is an important start, but will ultimately be fruitless unless we can also improve international politics. Even if a country is at peace with itself, it will face numerous risks if the countries around it are plunging deeper into chaos. Borders provide no respite from radioactive fallout, no shelter from extreme weather, and are of little use against determined cyber-intruders.

So let me rephrase the sentence with which I opened this book. There's no escape: the journey to a healthier society inevitably involves *international* politics. More precisely, that journey involves the positive technoprogressive transformation of international politics.

If successful, this vision will slow down and then stop those existing political initiatives that are pulling humanity in separate, fractious directions; instead, it will enable a renewed focus on building a comprehensively better future in which everyone benefits.

Assessing international politics

As a prelude to discussing international politics, let's briefly remind ourselves of the constructive role that politics can play in society. Politics is the process of collectively agreeing which constraints we put on each other's freedom.

Thus, as members of society, we have the freedom to drive motor vehicles from A to B, but we are constrained by speed limits and other traffic regulations. We have freedom of speech, but are constrained not to whimsically shout out "fire, fire!" in crowded locations. We have the freedom to develop and market new products and services, but we are constrained by various standards of health and safety. We have the freedom to keep a portion of what we earn in employment, but we are constrained to pass a specific portion of these earnings to central authorities by way of taxes. We have the freedom to hire and fire employees, but we are constrained by legislation covering discrimination and unfair dismissal. We have the freedom to prepare to defend ourselves against violent attack, but we are constrained not to exercise disproportionate force in any such defence. All these constraints annoy us or frustrate us from time to time. However, we generally accept that it is better for society that *some* constraints exist. It's the (hard) task of politics to figure out which are the right constraints at any one time – and then to oversee their enforcement.

International politics follows these same principles, not at the level of individuals within a local society, but at the level of societies within a global community. International politics is the process of collectively agreeing on constraints we put on national sovereignty.

Thus, nations can prepare to defend themselves against violent aggressors, but are constrained not to carry out certain kinds of tests of nuclear weaponry. Nations have the freedom to exploit the natural resources at their disposal, but are constrained not to unduly damage the international environment as a side-effect. Nations can use measures such as tax relief to support businesses working in their countries, but within constraints so as not to unfairly distort international market dynamics. Nations can determine their own policies on research and development of new products, but are constrained by international moratoria to avoid particularly risky fields of investigation. Just as for the constraints imposed by local politics, these international constraints from time to time cause annoyance and frustration. Nevertheless, most countries recognise that, in principle, greater safety, stability, and prosperity should follow from adoption of appropriate constraints on sovereignty. Just as for local politics, the dilemma is how to agree these constraints – and how to ensure they are fairly enforced.

The extra complication for international politics is that, unlike the level of the nation state, there is no overall governing structure for global relationships. There is no global police force to track down violators to ensure compliance. There is no process of democracy whereby one set of global politicians can be voted out of office, if they are perceived as having failed in their leadership roles. Existing international bodies, such as the United Nations, and the International Criminal Court located in The Hague, have limited powers, which individual countries seem to be able to ignore with impunity.

Some thinkers express gratitude for this lack of an international government. Prime sovereignty, they argue, should remain at the level of the nation state. No international government could be trusted to operate in a way that gains and keeps the assent of the various leading countries of the world. Any such body would be inclined to add extra layers of bureaucracy and interference. It would likely mandate policies that would be an anathema to national self-determination. It would suck up extra taxes, away from local jurisdiction, to serve the needs of globe-trotting administrators and their far-flung interventionist projects. Therefore – according to this viewpoint – any moves to an international government should be resisted.

Similar opposition is often expressed to the idea of "super-state" conglomerations of neighbouring counties. The notion of a European Union committed to "ever closer integration" alarms many observers, who fear the imposition of alien values and the usurpation of local autonomy. These observers believe that citizens could never feel as much loyalty to the European Union as to their nation state (such as Germany, Spain, or the

United Kingdom). Thank goodness, they say, for the failures of super-states.

I say, in contrast, that these failures are to be regretted. Without effective, trustworthy mechanisms of global coordination, countries are driven to take matters into their own hands. We end up in a race to the bottom. This makes the world a more dangerous place for all of us.

Indeed, observers in various parts of the world are increasingly concerned about falling under the growing influence of strident "superpowers" such as China or the United States. A world where America politicians are pursuing an international policy of "America First", or where Chinese politicians are pursuing an international policy of "China First", is a perilous place for the smaller countries that may be caught in the crossfire or trodden underfoot. It's no surprise if countries such as Iran and North Korea seek powerful weaponry as bargaining chips against potential global steamrollers. Once grown accustomed to their new-found arsenals, these countries are in no hurry to disarm. Weapons of mass destruction, in the hand, seem to be worth far more than acres of pious hopes.

The prisoner's dilemma

Arms races involving military weaponry are one example of international politics failing. At each step in such a race, any country which perceives itself as falling behind its potential adversaries can see a logical case to improve its armaments, so as to reduce the chance of it being overpowered in conflict. At the *next* step in the arms race, the same cold logic applies again, to whichever country now perceives itself as laggard. "Keeping up with the Joneses" has a terrible meaning when each round of expenditure adds extra potency to a growing explosive stockpile. The individually logical steps add up to a tragically illogical outcome.

There can be arms races without earth-shattering physical explosives. Other forms of race include software malware or biological pathogens. Systems described as "defensive" can contribute to the escalation of a race, too; they may spur the other side to improve their offensive capability in order to circumvent the new defensive mechanisms.

Trade wars can, likewise, prove deeply damaging, with countries taking increasingly dramatic economic steps to seek competitive economic advantage.

These are all cases of the "prisoner's dilemma" model. This occurs when there are two (or more) participants, and the actions that are rationally the best for the individual participants add up to an outcome that is rationally poorer than what could have been achieved if the participants had collaborated.

In the example that gave the model its name, consider if two accomplices to a major crime are each being interrogated by police. The police are seeking evidence to mount a prosecution. If both prisoners keep quiet, and refuse to answer questions, the prosecution cannot proceed, and the two suspects will instead be sentenced for a comparatively minor crime, receiving a sentence of one year each. However, the police are offering each of the suspects a deal. If either suspect accepts the deal and reveals evidence incriminating his accomplice, the former will walk free, and the latter will receive a hefty ten year sentence. If both suspects incriminate the other, both will be sent to prison for five years.

The first prisoner can reason as follows. He should accept the deal, and give evidence against his accomplice. That makes sense whether or not his accomplice independently decides to accept the deal being offered to him. Specifically, if the accomplice remains silent, the first prisoner will go free, rather than receiving a one year sentence. And if the accomplice also accepts the deal, the first prisoner will face a prison sentence of five years, which is still less than the ten years he would otherwise receive.

The same logic applies to the second prisoner as well. As a result, they are likely to *both* offer evidence, and will *both* end up in a worse situation (five years in prison) than if they had been able to cooperate (one year in prison). It's in the interest of the police in this case to prevent any such cooperation, so that the full facts of the crime can be revealed.

There are *lots* of variants to this discussion[332]. Although these variants are interesting, we can skip to the conclusion. There are, indeed, many circumstances in which parties that are unable to trust each other end up in significantly worse outcomes than if trust were feasible.

We've already seen examples in previous chapters. Owners of cotton mills in the 1830s experienced a strong economic pressure to hire young children to work in their factories, lest they incur greater wages costs than their competitors. The solution to that dilemma was a system of legal regulations, coupled with inspectors to enforce the regulations. Companies that emit greenhouse gases as a side-effect of their operations experience a strong economic pressure to keep doing so, lest they cede advantage to competitors who avoid the costs of cleaner energy solutions. The solution in this case is a global system of carbon taxes, coupled with inspectors to enforce conformance. So long as there are significant risks of companies cheating on their obligations, it increases the pressure on other companies to cheat as well. So long as there are significant risks of countries cheating on their agreements to minimise dangerous armaments, it increases the pressure on other countries to cheat too.

It's similar to the observation made as far back as 1651 by English philosopher Thomas Hobbes in his pioneering work on political philosophy, *Leviathan*. In the absence of mechanisms establishing trust, all people are liable to suspect each other, being fearful that their possessions will be stolen, or that they'll suffer bodily harm[333]:

> In the nature of man we find three principal causes of quarrel: first, competition; secondly, diffidence [that is, apprehension]; thirdly, glory.
>
> The first maketh man invade for gain; the second, for safety; and the third, for reputation. The first use violence, to make themselves masters of other men's persons, wives, children, and cattle; the second, to defend them; the third, for trifles, as a word, a smile, a different opinion, and any other sign of undervalue, either direct in their persons or by reflection in their kindred, their friends, their nation, their profession, or their name.

The result, according to Hobbes, is a state of war "of every man against every man". We would never be sure who we could trust, and therefore, we would need to be ready for combat at all time. This would be a truly dismal situation, providing people little incentive to work hard and build up resources – since these resources could be stolen at any time. As a result, there would be no development of trade, knowledge, technology, art, or culture:

> In such condition there is no place for industry, because the fruit thereof is uncertain, and consequently no culture of the earth, no navigation nor use of the commodities that may be imported by sea, no commodious building, no instruments of moving and removing such things as require much force, no knowledge of the face of the earth; no account of time, no arts, no letters, no society, and, which is worst of all, continual fear and danger of violent death, and the life of man solitary, poor, nasty, brutish, and short.

Later writers have observed that humans have instincts towards cooperation as well as instincts towards competition. These biological instincts seem to allow the growth of peaceful communities, rather than a Hobbesian war of "every man against every man".

Nevertheless, such peace is only kept because the group as a whole makes the effort to punish and vilify any individuals who from time to time try to take undue advantage of circumstances. Our blood boils when we observe free-loaders and shirkers. Numerous religions and morality folk tales urge community members to prioritise the greater good of the tribe over their own self-interest. The "golden rule" of ethics, taught by philosophers worldwide, is that we should treat others in the way we would ourselves wish to be treated. Such admonitions help to strengthen the inner pangs of conscience that people are inclined to experience, whenever they are tempted to deceive or exploit their friends, family, or neighbours. They also strengthen the group's conviction that any such free-loading behaviour should not be tolerated.

Our instincts towards cooperation run into increasing tension when we encounter groups of people from outside our original tribe. Where people are perceived as being significantly different from us, we find it easier to treat them as "other". We feel fewer obligations towards them. Our religions and morality folk tales may tell us to love our neighbours as ourselves, but they are often vague on who counts as a neighbour. The Mosaic commandment "thou shalt not kill" co-exists in the opening books of the Bible with multiple tales of mass murders that apparently had priestly endorsement. Good neighbourliness has its limits.

For these reasons, Hobbes – and many after him – applauded the rise to power of kings and other national leaders, who could oversee a "commonwealth", namely a system of law and order with the purpose of maintaining peace. Any such commonwealth involves members of society giving up some of their own rights. As Hobbes remarks, it is as if each person in the commonwealth makes a covenant, saying to one another[334],

> I... give up my right of governing myself to... this assembly of men, on this condition, that thou give up thy right... in like manner.

The commonwealth ("this assembly of men") will succeed only if the set of restraints are reciprocal. Each member of the society needs to give up their individual rights "in like manner". Otherwise the system of trust will break down again.

Of course, governing systems have varied greatly in their effectiveness throughout history. Some "commonwealths" have brought peace and prosperity to their members, whereas others have brought increased suffering. As reviewed in the previous chapter, the nations in which citizens have flourished have generally been those in which the institutions were inclusive rather than extractive.

Whilst some nations have flourished, what about the international community as a whole? How is that coping with global variants of prisoner's dilemmas?

Globalisation unravelling

The fall of the Berlin Wall in November 1989 seemed at the time to herald an important new phase of positive international relationships. It was a dramatic milestone in a series of steps that collectively suggested a forthcoming convergence of aspirations around the world:

- The programmes of perestroika and glasnost, undertaken by Mikhail Gorbachev, appeared to dismantle the repressive state apparatus of the Soviet Union, allowing former captive nation states to choose their own paths forward, and enabling the adoption of free markets and liberal politics
- In China, Deng Xiaoping adopted politics of market liberalisation; his phrase "To get rich is glorious" encouraged waves of entrepreneurial activity
- The invention by Tim Berners-Lee of the World Wide Web, coincidentally also in November 1989, enabled increasing sharing of information and ideas across previous borders and obstacles
- The European Union grew in size from twelve countries in 1987 to twenty seven in 2007; prospects for future expansion and closer integration seemed high.

The American political scientist Francis Fukuyama forecast in his 1992 book *The End of History*[335] that

What we may be witnessing is not just the end of the Cold War, or the passing of a particular period of post-war history, but the end of history as such: that is, the end point of mankind's ideological evolution and the universalization of Western liberal democracy as the final form of human government.

Fifteen years later, in an essay in the Guardian, Fukuyama emphasised some clarifications[336]:

> In my book *The End of History and the Last Man* I argued that, if a society wanted to be modern, there was no alternative to a market economy and a democratic political system. Not everyone wanted to be modern, of course, and not everyone could put in place the institutions and policies necessary to make democracy and capitalism work, but no alternative system would yield better results…
>
> *The End of History* was never linked to a specifically American model of social or political organisation… I believe that the European Union more accurately reflects what the world will look like at the end of history than the contemporary United States. The EU's attempt to transcend sovereignty and traditional power politics by establishing a transnational rule of law is much more in line with a "post-historical" world than the Americans' continuing belief in God, national sovereignty, and their military.

Another prominent American writer, three time Pulitzer Prize winner Thomas Friedman of the New York Times, expressed a similar sentiment in his 2005 book *The World is Flat*[337]. The world is becoming a single entity, in which ever smaller roles are played by physical barriers such as mountains and oceans, by political barriers such as national boundaries and military forces, and by cultural barriers such as different religions and ideological divides. As countries see the advantages of free trade, import tariffs decline. People around the world are receiving an education that prepares them to take part in international workforces that are connected electronically. Local variations in accent or fashion add a dash of colour, but no longer divide people into alien groups.

It's as if the solution to the global prisoner's dilemma was available – people around the world could collectively trust in the "commonwealth" of liberal democracies and open markets, and would all benefit as a result.

By 2018, it's much rarer to hear that kind of optimism expressed. There have been some major bumps on the path to a flat world and the end of history:

- It has become apparent that the main financial benefits from globalised trade disproportionately reward a minority of participants; because these benefits are by no means evenly spread throughout the world, many countries have lost their enthusiasm for the globalisation project

- In the wake of the financial crash of 2007-9, economic growth has proceeded more slowly than previously; this has caused many observers to question, not only the wisdom and the capability of the leaders of the worlds of banking and finance, but also the very idea of ongoing economic growth

- Rather than a blossoming friendship between the former superpowers of Russia and America, as had been anticipated in the wake of glasnost and perestroika, there's been an avalanche of mutual criticism, with strongly divergent views over various regional military interventions

- China's apparent march towards adopting the same democratic political model as the West – expected at one time to be similar to its ongoing adoption of key aspects of the market economy – has stalled, with its one-party system remaining firmly in place

- Divergence of economic performance within the Eurozone, and the consequent tensions experienced by the euro, have dampened the appetite for other countries to join that zone

- Many countries have seen a resurgence of interest in the religion of Islam; these countries have failed to follow the apparent pattern of declining influence of religion that occurred in many other countries (including Western European countries in which Christianity used to be dominant)

- Heightened numbers of economic migrants and displaced refugees have stirred up tensions, especially when the incomers are perceived to adhere to beliefs and practice (for example, those of fundamentalist Islam) which are starkly different from those of the host nation

- What we have learned from the always-on connectivity provided by the World Wide Web, isn't that all groups of people are alike, but that there are huge differences in attitude and desire; rather than leading different groups to want to integrate more tightly, the result of this increase in information has often been to drive different groups further apart.

These escalating levels of mistrust make it much harder to establish mutually beneficial agreements. Rather than tensions being defused, it's more likely that various arms races will accelerate. To be clear, this is a precarious development.

Towards technoprogressive globalisation

The dangerous unravelling of globalisation can be reversed – but only if there are major changes within the globalisation project. Instead of a neoliberal globalisation, we need a technoprogressive globalisation.

The goal of globalisation cannot simply be greater amounts of trade and more regular elections. That approach has been tried in the global court of public opinion, and found wanting. That approach left too many people:

- Perceiving themselves as losers from the process

- Feeling alienated and disenchanted, searching for meaning and validation by other means

- Deeply apprehensive about further encroachment on personal liberty or national sovereignty from forthcoming new waves of globalisation

- Ready to support populist leaders offering divisive solutions.

Instead, here's what technoprogressive globalisation emphasises:

- The diverse fears held by different groups around the world – fears that presently lead people towards separation, hoarding, and factionalism – need to be heard, recognised, and addressed, rather than being airbrushed aside

- Technologies of abundance are on the point, *if well managed*, of delivering ample goods and services for people in all corners of the globe, and at all levels in society, so that everyone will have access to a quality of life far exceeding that of prior generations

- In order for some regions of the world to prosper, there's no need for other regions of the world to lose out; we're not in any zero-sum game, but rather in a situation where collaboration and respect can bring progress across the board

- The legitimate aspirations of different religious and ethnic groups around the world – the various aspirations for a profound sense of meaning beyond that available from consumer goods and material possessions – can be delivered by the technoprogressive roadmap.

I'll say more about the last of these points in the next chapter, "Humans and superhumans". But first, I need to make two important caveats about how we can transition from our present dysfunctional set of global organisations into their envisioned technoprogressive replacements.

This transition will not be easy. A great deal of work remains to be done, to flesh out the positive picture of a world of sustainable abundance, inclusive international institutions, enhanced democratic processes, and the seventeen principles of technoprogressive decision-making introduced in the previous chapter. This fleshing out will include an intensely practical side, namely, increasingly embodying these principles within new organisations that I expect to emerge, on both the local and international levels. These new bodies will shadow and support existing governance organisations, winning respect not just by *talking about* technoprogressive principles but by *applying them*, day by day, month by month, year by year.

In parallel – to come to the second caveat, which will take up the rest of this chapter – very serious work also needs to be done to constrain various cancerous political initiatives that are sowing mistrust, anarchy, and discord worldwide. That is, we cannot expect to see the dawn of a comprehensively better global society unless we are ready to deal with a number of poisons in our midst – poisons that often arise, as it happens, from misguided efforts to build a better society.

Curing the cancers

In a human body, cancer occurs when normal biological processes kick into overdrive. Cells that normally divide every now and then, start dividing at an accelerated pace, and overwhelm the responses of the body that would, ordinarily, limit such an excess.

It's much the same with cancerous political initiatives. These initiatives have their roots in social dynamics with which we can sympathise. They emerge from half-truths that are loudly trumpeted and, alas, blown out of proportion. Energised, the responses take on a chaotic life of their own.

For example, many politicians are fearful of the pace of change, of job losses caused by migrant workers, of cultural enclaves that pursue different lifestyle priorities, or of "reds under the bed" or other infiltrators. But when their responses are disproportionate, they stir up undue waves of enmity and hostility, and sow larger damage for the longer-term. Without question, we need to address the underlying issues causing the fear in the first place, but we also need to tackle and defuse the disproportionate responses. Unless these cancerous responses are addressed quickly, they poison the body politic.

Let's start with the "reds under the bed" scare from the 1940s onwards, in which many patriotic supporters of the United States became alarmed by the threat of subterfuge from people inspired by communism. The scare was legitimate, but the reaction turned out to be excessive.

At the close of the Second World War, numerous countries in Eastern Europe – countries with long multicultural histories – had been transformed into single-party police states that prohibited expressions of dissent. North Korea fell under the communist control of Kim Il Sung in 1948, and mainland China fell under the communist control of Mao Zedong in 1949. At around the same time, it became clear that a number of sleeper agents, loyal to Joseph Stalin, were working behind the scenes in the United States to undermine its military superiority by passing secrets to the Soviet Union.

Elizabeth Bentley, who had been born in 1908 in New Milford, Connecticut, caused a national sensation from 1948 onwards with a series of public confessions of a lurid life of spying. Bentley had an American pedigree extending back on her mother's side to 1632 and on her father's side to the US revolutionary war. Nevertheless, it turned out she had coordinated not just one but two separate Soviet spy rings in the eastern United States. Dissatisfied by how her Soviet handlers were treating her, Bentley had eventually undergone a change of heart, and flipped from being a staunch anti-American communist to being a staunch pro-American anti-communist. She had a story to tell, and she told it well.

In a review article, Elizabeth Kerri Mahon summarises the impact of Bentley's admissions of guilt[338]:

> On November 7, 1945, just after lunch Elizabeth Bentley walked into the FBI offices in New Haven, CT and proceeded to change the course of history. The agents in the office didn't know what hit them when this

rather mumsy woman walked in, but before the end of the day they knew that they had hit the mother lode. Elizabeth not only named names (the list eventually ran to almost 150 people) but she gave such extensive detail that the eventual report ran to 107 pages with an index. She had almost total recall, probably honed from the time when she had to memorize huge chunks of information in her work as a Soviet spy...

Elizabeth... was proof that communists looked just like everyone else. If an Upper Middle Class woman could be duped into spying for the Commies, who knew who else had been lured into their lair?

It was the beginning of the nation's paranoia of a communist around every corner. Elizabeth fed into this by insisting that the Communist party's mandate was for their members to spy for the Soviet Union. During her time testifying, she spoke without notes and without a lawyer present, impressing everyone with her poise and her ability to never waver from her story. She often seemed more capable and intelligent than the people interviewing her. She came across as cool and unflappable.

In return for her disclosures to the FBI, Elizabeth Bentley escaped criminal prosecution. A different fate befell husband and wife pair Julius and Ethel Rosenberg. Born in New York in 1918 and 1915 respectively, the couple were put to death by electric chair within minutes of each other on 19 June 1953. Their capital crime had been to pass specific information to the Soviet Union about the American development of the atomic bomb. In justifying the imposition of the death penalty, presiding judge Irving Kaufman gave the following stark comment[339]:

Citizens of this country who betray their fellow-countrymen can be under none of the delusions about the benignity of Soviet power that they might have been prior to World War II. The nature of Russian terrorism is now self-evident...

I consider your crime worse than murder. Plain deliberate contemplated murder is dwarfed in magnitude by comparison with the crime you have committed. In committing the act of murder, the criminal kills only his victim. The immediate family is brought to grief and when justice is meted out the chapter is closed. But in your case, I believe your conduct in putting into the hands of the Russians the A-bomb years before our best scientists predicted Russia would perfect the bomb has already caused, in my opinion, the Communist aggression in Korea, with the resultant casualties exceeding 50,000 and who knows but that millions more of innocent people may pay the price of your treason.

Americans therefore perceived themselves at mortal threat from an enemy without and an enemy within. A Gallup poll conducted in America in November 1950 indicated that 81% of respondents viewed the Soviet Union as seeking world domination[340]. It seemed there were plenty of reasons for America to take defensive actions, to boost its security and protect its infrastructure. But in what will become a familiar pattern, the reaction to the looming threat grew into a cancer in its own right.

Within the United States, Senator Joseph McCarthy, working in parallel with the House Un-American Activities Committee, conducted a hostile investigation of people with alternative political views. Many targets of this investigation were hounded out of work, particularly in Hollywood, on account of communist sympathies they had expressed many years previously. For a while, McCarthy benefited from the apparent tacit support of President Dwight Eisenhower. A Gallup poll in January 1954 indicated approval of McCarthy by 50% of Americans; only 29% viewed him unfavourably. Nevertheless, there was growing disquiet about McCarthy's steamroller tactics, his dishonesty, his high-handed disrespect for the due process of legal review, and his reliance on innuendo. Renowned CBS broadcaster Edward Murrow dedicated an episode of his show in March 1954 to criticise McCarthy's brazen fearmongering[341]:

> The line between investigating and persecuting is a very fine one and the junior Senator from Wisconsin [McCarthy] has stepped over it repeatedly. His primary achievement has been in confusing the public mind, as between the internal and the external threats of Communism.
>
> We must not confuse dissent with disloyalty. We must remember always that accusation is not proof and that conviction depends upon evidence and due process of law. We will not walk in fear, one of another. We will not be driven by fear into an age of unreason, if we dig deep in our history and our doctrine, and remember that we are not descended from fearful men – not from men who feared to write, to speak, to associate and to defend causes that were, for the moment, unpopular.
>
> This is no time for men who oppose Senator McCarthy's methods to keep silent… We can deny our heritage and our history, but we cannot escape responsibility for the result. There is no way for a citizen of a republic to abdicate his responsibilities. As a nation we have come into our full inheritance at a tender age. We proclaim ourselves, as indeed we are, the defenders of freedom, wherever it continues to exist in the world, but we cannot defend freedom abroad by deserting it at home.

Historian Ellen W. Schrecker of the University of Yeshiva gave the assessment that[342],

> McCarthyism did more damage to the constitution than the American Communist party ever did.

The excesses of McCarthyism within the United States were soon reined back. McCarthy overreached himself in hearings that were broadcast live on TV. His popularity dwindled in the visible light of his aggressive approaches to interrogating witnesses. The public came to accept the essence of criticisms made by previous president, Harry Truman, regarding the approach of the Eisenhower administration[343]:

> It is now evident that the present Administration has fully embraced, for political advantage, McCarthyism... It is the corruption of truth, the abandonment of the due process law. It is the use of the big lie and the unfounded accusation against any citizen in the name of Americanism or security. It is the rise to power of the demagogue who lives on untruth; it is the spreading of fear and the destruction of faith in every level of society.

An astute political operator, Eisenhower moved deftly behind the scenes to undermine the little political capital retained by McCarthy. McCarthy was soon a shadow of his former self, dying in 1957 at the age of 48 from diseases related to alcoholism. His replacement in the US Senate, William Proxmire, scornfully criticised his predecessor as "a disgrace to Wisconsin, to the Senate, and to America"[344].

But whereas methods used to combat communism were toned down within the United States, a rougher, harsher set of principles continued to apply overseas. Overseas, the methods employed by the CIA and the American military arguably contributed as much to global dysfunction as did the communist insurgencies they sought to contain. The "cure" gave rise to as many problems as the original cancer.

Divergence of vision and practice

The inaugural address of US President John F. Kennedy is well-known for the stirring words of its climax[345]:

> My fellow Americans: ask not what your country can do for you – ask what you can do for your country.

My fellow citizens of the world: ask not what America will do for you, but what together we can do for the freedom of man.

These aspirations, for people around the world to set their vision higher than self-interest, still resonate today, nearly six decades after their January 1961 proclamation.

Earlier in his address, Kennedy had spelt out reasons why America should take a positive interest in improving the experiences of people experiencing poverty and oppression worldwide:

> To those people in the huts and villages of half the globe struggling to break the bonds of mass misery, we pledge our best efforts to help them help themselves, for whatever period is required – not because the communists may be doing it, not because we seek their votes, but because it is right. If a free society cannot help the many who are poor, it cannot save the few who are rich.

> To our sister republics…, we offer a special pledge – to convert our good words into good deeds – in a new alliance for progress – to assist free men and free governments in casting off the chains of poverty.

Kennedy also envisioned improved cooperation between the world's superpowers:

> Let us begin anew – remembering on both sides that civility is not a sign of weakness, and sincerity is always subject to proof. Let us never negotiate out of fear. But let us never fear to negotiate.

> Let both sides explore what problems unite us instead of belabouring those problems which divide us…

> And if a beachhead of cooperation may push back the jungle of suspicion, let both sides join in creating a new endeavour, not a new balance of power, but a new world of law, where the strong are just and the weak secure and the peace preserved.

Kennedy was by no means the first US President to set out lofty ideals for American involvement in global politics. In January 1918, as the First World War was raging, Woodrow Wilson gave a speech to a joint session of the United States Congress, setting out principles of international politics that ought to apply in the wake of the war. The speech identified justice for all peoples of the world as the basis for lasting peace[346]:

> What we demand in this war… is that the world be made fit and safe to live in; and particularly that it be made safe for every peace-loving nation which, like our own, wishes to live its own life, determine its own

institutions, be assured of justice and fair dealing by the other peoples of the world, as against force and selfish aggression.

All the peoples of the world are in effect partners in this interest, and for our own part we see very clearly that unless justice be done to others it will not be done to us.

Wilson then enumerated a total of "14 points" that would deliver the envisioned "program for peace". These included a principle of open diplomacy (decrying secretive agreements) and a principle of respect for populations currently under colonial control:

1. Open covenants of peace must be arrived at, after which there will surely be no private international action or rulings of any kind, but diplomacy shall proceed always frankly and in the public view...

5. A free, open-minded, and absolutely impartial adjustment of all colonial claims, based upon a strict observance of the principle that in determining all such questions of sovereignty the interests of the population concerned must have equal weight with the equitable claims of the government whose title is to be determined.

Wilson's set of principles gained admiration around the world, especially among populations who considered themselves unduly oppressed by colonial powers. The US President was therefore highly sought after, as he spent time in Paris during the negotiation of the Treaty of Versailles at the end of the war.

Amongst those who tried to meet Wilson in Paris was a youthful Ho Chi Minh – who would become in 1945 the first leader of North Vietnam. Ho presented Wilson's advisors with a petition seeking Vietnamese self-determination from French imperial control[347]:

Since the victory of the Allies, all the subject peoples are frantic with hope at prospect of an era of right and justice which should begin for them by virtue of the formal and solemn engagements, made before the whole world by the various powers of the entente in the struggle of civilization against barbarism.

While waiting for the principle of national self-determination to pass from ideal to reality through the effective recognition of the sacred right of all peoples to decide their own destiny, the inhabitants of the ancient Empire of Annam [Vietnam], at the present time French Indochina, present to the noble Governments of the entente in general... the following humble claims:

(1) General amnesty for all the native people who have been condemned for political activity.

(2) Reform of Indochinese justice by granting to the native population the same judicial guarantees as the Europeans have...

(3) Freedom of press and speech.

(4) Freedom of association and assembly.

(5) Freedom to emigrate and to travel abroad.

(6) Freedom of education, and creation in every province of technical and professional schools for the native population.

(7) Replacement of the regime of arbitrary decrees by a regime of law...

On the face of things, there could have been a profound meeting of minds here. The visions of Vietnam's Ho Chi Minh and America's Woodrow Wilson were broadly aligned. Nevertheless, history followed a different trajectory. The winning powers of the First World War showed little interest *in practice* in the self-determination of the Vietnamese – nor in the self-determination of many other countries.

What's more, the winning powers imposed punitive reparations payments on the losers of the war, storing up longer-term troubles that increased the likelihood of a future World War. Famously, that dismal outcome was predicted at the time, in a cartoon by the Australian artist Will Dyson that appeared in the British Daily Herald newspaper on 13 May 1919[348]. The cartoon, "Peace and future cannon fodder", depicted the leaders of France, Britain, and Italy (with Woodrow Wilson of the United States several steps behind), apparently pleased with themselves for having drafted the Versailles peace treaty. But the French leader, Georges Clemenceau, remarks to his colleagues, "Curious! I seem to hear a child weeping!" Hidden behind a pillar, a naked child is indeed weeping, next to a discarded copy of the peace treaty. The child is labelled "1940 class", meaning someone who could expect to start university in 1940, but who was also liable for conscription as "cannon fodder" in a future war at that time. The cartoon was strikingly prescient.

Evidently, it takes more than high-minded idealism, of the sort articulated by both Wilson (1918) and Kennedy (1961), to actually impact international politics. Formidable real-world practicalities get in the way:

1. It takes significant effort to oversee and police conformance to the high-minded principles. Although President Wilson was one of the

main champions of the idea of creating the League of Nations as part of the Versailles Treaty, the United States Senate refused to allow the United States to join the organisation. The country preferred its history of isolationism

2. The League of Nations soon faced its own problems of impotency, as summarised in a comment made by Italian dictator Benito Mussolini while Italian troops were using poison gas with impunity against Ethiopians[349]: "the League is very good when sparrows shout, but no good at all when eagles fall out"

3. The idealist motive of promoting local self-determination clashed with short-term commercial motivations: colonial powers expected better financial results if they retained control over subsidiary states

4. Another clashing motivation was the overriding desire to prevent the further expansion of the communist sphere. America adopted the principle of "containment", fearing a cascading tumble of a series of "dominos" – the fall of South Vietnam to troops led by Ho Chi Minh from Hanoi was expected to lead in turn to the imposition of communism in Laos, Cambodia, Thailand, Malaysia, India, and so forth

5. A "military industrial complex" gained increasing influence over the policies of countries including America, causing decisions to be made that would benefit military forces, but which would not always be in the genuine interest of international peace.

The topic of the military industrial complex brings us back to the metaphor of cancer – an animated reaction that takes on a life of its own. So long as a cancer's growth is unchecked, the wellbeing of the body as a whole is jeopardised.

Recognising and overcoming complexes

The concept of the military industrial complex featured in the farewell speech made by President Eisenhower in January 1961. Eisenhower issued a profound warning that the complex posed a growing threat to America's liberty and democracy[350]:

> Until the latest of our world conflicts, the United States had no armaments industry. American makers of ploughshares could, with time and as required, make swords as well. But now we can no longer risk emergency

improvisation of national defence; we have been compelled to create a permanent armaments industry of vast proportions. Added to this, three and a half million men and women are directly engaged in the defence establishment. We annually spend on military security more than the net income of all United States corporations.

This conjunction of an immense military establishment and a large arms industry is new in the American experience. The total influence – economic, political, even spiritual – is felt in every city, every Statehouse, every office of the Federal government. We recognize the imperative need for this development. Yet we must not fail to comprehend its grave implications. Our toil, resources and livelihood are all involved; so is the very structure of our society.

As a distinguished former military general, Eisenhower spoke with evident authority on this topic:

In the councils of government, we must guard against the acquisition of unwarranted influence, whether sought or unsought, by the military-industrial complex. The potential for the disastrous rise of misplaced power exists and will persist.

We must never let the weight of this combination endanger our liberties or democratic processes. We should take nothing for granted. Only an alert and knowledgeable citizenry can compel the proper meshing of the huge industrial and military machinery of defence with our peaceful methods and goals, so that security and liberty may prosper together.

It's one thing to be aware of the risks posed by a military industrial complex (and the associated trade in armaments). It's another thing to successfully manage these risks. The same risks apply as for other vested interest "complexes" that have featured in previous chapters of this book:

- A *carbon energy complex*, which earns huge profits from the ongoing use of carbon-based fuels, and which is motivated to minimise appreciation of the risks to climate from continuing use of these fuels

- A *financial complex*, which (likewise) earns huge profits, by means of complicated derivative products that are designed to evade regulatory scrutiny whilst benefiting in cases of financial meltdown from government handouts to banks that are perceived as "too big to fail"

- An *information technology complex*, which collects vast amounts of data about citizens, and which enables unprecedented surveillance, manipulation, and control of people by corporations and/or governments

- A *medical industrial complex*, which is more interested in selling patients expensive medical treatment over a long period of time than in low-cost solutions which would prevent illnesses in the first place (or cure them quickly)

- A *political complex*, which seeks above all else to retain its hold on political power, often by means of undermining a free press, an independent judiciary, and any credible democratic opposition.

In all six cases, the goals of the complex are generally only weakly aligned with the goals of society as a whole. If society is not vigilant, the complex will subvert the better intentions of citizens. The complex is so powerful that it cannot be controlled by mere words of advocacy.

To guard against any such complex becoming too powerful, society needs to embody a number of vital technoprogressive principles (these are a subset of the ideas promoted in earlier chapters):

- *Transparency*: The operations of the various complexes need to be widely publicised and analysed, bringing them out of the shadows into the light of public understanding

- *Disclosure*: Conflicts of interest must be made clear, to avoid the public being misled by individuals with ulterior motives

- *Accountability*: Instances where key information is found to have been suppressed or distorted need to be treated very seriously, with the guilty parties having their reputations adjusted and their privileges diminished

- *Assessment of externalities*: Evaluation systems should avoid focussing too narrowly on short-term metrics (such as financial profit) but should take into full account both positive and negative externalities – including new opportunities and new risks arising

- *Sustainable abundance for all*: It should become widely understood that there is no need for decisions to be "zero sum", in which a benefit for one party is always matched by a loss for another party; instead, via wise and profound adoption of technologies of abundance, sufficient goods can be created that the quality of life can be significantly improved, for everyone, on a long-term basis

- *Transcending factionalism*: The technoprogressive vision of a comprehensively better society can appeal to people with widely differing backgrounds, enabling them to work together, in pursuit of the abundance of health and vitality that can be generated

- *Robust defence against diminutive visions*: So long as groups of people remain stuck in smaller visions of the potential future (visions for example in which "greatness" will be restricted to particular groups, classes, religions, or nations; or visions tied to individual charismatic leaders rather than to an independent set of science-based ideas), it is advisable to minimise the influence of these groups – by robustly critiquing their ideas and offering an integrative alternative

- *Build bridges rather than walls*: Potential conflicts should be handled by diplomacy, negotiation, and seeking a higher common purpose, rather than by driving people into antagonistic rival camps that increasingly bear hatred towards one another

- *Leanness:* Decisions should focus on questions that matter most, rather than dictating matters where individual differences can easily be tolerated

- *Democratic oversight*: People in leadership positions in society should be subject to regular assessment of their performance by a democratic review, that involves a dynamic public debate aiming to reach a "convergent opinion" rather than an "average opinion"

- *Tech-embracing:* All the above principles can be assisted by smart adoption of collabtech – including wikis (or similar) that map out the landscape of decisions, automated logic-checkers, and modelling systems.

One of the areas that do "matter most" is that of the preservation of autonomous democracy. A growing confusion about the merits of democracy is one of the social cancers that need to be actively addressed. Unless this cancer is handled quickly, society stands poised to plunge into deeper turmoil.

Democracy undermined

Two sets of votes in 2016 were close-run affairs. In Britain, on June 23rd, electors voted by 51.89% to 48.11% to leave the EU. In the United States, on November 8th, 48.2% of the votes in the presidential election were cast for Hillary Clinton, compared to 46.1% for Donald Trump, but due to the mechanics of the US Electoral College, including "winner takes all" dynamics for individual states, Donald Trump emerged victorious as the new president.

In both cases, it has been widely alleged that the votes were distorted by external influence. For example, a report issued by the Office of the Director of National Intelligence on 6th January 2017 contained the following assessment[351]:

> Russian efforts to influence the 2016 US presidential election represent the most recent expression of Moscow's longstanding desire to undermine the US-led liberal democratic order, but these activities demonstrated a significant escalation in directness, level of activity, and scope of effort compared to previous operations.

> We assess Russian President Vladimir Putin ordered an influence campaign in 2016 aimed at the US presidential election. Russia's goals were to undermine public faith in the US democratic process, denigrate Secretary Clinton, and harm her electability and potential presidency. We further assess Putin and the Russian Government developed a clear preference for President-elect Trump...

> We also assess Putin and the Russian Government aspired to help President-elect Trump's election chances when possible by discrediting Secretary Clinton and publicly contrasting her unfavourably to him...

> Moscow's approach evolved over the course of the campaign based on Russia's understanding of the electoral prospects of the two main candidates. When it appeared to Moscow that Secretary Clinton was likely to win the election, the Russian influence campaign began to focus more on undermining her future presidency...

> Moscow's influence campaign followed a Russian messaging strategy that blends covert intelligence operations—such as cyber activity—with overt efforts by Russian Government agencies, state-funded media, third-party intermediaries, and paid social media users or "trolls."

As an indication of the authority behind this report, note the following introductory sentence:

This report includes an analytic assessment drafted and coordinated among The Central Intelligence Agency (CIA), The Federal Bureau of Investigation (FBI), and The National Security Agency (NSA), which draws on intelligence information collected and disseminated by those three agencies.

The report contains this warning about potential future threats to the democratic process:

We assess Moscow will apply lessons learned from its Putin-ordered campaign aimed at the US presidential election to future influence efforts worldwide, including against US allies and their election processes.

Information about Russian interference in the UK's Brexit vote has become clearer as time has passed since that referendum. The Times carried a report "Russia used Twitter bots and trolls 'to disrupt' Brexit vote" on 15th November 2017[352]:

Russian Twitter accounts posted more than 45,000 messages about Brexit in 48 hours during last year's referendum in an apparently co-ordinated attempt to sow discord, *The Times* can reveal.

More than 150,000 accounts based in Russia, which had previously confined their posts to subjects such as the Ukrainian conflict, switched attention to Brexit in the days leading up to last year's vote, according to research for an upcoming paper by data scientists at Swansea University and the University of California, Berkeley.

Russian activity spiked on June 23, the day of the referendum, and on June 24 when the result was announced. From posting fewer than 1,000 tweets a day before June 13, the accounts – many of which are virulently pro-Putin – posted 39,000 tweets on June 23-24.

Tho Pham, a researcher from Swansea University whose analysis was featured in the report in the Times, gave this summary:

The main conclusion is that bots were used on purpose and had influence.

For an indication of the apparent industrial scale of Russian-backed manipulation of social media in both the US and the UK, it's worth reading an account, in NBC News, of the activities of a former employee of the company "Internet Research Agency"[353]:

For months, Vitaly Bespalov, 26, was one of hundreds of workers pumping out misinformation online at the Internet Research Agency, the Russian troll factory responsible for explosive content seen by 126 million Americans in the run-up to the U.S. presidential election.

In many ways, the IRA was like a normal IT facility, Bespalov told NBC News in an exclusive broadcast interview. There were day shifts and night shifts, a cafeteria, and workers were seated at computers in a large open floor plan.

But in the squat, four-story concrete building on Savushkina Street in St. Petersburg, secured by camouflaged guards and turnstiles, bloggers and former journalists worked around the clock to create thousands of incendiary social media posts and news articles to meet specific quotas.

The article detailed the breakdown of work at Internet Research Agency between various projects:

Bespalov described how his own work centred on discrediting Ukraine, but that others in the building focused solely on the U.S.

Workers in the "American department" were paid the equivalent of between $1,300 to $2,000 a month for sparking social media uproar. Entry level trolls got only about $1,000 a month with paid bonuses.

Writers were separated by floor, with those on the third level blogging to undermine Ukraine and promote Russia. Writers on the first floor – often former professional journalists like Bespalov – created news articles that referred to blog posts written on the third floor. Workers on the third and fourth floor posted comments on the stories and other sites under fake identities, pretending they were from Ukraine. And the marketing team on the second floor weaved all of this misinformation into social media.

Bespalov's work at the Internet Research Agency had started in 2014:

Following Russia's annexation of the Crimean peninsula of Ukraine in 2014 – and Russia's subsequent suspension from the G8, plus heavy international sanctions – Bespalov was hired at the troll factory to rewrite articles about Ukraine for a site that was designed to look like it was based out of that country, not St. Petersburg, Russia.

The facts were to remain the same, but with a few key words swapped out. "Terrorist" became "militia men". "Ukrainian Army" became "national guard". Russia couldn't be criticized.

The objective was to have the articles be "70 percent" original text and get them to the top of search engine results, Bespalov said…

"We were told that girls' accounts are looked at more often," Bespalov told NBC News. "We would put Name, Surname, City... any photo of an attractive girl that I would have managed to find on the internet and then links – all sorts of links and links. Then the girls would get blocked eventually and you would start afresh."

UK-based researchers who have unearthed disturbing evidence of the scale of manipulation of social media in the run-up to the Brexit vote include former metropolitan police officer JJ Patrick[354] and award-winning[355] Observer journalist Carole Cadwalladr[356].

I used the adjective "disturbing" for the evidence of overseas interference in the political processes of the US and the UK. But not everyone shares this assessment. No fewer than six types of sceptical response to this suite of evidence deserve attention.

To briefly anticipate the sixth of the responses, some critics may say that any analysis of the extent of Russian influence is a distraction from the home-grown factors causing voters to prefer Trump and Brexit. For example, pro-democracy campaigner Naomi Klein states in her electrifying 2017 book *No Is Not Enough: Resisting Trump's Shock Politics and Winning the World We Need* that, whilst it is right that a special investigation proceeds into possible collusion between Trump and Russia, more attention should be given to collusion between Trump and the oil industry[357]:

> Make no mistake: Trump's collusion with the fossil fuel industry is the conspiracy hiding in plain sight.

However, my view is that it's worth going into all six of these responses with some care. The resulting discussion sheds important light on the challenges that a collaborative democratic process faces. We would be naive to look away from it.

The debate over external interference

The *first* sceptical response is to declare, "Fake news". Accounts by people such as Vitaly Bespalov, the 26 year old employee in St Petersburg, are probably exaggerated, self-serving, and misleading. The people who have an interest in promoting such stories cannot be trusted. It's as stated earlier: there are various complexes which are keen to distort public discussion. This includes the military industrial complex, with an interest to make potential enemies appear more dangerous and capable than reality, in order to secure more funding and power for themselves. A subset of the military industrial complex has been dubbed "the deep state", and includes many parts of the intelligence community. Since reports by the likes of Vitaly Bespalov play into the narrative advocated by the intelligence community, we should disregard them.

My response to this response is to say: *Not so fast*. We cannot sweep away all the evidence of foreign interference quite so quickly. We need to look more carefully at the evidence itself.

Just because a piece of evidence appears to support the position of an agency with a vested interest – such as the military industrial complex – that's no reason to discard the evidence. One of the core principles of science is that we should make all efforts to assess evidence independently of which conclusions might (or might not) be bolstered by that evidence.

What's more, just because *some* aspects of a story turn out to be exaggerated or misconceived, it fails to follow that the story should be rejected *in its entirety*.

My own considered judgement on this matter is the same as expressed in a Politifact article from 12th December 2017, namely, that the description of Russian election interference as a "made-up story" (that is, "fake news") itself deserves the label "2017 Lie of the Year"[358]:

> A mountain of evidence points to a single fact: Russia meddled in the U.S. presidential election of 2016.
>
> In both classified and public reports, U.S. intelligence agencies have said Russian President Vladimir Putin ordered actions to interfere with the election. Those actions included the cyber-theft of private data, the placement of propaganda against particular candidates, and an overall effort to undermine public faith in the U.S. democratic process...
>
> Facebook, Google and Twitter have investigated their own networks, and their executives have concluded – in some cases after initial foot-dragging – that Russia used the online platforms in attempts to influence the election.
>
> After all this, one man keeps saying it didn't even happen...
>
> Trump continually asserts that Russia's meddling in the 2016 election is fake news, a hoax or a made-up story, even though there is widespread, bipartisan evidence to the contrary.
>
> When the nation's commander-in-chief refuses to acknowledge a threat to U.S. democracy, it makes it all the more difficult to address the problem. For this reason, we name Trump's claim that the Russia interference is a hoax as our Lie of the Year for 2017.

The *second* sceptical response is to deny the scale of the actual impact of any interference in social media. According to this viewpoint, voters in the US and UK knew their own minds, and had their own reasons for voting in particular ways. This view states that it's insulting to suggest that messages from Russian agents could persuade voters to change their minds in any significant way. Voters are more robust, and have more autonomy. To suggest otherwise is to belittle these voters, and to cast undue doubts on the value of democratic votes.

My response to this response is to point to the size of the advertising industry. The huge spend of this industry is predicated on the belief that messages *can* change people's minds – persuading them to:

- Buy goods or services they were not previously considering buying

- Pay a higher price, for an apparent "premium offering", than they were previously considering paying

- Identify themselves as part of a particular community, in ways that previously hadn't appeared so important

- Pass on messages to others in their own networks, with a growing sense of urgency and importance.

In many cases, the adverts leave people believing that their choices were all made by free will. They may even forget having seen the advert.

Of course, considerable amounts of advertising spend is wasted. Perhaps more often than not, adverts fall on deaf ears. But the industry operates on the assumption that its messages hit home sufficiently often. The advertising which fails is compensated by the advertising that succeeds. It's the same with interference by foreign powers in domestic democratic processes.

A follow-up to this discussion will insist that advertising – whether commercial or political – is unable to persuade people towards courses of action to which they are fundamentally opposed. In this case, all that a message can do is to accelerate someone towards a decision that was already latent within them. However, my response is that many electors contain a bundle of different inclinations, co-existing uneasily with each other. Depending on circumstances and mood, these electors could tip towards being pro-EU or anti-EU. Again, they might tip towards being pro-Trump or anti-Trump. A well-targeted message on social media can result in an unconscious decision between these different tendencies.

In short, what this second response does is to insult, not the intelligence of the average voter, but the intelligence of the state apparatus that seeks to interfere in foreign elections. That state apparatus is surely well aware of the kind of impact which can result from their activity. They wouldn't be spending so much time and effort in that activity unless they observed at least some results arising that promoted their goals.

The question remains as to the implications of voters being persuaded to change their minds, by cleverly positioned social media content. What does this observation imply about the value of democracy? Should we therefore conclude that democracy is of little importance?

As it happens, promoting such a conclusion is one of the goals of the external manipulators of US and UK public opinion. These manipulators want to undermine not only the *operation* of democracy but also the *reputation* of democracy. Autocratic leaders want people to think that democracy isn't anything special – it's not something worth fighting hard to preserve. In this view, a genuinely free press is a hindrance on effective government, rather than a positive for democracy. Independent judiciary impedes decisive government action. Government with strong leaders – such as Vladimir Putin – is a much more important social goal, in this line of thinking, than all the bother and hassle of democratic institutions.

However, a better answer is as follows. Yes, democracy, as currently practiced, is falling far short of ideal. Yes, too many voters can have their opinions swayed too easily. But that's no reason to abandon the vision of democracy. As described in the previous chapter, democracy is the best guarantee of inclusive progress within society. When properly supported with technoprogressive institutions and tools, democracy will reduce the risk that:

- Groups of people will be left behind as technology provides new products and solutions

- Ideas will be drawn only from limited sections of society

- Vested interests will remain far too long in dominant positions, preventing others from superseding them.

Recognising the problems faced by present-day democracy ought therefore to be a prelude, not to *losing faith* in democracy, but to smarter and stronger initiatives to *improve* democracy.

This brings me to the *third* sceptical response to evidence of widespread Russian interference in overseas democracies. The whole idea smacks of conspiratorial thinking. The path taken by Donald Trump to the White House involved a long series of improbable events. If any one of these events had transpired differently, the 45th president of the United States would have been someone other than Trump. Likewise with the UK vote in favour of Brexit. Is it really to be believed that the Russian operatives had the long-term foresight to court Donald Trump from as early as 1986 (when Trump first had lunch with the US ambassador from the Soviet Union)[359], with an eye to eventually making him the US President? It stretches credibility to suppose that the Russian state could successfully envisage and then execute such a lengthy multi-stage operation of interference and manipulation.

My response to this response is that we need a better understanding of the goals of the Russian interventions. These goals were not, primarily, to put Donald Trump into the White House, nor to cause the UK to exit from the EU. Instead, the goals were broader:

- To weaken institutions and countries that oppose Russian expansionism

- To cast doubt on the notion that full democracy is a better system of government than the strong-arm tactics pursued by Putin

- To damage the reputation of individuals who speak out against Russian abuses of power

- To encourage initiatives that would fracture the resilience of institutions and countries standing in the way of the goals of the Russian government.

In support of these goals, Russian agents pursued a large number of tactical projects, maintaining flexibility as to where they would invest the most effort. They had no need to succeed in all of these projects. They ended up being lucky with their support of Donald Trump, and in their support of Brexit.

In other words, rather than executing a single massive masterplan, lasting many years, what Russian agents were able to do is to identify a strategic direction, and then find a number of successful tactical objectives in support of their goals. That's a much more credible analysis. There's no need to invoke fantastical detailed long-term planning.

It also seems that a number of developments in recent years magnified the desire of the Russian government to weaken their perceived enemies – developments that were deeply frustrating to Putin and his allies:

- Publication in early April 2016 of the "Panama Papers", that indicated how members of Putin's inner circle have become extraordinarily wealthy[360]

- Passage by the US congress in 2012 of the Magnitsky Act[361] which froze the financial assets of a number of Russian officials, in response to information shared by Bill Browder (who was at one time the largest foreign investor in Russia) about large-scale state-sanctioned financial and judicial manipulations inside Russia, including the murders of journalists, lawyers, and other whistleblowers who dared to try to publicise these distortions

- Imposition by the EU, from September 2014 onwards, of a wide range of sanctions on Russian organisations and individuals in the wake of Russian support for separatists in eastern Ukraine[362]; these sanctions were one of the factors behind the financial crisis experienced in Russia starting in 2014[363].

It's no wonder that the Russian state apparatus has become more animated.

The *fourth* sceptical response says: "What Russia is doing is no different from what America and Britain have been doing for decades". Interference in foreign politics is nothing new. It's hypocritical of US and UK observers to criticise Russia for trying to influence elections in other countries.

There's considerable force in this response. There's good evidence that covert operations involving American and British agents took place over the years in countries as varied as Cuba, the Dominican Republic, Guatemala, El Salvador, Haiti, Honduras, Panama, Brazil, Congo, Egypt, Greece, Italy, Poland, Malta, Slovakia, Romania, Bulgaria, Albania, Iran, Indonesia, Vietnam, Laos, and Cambodia[364]. These operations included intended assassinations and coups d'état. Indeed, the creation of the Soviet Union in 1917 was followed by a concerted effort by British and American forces (amongst others) to strangle the communist revolution in its infancy. The resulting civil war is noted by Guinness World Records as being "the world's costliest civil war"[365]:

The world's costliest civil war, in terms of the number of lives lost during combat and in events relating to the war, is the Russian Civil War of 1917-22. It is estimated that the former Soviet Union lost some 1.5 million combatants, and around 8 million civilians died following armed attacks, famine and disease.

That war was one factor causing deep anti-western sentiment in the Soviet Union in the decades that followed.

A 2006 report to the US Congress, prepared by the Congressional Research Service, confirmed the role in "special operations" of a clandestine subset of the CIA known as "Special Operations Forces"[366]:

> The U.S. strategy in pursuing the war on international terrorism involves a variety of missions conducted by military and civilian intelligence personnel characterized as "special operations" or paramilitary operations...

> The Department of Defense (DOD)... defines special operations as "operations conducted in hostile, denied, or politically sensitive environments to achieve military, diplomatic, informational, and/or economic objectives employing military capabilities for which there is no broad conventional force requirement"...

> DOD special operations are frequently clandestine – designed in such a way as to ensure concealment... The CIA conducts covert and clandestine operations to avoid directly implicating the U.S. Government.

In some cases, units of the CIA were probably involved in drug trafficking, in order to channel funds to resistance groups opposed to the official governments in various parts of the world[367].

And in some recent cases, Americans intervened right on the doorstep of Russia – such as with civil protests in Ukraine[368]. Even closer, the re-election of Boris Yeltsin as Russian President in 1996 is widely thought to have been enabled by western interference[369].

Isn't it therefore two-faced for observers to criticise the actions of Russian operatives who, in similar ways, have their own interest in opposing the official governments in parts of the world?

My response to this response is to insist that nefarious activities should be exposed and critiqued, *regardless of which group is conducting them*. Just as counter-democratic actions of Russian operatives deserve to be revealed and spotlighted, so do those of British and American operatives. Indeed, cutting corners in the name of "defending democracy" is a short-sighted policy. As covered earlier in this chapter, if a response to a perceived cancer is too aggressive and simple-minded, it can become like a cancer in its own right. The intended cure stores up more problems. Accordingly, technoprogressives seek maximum transparency about operations. Politicians should state intent and policy as clearly as possible, without trying to hide or distort processes.

But at the same time, we need to be ready to recognise a difference in degree. Just because two sets of agents are each liable to criticism, it does not mean they are *equally* liable to criticism. Just because all political regimes have defective elements, it does not mean that all political regimes are equally defective. Far from it.

It's worth taking the time to read the accounts of Russian state malfeasance in the 2015 book *Red Notice*[370] by Bill Browder, who I mentioned earlier in connection with the Magnitsky Act. Browder's book provides ample documentation of many shocking abuses of power.

Browder himself is no angel. He has an intriguing personal back story, which takes up the first half of his book. These chapters explain how Browder's company Hermitage Capital came to be the leading foreign participant in many Russian investment schemes following the wave of post-Soviet privatisations. It also explains Browder's fierce legal conflicts with some of the Russian oligarchs, as he fought to prevent further fleecing of the assets of companies in which he had invested.

For a while, it seems that Putin supported what Browder was doing. But then Browder became an increasing annoyance to the Kremlin. What happened next is alarming, by any measure. It's no surprise that Browder has been called "Putin's No. 1 enemy". A good flavour is conveyed by a review of *Red Notice* by Luke Harding in the Guardian[371]:

> In 2008 a young Russian lawyer called Sergei Magnitsky uncovered a massive tax fraud. He found evidence that a group of well-connected Russian officials had stolen a whopping $230m. The same officials had Magnitsky arrested; he was tossed into a freezing cell and refused medical treatment. Magnitsky – who suffered from pancreatitis and gall stones – spent months in pain. This state-sanctioned torture was meant to make him withdraw his testimony. He didn't. One day his condition grew critical. Guards put him in an isolation cell. There, they beat him to death.
>
> Magnitsky's case was to become the most notorious and best-documented example of human rights abuse in Vladimir Putin's Russia. That this

happened was down to one man: Bill Browder, a US-born financier and the CEO of a successful asset management company. Once a Putin fan, Browder found himself in trouble in 2005 when he was deported from Russia. He hired a team, including Magnitsky. When the Kremlin got nasty, most of the lawyers fled. Magnitsky – a family man with two small boys, who liked Beethoven – refused to leave. He believed the law would protect him, that Russia had said farewell to its Soviet ghosts. It was a tragic misjudgment…

This takes me to the *fifth* sceptical response in this series. What's the value in stoking anti-Russian sentiment? Aren't these nationalistic sentiments a dangerous throwback to a time when a misguided sense of "my country, right or wrong" led to so many pointless wars? Isn't it absurd – and repugnant – to group all Russians under the same critical brush?

My response to this response is that it confuses opposition to a government with opposition to a country. Emphatically, my objection is to the practices adopted by the circle around Putin, not to the aspirations and wellbeing of the Russian people as a whole.

We should not allow a commendable positive impulse for good relations with all groups of people around the world (including Russians) to blind us to troublesome features of the current Russian state apparatus. Friendship is not about ignoring character flaws. It's about finding the right time and place to address these issues – and about ensuring that they don't cause undue problems in the meantime. That's why we need to strengthen societies around the world against manipulation by counterfeit news stories, corrosive sloganeering, and anti-democratic impulses. And that's why we need to be acutely aware of what's actually happening, rather than sliding down a rose-tinted naivety to a world in which might is right, and strong-arm state suppression overpowers independent reasoning.

However, it's also vital that we seek to engage creatively and sympathetically with people at all levels of the Russian state. We should recognise the pernicious challenges they have inherited from the past – especially the chaos of the Yeltsin years, when neoliberal policies championed by westerners produced such harmful effects. We need to be careful to avoid provoking people to make violent anti-Russian actions. I anticipate that, with wise bridge-building, Russia will play a very substantial positive role in the achievement of the technoprogressive vision.

The *sixth* sceptical response takes a different tack. Why focus on Russian manipulation of western political opinion, when that's only one of many factors leading electors to vote for Trump (in the US) and Brexit (in the UK)? Perhaps that manipulation caused an increase in support for a disruptive viewpoint from 48% to 52%. But in that case, isn't it more important to understand the factors leading 48% to support the viewpoint, rather than to agonise over the incremental 4%?

My response to this response is… to agree. At the same time as we explore how democracy is being damaged by external forces, we also need to look more closely at the other factors leading to wide public discontent with the status quo (establishment presidential candidates in the US, and continuing EU membership in the UK).

In Chapter 3 of this book, "Fear and outrage", I covered in general terms the factors that are causing increasing number of electors worldwide to feel deeply apprehensive about the future and alienated from the policies of mainstream politicians. To close this chapter, I'll review in more detail the specific factors leading to disenchantment in the UK with the EU project. That discussion will also point the way towards a healthier, invigorated set of international institutions. But, first, I want to say a few words on the positive case for the UK remaining within the EU.

About platforms

One important lesson I've learned from my career – both as a smartphone technologist, and, later, as a futurist – is that collaboration is hard. Collaboration necessarily involves compromise. It involves the inconvenience of submitting to protocols and standards which probably don't match your first thought on how you'd like to operate.

If you're in a hurry, you generally don't want to spend time agreeing how everyone's going to collaborate together. You'll be tempted to try to handle the job yourself. It's as in the first phrase of what is widely said to be an African proverb[372]: "If you want to go fast, go alone."

The conclusion of the proverb, however, indicates the merit of a collaborative approach: "but if you want to go far, go together". That was the approach I sought to adopt, several times over, during my days as an executive within the smartphone OS company Symbian (and previously within the PDA manufacturer Psion)[373]:

- Whereas some of my colleagues preferred to keep the size of the software engineering team small, and to rely on the heroics of individual superstar developers, I argued for taking the time to recruit and train and organise a larger workforce

- Whereas, at a later phase, some of my colleagues preferred to create as many components as possible of our operating system inside the company, I argued for taking the time to build an extended community of partner companies, who would have the capability and motivation to provide solutions to plug into the operating system

- Whereas some of my colleagues preferred to hurry along and enable the creation of individual robust, attractive smartphones, I argued for taking the time to design and support application programming interfaces which could then be leveraged by independent application developers.

Collaboration on any complicated initiative requires agreement on an underlying *platform* – a shared set of vocabulary, assumptions, tools, techniques, resources, and services. A platform identifies roles and responsibilities: if someone follows a certain set of rules, they will gain a certain set of benefits. Break these rules, however, and you'll be on your own.

Platforms – whether mobile operating systems like Symbian OS and Android, communications protocols like USB and Wi-Fi, programming languages such as Java and Scala, or content platforms like HTML and LaTeX – all have their drawbacks as well as their benefits. Over time, to cope with changing circumstances and new requirements, platforms need to adapt and evolve, lest their drawbacks come to outweigh the benefits. In due course, the flexibility in a platform can be used up, and it moves into an architectural dead-end. In that case, evolution can become slower and more cumbersome, prompting calls to ditch a platform altogether. The mammals replaced the dinosaurs. Arabic numerals replaced Roman numerals. Google's Android and Apple's iOS replaced the less flexible operating systems from Symbian, Palm, and BlackBerry.

But notice that the process of switching to a brand new platform can be fraught with danger. Self-confident managers of technology companies often overestimate the speed at which they can execute a platform change:

- The grass seems greener on the other side of an envisioned platform transition, but such perceptions are often misleading

- New platforms often have their own major shortcomings, that were not apparent from optimistic marketing presentations

- Existing platforms enable lots of positive solutions that have become taken for granted, but which will suddenly be remembered once they fail to operate inside the new platform.

I've had the misfortune to observe several smartphone management teams make a huge mess of attempted platform transitions. My 2014 book *Smartphones and Beyond* contains my analysis of Nokia's struggle from 2010 onwards to migrate from its existing operating systems to Microsoft Windows Phone – a struggle that led, sadly, to dramatic market decline for that once high-flying company[374].

The Nokia executives were no fools. They realised in advance that the transition would be deeply challenging. They knew that the current incarnation of Windows Phone lacked many of the key features of Symbian OS, and that the process to upgrade to later versions of Windows Phone would be bumpy. However, they underestimated the *scale* of these difficulties. Working with Microsoft turned out to be considerably harder than they had imagined. And several of the core difficulties of their previous (pre-Microsoft) projects remained in place even after the transition, whereas they had been naively expected to evaporate in the process. They had scapegoated their previous platforms, without accepting that their issues with project execution had wider causes.

As for technology systems, so also for political systems. Networks of international alliances rise and fall, and change their shape over time. In the heat of a moment, some of the drawbacks of an international alliance can loom large in mind, and can cause people to overlook the benefits of the alliance. In the presence of media distortions, this imbalance of perceptions can become magnified, and persist for longer periods of time. The alliance can easily become the scapegoat for issues that actually have origins elsewhere. That is what has happened with the perception of the EU within the UK:

- Unfairly hostile characterisations of continental European politicians – such as Germans and Belgians – have damaged the potential for constructive UK engagement with our EU partners

- Distortions of many matters of fact about EU policy and governance structure have amplified that ill will

- Attention has been diverted from areas in UK politics that are the actual causes of problems that are, incorrectly, blamed on the EU

- Lengthy efforts to "square the circle" in negotiating Britain's exit from the EU are consuming vital parliamentary time that would much better be spent on many of the other pressing issues covered elsewhere in this book.

To be clear, the EU platform has a wide range of faults. Like many other platforms – both technological and political – it has proven slow to adapt. It has frequently been the victim of its own inertia. Nevertheless, if all the effort spent on negotiating the details of Brexit were instead applied to reforming the EU, I expect that significant improvements would be made. The election of Emmanuel Macron as the new President of France, along with other winds of change, can provide the opportunity for faster reform of the EU into a multi-level organisation, with some countries in an inner core, using the Euro currency, and with other countries forming two or more surrounding rings. That would be far preferable, in my view, to the chaos of the UK altogether abandoning the collaborative EU platform.

A tangled isolationist alliance

It's not just Russian operatives, organising a vast online network of troll accounts, that distorted the debate in the UK over the merits of EU membership. An even bigger distortion was applied by top-selling British newspapers such as the Daily Mail and the Daily Express.

A review article by journalist Jane Martinson, published the day after the Brexit referendum, analysed the impact of regular anti-EU polemic in leading British newspapers[375]:

> Was it the Sun wot won it? The Sun, which came out last week with a union jack-draped front cover urging its readers to "BeLeave in Britain" and at 6am on Friday published "See EU later", did not rise against the EU alone. British newspapers were overwhelmingly in favour of Brexit, with the Mail, Telegraph, Express and Star accounting for four times as many readers and anti-EU stories as their pro-remain rivals.

"If you believe in Britain, vote leave," urged the Mail on Wednesday, lambasting the "lies" and "greedy elites" of a "broken, dying Europe" on its front page.

Such headlines were not just the hallmark of an increasingly bitter referendum campaign – with its relentless focus on anti-immigration stories – but came after years of anti-EU reporting in most of the British press.

In February, the Mail front page asked simply "Who will speak for England?" – highlighting the causes of independence and nationhood that have so helped the leave campaign.

In September of that year, SubScribe published a major review of how the subject of immigration has been treated by popular newspapers[376]. The review contains numerous collages of front pages that vilified immigrants:

> The Leave campaign in the EU referendum and its newspaper supporters made great play of immigration and of how leaving the community would give Britain back control of its borders – and there has been strong evidence of a rise in racist or "hate" crimes since the vote in June.
>
> A certain section of our society appears to have believed that the moment the votes had been counted, all foreigners would be put on the next boat and that any who remained were fair game. It is frightening.
>
> Going through the Sun's coverage of the issue so far this year, SubScribe had collated 120 almost entirely negative news reports and opinion pieces before [a single positive] one from June 28 turned up...
>
> For the Daily Express, all foreigners are a problem and everything is Europe's fault. Since the Cameron became Prime Minister in 2010, the paper has splashed on migration issues on 179 occasions... with a marked acceleration since the run-up to January 2014, when Romanians and Bulgarians were given full access to the UK.

The article concludes that the torrent of negative headlines adds up to a single message: "Refugees not welcome".

Just as we should understand the underlying motivations of the Russian operatives – namely, to weaken an institution, that is the EU, which was providing effective opposition to Russian abuses of power – we should also understand the underlying motivations of the owners of the newspapers that have campaigned most vigorously for Britain to leave the EU.

Writing in the Evening Standard, Anthony Hilton recalled a conversation with Rupert Murdoch, the billionaire newspaper proprietor[377]:

I once asked Rupert Murdoch why he was so opposed to the European Union. "That's easy," he replied. "When I go into Downing Street they do what I say; when I go to Brussels they take no notice."

In view of potential government enquiries into the takeover of Sky by Fox, Murdoch subsequently claimed "I have never uttered these words". But as reported by the Guardian, Anthony Hilton has stuck to his version[378]:

> When asked by the Guardian, Hilton said: "I stand by my story." He said Murdoch made the remarks in a conversation in the early 1980s, when Hilton was city editor of the Times. Hilton, now a columnist for the Evening Standard, has referred to the anecdote several times over the years without either a denial or a complaint from his former boss, until now.

Rupert Murdoch is far from being alone as an "elite" member of society who is a strong supporter of Brexit. In his 2017 book *How To Stop Brexit – And Make Britain Great Again*, former UK Deputy Prime Minister Nick Clegg provides a useful analysis of the Brexit elite[379]. He starts with some remarks about Nigel Farage, long-time head of UKIP, the United Kingdom Independence Party:

> In a speech in Mississippi in support of Donald Trump's presidential campaign, Nigel Farage hailed the vote for Brexit as a victory for the 'little people, the real people … the ordinary, decent people'. A few months later Mr Farage, a privately educated ex-City trader with a taste for a post-prandial glass of port, flew across the Atlantic to join President Trump at the billionaire's victory party. There is a famous photo of the pair celebrating in front of one of Trump Tower's gold-plated lift doors. The little people must have been just out of shot.
>
> The image was comical, but that meeting of narrow minds was an insight into a far darker aspect of the Brexit vote. For when the champions of the Leave vote insist that the referendum result must for ever be venerated as the will of the people, what they don't tell you is that a small, mostly elderly, mostly male collection of party donors, media barons, obsessive newspaper editors and opportunist hedge-fund managers have been driving the Brexit agenda, it would appear largely for their own ends. The best way to describe them is, as it happens, as an elite.

Clegg quickly provides an important clarification:

> This is not an attempt to suggest that the Brexit eruption was not fuelled by grass-roots discontent. It was, of course – but the ideas, money and

propaganda that turbocharged the campaign were provided by an unaccountable array of vested interests, none of whom could ever claim to be representatives of ordinary people.

He then moves on to give more details about the Brexit elite:

Over the years, the same names just keep on coming up. Rarely straying from the shadows, a handful of multimillionaire businessmen have, in some cases for thirty years or more, bankrolled whichever party or politician or think tank or campaign group stands on the most aggressive EU-bashing platform. Time and again, this small cast list – amongst them Paul Sykes, Peter Cruddas, Stanley Kalms, Stuart Wheeler, Michael Hintze and Patrick Barbour – repeatedly emerge as major Eurosceptic donors and backers of either the Conservative Party or UKIP.

The City of London is largely portrayed as pro-EU, or at least pro-Single Market, but some very rich City men began to push game-changing sums towards the Leave side of the campaign. Why were they so interested in securing a particular result? In part, it seems, for reasons of self-interest: these phenomenally wealthy men view the financial regulations of the EU as burdensome and want to see the UK reinventing itself as a low-tax/ low-regulation economy that is no longer bound to work with our European allies and no longer beholden to a set of shared standards.

This analysis is supported by a recent Guardian analysis of elements of the Paradise Papers[380]:

Many of the most powerful supporters of the Brexit campaign appear in the Paradise Papers because of their offshore interests. There is nothing illegal about their arrangements.

But many of these same voices have urged a "hard Brexit" – which could see the UK ripping up its economic model and in effect becoming a tax haven on the borders of Europe.

That might suit Brexiters, many of whom have either made their money, or keep their money, or live, offshore.

We can therefore discern three elements of an anti-EU alliance:

1. Many voters who felt that mainstream politicians had ignored them, and who wished to register a strong anti-establishment protest vote

2. Wealthy members of a Brexit elite, who wish freedom from EU regulations in order to maximise their own profit-making potential (regardless of the negative externalities that may arise); cleverly,

they adopted the slogan "take back control" to indicate that the UK should no longer be liable to such regulations, without mentioning the many benefits of agreed regulatory frameworks

3. Operatives backed by Russia (and, perhaps, by other anti-western regimes) who sought to weaken or paralyse the EU.

To this we should add in an element whose size is difficult to assess. That's the portion of the UK voters who harbour significant racist or xenophobic sentiments. To be clear, I'm not implying that all Brexit voters are racists. However, the reverse implication is strong: nearly all voters with latent racist views are Brexit voters. And newspapers such as the Daily Mail were adept at triggering such views, without readers having to think of themselves as being overt racists.

Yet another element is the proportion of people who have fallen victim at some time in their life to EU administrative straitjackets or bureaucratic ineptitude – and who have chosen to generalise from that particular experience to a theory that the EU is somehow incapable of meaningful reform. (One reason for them choosing this interpretation is the grossly distorted media coverage of EU operations.)

A final part of what amounts to a rather tangled isolationist alliance goes by the label "Lexit", meaning people who have left-wing reasons for supporting Brexit. To an extent, the Lexit group overlaps with the previous category, in thinking that the EU is incapable of meaningful reform – though in the Lexit case, it's left-wing reform that they want to see (and believe cannot happen).

For a useful introduction to both the strengths and weaknesses of Lexit, I recommend the breezy article "Everything you need to know about Lexit" by the editor of Politics.co.uk, Ian Dunt[381]. As Dunt explains (referring to politicians within the UK):

> Most left-wing figures in politics, journalism, academia and trade unionism are very critical of Brexit. But [Lexit is] a significant minority view and one that dominates in the Labour leadership. Left-wing attacks of the EU have a long political heritage and include some much-loved figures on the left, like Tony Benn. They're not without content either. There are some powerful left-wing critiques of the project.

The first set of Lexit arguments cover "freedom of movement for employers", whereby EU regulations can enable so-called "social dumping" by employers:

> It's about undercutting local wages and conditions by shipping in workers from overseas or basing your company's legal status on wherever saves you the most money.

Dunt gives the example of Finnish ferry company Viking Line[382]:

> Viking Line operated a ferry between Finland and Estonia, under a Finnish flag and an arrangement with the Finnish Seaman's Union. It paid high Finnish wages and abided by high Finnish worker standards and, as a consequence, it made a loss. So they came up with a sneaky idea. They reflagged the ferry the other way round. The Finnish union got terribly upset about it and won support from the International Transport Workers' Federation, which asked all affiliated unions not to negotiate with Viking Line. The company backed down…

> But then Estonia joined the EU. This allowed the firm to take its case to court and say that the unions had contravened their freedom of establishment, which is guaranteed under EU law.

> [The ECJ – the European Court of Justice] ruled that strikes have to be compatible with EU law, so where they had the effect of limiting freedom of movement or association, they were unlawful.

Is this is good enough reason for left-leaning politicians to push for the UK to leave the EU? Hardly. Dunt observes:

> There's pretty widespread recognition that the ECJ got the balance wrong here. The underlying posted worker system is being reformed. New French president Emmanuel Macron has managed to secure quite extensive changes to improve the system.

In other words, the EU has the ability to reform and evolve itself.

A similar analysis applies for two more sets of Lexit arguments covered by Dunt – those concerning "freedom of movement for workers" and "state aid". To cut to the overall conclusion:

> The EU is basically a social democrat project, based along German or Scandinavian lines. That's probably too right-wing for some people, and it's certainly too left wing for others. But it has a lot of space there for a wide range of political arrangements, covering the vast majority of political views in the UK. It doesn't always get the relationship right between abiding by EU rules and workers' rights, but you have to be a very stern

observer to conclude from these fairly limited problems that we should take the massive risk of leaving the EU altogether...

Dunt's final point from this article deserves double underlining:

But still, we shouldn't write off left wing criticisms of the EU. Many of them are perfectly valid. Remainers would do well to address them, rather than dismiss them.

An integrative technoprogressive alliance

It's time to draw some conclusions of my own. In reviewing the UK's decision to leave the EU, I've by no means explored all the relevant lines of discussion. However, I offer the following overall opinions:

- The EU has greater ability to adapt and evolve that many of its critics imagine

- Many politicians and civil servants who work for the EU and who were previously unwilling to contemplate democratic reform of the organisation, have been awakened from their complacency by recent turns of event, and are now more open to positive evolution

- The EU provides numerous benefits to its member states, that critics in the UK have overlooked or forgotten

- Mainland Europeans often have a greater warmth of feeling towards the EU project than UK-based critics realise; this warmth – born out of decades (indeed centuries) of preceding wars and conflicts – gives the EU deep resilience against the shocks it faces

- The landscape of conversation around Brexit has been deliberately and extensively distorted, by participants *on both sides* of the debate, in ways that are really unhelpful

- Vast energies are being deployed, both in the UK and in the other EU members, in negotiations and preparations, that could far better be spent on positive collaborative reforms of the EU, not to mention other existential risks and existential opportunities

- A debilitating inertia prevails, which means that "good money is being spent after bad money", with politicians unable or unwilling to admit previous mistakes, similar to the way that countries persist in disastrous overseas wars (such as the Vietnam War) long after an objective analysis would have resulted in withdrawal or reversal.

My reasons for covering this sorry state of affairs are not just because I think a major mistake is being made in this instance – a mistake with profoundly damaging consequences for global relationships. It's also because this example illustrates the stark set of challenges facing international politics:

- Politicians and electors, alike, tend to underrate the value and importance of existing international organisations; they see the drawbacks of these organisations, but aren't reminded sufficiently often of their benefits

- There's a lack of a clear, credible roadmap for positive evolution of these organisations and institutions

- Discussion of options for improved international relations is often blighted by deliberate distortions

- There's little agreement on the overall principles by which international organisations should operate; instead, debates are dominated by pragmatic, incremental, incidental considerations

- As a result, inertia prevails; Nero fiddles while Rome burns.

However, an emerging technoprogressive alliance can take some inspiration from what has been achieved by the long-time supporters of Brexit. The tangled isolationist alliance in favour of the UK exiting the EU can serve as a positive model for what technoprogressives need to do:

- The Brexit vision that British politicians might become free from the limitations imposed by EU regulations prefigures the technoprogressive vision of forthcoming sustainable abundance, in which people in all sectors of life will become free from the limitations imposed by scarcity

- The inspirational Brexit slogan of "take back control" therefore prefigures the technoprogressive vision of "take back humanity"

- The decades-long commitment by the Brexit elite to promoting their cause, through thick and thin, should find echoes in commitments by technoprogressive supporters to keep the challenges and opportunities of accelerating technology firmly in the public mind – through thick and thin, year out and year in.

But there need to be key differences as well. The Brexit elite have made their peace with the practice of speaking untruths to electors. Dominic Cumming, director of Vote Leave, included in a lengthy review of the Brexit campaign the admission that[383]:

The £350 million / NHS argument was necessary to win...

Would we have won without £350m/NHS? All our research and the close result strongly suggests No.

This is despite the figure of £350 million per week – painted on a red bus that travelled nationwide during the campaign – being widely debunked as a misleading estimate for the net spend by the UK in the EU.

In contrast, the technoprogressive campaign should seek maximum openness, maximum candour, and maximum accessibility for its analysis. Rather than viewing citizens as people to be manipulated and bamboozled, it should expect – and take steps to enable – a truthful, sincere dialogue. Rather than seeing all the insight as being on a single side of an argument, it should be ready to hear wisdom from multiple parties in a dispute. Rather than seeing some citizens as hostile enemies, and desiring to outsmart them or destroy their reputations, it should aspire to transcend factionalism. Rather than seeing every interaction as necessarily involving a loser as well as a winner, it should champion a vision of radical abundance in which there's room for everyone to flourish.

I'll come back to this vision in the final chapter of this book. But first, let's consider whether it's really credible to expect the best of citizens – all citizens. Wouldn't it be more practical to seek to muddle along through, horse-trading and power-broking, sensibly accommodating human foibles? Indeed, might a vision of improved citizenry itself be a mortal danger, recalling the horrific history of Cambodia's Year Zero, Mao Zedong's Cultural Revolution, or the New Man of the Nazi master race?

12. Humans and superhumans

Is it possible to significantly improve politics, over the course of, say, the next dozen years, without first significantly improving human nature?

In this chapter, I'll look at four different answers to this question:

1. We shouldn't try to improve human nature; that's the route to hell

2. We can have a better politics without any change in human nature

3. Improving human nature will turn out to be relatively straightforward; let's get cracking

4. Improving human nature will be difficult but is highly desirable; we need to carefully consider the potential scenarios, with an open mind, and then make our choices.

Angels and demons

We humans are sometimes angelic, yet sometimes diabolic.

On occasion, we find ways to work together on a transcendent purpose with wide benefits. The huge collaborative effort of the Apollo project led, not only to twelve astronauts walking on the Moon, 240 thousand miles distant from the Earth, but also to improvements in some 6,300 technologies, including the CAT scanner, cordless tools, freeze-dried foods, scratch-resistant lenses, and satellite television[384]. The Marshall Plan[385], with investment by the United States after the end of the Second World War of some $12B (equivalent to around $120B in 2018 terms), enabled the positive rebuilding of Western European economies after the ravages of wartime; in contrast to the punitive Versailles peace treaty after the First World War, mentioned in the previous chapter, this demonstrated a far-sighted magnanimity that was to turn former bitter enemies into long-term allies. In the UK, the project to create the National Health Service, with its vision of healthcare available to every citizen, set aside short-term commercial considerations in favour of broader, long-lasting social benefit; the UK government spent £11.4B on the NHS in its first year alone (1948)[386].

But on other occasions, we treat each other abominably. Not only do we go to war with each other, but our wars are often accompanied by hideous so-called "war crimes". Our religious crusades, whilst announced in high-minded language, have involved the subjugation or extermination of hundreds of thousands of members of opposing faiths. The twentieth century saw genocides on a scale never before experienced, including (by some estimates)[387] eight hundred thousand Tutsi in Rwanda, one and a half million Armenians in Turkey, two million Cambodians under Pol Pot, six million Jews in the Nazi holocaust, and up to seven million Ukrainians in the deliberate "Holodomor" famines arising from Stalin's policies between 1932-33. For a different example of viciousness, the comments attached to YouTube videos frequently show intense hatred and vitriol[388].

As technology puts more power in our hands, will we become more angelic, or more diabolic? *Probably both, at the same time.*

A nimbleness of mind can coincide with a harshness of spirit. Just because someone has more information at their disposal, that's no guarantee the information will be used to advance beneficial initiatives. Instead, that information can be mined and contoured to support whatever course of action someone has already selected in their heart.

Great intelligence can be coupled with great knowledge, for good but also for ill. The outcome in some sorry cases is greater vindictiveness, greater manipulation, and greater enmity. Enhanced cleverness can make us experts in techniques to suppress inconvenient ideas, to distort inopportune findings, and to tarnish independent thinkers. We can find more devious ways to mislead and deceive people – and, perversely, to mislead and deceive ourselves. In this way, we could create the mother of all echo chambers. It would take only a few additional steps for obsessive human superintelligence to produce unprecedented human malevolence.

Transhumanists want to ask: can't we find a way to alter the expression of human nature, so that we become less likely to use our new technological capabilities for malevolence, and more likely to use them for benevolence? Can't we accentuate the angelic, whilst diminishing the diabolic?

To some critics, that's an extremely dangerous question. If we mess with human nature, they say, we'll almost certainly make things worse rather than better.

Far preferable, in this analysis, is to accept our human characteristics as a given, and to evolve our social structures and cultural frameworks with these fixed characteristics in mind. In other words, our focus should be on the likes of legal charters, restorative justice, proactive education, multi-cultural awareness, and effective policing.

My view, which I'll explain in this chapter, is that these humanitarian initiatives towards *changing culture* need to be complemented with transhumanist initiatives to *alter the inclinations inside the human soul*. We need to address nature at the same time as we address nurture. To do otherwise is to unnecessarily limit our options – and to make it more likely that a bleak future awaits us.

The good news is that, for this transhumanist task, we can take advantage of a powerful suite of emerging new technologies. The bad news is that, like all new technologies, there are risks involved. As these technologies unfold, there will surely be unforeseen consequences, especially when different trends interact in unexpected ways.

As I'll indicate shortly, transhumanists have long been well aware of the risks in changing the expression of human nature. But these risks are no reason for us to abandon the idea. Instead, they are a reason to exercise care and judgement in this project.

That's because, to accept the status quo, without seeking to change human nature, is itself a highly risky approach. Indeed, there are *no* risk-free options in today's world. If we want to increase our chances of reaching a future of sustainable abundance for all, without humanity being diverted en route to a new dark age, we should leave no avenue unexplored.

The new human in history

For as long as history has been recorded, humans have been turning over new leaves in their lives. As a result of a dramatic personal experience – perhaps involving a shock or disappointment, or seeing the inspiring example of someone else, or finding a novel way of looking at the world – people have set aside former habits and attitudes.

Christianity has the concept of someone being "born again". It celebrates the dramatic conversion stories of figures such as Saul of Tarsus, Augustine of Hippo, and John Wesley (the founder of Methodism). With a new sense of purpose and meaning, and with the support of a broader community, converts can find inner strength to set themselves on different personal trajectories. Buddhism points to life-altering examples of people gaining what they discern to be enlightenment. Mindfulness can improve our ability to resist the winds of desire. Other religions have their own approaches to encouraging personal transformation. Outside of religion, additional triggers for "rebirth" include new romantic relationships, insight from sessions with psychotherapists, and the adoption of secular ideologies.

As it happens, various ideologies have their own theories about factors that enable the emergence of improved human character. Christianity has the idea that, to escape from a maelstrom of inner hatefulness, and to be able to forgive others for their misdeeds against us, it helps to have a strong sense of our own state of being forgiven. To quote from the New Testament[389]:

> Be kind and compassionate to one another, forgiving each other, just as in Christ God forgave you.

Marxists have a different theory, according to which we humans are "alienated" or "estranged" from our real potential, by virtue of dysfunctions in our economic relationships[390]. In our workplaces, we frequently create goods for which we feel little rapport. A disproportionate share of the fruits of our labour is taken by our employer. We are obliged to compete with other workers for a limited number of employment opportunities. And as consumers, we are bombarded with messages telling us we will miss out, unless we purchase the latest products. All this makes us unnecessarily anxious, envious, prone to hoarding, and slyly competitive. In this analysis, the route to an improved human nature is to transform society's economic relationships – as summarised by phrases such as transferring the "means of production" into "collective ownership".

Specific Marxist leaders took that analysis further. The far-reaching goals of the 1917 Bolshevik revolution included, not merely improved management of the economy, but also the creation of what Leon Trotsky called "a superman"[391]:

> Man will make it his purpose to master his own feelings, to raise his instincts to the heights of consciousness, to make them transparent, to extend the wires of his will into hidden recesses, and thereby to raise himself to a new plane, to create a higher social biologic type, or, if you please, a superman...
>
> Social construction and psychophysical self-education will become two aspects of one and the same process...
>
> Man will become immeasurably stronger, wiser, and subtler; his body will become more harmonic, his movements more rhythmic, his voice more

musical. The forms of life will become dynamically dramatic. The average human being will rise to the heights of an Aristotle, a Goethe, or a Marx.

Mark Cooray from Macquarie University, Sydney, Australia draws further attention to the idea of "New Soviet Man"[392]:

The essential danger and destructiveness of the communist state… is that it has not been satisfied only with controlling the political and economic affairs of society. In its totalitarian form, the communist state extends its domination into the personal and cultural being of man…

Lenin and the Bolsheviks seized power in 1917, not merely to nationalise the means of production and direct the economy through central planning. Their goal was wider than that: the creation of a New Soviet Man, freed from the bourgeois prejudices of the past.

The "New Man" was to be altruist in spirit, communal in outlook, sacrificial in his labour for the common good, boundless in his fight for world revolution.

Referring to analysis in the 1985 book *Cogs in the Wheel: The Formation of Soviet Man* by Russian emigré dissident historian Mikhail Heller[393], Cooray lists three steps taken by the Bolshevik regime to produce the new man:

The first step was total destruction of the old social order and all of the social and cultural institutions that surrounded and protected the individual. Heller refers to this as the process of culturally stripping the individual naked and atomising him so he is defenceless and mouldable by the state in each and every corner of social life.

The next step was the "nationalisation of time" through central planning…

Finally came "ideologization", the process through which the Soviet State attempted to fill the content of men's minds and influenced the language and thought patterns of "the people" in whose name the leaders undertook this grand scheme. Under this heading Heller details the state's control and direction of literature, the arts, education, and the all-pervasive din of propaganda through every mode of communication. Nor does Heller ignore the role of fear, intimidation, and terror as practised by the secret police.

In China, Mao Zedong gave Marxist ideas a further twist by viewing countryside peasantry as the class that could propel forward a better future. True education, in this view, took place in rural farms. As part of the Chinese "Cultural Revolution", Mao launched a movement with the name

"Up to the Mountains and Down to the Countryside". A article he wrote in the Chinese People's Daily in 1968 contained the followed admonitions[394]:

> We too have two hands; let us not laze about in the city... The intellectual youth must go to the country, and will be educated from living in rural poverty.

This fit the wider pattern of Maoist criticism of "the Four Olds" – old customs, old habits, old culture and old thinking. The pernicious effect of these "olds" would, Mao thought, be undone in the transformational context of agricultural grit and toil. New humans would emerge from the cauldron of pure labour.

Nowadays, Chinese people regard the 17 million youths who were displaced in this way, from cities into the countryside, as "the lost generation" – separated from their families and denied access to university education. One of the participants, Hu Rongfen, previously a top student in her class in Shanghai in 1971, gave her story to CNN in 2012[395]:

> "We were told that city dwellers never move their limbs and could not distinguish different crops," says Hu, now 58. "So we were banished to labour and learn skills and grit from peasants." Hu spent four years (1971-1974) planting rice, spreading cow dung and chopping wood in Jin Xian, a mountainous county...
>
> "I still can't bear to recall my youth spent on the farm," she says.
>
> One of Hu's most vivid memories was working in rice fields in early spring in freezing water, on which lumps of ice still floated. There, she would bend down to seed for more than ten hours. She would slap her legs madly to rid herself of the leeches clinging to her limbs. Blood would ooze from her wounds and mingle with the dirt and water.
>
> Another time, she recalled walking 40 kilometres along mud paths against bone-chilling winds to the nearest bus station on Chinese New Year's Eve to catch a ride to the train station to go back to Shanghai to see her parents.

On a positive note:

> She confesses she did gain something – an iron will to live through the toughest conditions.

What's more, she did live to tell her tale. That's in contrast with up to two million other people caught up in the Cultural Revolution. That campaign was conceived to inject new life into Maoism, but ended up creating chaos. Beijing-based Guardian journalist Tom Phillips gives this summary[396]:

> When the mass mobilisation kicked off party newspapers depicted it as an epochal struggle that would inject new life into the socialist cause. "Like the red sun rising in the east, the unprecedented Great Proletarian Cultural Revolution is illuminating the land with its brilliant rays," one editorial read.
>
> In fact, the Cultural Revolution crippled the economy, ruined millions of lives and thrust China into 10 years of turmoil, bloodshed, hunger and stagnation.
>
> Gangs of students and Red Guards attacked people wearing "bourgeois clothes" on the street, "imperialist" signs were torn down and intellectuals and party officials were murdered or driven to suicide.
>
> After violence had run its bloody course, the country's rulers conceded it had been a catastrophe that had brought nothing but "grave disorder, damage and retrogression".

The human horrors of the Cultural Revolution are themselves put into the shade by even larger suffering in China during the "Great Leap Forward" that preceded it. It is estimated that forty five million Chinese succumbed in the upheavals and the subsequent famine.[397]. Historian Frank Dikötter from the University of Hong Kong notes the following in the preface of his 2010 book *Mao's Great Famine*[398]:

> Between 1958 and 1962, China descended into hell. Mao Zedong, Chairman of the Chinese Communist Party, threw his country into a frenzy with the Great Leap Forward, an attempt to catch up to and overtake... [the West] in less than 15 years By unleashing China's greatest asset, a labour force that was numbered in the hundreds of millions, Mao thought that he could catapult his country past his competitors.
>
> Instead of following the Soviet model of development, which leaned heavily towards industry alone, China would 'walk on two legs': the peasant masses were mobilised to transform both agriculture and industry at the same time, converting a backward economy into a modern communist society of plenty for all. In pursuit of a utopian paradise, everything was collectivised, as villagers were herded together in giant communes which heralded the advent of communism.
>
> People in the countryside were robbed of their work, their homes, their land, their belongings, and their livelihood. Food, distributed by the spoonful in collective canteens according to merit, became a weapon to

force people to follow the party's every dictate. Irrigation campaigns forced up to half the villagers to work for weeks on end on giant water-conservancy projects, often far from home, without adequate food and rest. The experiment ended in the greatest catastrophe the country had ever known... at least 45 million people died unnecessarily...

The full magnitude of the disaster of the Great Leap Forward was deliberately hidden for many years afterwards. Only with the relatively recent opening of party records within China have many details become apparent. Dikötter comments:

Thanks to the often meticulous reports compiled by the party itself, we can infer that between 1958 and 1962 by a rough approximation 6 to 8 percent of the victims were tortured to death or summarily killed – amounting to at least 2.5 million people. Other victims were deliberately deprived of food or starved to death. Many more vanished because they were too old, sick or weak to work – and hence unable to earn their keep. People were killed selectively because they were rich, because they dragged their feet, because they spoke out, or simply because they were not liked, for whatever reason, by the man who wielded the ladle in the canteen.

Two individual examples recounted by Dikötter give an idea of the horror experienced[399]:

When a boy stole a handful of grain in a Hunan village, local boss Xiong Dechang forced his father to bury him alive. The father died of grief a few days later.

The case of Wang Ziyou was reported to the central leadership: one of his ears was chopped off, his legs were tied with iron wire, a ten kilogram stone was dropped on his back and then he was branded with a sizzling tool – punishment for digging up a potato.

The damage inflicted on China by this "Great Leap Forward" extended beyond bodily mutilation and the loss of life. Dikötter chronicles evidence of adverse impact on infrastructure and on nature:

Up to a third of all housing was turned to rubble and the land savaged in the maniacal pursuit of steel and other industrial accomplishments.

Dikötter concludes that these four years saw:

The greatest demolition of real estate – and catastrophe for the natural environment – in human history

Year Zero

A healthy open society depends on elements – journalists and other researchers – that determinedly seek out evidence of the actual impact of government policies. It does not rely simply on official accounts.

Mao's China was far from being an open society. As a result, it was possible for many observers to put onto a false pedestal Mao's model for the dual transformation of society and individuals, and to conclude, incorrectly, that model should be applied in their own country.

One such observer was the Cambodian, Pol Pot. The havoc he was to inflict on his country exceeded, in proportion terms, that even of Mao. Once again, the havoc had its roots in a flawed idealistic vision of human transformation.

Pol Pot grew up in a farming family in Kompong Thom in central Cambodia, before winning a scholarship to study radio electronics in Paris in 1949. While overseas, he made little progress with his formal studies – he failed his exams three years in a row – but he developed an increasing fascination with Marxism. He returned to Cambodia in 1953 and was soon active in the underground communist movement. By 1965, as the general secretary of what would later become known as the Khmer Rouge, he travelled secretly to Beijing, apparently hiking through jungles to evade detection[400]. Over three months, Pol Pot met most of the Chinese leadership, courting support for his party's activities. He absorbed yet more Maoist ideology in another extended visit to China in 1968. By the time the Khmer Rouge had seized power in Cambodia, they proudly referred[401] to the "fierce gains" that "have been achieved because of 'The Super Great Leap Forward'" – the adjective 'Super' implying they had copied yet outdone Mao's accomplishments with his "Great Leap Forward".

One outcome of the "Super Great Leap Forward" was that nearly two million Cambodians died between 1975 and 1979 – representing around one quarter of the population of that country.

Journalist Dan Fletcher provides insight into the vision that motivated Pol Pot[402]:

> During the Khmer Rouge's nascent days, the movement's leader, Pol Pot, had grown to admire the way the tribes on the outskirts of Cambodia's jungles lived, free of Buddhism, money or education, and now he wanted to foist the same philosophy on the entire nation. Pol Pot envisioned a

Cambodia absent of any social institutions like banks or religions or any modern technology. He sought to triple agricultural production in a year, absent the manpower or means necessary. On a visit to China in 1975, two Khmer Rouge members bragged they would "be the first nation to create a completely Communist society without wasting time on intermediate steps".

It was deadly arrogance. With the cities emptied and the population under Khmer Rouge control, Pol Pot's means of implementation was to begin exterminating anyone who didn't fit this new ideal. He declared that he was turning Cambodia – now renamed the Democratic Republic of Kampuchea – back to "Year Zero," and intellectuals, businessmen, Buddhists and foreigners were all purged. "What is rotten must be removed," read a popular Khmer Rouge slogan at the time, and remove they did, often by execution but sometimes simply by working people to death in the fields.

In November of 2017, I took the opportunity to visit the notorious Tuol Sleng "S-21" prison in Phnom Penh, where it is estimated that 12,000 inmates died between 1975 and 1979. Only 15 of the prisoners survived their incarceration. Two of them still visit the prison every day, talking to shocked tourists about their ordeals. Their stories are heart-breaking[403].

Preserved as a stark reminder, a sign remains in place in the prison courtyard, giving instructions to the inmates in three languages – Cambodian, French, and English – about how they should respect prison officials:

1. You must answer accordingly to my questions – don't turn them away.
2. Don't try to hide the facts by making pretexts this and that. You are strictly prohibited to contest me.
3. Don't be fool for you are a chap who dare to thwart the revolution.
4. You must answer immediately my questions without wasting time to reflect.
5. Don't tell me either about your immoralities or the essence of the revolution.
6. While getting lashes or electrocution you must not cry at all.
7. Do nothing, sit still and wait for my orders. If there is no order, keep quiet. When I ask you to do something, you must do it right away without protesting.

8. Don't make pretext... [by talking about alleged divisions within the Khmer Rouge] in order to hide your secret or traitor.

9. If you don't follow all the above rules, you shall get many lashes of electric wire.

10. If you disobey any point of my regulations you shall get either ten lashes or five shocks of electric discharge.

Many of the actual deaths took place at so-called "killing fields" outside of the cities. Today, memorials have been erected at some of these locations, containing vast collections of human skulls. Behind panes of glass, colour-coded annotations indicate abrasions on the skulls that suggest the particular manner in which their unfortunate owners were bludgeoned. To save money, the Khmer Rouge guards avoided the use of bullets. Instead, they wielded agricultural implements as deadly weapons.

Anyone who wore glasses, or who understood French or English, was viewed with great suspicion by the Khmer Rouge and was liable to summary execution. These were signs of being educated and, therefore, independent-minded. Similarly, Cambodians with knowledge of western medicine did their best to hide this fact, even if this meant that their family members would die from ailments they could have cured.

One example is Dr. Haing Ngor, who trained as a surgeon and gynaecologist before the Khmer Rouge came to power. Ngor and his wife Houy were among millions of others who were forcibly relocated from Phnom Penh into a concentration camp where inmates laboured long hours in rice fields. Ngor managed to survive the ordeal, but his wife died at the camp during childbirth complications in 1975. After the demise of the regime, Ngor emigrated to the USA, and gained renown as the co-starring actor in the 1984 film "The Killing Fields"[404]. But to compound his earlier tragic experiences, Ngor was the victim of a street robbery gone wrong in 1996 outside his Los Angeles residence. He handed over money to his assailants but held on tightly to a gold locket containing a treasured picture of his deceased wife. In the ensuing struggle, Ngor was fatally injured. As reported by court journalist Kenneth Ofgang, the couple's niece presented evidence at the subsequent murder trial[405]:

> Houy Ngor died in childbirth in 1975 while she and her husband were in forced labour in the rice fields. Their niece... explained that while Ngor was a gynaecologist, he did not attempt to deliver the child himself for fear that the entire family would be massacred if the ruling Khmer Rouge – a

peasant-based Communist movement that was responsible for perhaps two million deaths and despised city-dwellers, educated people, and western influences, including western medicine – realized that he was a doctor.

There was no space for western medicine in the Cambodian Year Zero rebirth project.

The children of "enemies of the people" were themselves regarded as "enemies of the people" – since they might grow up with a desire to exact vengeance on their parents' killers. The commandant of the S-21 prison confirmed this assessment in evidence he gave at his own trial at a genocide tribunal in 2009. As reported by journalist Andrew Buncombe[406]:

> The former head of a prison run by the Khmer Rouge has confessed to one of the darkest crimes committed during the regime's brutal rule – smashing the skulls of babies and children against the trunks of trees.
>
> In testimony before a genocide tribunal in Cambodia, Kaing Guek Eav, better known as Duch, said that the children were executed to prevent them seeking revenge. Always watchful to save bullets, executioners would hold the youngsters by their legs or feet and smash their heads against tree trunks located in now notorious "killing fields" on the edge of Phnom Penh.
>
> "I am criminally responsible for killing babies, young children and teenagers," said Duch, referring to photographs he was shown of how the children were killed...
>
> On a court-ordered visit to the killing fields, Duch fell to his knees and wept, first as he passed the tree where the children were killed and again when he stopped at a stupa in which are held the remains of around 80,000 skulls, all of them victims of the regime.

Utopia and Extropia

Do utopian experiments always turn out bad? What is the right conclusion to draw from the dreadful examples of the Khmer Rouge in Cambodia, Maoist experimentation in China, and the Bolshevik revolution in the Soviet Union? And for that matter, what about:

- The Nazi drive towards a "pure" Aryan race – including control over human reproduction
- The theocratic Taliban regime in Afghanistan, with its belief in rigid adoption of sharia law

- The revolutionary "socialism for the 21st century" vision of Hugo Chávez in Venezuela
- The fanatical "juche" self-reliance philosophy of the autocratic Kim dynasty in North Korea?

It would be lazy to conclude that, because a number of idealistic initiatives to improve society and humanity have gone horribly wrong, therefore *all* such initiatives will go horribly wrong.

Here is a better set of conclusions:

- Idealistic initiatives to improve society and humanity involve large risks, and need to be approached with correspondingly large amounts of caution

- To reduce the risks from future initiatives going wrong, society needs to study in considerable detail the actual history of previous transformational initiatives – digging far deeper than the content of the brief sketches given earlier in this chapter, for fuller insight

- A major drawback of all the initiatives covered so far was their opposition to openness: the regimes imposed limits on objective research and debate, treating official party rhetoric as sacrosanct

- Another core issue with all these initiatives is that their analysis of the human condition was flawed; they had a wrong (or incomplete) diagnosis of the causes of inhuman behaviour, and, therefore, a wrong (or incomplete) prescription of how to fix matters.

To expand the last of these points, note how the various initiatives assessed complex social forces in grossly one-sided ways. They highlighted drawbacks of a market economy, as well as the difficulties of controlling a society in which there are many independent schools of thought, without also recognising the many benefits of free markets and free thinking. And they over-estimated the extent to which changing the environment would, by itself, change human character.

Just because a number of social reform initiatives were based on assumptions that turned out to be wrong, it does not follow that all subsequent initiatives will likewise fail. That would be like concluding, at the start of the twentieth century, that since all attempts at powered human flight had failed up to that time – and many lives had been lost in the process – powered flight would therefore forever remain beyond human capability. Instead, what was lacking, before the breakthrough success of the Wright brothers, was a sufficient understanding of the science of aerodynamics, new ideas on how to balance and steer an airplane once it was airborne, and improvements in the design of the airplane itself and its engine. Once the preconditions had been assembled, progress with powered flight came remarkably quickly[407].

The Wright brothers built upon the earlier work of ballooning pioneers such as the Montgolfier brothers and gliding pioneers like Otto Lilienthal. In the same way, the forthcoming technoprogressive transformation of society and politics can draw inspiration from earlier progressive politicians, who achieved in various ways social transformations that in turn enabled wider human flourishing. Citizens of all ages grew healthier and smarter as a result of legal reforms addressing universal education, pensions, access to healthcare, food hygiene, drug safety, environmental protection, advertising standards, maternity relief, discrimination on account of race, gender, or age, curtailment of the power of cartels and monopolies, and much more. In each case, these social initiatives freed individuals from some of the hazards of ordinary living, and gave them the means to attain richer levels of human experience.

Transhumanists maintain that these past examples could be radically surpassed, in the next few decades, by initiatives that will free individuals more comprehensively from the hazards of life, and enable yet richer states of consciousness and wellbeing. This may sound like a utopian vision, but transhumanists prefer a different adjective, "extropian".

The term "extropian" first featured in the magazine "Extropy: Vaccination for Future Shock" launched by philosophers Tom Morrow and Max More in August 1988[408]. Before discussing "extropian", let's consider the root term "extropy". "Extropy" is itself positioned as a metaphorical opposite of entropy, which is a scientific measurement of the degree of disorder of a system. The celebrated Second Law of Thermodynamics states that the entropy of an isolated system never decreases over time. This gives mathematical expression to the observed general trend of matter and energy towards chaos and disorder.

For systems that are *not* isolated – where interchange of energy and matter can take place with the wider environment – it *is* possible for entropy to decrease. Living entities are an important example, with we humans having particular ability to remake our environment. Hence the term extropy, signifying "the extent of a system's intelligence, information, order, vitality, and capacity for improvement"[409].

Under the primary authorship of Max More, the statement of Extropian Principles evolved over the years, culminating in 2003 in version 3.11. This version lists seven principles[410]:

1. **Perpetual Progress**: Extropy means seeking more intelligence, wisdom, and effectiveness, an open-ended lifespan, and the removal of political, cultural, biological, and psychological limits to continuing development. Perpetually overcoming constraints on our progress and possibilities as individuals, as organizations, and as a species. Growing in healthy directions without bound.

2. **Self-Transformation**: Extropy means affirming continual ethical, intellectual, and physical self-improvement, through critical and creative thinking, perpetual learning, personal responsibility, proactivity, and experimentation. Using technology – in the widest sense to seek physiological and neurological augmentation along with emotional and psychological refinement.

3. **Practical Optimism**: Extropy means fuelling action with positive expectations – individuals and organizations being tirelessly proactive. Adopting a rational, action-based optimism or "proaction", in place of both blind faith and stagnant pessimism.

4. **Intelligent Technology**: Extropy means designing and managing technologies not as ends in themselves but as effective means for improving life. Applying science and technology creatively and courageously to transcend "natural" but harmful, confining qualities derived from our biological heritage, culture, and environment.

5. **Open Society – information and democracy**: Extropy means supporting social orders that foster freedom of communication, freedom of action, experimentation, innovation, questioning, and learning. Opposing authoritarian social control and unnecessary hierarchy and favouring the rule of law and decentralization of power and responsibility. Preferring bargaining over battling, exchange over extortion, and communication over compulsion. Openness to improvement rather than a static utopia. Extropia ("ever-receding stretch goals for society") over utopia ("no place").

6. **Self-Direction**: Extropy means valuing independent thinking, individual freedom, personal responsibility, self-direction, self-respect, and a parallel respect for others.

7. **Rational Thinking**: Extropy means favouring reason over blind faith and questioning over dogma. It means understanding, experimenting, learning, challenging, and innovating rather than clinging to beliefs.

As well as the lexical contrast to entropy, the distinction between "extropia" and "utopia" was also deliberate. The extended description of the extropian principle of "Open Society" makes this clear:

> Open societies avoid utopian plans for "the perfect society", instead appreciating the diversity in values, lifestyle preferences, and approaches to solving problems. In place of the static perfection of a utopia, we might imagine a dynamic "extropia" – an open, evolving framework allowing individuals and voluntary groupings to form the institutions and social forms they prefer. Even where we find some of those choices mistaken or foolish, open societies affirm the value of a system that allows all ideas to be tried with the consent of those involved.

> Extropic thinking conflicts with the technocratic idea of coercive central control by insular, self-proclaimed experts. No group of experts can understand and control the endless complexity of an economy and society composed of other individuals like themselves. Unlike utopians of all stripes, extropic individuals and institutions do not seek to control the details of people's lives or the forms and functions of institutions according to a grand over-arching plan.

> Since we all live in society, we are deeply concerned with its improvement. But that improvement must respect the individual. Social engineering should be piecemeal as we enhance institutions one by one on a voluntary basis, not through a centrally planned coercive implementation of a single vision. We are right to seek to continually improve social institutions and economic mechanisms. Yet we must recognize the difficulties in improving complex systems. We need to be radical in intent but cautious in approach, being aware that alterations to complex systems bring unintended consequences. Simultaneous experimentation with numerous possible solutions and improvements – social parallel processing – works better than utopian centrally administered technocracy.

Returning to the topic of "from Utopia to Extropia" in the course of a 2009 essay, More sought to correct a number of popular misunderstandings about transhumanism. In each case, the correction sees transhumanism as being less utopian than various critics suppose[411]:

- Transhumanism is about continual improvement, not perfection or paradise.

- Transhumanism is about improving nature's mindless "design", not guaranteeing perfect technological solutions.

- Transhumanism is about morphological freedom, not mechanizing the body.

- Transhumanism is about trying to shape fundamentally better futures, not predicting specific futures.

- Transhumanism is about critical rationalism, not omniscient reason.

Pragmatically envisioning better humans

The technoprogressive transformation of society and human nature that I envision will build upon the important insights of the extropian principles. It also builds upon the product management insight that it's more important to analyse the intended outcome of a transformation than to become over-enthused by potential means to carry out that transformation. That is, the specification must come first, and then the implementation. Otherwise the implementation might develop inertia of its own. In that case, we'll get technology for technology's sake – answers looking for questions, rather than the other way round.

Accordingly, let's now take a moment to explore features of the human character that there's a strong case to seek to improve. Then we can move on to consider potential ways to carry out such improvements.

The character features I'm aiming to list are those which, if they are not tamed, threaten to combine in devastating ways with the greater powers that technology as a whole is putting in our hands. These features include:

- *Dysfunctional emotions*: we are prone to being dominated by emotional spasms – of anger, self-righteousness, possessiveness, anxiety, despair, etc – to the extent that we are often unable to act on our better judgements

- *Overconfidence*: we tend to assess ourselves as having above-average abilities; we also often assume that our core beliefs are more likely to be true than an objective evaluation would suggest

- *Confirmation bias*: we divert our attention from information that would challenge or negate our own pet theories or the commonly accepted paradigms of our culture; we clutch at any convenient justification for ignoring or distorting such information

- *Abuse of power*: we are too ready to exploit the power we temporarily hold, for example in personal relationships with subordinates or colleagues, and in the process damage other people – and often our own longer-term interests too

- *In-group preference*: we are liable to prejudice in favour of people who seem "like us" (by whatever criteria), and against people who appear to fall outside our group; this drives unnecessary conflict, and can also mean we miss the best opportunities

- *Over-attachment*: we cling onto things that might conceivably be useful to us at some time in the future, even if these attachments reduce our room for manoeuvre or damage our openness to new experiences

- *Herd mentality*: we too readily fall into line with what we perceive our peers are thinking or doing, even though our conscience is telling us that a different path would be better

- *Loss of perspective*: we fail to pay attention to matters that should be of long-term importance to us, and instead become dominated by grudges, personal vindictiveness, fads, and other distractions.

Many of these characteristics are likely to have bestowed some evolutionary advantage to our ancestors, in the very different circumstances in which they lived. They are far less useful in today's world, with its vastly increased complexity and connectivity, where individual mistakes can be magnified onto a global scale.

Other characteristics on the list probably never had much direct utility, but they existed as side-effects of yet other character traits that were themselves useful. Evolution was constrained in terms of the character sets it could create; it lacked complete flexibility. However, we humans possess a much greater range of engineering tools. That opens the way for the conscious, thoughtful re-design of our character set.

Some critics of transhumanism respond that they prefer to keep human nature as it is, thank you very much, with all our quirks and foibles. These features are said to enable creativity, fun, imagination diversity, and so on. My response is to point again to the character flaws listed earlier. These are *not* "quirks" or "foibles". Nor can they be described as "allowable weaknesses". They are *dangerous* weaknesses. And as such, they deserve serious attention from us. Can we find ways to dial down these character flaws, without (at the same time) inducing adverse side-effects?

Transhumanists are by no means the first set of thinkers to desire these changes in human nature. Philosophers, religious teachers, and other leaders of society have long called for humans to overcome the pull of "attachment" (desire), self-centredness, indiscipline, "the seven deadly sins" (pride, greed, lust, envy, gluttony, wrath, and sloth), and so on. Where transhumanism goes beyond these previous thinkers is in highlighting new methods that can now be used, or will shortly become available, to assist in the improvement of character.

Collectively these methods can be called "cognotech". They will boost our all-round intelligence: emotional, rational, creative, social, spiritual, and more. Here are some examples:

- New pharmacological compounds – sometimes called "smart drugs"

- Gentle stimulation of the brain by a variety of electromagnetic methods – something that has been trialled by the US military[412]

- Alteration of human biology more fundamentally, by interventions at the genetic, epigenetic, or microbiome level

- Vivid experiences within multi-sensory virtual reality worlds that bring home to people the likely consequences of their current personal trajectories (from both first-person and third-person points of view), and allow them to rehearse changes in attitude

- The use of "intelligent assistance" software that monitors our actions and offers us advice in a timely manner, similar to the way that a good personal friend will occasionally volunteer wise counsel; intelligent assistants can also strengthen our positive characteristics by wise selection of background music, visual imagery, and "thought for the day" aphorisms to hold in mind.

Technological progress can also improve the effectiveness of various traditional methods for character improvement:

- The reasons why meditation, yoga, and hypnosis can have beneficial results are now more fully understood than before, enabling major improvements in the efficacy of these practices

- Education of all sorts can be enhanced by technology such as interactive online video courses that adapt their content to the emerging needs of each different user

- Prompted by alerts generated by online intelligent assistants, real-world friends can connect at critical moments in someone's life, in order to provide much-needed personal support

- Information analytics can resolve some of the long-running debates about which diets – and which exercise regimes – are the ones that will best promote all-round health for given individuals.

The case for being open to the merits of a variety of interventions to improve human character is made in a 2012 article in Philosophy Now by professors Julian Savulescu (Oxford) and Ingmar Persson (Gothenburg)[413]:

> For the vast majority of our 150,000 years or so on the planet, we lived in small, close-knit groups, working hard with primitive tools to scratch sufficient food and shelter from the land. Sometimes we competed with other small groups for limited resources. Thanks to evolution, we are supremely well adapted to that world, not only physically, but psychologically, socially and through our moral dispositions.
>
> But this is no longer the world in which we live. The rapid advances of science and technology have radically altered our circumstances over just a few centuries. The population has increased a thousand times since the agricultural revolution eight thousand years ago. Human societies consist of millions of people. Where our ancestors' tools shaped the few acres on which they lived, the technologies we use today have effects across the world, and across time, with the hangovers of climate change and nuclear disaster stretching far into the future. The pace of scientific change is exponential. But has our moral psychology kept up?
>
> With great power comes great responsibility. However, evolutionary pressures have not developed for us a psychology that enables us to cope with the moral problems our new power creates. Our political and economic systems only exacerbate this.

Savulescu and Persson go on to highlight grave risks to humanity posed by international war and climate change. Our current psychology, they argue, is far from adequate to the collective challenges we now face. They make the following recommendations:

> Our moral shortcomings are preventing our political institutions from acting effectively. Enhancing our moral motivation would enable us to act

better for distant people, future generations, and non-human animals. One method to achieve this enhancement is already practised in all societies: moral education. Al Gore, Friends of the Earth and Oxfam have already had success with campaigns vividly representing the problems our selfish actions are creating for others – others around the world and in the future.

But there is another possibility emerging. Our knowledge of human biology – in particular of genetics and neurobiology – is beginning to enable us to directly affect the biological or physiological bases of human motivation, either through drugs, or through genetic selection or engineering, or by using external devices that affect the brain or the learning process. We could use these techniques to overcome the moral and psychological shortcomings that imperil the human species.

We are at the early stages of such research, but there are few cogent philosophical or moral objections to the use of specifically *biomedical* moral enhancement – or *moral bioenhancement*. In fact, the risks we face are so serious that it is imperative we explore every possibility of developing moral bioenhancement technologies – not to replace traditional moral education, but to complement it. We simply can't afford to miss opportunities.

Once again, it's worth stressing some key differences between this kind of transhumanist initiative, on the one hand, and the idealist political campaigns of Stalin, Hitler, Mao, Pol Pot and others covered earlier in this chapter. The transhumanist initiative is committed to:

- Open review, so that problems arising can be noticed and addressed promptly

- An experimental approach, to discover what actually works in reality, rather than just sounding good in theory

- An agile framework, in which feedback is sought on a regular basis, so that knowledge can accumulate quickly via a "fail fast" process

- Easy access by all members of society to the set of ideas that are under discussion, in order to promote a wider appreciation of any emerging risks or opportunities

- Giving priority to data, rather than to anecdote, supposition, or ideology

- Embracing diversity as far as possible, with hard constraints being imposed only when matters are seen to be particularly central

- Integrating viewpoints from many different perspectives, rather than insisting on there being only "one true way" forwards.

The technoprogressive feedback cycle

One criticism of the initiative I've just outlined is that it puts matters the wrong way round.

I've been describing how individuals can, with the aid of technology as well as traditional methods, raise themselves above their latent character flaws, and can therefore make better contributions to the political process (either as voters or as actual politicians). In other words, we'll get better politics as a result of getting better people.

However, an opposing narrative runs as follows. So long as our society is full of emotional landmines, it's a lot to expect people to become more emotionally competent. So long as we live in a state of apparent siege, immersed in psychological conflict, it's a big ask for people to give each other the benefit of the doubt, in order to develop new bonds of trust. Where people are experiencing growing inequality, a deepening sense of alienation, a constant barrage of adverts promoting consumerism, and an increasing foreboding about an array of risks to their wellbeing, it's not reasonable to urge them to make the personal effort to become more compassionate, thoughtful, tolerant, and open-minded. They're more likely to become angry, reactive, intolerant, and closed-minded. Who can blame them? Therefore – so runs this line of reasoning – it's more important to improve the social environment than to urge the victims of that social environment to learn to turn the other cheek. Let's stop obsessing about personal ethics and individual discipline, and instead put every priority on reducing the inequality, alienation, consumerist propaganda, and risk perception that people are experiencing. Instead of fixating upon possibilities for technology to rewire people's biology and psychology, let's hurry up and provide a better social safety net, a fairer set of work opportunities, and a deeper sense that "we're all in this together".

I answer this criticism by denying that it's a one-way causation. We shouldn't pick just a single route of influence – either that better individuals will result in a better society, or that a better society will enable the emergence of better individuals. On the contrary, there's a two way flow of influence.

Yes, there's such a thing as psychological brutalisation. In a bad environment, the veneer of civilisation can quickly peel away. Youngsters who would, in more peaceful circumstances, instinctively help elderly strangers to cross the road, can quickly degrade in times of strife into obnoxious, self-obsessed bigots. But that path doesn't apply to everyone. Others in the same situation take the initiative to maintain a cheery, contemplative, constructive outlook. Environment influences the development of character, but doesn't determine it.

Accordingly, I foresee a positive feedback cycle:

- With the aid of technological assistance, more people – whatever their circumstances – will be able to strengthen the latent "angelic" parts of their human nature, and to hold in check the latent "diabolic" aspects

- As a result, at least some citizens will be able to take wiser policy decisions, enabling an improvement in the social and psychological environment

- The improved environment will, in turn, make it easier for other positive personal transformations to occur – involving a larger number of people, and having a greater impact.

One additional point deserves to be stressed. The environment that influences our behaviour involves not just economic relationships and the landscape of interpersonal connections, but also the set of ideas that fill our minds. To the extent that these ideas give us hope, we can find extra strength to resist the siren pull of our diabolic nature. These ideas can help us focus our attention on positive, life-enhancing activities, rather than letting our minds shrink and our characters deteriorate.

This indicates another contribution of transhumanism to building a comprehensively better future. By painting a clear, compelling image of sustainable abundance, credibly achievable in just a few decades, transhumanism can spark revolutions inside the human heart.

In this sense, transhumanism has *some* similarities to religion. Transhumanism can provide a vivid common purpose that transcends the concerns of everyday living. It can generate a profound sense of meaning and purpose in people's lives, spurring them to remarkable effort.

Indeed, transhumanism holds out the prospect of realising goals that were, formerly, hallmarks of religious thinking:

- Omniscience – or, at least, radically increased knowledge

- Omnipotence – or, at least, the capture and redeployment of enough energy from the sun to meet all human needs

- The creation of life – via the capabilities of synthetic biology

- Personal rebirth – via the enhancement technologies listed earlier

- Immortality – or, at least, the prospect of indefinite youthfulness[414]

- Resurrection – via the future reanimation of people placed at the point of their legal death into ultralow-temperature cryonic suspension[415], and perhaps even via eventual reconstitution by future technology of the minds of people whose bodies have long since disintegrated[416].

The comparison between transhumanism and religion alarms some critics. These critics assert that transhumanists demonstrate not only the positive characteristics of religion but also its negative aspects. Specifically, they suggest that[417]:

- An alluring sense of purpose may cause transhumanists to leave careful rationality behind

- A sense of "worship" may develop, of core texts or semi-messianic individuals (it is sometimes implied that transhumanists treat the pronouncements of futurist Ray Kurzweil with uncritical awe[418])

- Transhumanism distracts adherents with a naïve "pie in the sky" vision, whereas there are many more practical steps that ought to be taken to provide real-world solutions for pressing social issues.

I see these criticisms as unfair. I don't deny that *some* people embrace transhumanist ideas uncritically. They let their optimism run ahead of their rationality. They become over-excited. But every philosophy has its share of uncritical adherents. That fact, by itself, is no reason to reject any philosophy. Indeed, the mainstream of transhumanism has a rich self-awareness of the potential dangers of over-enthusiastic adoption of accelerating technology. To see that, let's now turn to the nearest thing that transhumanism has to a canonical text.

The Transhumanist Declaration

The Transhumanist Declaration was the fruit of an open collaborative process. The first published version dates from July 1998[419]. That version names twenty four people as having contributed to the document. The twenty four include:

- The publishers of the Extropy magazine – Max More and Tom Morrow

- The co-founders of the World Transhumanist Association – Nick Bostrom and David Pearce

- Natasha Vita-More, who had authored a "Transhumanist Art Statement" as early as January 1982[420].

Revised versions of the Declaration were agreed and published by the World Transhumanist Association in 2002 and in 2009[421]. The 2009 version contains eight clauses. No fewer than four of these clauses address the topic of risks arising from new technologies.

The first two clauses of the Declaration outline a vision of the scale of potential changes ahead:

(1) Humanity stands to be profoundly affected by science and technology in the future. We envision the possibility of broadening human potential by overcoming aging, cognitive shortcomings, involuntary suffering, and our confinement to planet Earth.

(2) We believe that humanity's potential is still mostly unrealized. There are possible scenarios that lead to wonderful and exceedingly worthwhile enhanced human conditions.

The Declaration then introduces the topic of "serious risks, especially from the misuse of new technologies":

(3) We recognize that humanity faces serious risks, especially from the misuse of new technologies. There are possible realistic scenarios that lead to the loss of most, or even all, of what we hold valuable. Some of these scenarios are drastic, others are subtle. Although all progress is change, not all change is progress.

Next, the Declaration makes a series of proposals for how to address both the risks and the opportunities arising:

(4) Research effort needs to be invested into understanding these prospects. We need to carefully deliberate how best to reduce risks and expedite beneficial applications. We also need forums where people can

constructively discuss what should be done, and a social order where responsible decisions can be implemented.

(5) Reduction of existential risks, and development of means for the preservation of life and health, the alleviation of grave suffering, and the improvement of human foresight and wisdom should be pursued as urgent priorities, and heavily funded.

The Declaration is clear that the identification of the best outcomes involves much more than simply a focus on technological possibility:

(6) Policy making ought to be guided by responsible and inclusive moral vision, taking seriously both opportunities and risks, respecting autonomy and individual rights, and showing solidarity with and concern for the interests and dignity of all people around the globe. We must also consider our moral responsibilities towards generations that will exist in the future.

The Declaration goes on to discuss implications for sentient beings other than humans:

(7) We advocate the well-being of all sentience, including humans, non-human animals, and any future artificial intellects, modified life forms, or other intelligences to which technological and scientific advance may give rise.

Finally, the Declaration emphasises the key value of personal choice:

(8) We favour allowing individuals wide personal choice over how they enable their lives. This includes use of techniques that may be developed to assist memory, concentration, and mental energy; life extension therapies; reproductive choice technologies; cryonics procedures; and many other possible human modification and enhancement technologies.

The principles in the Transhumanist Declaration stand opposed to any blind techno-optimism. There's nothing in these principles about "technology for technology's sake". Rather than technology, the central pivot of the Declaration is humanity. Indeed, the very first word in the document is "Humanity", and humanity features again and again in the various clauses.

Nor does the Declaration set out the future as being somehow inevitable or fore-ordained. In distinction from religions which seek to reassure adherents with prophetic visions of a sure salvation ahead, transhumanism indicates that the future is something very much under the influence of present-day human actions.

Nevertheless, I quite often hear speakers at meetings pour scorn on the concept of transhumanism, alleging that the philosophy is obsessed with technology, efficiency, and certitude. It's my observation that these speakers have painted a straw man target for their own purposes. When I query these speakers about the Extropian Principles or the Transhumanist Declaration, they frequently don't have the first notion of the content of these documents. What these speakers are actually criticising is something different from transhumanism. They're criticising the opinions that are sometimes expressed by technology enthusiasts outside of the transhumanist community itself, or who only have a peripheral foothold in that community.

I don't expect such criticisms to abate any time soon. The straw man transhumanist is such an easy target for lazy writers and speakers that it's no wonder that they like to attack it from time to time. The attack makes them feel virtuous.

What *will* accelerate a change in mind is when transhumanism can point to notable real-world results. The debate about ideas is important, which is why I've written this book – with the aim of conveying to a wider audience a richer description of what transhumanists can hope to accomplish. But the ideas will become more credible when they can be matched by at least some initial demonstrations of people with superhuman characteristics.

Practical transhumanism

One of the most important developments within the overall transhumanist community, in the last few years, has been the growth of workshops and summits dedicated to "biohacking". Biohacker summits with multiple speakers have taken place at Helsinki (on several occasions), London, and Stockholm. As a flavour of the content, here's a listing of the presentation titles from the Stockholm summit of May 2017[422]:

- Better Living Through Science, Technology & Nature
- Upgrade Yourself: Be Smarter, Sharper and Healthier
- Timeless: How I learned to Time Travel [a talk about mindfulness]
- The Current Landscape for Human Augmentation
- Being Transhuman In a Post-Human Age
- Sweet Tooth: How to Overcome Sugar Addiction

- An Introduction to Low Level Laser Therapy in Pain Management
- Hacking Your Biology With Nutrition
- Optimizing Neurotransmitters for Cognitive Health and Performance
- Fasting Routines for Improved Immunity and Optimal Health
- Biohacking Your Genital Area for Longevity and Health
- Biohacking Physical Exercise
- Beauty Technology: Hack Your Body With Cosmetics
- The 6 Keys to Become a Master Learner
- Towards an Upgraded Life

Many of the world's leading companies have become interested in the potential of methods for their employees to become more creative, more resilient, more thoughtful, more collaborative, and more effective. Their interest arises because of the potential to improve the financial results of the company, to generate product innovations more quickly, and to enable employees to experience a greater sense of fulfilment.

For example, Google in 2007 supported the desire of one of their first employees, Chade-Meng Tan, to create an internal training course covering mindfulness, neuroscience, and emotional intelligence. The course deliberately adopted language that resonated with engineers: it talked about humans inspecting and debugging their own brain processes. A book followed in 2012, with a title that played upon Google's dominance of the search industry: *Search Inside Yourself.* The book's subtitle is provocative and spirited: "The unexpected path to achieving success, happiness (and world peace)"[423].

The book's website makes some big claims[424]:

Early Google engineer and personal growth pioneer Chade-Meng Tan first designed *Search Inside Yourself* as a popular course at Google intended to transform the work and lives of the best and brightest behind one of the most innovative, successful, and profitable businesses in the world – and now it can do the same for you. Meng has distilled emotional intelligence into a set of practical and proven tools and skills that anyone can learn and develop.

Created in collaboration with a Zen master, a CEO, a Stanford University scientist, and Daniel Goleman (the guy who literally wrote the book on emotional intelligence), this program is grounded in science and expressed in a way that even a sceptical, compulsively pragmatic, engineering-oriented brain like Meng's can process. Whether your intention is to reduce stress and increase well-being, heighten focus and creativity, become more optimistic and resilient, build fulfilling relationships, or make a profit, the skills provided by *Search Inside Yourself* will prove invaluable for you. This is your guide to enhancing productivity and creativity, finding meaning and fulfilment in your work and life, and experiencing profound peace, compassion, and happiness while doing so.

Search Inside Yourself reveals how to calm your mind on demand and return it to a natural state of happiness, deepen self-awareness in a way that fosters self-confidence, harness empathy and compassion into outstanding leadership, and build highly productive collaborations based on trust and transparent communication. In other words, *Search Inside Yourself* shows you how to grow inner joy while succeeding at your work. Meng writes: "Some people buy books that teach them to be liked, others buy books that teach them to be successful. This book teaches you both. You are so lucky."

Search Inside Yourself is now an independent organisation, and reports that 13,000 people have participated in its courses, with measurable improvements in stress management (avoiding emotional drain), productivity (avoiding distractions), and healthcare costs (on average, participants spent $3,000 per annum less after the course than before it)[425].

A more recent book for which even bigger claims have been made is *Stealing Fire*, co-authored by Steven Kotler and Jamie Wheal[426]. The subtitle of this book indicates what it covers: "How Silicon Valley, the Navy SEALs, and Maverick Scientists Are Revolutionizing the Way We Live and Work". Jason Silva, a filmmaker and public speaker, produced a full-hearted video endorsement of that book. Here are some excerpts from his transcript[427]:

> People talk about happiness. Certainly the self-help section in the book store is full of books telling you how to tap into that happiness, how to be happy, how to "think and grow rich," and so on and so forth, but what I think is ultimately more interesting, my friends, is those states North of happy.

> Jamie Wheal and Steven Kotler are the co-founders of the Flow Genome Project. The Flow Genome Project aims to deconstruct the elusive and mystical flow state.

In the field of positive psychology, a flow state is a state of consciousness in which you feel your best and you perform your best. Think of the athlete in the zone, think of the jazz musician in the pocket, think of the surfer catching that perfect wave.

Silva explains the 'STER' framework that Wheal and Kotler use in their book to analyse the higher states of consciousness characterised by flow:

These states of consciousness, in which you feel your best and you perform your best, are characterized by the acronym STER, which stands for: Selflessness – the self vanishes; Timelessness – your sense of time dilates and dissipates; Effortlessness – the activity just kind of flows magically; and information Richness – there's this feeling of a high-res download of realization and possibility that seems to kind of emerge from the world around you.

These states of consciousness have always been elusive; they're like quasi mystical states of ecstasis, as the Greeks described them. Jamie Wheal and Steven Kotler's new book, *Stealing Fire*, alluding of course to Prometheus who stole fire from the gods, is about the fact that finally for the first time in history, ecstasis is understandable. Ecstasis is reproducible. Flow can be had on tap.

Silva ends his endorsement with an echo of the famous "Ask not" quote from John F Kennedy's 1961 presidential inauguration address:

Ask not what the world needs, ask instead what makes you come alive, because what the world needs, is more people who have come alive. And this book, *Stealing Fire*, is going to bring that to you folks…

Mystical states on tap for everyone. Let's democratize nirvana, let's democratize ecstasis and let's upgrade the world.

It's lyrical language. But do the claims withstand scrutiny?

Online reviewers of the books *Stealing Fire* and *Search Within Yourself* make many criticisms of these volumes. It's said there's too much hype, too much wishful thinking, too much self-congratulation, and insufficient real-world guidance. Evidence is treated selectively. The anecdotes the books include are capable of multiple interpretations. The books, critics suggest, are just extended advertisements for expensive courses.

My advice is to avoid strict black-or-white conclusions. No doubt many of the claims made for individual techniques are exaggerations. Yes, some companies – including the sponsors of the Biohacker summits – are closely monitoring sales figures for their products. They have commercial imperatives to position their products in an attractive light. However, just because an industry contains *some* hype is no reason to dismiss *all* the claims made in that industry. Instead, we need to use our judgement. We need to take the time to collectively explore, with an open mind and a sceptical eye, which products and techniques work in which situations.

From having watched this field for more than a decade, it's my judgement that it's likely to experience a significant transformation in the next few years. Just as practical uses of artificial intelligence have emerged in the last few years from preceding fallow periods, known as "AI winters", I expect we'll shortly see increasingly practical applications of biohacking. First, however, there's one more hurdle that needs to be overcome – the hurdle of over-restrictive legislation.

Legislation impacting transhumanism

One complaint made by reviewers of the book *Stealing Fire* is that several of the recommendations it contains fall foul of local or national laws. The rich, powerful, and resourceful people covered in the book have their own means of acquiring the smart drugs championed by the authors. But many readers aren't in such a position.

For example, readers in search of reliable providers of various smart drugs may come across the website nootropics.com. At first glance, things look encouraging. Here are some answers from the FAQ on the website[428]:

Nootropics are compounds that show evidence of improving the cognitive abilities of healthy individuals…

Nootropics can be used for many different things including: focus, sociability, anti-anxiety, and sleep quality.

We've extensively researched all of our products and have come up with a number of categories to help you find exactly what you're looking for.

The website also explains the company's approach to quality assurance:

Testing, testing, and more testing.

All of our products are tested once after being manufactured, and then undergo a stringent process of quality assurance by our friends at Ceretropic.

No method on its own is absolute, which is why we use multiple methods to make sure that everything we sell is what we say it is, is of the highest purity, and most importantly is safe.

We test for identity, purity, and an array of heavy metals using FTIR and HPLC.

Encapsulation is an important part of the process, and presents an opportunity to give you that extra bit of confidence in us. For this reason our products are encapsulated at an FDA registered and cGMP certified facility that has been in operation for over 25 years.

But the website has some bad news for many potential customers. Here's the answer to the question "What countries do you ship to?"

Due to troubles with customs and a high number of packages being seized, we do not ship to these countries: Afghanistan, Argentina, Austria, Belgium, Brazil, Cuba, Germany, Ireland, Italy, Morocco, Norway, Sweden, Sudan, Syria, UAE, and UK.

And there's an extra reason the company doesn't ship products to the UK:

Due to the recent Psychoactive Substances Bill, unfortunately we cannot ship to the UK.

The bill mentioned came into force throughout the United Kingdom on 26 May 2016[429]. The intent of the bill is good: to reduce the number of deaths or impairments occurring from people using so-called "legal high" drugs. The complication is that there's no clear boundary definition of this category of drugs. It's not possible to create a full list of all such drugs, since people with knowledge of chemistry frequently create new molecules with similar psychoactive impact to previous drugs. For this reason, the 2016 bill takes a blanket approach. The bill:

Makes it an offence to produce, supply, offer to supply, possess with intent to supply, possess on custodial premises, import or export psychoactive substances; that is, any substance intended for human consumption that is capable of producing a psychoactive effect

The bill recognises, however, that this definition is far too broad, since it encompasses many substances that have a long history of legal usage. Accordingly, the bill:

Excludes legitimate substances, such as food, alcohol, tobacco, nicotine, caffeine and medical products from the scope of the offence, as well as controlled drugs, which continue to be regulated by the Misuse of Drugs Act 1971

Yet another exclusion is defined in the very next clause of the bill, which

> Exempts healthcare activities and approved scientific research from the offences under the act on the basis that persons engaged in such activities have a legitimate need to use psychoactive substances in their work.

Despite these exceptions, the bill has received a torrent of criticism that it is too heavy-handed. The government's own Advisory Council on the Misuse of Drugs (ACMD), which is composed of independent experts, made no fewer than eight substantive criticisms of the bill, only some of which were addressed in subsequent changes in its text. Here are some extracts from a letter sent to the government by the Chair of the ACMD, Professor Les Iversen[430]:

> The ACMD… cautions against a blanket ban on all psychoactive substances. It is almost impossible to list all possible desirable exemptions under the Bill. As drafted, the Bill may now include substances that are benign or even helpful to people including evidence-based herbal remedies that are not included on the current exemption list.

> The psychoactivity of a substance cannot be unequivocally proven. The only definitive way of determining psychoactivity is via human experience, which is usually not documented…

> The Bill has the potential to both criminalise and apply disproportionate penalties to many otherwise law abiding young people and adults…

> The Bill would have a substantial impact on the sale of many herbal medicines… Purchasing a benign, possibly evidence-based herbal product from a website outside the UK would appear to attract a seven year prison tariff.

New Scientist writer Clare Wilson summarised the new law as "one of the most unhelpful laws ever passed"[431]:

> It's official – the UK ban on legal highs… is going to be one of the stupidest, most dangerous and unscientific pieces of drugs legislation ever conceived.

> Watching MPs debate the Psychoactive Substances Bill yesterday, it was clear most of them hadn't a clue. They misunderstood medical evidence, mispronounced drug names, and generally floundered as they debated the choices and lifestyles of people who are in most cases decades younger than themselves.

It would have been funny except the decisions made will harm people's lives and liberty.

Wilson went on to draw an analogy with other failed prohibition laws:

The bill is an attempt to clamp down on substances that mimic the effects of drugs like cannabis and ecstasy. It stems from the media hysteria a few years ago over one of the best known ones, mephedrone, or meow meow, which was linked with some deaths. Mephedrone was banned, but new compounds can be made rapidly and other legal highs soon took its place. These can be openly sold on the internet and in "head shops", seedy-looking stores found in most towns and cities.

So "ban everything that gets you high" was the government's reaction – and this bill is the result. The idea of a blanket prohibition is superficially appealing – yet fundamentally flawed. Banning something people enjoy does not mean they will stop doing it. It just means that instead of buying what they want from shops and legal websites, they now need to trade with criminals. Criminals have much less incentive to make sure their products are genuine and unadulterated or to refuse sales to minors.

Prohibition didn't work with alcohol in 1920s America, it hasn't worked with heroin today and it won't work with anything else people get high on either.

Wilson then made a prediction whose accuracy is borne out by the current non-availability of nootropics in the UK from companies like nootropics.com:

A ban on all things psychoactive will also unintentionally snare other generally harmless substances that were never the intended targets. If this bill has highlighted anything, it is the ubiquity of the human desire to tweak brain chemistry in satisfying ways. Special exemptions have already had to be made for caffeine, nicotine, and of course, the world's number one recreational drug of choice: alcohol.

To MPs, sinking a few bottles of good claret with chums at the end of a hard day is perfectly normal and acceptable, and is a world away from the chemical adventures of 20-year-olds. Yet both involve deliberately altering brain chemistry. Both have risks if overdone. You could argue the law's stance all comes down to the history and popularity of your chosen method of drug use.

The Psychoactive Substances Bill exemplifies legal obstacles facing other potential transhumanist enhancements – not just mind enhancements:

- The politicians debating the issue had a very limited understanding of the field – mispronouncing drug names, and (in the words of Clare Wilson) "generally floundering" during the debate

- The politicians gave undue precedence to the status quo – the acceptability of using drugs such as alcohol and tobacco – as opposed to newer drugs that are arguably not only more effective but also safer

- The politicians were overly influenced by "media hysteria" from conservative-leaning press, in which a number of unfortunate individual cases were given especial prominence, without a wider context.

The former Chair of the UK government's ACMD (Advisory Council on the Misuse of Drugs), Professor David Nutt, reports a conversation he has had in similar forms with many MPs, including the Home Secretary at the time, Jacqui Smith. The conversations arose because of a provocative analysis by Nutt giving the factually accurate statistic that horse riding was more dangerous than taking the drug ecstasy. Guardian writer Decca Aitkenhead describes the conversation[432]:

> [Nutt] was, he happily admits, probably naive when he accepted the chair of the ACMD. "I genuinely thought reason would eventually prevail." Within 12 months of his appointment he published a paper that found horse riding to be more dangerous than taking ecstasy – and probably, he suspects, triggered his dismissal nine months later.
>
> "It's funny how the horse riding line really bugged them," he reflects, still looking bemused. "I thought that paper would allow people to engage in a rational debate… But what it did was the opposite: it just riled them, because they cannot think logically about drugs."
>
> He describes a truly surreal exchange with the then home secretary, Jacqui Smith, who told him: "You cannot compare the harms of an illegal activity with a legal one." But don't we need to compare the harms, he asked her, in order to see if something should be illegal? "And there was this long pause. And she said, 'You can't compare the harms of an illegal activity with a legal one.' And this is the problem. Many politicians seem to think that once something is illegal, job done."

Nutt has some even more critical words about a subsequent Home Secretary, Theresa May – who was later to become Prime Minister. George Bowden of the Huffington Post reported in February 2017[433]:

Theresa May's religious beliefs have made her an "extremist" on drugs policy, according to Professor David Nutt.

Nutt, the former government advisor who was sacked in 2009 after describing ecstasy as no more dangerous than horse riding, told *The Huffington Post UK* that May has consistently stifled the debate on drugs in Britain over the last six years.

He alleged that she had "actively excluded evidence and common sense" over drugs policy in her time as Home Secretary between 2010 and 2016 and that, as Prime Minister, things under her premiership could get worse.

"She comes from quite a religious background and she has a religious, what you might call an extremist position, about drugs, except alcohol," Nutt said. "So she has made the situation worse because she has actively excluded evidence and common sense from the Home Office."

One of Theresa May's colleagues in the Cabinet at that time, Nick Clegg (from a different party than May in the coalition government) has put on record that the Home Secretary worked strenuously to doctor the output of a Home Office report into the effectiveness of hard drug laws. The team working on the report found the laws actually had no impact on the level of drug use. This evidence contradicted May's personal philosophy, which led her into "an endless wrangle" to try to suppress some of the findings[434].

George Bowden continues his analysis:

Nutt said there is a wider effort on the part of tabloid newspapers to whip up frenzied "hysteria" to ban drugs that have been used with little harm for decades…

Nutt believes banning a drug is seen as a "badge of honour" by newspaper editors…

"Basically you create false stories, you create false fears, it's been done for the last hundred years," he added. "The public should wake up. This is really the classic example of 'alternative truth'".

Towards enhancement

Underlying much of the legislative opposition to transhumanist technologies, such as smart drugs, is the philosophical viewpoint that claims there's a fundamental distinction between "therapies" and "enhancement":

- Therapies can repair humans to a normal state of health and functioning, and are to be encouraged

- Enhancement would bring humans to levels of health and functioning beyond what is normal, and are to be resisted.

For example, this philosophy would accept the use of specific drugs to treat individual diseases – and, accordingly, to extend the lifespans of people afflicted by these diseases. However, as advocated by two of the speakers at a 2016 Intelligence Squared debate[435], this philosophy would *not* accept the use of these drugs with the *primary* goal to extend human lifespans.

Again, it would be acceptable for a drug like Viagra to address problems of erectile dysfunction, restoring someone's sexual potency to a level experienced earlier in their life. But, in this philosophy, it would be wrong for people to use Viagra to reach superhuman levels of sexual performance.

Here's how the renowned American philosopher Francis Fukuyama expressed his opposition to the transhumanist project of human enhancement[436]:

> For the last several decades, a strange liberation movement has grown within the developed world. Its crusaders aim much higher than civil rights campaigners, feminists, or gay-rights advocates. They want nothing less than to liberate the human race from its biological constraints. As "transhumanists" see it, humans must wrest their biological destiny from evolution's blind process of random variation and adaptation and move to the next stage as a species...

> The human race, after all, is a pretty sorry mess, with our stubborn diseases, physical limitations, and short lives. Throw in humanity's jealousies, violence, and constant anxieties, and the transhumanist project begins to look downright reasonable. If it were technologically possible, why wouldn't we want to transcend our current species?

Having described transhumanism, Fukuyama went on to criticise it as having a "frightful moral cost":

> The seeming reasonableness of the project, particularly when considered in small increments, is part of its danger. Society is unlikely to fall suddenly under the spell of the transhumanist worldview. But it is very possible that we will nibble at biotechnology's tempting offerings without realizing that they come at a frightful moral cost.

> The first victim of transhumanism might be equality. The U.S. Declaration of Independence says that "all men are created equal," and the most

serious political fights in the history of the United States have been over who qualifies as fully human. Women and blacks did not make the cut in 1776 when Thomas Jefferson penned the declaration. Slowly and painfully, advanced societies have realized that simply being human entitles a person to political and legal equality. In effect, we have drawn a red line around the human being and said that it is sacrosanct.

Underlying this idea of the equality of rights is the belief that we all possess a human essence that dwarfs manifest differences in skin colour, beauty, and even intelligence. This essence, and the view that individuals therefore have inherent value, is at the heart of political liberalism. But modifying that essence is the core of the transhumanist project. If we start transforming ourselves into something superior, what rights will these enhanced creatures claim, and what rights will they possess when compared to those left behind? If some move ahead, can anyone afford not to follow? These questions are troubling enough within rich, developed societies. Add in the implications for citizens of the world's poorest countries – for whom biotechnology's marvels likely will be out of reach – and the threat to the idea of equality becomes even more menacing.

Fukuyama's criticisms need to be taken seriously. Indeed, the greater the degree of enhancement that is adopted by some humans, the bigger the differential in capability will result. Unmodified humans will increasingly be unable to compete. Those humans who wish to exercise their fundamental right not to become enhanced may, therefore, increasingly see enhanced humans as threats.

But this, by itself, is no reason to oppose the transhumanist initiative. A similar complaint could have been levied at any past initiative that enabled people to reach to higher levels of performance:

- Teaching literacy – enabling people to read and write (and therefore putting the illiterate at an increasing disadvantage)

- Providing better diet and exercise (putting at a disadvantage those people who choose an unhealthy diet or exercise regime)

- Distribution of reliable means of contraception, allowing women to make their own choices about the timing of pregnancies and, therefore, the interruption of their careers

- Adoption of railways, interstate highways, broadband, and so on, benefiting those willing to embrace new technology more than the innately conservative among us.

It is the clear goal of transhumanism to make "biotechnology's marvels" (in Fukuyama's wording) – and all other technologies of enhancement – available to anyone who wishes to access them. Rather than equality at a reduced level, in which enhancement therapies are banned, transhumanism envisions an equality of opportunity at a higher level.

Any proposed hard boundary line between "therapy" and "enhancement" moves over time. What one generation regards as an enhancement is viewed by a later generation as a given. New forms of clothing, new forms of transport, new aides to memory, and so on, were all novel at a time – and opposed as such. The celebrated Socrates, who is usually seen as far-sighted, is an example of opposition to a new practice, namely literacy. He decried the need for people to learn to read and write. As described by Betsy McKenzie from Suffolk University, Boston[437]:

> [Socrates] worried that reliance on writing would erode memory (it has!), but also, and maybe more importantly, that reading would mislead students to think that they had knowledge, when they only had data.

To fully answer the objections of Fukuyama and others against the transhumanist project, it will be necessary to demonstrate that three robust mechanisms are in place. The mechanisms are answers to three legitimate concerns:

1. The concern that transhumanists underestimate the dangers of tampering with human nature, and will allow a fascination with technological possibilities to cloud their judgements

2. The concern that transhumanist technology will only be available to elite or wealthy members of society, leading to an increase in inequality and, potentially, a "transhumanism for the 1%"

3. The concern that transhumanism will force people into adopting new lifestyles and practices against their will, in order not to be ejected into some kind of backwater wilderness.

If you have made it to this late stage of my book, my responses to these three concerns will not surprise you. The mechanisms we need to advocate and advance, in response to these concerns, are:

1. *Enhanced foresight*, in which the risks and opportunities from new technologies are considered and debated in ways that are more rational, more agile, and more inclusive than at present

2. *Enhanced democracy*, in which all members of society have full opportunities to participate, rather than people having to rely on fortuitous provisions from the market place, large corporations, and other self-interested complexes

3. *Enhanced diversity*, in which society supports a rich variety of lifestyle choices (think of the Amish), without isolating people in any group from the overall benefits of the new technologies of abundance.

It will take time to fully establish these mechanisms. They won't appear fully formed overnight. We'll build them in stages. As the technoprogressive worldview gains fuller support, politics will improve step by step. That process will be the subject of the final chapter of this book.

By the way, in case you're in any doubt, here's my answer to the question from the start of this chapter, "Is it possible to significantly improve politics, over the course of, say, the next dozen years, without first significantly improving human nature?" The answer has three parts:

- Any project to improve politics without addressing human nature is likely to make only limited progress

- Improving human nature is a risky endeavour too, but is highly desirable, and we have good insights as to how to move forwards

- By keeping the best characteristics of present-day humanity to the fore, we can take advantage of science and technology to make two sets of improvements in tandem: better humans *and* better politics.

13. Politics and leadership

Chiselled in gold letters on a granite monument in Highgate Cemetery, North London, one of the most famous sayings of Karl Marx echoes from beyond the grave[438]:

> The philosophers have only interpreted the world in various ways. The point is to change it.

The preceding chapters of this book contain their fair share of interpretation. *But what next?* If someone is at least broadly sympathetic to the technoprogressive vision I have outlined, and would like to hasten the accomplishment of that vision, what steps should they take?

The suggestions I make in this final chapter belong under three headings: connect, act, and iterate:

- *Connect* – find and join communities of people whose goals and projects resonate with you, and where your own efforts can be meaningfully amplified

- *Act* – identify useful individual tasks where you can make a difference, and become involved

- *Iterate* – be ready to start small, to venture outside of your comfort zone, to set and respect deadlines by when you will review progress with community members, to learn from both the failures and successes you experience, and to repeat the whole process, again and again, gaining more and more insight and effectiveness.

A simple way to move forwards, on all three of these headings, is to visit the Transpolitica projects webpage[439], transpolitica.org/projects, find something on that page that appeals to you, get started, and reconnect regularly.

Alternatively, you may prefer to become involved in projects taking place outside the Transpolitica umbrella. I give many examples in the *Afterword* that follows this chapter.

This chapter also contains some recommendations on how to connect, act, and iterate in more effective ways – ways that benefit from technoprogressive technologies and culture. At the same time, I fill in a few gaps left over from discussions in earlier chapters.

Towards super-collaboration

Of the many sets of technology that I've mentioned in this book, perhaps the most important is collabtech – technology that will improve our ability to collaborate with one another.

With the right kind of collaboration, the different skills and insights that are possessed by people around the world can add up to an extraordinary technoprogressive force. Many hands will make light work. But in the absence of such collaboration, people will talk past each other, waste time and resources re-inventing wheels, find unnecessary fault in each other's ideas, become absorbed in fruitless arguments, and generally go round in circles. Too many cooks will spoil the broth. Civilisation will burn while we all gesticulate from the sidelines.

Let's take a closer look at the components of collabtech. Various information processing tools that can enhance collaboration include:

- *Wikis or other distributed databases* that enable many contributors to build on each other's work, as happens so well in Wikipedia

- *Reputation management systems* that make it clear to a community which participants have a track record of providing helpful input, and which have unknown reliability or a negative history

- *Fact-checking tools* that alert participants when information is suspect

- *Logic-checking tools* that alert participants when an argument is suspect

- *Provenance-checking tools* that alert participants when a contribution has a different source than what first seems to be the case

- *Shared decision-making tools* that guide a community through a process of collective judgement – for example, via iterated voting

- *Task decomposition tools* that break down large projects into manageable chunks of activity

- *Modelling tools* that enable rich simulations of scenarios, to allow decision-makers to anticipate likely developments ahead of real-world deployment

- *Librarian tools* that monitor the state of collaborative decision systems, and take action to tidy content or update linkages

- *Smart communications tools* that guide participants how to express themselves in ways that aid positive team dynamics

- *Translation tools* that help people to communicate, not just across different spoken languages, but also across conceptual divides and alternative paradigms

- *Educational tools* that help people to understand and make full use of the other elements of collabtech listed above.

Tools are a good start, but for successful collaboration, human skills are important too. For best results, people need to be:

- Able to put aside their egos and personal hobby horses, and to adopt tasks which objectively need people working on them

- Willing to take small steps, in an uncertain environment, rather than being dominated by "analysis paralysis" or waiting indefinitely for a seemingly perfect proposal to fall into their laps

- Future-focused, anticipating new activities, rather than past-bound, repeatedly re-celebrating previous accomplishments

- Ready to challenge unruly behaviour and adverse personalities in a group, in order to avoid positive teams from degenerating

- Skilled in diplomacy, speaking and acting in ways that are constructive as well as truthful, in order to preserve as much good will as possible

- Sufficiently self-aware in order to make commitments that they have a realistic chance of keeping – rather than falling victim to over-confidence and self-deception.

At a broader level, the human skill of community management is particularly important. It involves the more established members of a community taking the time to:

- Welcome and mentor less experienced participants

- Identify community members who have special abilities that deserve to be encouraged

- Suggest matches between participant and task, that will allow participants to grow in experience and confidence

- Create sub-teams of people that are suited to working and growing together on particular projects, and who can inspire each other to greater effort

- Delegate project tasks in a way that empowers and motivates team members yet avoids cataclysms – in business parlance, this is known as "hands off but eyes open"

- Intervening promptly when tasks are going haywire – so that the community as a whole can "fail fast" rather than "fail fatally".

In summary, collaborations are more likely to be fruitful when a participant brings the above attitudes and skills to the table, and where the community already embodies at least some of the practices listed.

This set of tools and skills may appear daunting. But as with any other large task, the trick is to break things down into smaller steps, and make regular progress.

Four breakthroughs ahead

I'm not aware of any community that scores well on all the above points, but what's important is that a community is moving in the right direction. At the end of this book, I'll provide some pointers to technoprogressive communities I believe are well worth attention and support.

However, the whole landscape of different communities is itself evolving quickly. A community that is vibrant at one time may fall stagnant at a later date. Sometimes this change is due to personality issues. Sometimes the cause may be unpredictable "butterfly" effects, in which random small actions escalate in unexpected ways, like a butterfly flapping its wings might give rise to a hurricane on the other side of the planet. But I foresee four ongoing breakthroughs in technology platforms that are likely to cause shake-ups in levels of community activity. The communities that manage these breakthroughs most effectively will likely be the ones to flourish in the years ahead.

The first of these breakthroughs is the cognotech revolution covered in the previous chapter: people using biohacking and brainhacking in order to reach higher levels of both personal and group effectiveness.

The second is the revolution in artificial intelligence and deep machine learning covered in Chapters 4 and 5: people taking advantage of smart automation systems to (again) reach higher levels of both personal and group effectiveness.

The third is the revolution in decentralised databases known variously as "blockchain" and "DLT" (distributed ledger technology). I'll have more to same on this topic in the next section.

The fourth is a revolution, not so much in technology itself, but in the public understanding of both technology and the rate of change. As the public recognises more fully the scale of the potential disruptions of the next few decades – both the potential upsides and the potential downsides – they'll be less tolerant of worldviews that advocate only modest amounts of change. "Keep calm and muddle through" may have been a fine motto in times past, but today's population increasingly realise this advice has passed its "sell by" date. "More of the same" is no longer sufficient. The suggestion to "Trust the establishment; they'll sort things out" is increasingly scorned – both in people's minds, and at ballot boxes.

The implication of this final breakthrough is that the time for "slow-paced futurism" is quickly passing.

As someone who's had the word "Futurist" on my business card since early 2009, I've been inspired since that time to see more and more people taking the subject of futurism seriously. Thankfully, there's a growing awareness, nowadays, that it's important to analyse future scenarios. It's increasingly recognised that, if people spend time thinking about the likely developments of current trends, they'll be better prepared to try to respond to these trends. Instead of being shocked when disruptive forces burst through from being "under the radar" to having major impacts on lifestyles and society, they'll have been acting beforehand to influence the outcome – pushing hard to increase the likelihood of positive changes, and to decrease the likelihood of negative changes.

But it's my observation that, in too many of the meetings I attend and the discussions I observe, the futurism on display is timid and conservative. Well-meaning speakers contemplate a future, ten or twenty years ahead, that is 95% the same as today, but with, say, 5% changes. In these modestly innovative future scenarios, we might have computers that are faster than today's, screens that are more ubiquitous than today's, and *some* jobs will have been displaced by robots and automation. But human nature will be the same in the future as in the past, and the kinds of thing people spend their time doing will be more-or-less the same as they have been doing for the last ten or twenty years too (except, perhaps, faster).

In contrast, people not locked into the status quo are increasingly aware that momentous changes in human nature and human society are at hand:

- Robots and other forms of automation are on the point of displacing perhaps 90% of human employees from the workforce – with "creative" jobs and "managerial" jobs being every bit as much at risk as "muscle" jobs

- Enhanced suites of medical therapies are poised to enable decades of healthy life extension and an associated "longevity dividend" financial bonanza (since costs of healthcare will have plummeted)

- Genetic editing will allow not only "designer babies" and "super Olympians" but the creation of multiple new forms of life

- Systems that exist both inside and outside of the human brain will soon be able to dramatically increase multiple dimensions of our intelligence

- Virtual reality and augmented reality will shortly be every bit as vivid and compelling as "natural reality"

- Artificial general intelligence software may soon be providing convincing new answers to long-standing unsolved questions of science and philosophy

- Cryonic suspension of people on the point of death might become pervasive, as the credibility of the possibility of reanimation by future science grows higher, and as people discern the benefits of hitching themselves into an "ambulance to the future"

- Second and third order crossover impacts among the above items are likely to cause yet more turmoil.

So whilst I cautiously welcome the slow-paced futurists, I hope that more of them will soon realise the immensity of the transformations ahead, and become fast-paced futurists. Communities that are too dominated by present-day concerns and incremental thinking, and which are dependent on financial support from similarly slow-paced sponsors, are likely to be disrupted by newcomers – new communities that are more receptive to the accelerating pulse of transformation, and which can provide a set of ideas, such as transhumanism, which compellingly make sense of what people can see happening.

Friction and decentralisation

At the same time as we talk about the potential for disruption, we should also talk about the potential of the opposite of disruption, namely stasis.

Stasis is when communities become stuck, or, less dramatically, when they take a long time to change. To extend the metaphor, stasis arises when there's too much friction, that is, resistance to change. In such circumstances, decision processes are lengthy, and require the consent of several different parties who are difficult to corral. Key members of the community are preoccupied with preserving what the community is already doing well. Rather than enabling change, the hub of the community disables it. The hub is more interested in continuing to enjoy present-day benefits (even if these may be dwindling) than in risking their positions with potential risky initiatives into new fields. And since every initiative has risks, hubs that are indisposed to change can find plenty of reasons to avoid meaningful evolution.

This is one of the reasons why the notion of *decentralisation* is growing in popularity. If a community can operate without the bottleneck of an uncooperative hub, it can evolve more quickly.

An evocative metaphor for decentralisation is contained in the 2006 book by Ori Brafman and Rod Beckstrom, *The Starfish and the Spider: The Unstoppable Power of Leaderless Organizations*[440]:

> If you cut off a spider's leg, it's crippled; if you cut off its head, it dies. But if you cut off a starfish's leg it grows a new one, and the old leg can grow into an entirely new starfish...

> *The Starfish and the Spider* argues that organizations fall into two categories: traditional "spiders," which have a rigid hierarchy and top-down leadership, and revolutionary "starfish," which rely on the power of peer relationships.

The book attributed the success of many communities – both in recent times (such as Wikipedia, eBay, and Skype) and earlier in history (such as the abolition of slavery) – to their starfish-like characteristics. There's a lot of merit in this assessment.

A significant example of the power of decentralisation can be seen in the rise of open-source software. Rather than being kept private, under the control of a single company, open source software is available for anyone interested in it to download, study, tinker with, modify, and recompile into alternative versions. Software developed as open source includes the Firefox web browser, the Apache web server, the Linux operating system that powers Android smartphones, and the MediaWiki software that powers Wikipedia.

One strong feature of open-source software is that a community is able to "fork" the software, building it in a different way to an earlier version, without needing any special permission. A 2008 blogpost on the Pingdom website describes "10 interesting software forks", including Ubuntu from Debian, Firefox from Mozilla Application Suite, and Webkit from KHTML[441]. The blogpost finishes with this comment:

> Judging from these ten software forks, common causes of forks are disagreements (sometimes purely ideological) and personality clashes, though more practical reasons are also common (such as the Webkit and Firefox examples). It is also interesting to see that many times the forks have surpassed the original software in popularity.

Distributed ledger technology (DLT) can be viewed as an extension of the same set of ideas. The goal is to avoid control points which might unnecessarily delay or subvert an intended transaction or transformation.

Whereas open-source software stores sets of instructions (algorithms), a DLT can store any kind of data. Ledgers themselves go back to the beginning of recorded history, when clay tablets were used to record details of property or trade. Over the millennia, clay tablets were replaced by papyrus, then by paper, and more recently by computers, by which time the more modern word "database" was often used instead of "ledger". A ledger is "distributed" if there are multiple copies of it, which are kept synchronised by connections between them. For a ledger to be useful, there need to be rules about which changes can be made in it. As an example, the registry ledger that records land ownership can only be updated by certified officials. The ledger that records my bank balance can only be updated by processes approved by my bank; I cannot edit that ledger at a whim to double the amount of money supposedly in my possession.

Where things become interesting is that modern DLT systems add extra capabilities:

- The ledger contains a tamper-proof historical archive of all changes that have been made in the ledger; the previous contents of this archive cannot be altered, even by a central authority

- The ledger can contain rules, sometimes called "smart contracts", that are triggered automatically when certain conditions apply, without the need for any human intervention

- Trust in the authenticity of the content of the ledger is derived, not from the say so of any central authority such as banking officials, but from the inherent structure of the ledger itself, as protected by secure cryptography.

In the words of technology commentator Andreas Antonopoulos, what we have here is the possibility of "A shift from trusting people to trusting math"[442]. Antonopoulos explains it as follows:

> Here's the most important effect of this new trust model of trust-by-computation: no one actor is trusted, and no one needs to be trusted. There is no central authority or trusted third party in a distributed consensus network.

> That fact opens up a completely new network model, as the network no longer needs to be closed, access-controlled or encrypted. Trust does not depend on excluding bad actors, as they cannot "fake" trust. They cannot pretend to be the trusted party, as there is none. They cannot steal the central keys as there are none. They cannot pull the levers of control at the core of the system, as there is no core and no levers of control.

> As a result, the network can be open to all; the transactions can be broadcast on any medium, unencrypted; and applications can be added at the edge without vetting or approval.

The best known DLT is the blockchain mechanism that underpins the bitcoin cryptocurrency. In this case, the ledger is composed of a set of "blocks" that are added over time, with each block referring to previous blocks, thereby forming an ever-growing *chain of blocks*. The individual blocks in turn contain records of financial transactions: the transfer of a given amount of bitcoin between two accounts associated with unique identifiers.

Keep in mind that a blockchain can be used to contain other sorts of records, apart from bitcoin transactions, and that there are many other kinds of DLT apart from blockchain itself. In some cases, a DLT allows anonymous third parties to update the ledger, without requiring any pre-validation. This is known as a "permissionless" ledger. In other cases – known as "permissioned" – access is restricted to approved "trusted parties" that meet various conditions specified by the operator of the ledger. Permissioned DLTs are expected to enable improvements in processing efficiency, and are being studied with great interest by banks and other financial institutions. For example, here is how the R3 consortium describes itself and its "Corda" product[443]:

> Launched in September 2015, R3 was born out of a common frustration amongst banks and other financial institutions with multiple generations of disparate legacy financial technology platforms that struggle to interoperate, causing inefficiencies, risk and spiralling costs.

> Recognizing the power of distributed ledger technology lies in its network effect, we worked with the industry to build the largest collaborative group of its kind in financial markets.

> Since then R3 has grown from a staff of eight finance and technology veterans with nine bank members to a global team of over 125 professionals serving over 100 global financial institutions and regulators on six continents. Our work is further supported by over 2,000 technology, financial, and legal experts drawn from our global member base...

> Corda is a distributed ledger platform that is the outcome of over two years of intense research and development by R3 and 80 of the world's largest financial institutions. A financial grade ledger, Corda meets the highest standards of the banking industry, yet it is applicable to any commercial scenario...

> With Corda, participants can transact without the need for central authorities, creating a world of frictionless commerce.

Blockchain and politics

If DLTs can enable "frictionless commerce", could they also enable "frictionless governance" and "frictionless politics"?

Los Angeles based attorney Shiva Bhaskar has suggested, in an article entitled "How Blockchain Can Improve Politics", that blockchain might have applications in[444]:

- Counting votes more reliably, to avoid issues with recounts and the notorious "hanging chads"

- Making clear the provenance of news stories, in order to reduce instances of voters being misled by "fake news"

- Helping voters to collaborate with government administrators to propose changes in legislation.

Researcher Marcella Atzori from the UCL Center for Blockchain Technologies offers this assessment[445]:

> The blockchain technology potentially allows individuals and communities to redesign their interactions in politics, business and society at large, with an unprecedented process of disintermediation on large scale, based on automated and trustless transactions. This process might rapidly change even the tenets that underpin existing political systems and governance models, calling into question the traditional role of State and centralized institutions.
>
> Indeed, many blockchain advocates claim that the civil society could organize itself and protect its own interests more effectively, by replacing the traditional functions of State with blockchain-based services and decentralized, open source platforms (e.g. Ethereum, Omni Layer, Eris). Driven by the enthusiasm for the new possibilities offered by information technology, along with a profound dissatisfaction with the current political systems, they hence encourage citizens to be part of the blockchain revolution and self-create their own systems of governance, in which centralization, coercion and hierarchies are replaced by mechanisms of distributed consensus.

Vinay Gupta, a long-time enthusiast for digital currencies and public-key cryptography, who was subsequently involved in the public launch of Ethereum ("a second generation blockchain")[446], has suggested that blockchain will allow more and more areas of life to move from being controlled by government to being under the decentralised control of the population as a whole.

In a 2014 video interview with BraveTheWorld, Gupta pointed to the example of paper size (A4, US Letter Size, etc) as having a set of co-existing standards that people use without any government scrutiny. "It's essentially apolitical", he said. Why can't this happen with other goods and services? He continued as follows[447]:

> My basic philosophy is that, as far as possible, what we want to do is to de-governance things. We want to take a thing that *used to* require state

intervention, find a way of doing it that's equitable to everyone, but doesn't require the state, and then just get on with doing it...

As you move further down the path of technological progress, more and more things that used to require a state actor to back them become things that can be done by the market; if you go further, more and more things that used to be done by the market can be done by individuals basically in free association networks.

Referring to examples such as 3D printing and solar electricity shared off-grid, Gupta drew this conclusion:

That process – of something that would have taken state power, then it would have taken market power, and now it's something that can be done at home – is a process where you get less and less dependent on other people, and less and less dependent on these complex social structures that never really represent you. You're de-governancing this stuff, and get more autonomy and more autarky.

Gupta went on to give this definition of the role of politics in society:

Fundamentally, politics is simply about allocating scarcity. You've got different systems that figure out who will starve and who will eat – systems with names like capitalism, socialism, communism, and fascism. But if you take the scarcity out of the system, it doesn't really matter who is in charge, because nobody is going to starve and nobody is going to die... If we could just get rid of the scarcity, politics would be fundamentally less important.

For the particular scarcity of "verified true facts", Gupta suggests that a single worldwide blockchain could prove to be a vital asset. Here's an extract from a talk he gave at OuiShareFest in 2016[448]:

With all that information logged into a global system, we could then also potentially... have one person, one vote, for the entire world, to decide what we're going to do about this set of facts. The lifeblood of democracy is truth. Without truth, there is no democracy. And... we have a very hard time reaching the truth these days, because of the massive monopolisation of the media by large corporate interests...

So if we start putting the facts of the situation onto blockchain, so that there is one truth the entire world can see, it becomes imaginable that you could then have democratic decision making at the global level.

Here's my own assessment of the transformational promise of blockchain:

- There's a lot here that's worth investigating for its potentially profound beneficial effects

- There's also a lot here that's wishful thinking – ideas that are being hyped up in order to inflate share prices and the values of various cryptocurrencies

- There's even a lot of dangerous thinking here, which could lead society to bitterly regret naively trusting these systems.

In more detail:

- The variants of blockchain that operate bitcoin – as well as many other cryptocurrencies – face growing problems with excess energy usage, exponentially increasing data storage, and slow confirmation of transactions; the blockchain community has various ideas on how to bypass these problems but, at time of writing, these ideas remain speculative[449]

- Many of the proposed use cases for blockchain can be implemented, more easily and more effectively, with simpler database systems than the full blockchain apparatus

- The various specific potential applications of blockchain mentioned above – improvements in counting votes, identifying fake news, and the collaborative drafting and review of new policies – would require changes in human practice and social institutions as well as in the technology adopted, and might in that case be better implemented *without* moving all the way to a resource-intensive blockchain

- Blockchain is no more of a panacea – a magic "cure all" solution – than was open-source software before it; many ailing projects that hope to revive their fortunes by converting to open-source and/or blockchain will discover their issues cannot be solved so simply

- The idea that blockchain is inherently beneficial is as misguided as the idea that artificial intelligence is inherently beneficial; in both cases, the systems need wise human design and human supervision

- Systems of unstoppable self-executing code, such as smart contracts, depend on various assumptions which may turn out to be false in the actual circumstances when the code is triggered in the future

- Although the distributed ledger itself may be immune from sabotage from "bad actors" (of either the malicious or incompetent types), the ledger is generally embedded in wider systems which *are* vulnerable to exploitation, subversion, or sabotage

- Blockchain advocates sometimes just see the downsides of central governance, and fail to give proper recognition to the many upsides that governments can bring

- Any suggestion that the problem of scarcity has already been solved, and that it's only self-interested politicians which perpetuate systems of scarcity, fails to appreciate that many types of service (including medical treatments) still do remain fundamentally expensive[450].

I am struck by the prescience of Harvard Law Professor Lawrence Lessig, who wrote the following words in an essay in 2000, referring at the time to the controversy about how society should regulate cyberspace, but his reasoning applies equally to the regulation of blockchain systems[451]:

We live in an era fundamentally sceptical about [government]. Our age is obsessed with leaving things alone. Let the Internet develop as the coders would develop it, the common view has it. Keep government out.

This is an understandable view, given the character of our government's regulation. Given its flaws, it no doubt seems best simply to keep government away. But this is an indulgence that is dangerous at any time. It is particularly dangerous now.

Our choice is not between "regulation" and "no regulation." The code regulates. It implements values, or not. It enables freedoms, or disables them. It protects privacy, or promotes monitoring. People choose how the code does these things. People write the code. Thus the choice is not whether people will decide how cyberspace regulates. People – coders – will. The only choice is whether we collectively will have a role in their choice – and thus in determining how these values regulate – or whether collectively we will allow the coders to select our values for us.

For here's the obvious point: when government steps aside, it's not as if nothing takes its place. It's not as if private interests have no interests; as if private interests don't have ends that they will then pursue. To push the anti-government button is not to teleport us to Eden. When the interests of government are gone, other interests take their place. Do we know what those interests are? And are we so certain they are anything better?

Here's Lessig's conclusion:

Our first response should be hesitation. It is proper to let the market develop first. But as the Constitution checks and limits what Congress does, so too should constitutional values check and limit what a market does. We should test both the laws of Congress and the product of a market against these values. We should interrogate the architecture of cyberspace as we interrogate the code of Congress.

UCL researcher Marcella Atzori, already mentioned above, gives this summary of risks of using blockchain for government services[452]:

The benefits of open, unpermissioned blockchains for government services seems to be offset by several risks, related to:

- Moral hazard, scalability problems, trend towards centralization and likely dependency of networks on private oligarchies, such as miner corporations, which may rapidly conduct stock exchange mergers and acquisitions, gaining considerable power on global scale;

- Domination of market logic over essential public services and citizens' rights, which should be rather protected [against] speculations…;

- Possible lack of service continuity and/or preservation of data in the medium-long run with no delineation of liability, due to market dynamics and/or serious technical flaws;

- Raising of a dominant techno-elite with growing supervisory powers over strategic services at global level, without the necessary formal legitimacy.

I share the sentiments expressed at the end of Atzori's paper:

It is the conscientious application of principles and rights enshrined in law that can really empower individuals – rather than the privatization of government services through market-driven decentralized platforms…

While the strong public dissent of techno-libertarians and cypherpunks is honourable, for it brings the issue of civil rights into focus, now more than ever the theoretical principles of the State should not be confused with bad governance or corrupted politicians…

The major challenge for global civil society will soon be to explore new political and social dimensions, with the aim of integrating the applications of disruptive technologies such as the blockchain with citizens' rights, equality, social cohesion, inclusiveness, and protection of public sector.

Such integration is vital and cannot be left to the (anti-) political engineering of IT experts, financial investors, and code developers: it requires indeed a mature and interdisciplinary effort by all the fields of human knowledge, with particular regard to political theory, humanities and social sciences, to best assess risks, benefits and outcomes of the new technologies.

In the very next future, this integration might be the only safeguard left against many possible technological dystopias.

Such integration is, perhaps needless to say, the prime concern of the technoprogressive project.

Action required

As I said at the start of this chapter, concrete progress with the technoprogressive project needs people willing to connect, act, and iterate.

The point of connecting is, emphatically, not just to circulate ideas in endless social media "sharing" or "retweeting". It's to join teams of people who are likely to progress some of the unfinished business of the technoprogressive initiative. There's plenty of real work that needs doing:

- Documenting and analysing the strengths and weaknesses of key policy ideas, and creating new policy proposals to fill urgent gaps

- Understanding more fully the risks and opportunities associated with various approaches to technological and political innovation

- Building bridges to potential allies

- Finding better ways to express technoprogressive ideas, so that they have greater impact on audiences (without being misleading, and without losing the longer term vision); this includes videos and graphics as well as text, memes as well as bulleted lists, evocative parables as well as detailed analysis, and broader works of art as well as linear prose

- Reducing public misunderstanding by responding skilfully and robustly to any misleading criticisms of the project, without unduly alienating the critics; ideally these critics will, upon a rethink, want to find a positive role for themselves inside the overall technoprogressive movement

- Developing and supporting spokespeople, who can ensure that important technoprogressive insights remain in the public mind

- Influencing the influencers and educating the educators – connecting with people who already have significant public standing, who may be receptive to adapting and sharing technoprogressive thoughts with their own audiences

- Trailblazing smart adoption of collabtech, cognotech, artificial intelligence, and blockchain, in order to improve the effectiveness of the community, and also to encourage adoption by wider society

- Developing examples of "shadow institutions" that can act as models and inspiration for the evolution of existing national and international bodies

- Considering various possible sequencing of different tasks, bearing in mind the dependencies between them.

Iterating towards the Singularity

I see the set of likely futures for humanity, around the middle of this century, as being split into two main groups. In one group of futures, society will reach a state of sustainable equitable abundance; in the other, it will plunge down into a new dark age of ignorance and destruction.

A potential middle path, in which society continues more or less the same as before, though with a few extra bells and whistles, has a low probability. That's on account of the fearsome disruptive power of the technologies that are fast developing. There is no easy way to turn off these powers. Once uncorked, the genie of radical exponential transformation cannot be returned into the confinement of a human-held bottle.

Unless humanity becomes collectively significantly wiser than before, we'll become significantly more foolish. Unless we attain higher states of enlightenment, we'll come to experience bitter states of depravity. Humanity is being put to a more demanding test of our capability than at any previous point in history.

To describe this fateful test, the word "Singularity" comes to mind. I hesitate to introduce it to the discussion, since it's a word that already has multiple meanings in a futurist context[453]. But it brings an important note of seriousness to the table. If humanity fails this test, there's no going back.

It needs to be emphasised, however, that this test isn't something that will take place on a single day. Nor is it something that will fall into the hands of a single person. Instead, humanity's path into the future involves numerous choices, in which we all have a chance to participate.

The metaphor of a tug of war is more appropriate than that of tossing a single coin. The red ribbon at the centre of the tug of war rope can be moved, centimetre by centimetre, by the collective effort of numerous rope-pullers. Each of us needs to find the best way to grasp the rope, and the best angle to exert effort, bearing in mind the overall landscape of the contest. As the rope moves over different terrain, we need to adjust our stance. As our colleagues wilt under the strain, we need to find new ways to encourage them, or to recruit new volunteers to join the campaign.

In reality, of course, things are by no means so straightforward. There is no red ribbon, nor a visible rope. The landscape is deeply more complicated. We live surrounded by distractions. Any time we think we see a rope worth pulling, plenty of voices will tell us we're mistaken. Warnings about "fake rope" will challenge our conviction.

The test facing us, therefore, involves brain as well as brawn – discernment as well as endeavour. To adapt the words of Stephen Covey, writer of a truly great book on personal effectiveness, *The Seven Habits of Highly Effective People*[454], we need skills in pulling ropes, but also the skill to know which ropes to pull.

The seventh of Covey's famous seven habits is "Sharpen the saw":

Suppose you were to come upon someone in the woods working feverishly to saw down a tree.

"What are you doing?" you ask.

"Can't you see?" comes the impatient reply. "I'm sawing down this tree."

"You look exhausted!" you exclaim. "How long have you been at it?"

"Over five hours," he returns, "and I'm beat! This is hard work."

"Well, why don't you take a break for a few minutes and sharpen that saw?" you enquire. "I'm sure it would go a lot faster."

"I don't have time to sharpen the saw," the man says emphatically. "I'm too busy sawing!"

Habit 7 is taking time to sharpen the saw. It… is the habit that makes all the others possible.

Sharpening the saw means taking the time for renewal – reflecting on what went well, and what went badly, in the preceding period of activity – and what, therefore should be the priorities in the next phase of activity.

Whether we as individuals end up being a force that elevates humanity towards a positive Singularity – or, instead, an impediment unwittingly dragging humanity towards a negative Singularity – depends in this analysis on three factors:

1. Did we discern sufficiently wisely the projects where our efforts should be applied?

2. Were our actions in support of these projects sufficiently potent?

3. Did we interleave our periods of forceful endeavour with periods of sage reflection and personal development, to improve both our discernment and our application of effort in subsequent periods?

The right choice of communities in which we spend our time will increase our likelihood of success on all three counts. It will make it more likely that humanity's journey avoids plunging into any negative Singularity and instead reaches a positive "Humanity+" Singularity.

Building bridges to better politics

Motivational speaker Jim Rohn offers a memorable statement about the impact on us of the people with whom we frequently interact[455]:

> You are the average of the five people you spend the most time with.

In other words, we should choose these five people carefully!

As a rough rule of thumb, if we spend time with unambitious people, our own ambition level will tend to drop. If we spend time with people who make quick, rash decisions, we'll be inclined to make our own decisions more quickly and more rashly. If our regular companions are focused on questions of the performance of different sports teams, we'll likely spend more of our own time keeping track of the ins and outs of sports contests. If we deepen our connections to a community that undertakes incremental projects towards an envisioned technoprogressive transformation of society, we'll be more likely to make regular contributions of our own towards such a goal.

It's as I said a few moments ago: the choice of communities in which we spend our time matters a great deal.

However, there is a potential dark side to any involvement in a given community: we risk becoming disconnected from wider initiatives. As the language and concepts of one community become like second nature to us, they might prevent us from properly understanding activities outside of that community. We may up in a bubble of self-congratulation – an echo chamber – impervious to the important insights of other groups.

It's part of our inherited human nature to be alert against potential dangers from outsiders. It's in our instinct to put up barriers to protect ourselves from people perceived as outsiders. Communities that, compared to us, seem to have different objectives, different beliefs, or different modes of operation, might appear alien and frightening. In that case, an initial disagreement can become a prelude to fierce opposition – even if, in reality, there is more that unites than divides two communities.

For this reason, the task of "connecting" which I have highlighted in this chapter, needs to extend beyond "connecting to a community where we feel at home" to "building bridges to other communities".

That is, whilst there will be times when we need lots of effort to pull in specific directions, against opposing forces – as in a tug-of-war contest – there will also be times when we need more effort to collaborate than to compete. The metaphor of the determined tug-of-war therefore needs to be complemented with the metaphor of painstaking bridge-building.

The complication, however, is that bridge-building is hard. Attempts to create dialogue across entrenched differences of opinion often make little progress. We may think we have offered a decisive response to a hostile opinion expressed by outsiders, but the outsiders seem hardly to notice what we have said. They continue with their opinions unscathed.

To understand what's happening, we need to distinguish *underlying motivation* from *supportive rationale*. In the vivid metaphor of the elephant and the rider, developed by social psychologist Jonathan Haidt in his remarkable 2006 book *The Happiness Hypothesis*[456], the conscious mind is akin to the human rider bestride a powerful elephant – the subconscious.

Haidt develops this analogy in the first chapter of his book[457]:

> Why do people keep doing… stupid things? Why do they fail to control themselves and continue to do what they know is not good for them? I, for one, can easily muster the willpower to ignore all the desserts on the menu. But if dessert is placed on the table, I can't resist it. I can resolve to

focus on a task and not get up until it is done, yet somehow I find myself walking into the kitchen, or procrastinating in other ways. I can resolve to wake up at 6:00 A.M. to write; yet after I have shut off the alarm, my repeated commands to myself to get out of bed have no effect…

It was during some larger life decisions, about dating, that I really began to grasp the extent of my powerlessness. I would know exactly what I should do, yet, even as I was telling my friends that I would do it, a part of me was dimly aware that I was not going to. Feelings of guilt, lust, or fear were often stronger than reasoning…

Modern theories about rational choice and information processing don't adequately explain weakness of the will. The older metaphors about controlling animals work beautifully. The image that I came up with for myself, as I marvelled at my weakness, was that I was a rider on the back of an elephant. I'm holding the reins in my hands, and by pulling one way or the other I can tell the elephant to turn, to stop, or to go. I can direct things, but only when the elephant doesn't have desires of his own. When the elephant really wants to do something, I'm no match for him.

The rider may think he or she is in control, but the elephant often has its own firm ideas, particularly in matters of taste and morality. In such cases, the conscious mind acts more like a lawyer than a driver. As Haidt continues:

Moral judgment is like aesthetic judgment. When you see a painting, you usually know instantly and automatically whether you like it. If someone asks you to explain your judgment, you confabulate. You don't really know why you think something is beautiful, but your interpreter module (the rider) is skilled at making up reasons… You search for a plausible reason for liking the painting, and you latch on to the first reason that makes sense (maybe something vague about colour, or light, or the reflection of the painter in the clown's shiny nose). Moral arguments are much the same: Two people feel strongly about an issue, their feelings come first, and their reasons are invented on the fly, to throw at each other. When you refute a person's argument, does she generally change her mind and agree with you? Of course not, because the argument you defeated was not the cause of her position; it was made up after the judgment was already made.

If you listen closely to moral arguments, you can sometimes hear something surprising: that it is really the elephant holding the reins, guiding the rider. It is the elephant who decides what is good or bad, beautiful or ugly. Gut feelings, intuitions, and snap judgments happen constantly and automatically... but only the rider can string sentences together and create arguments to give to other people. In moral arguments, the rider goes beyond being just an advisor to the elephant; he becomes a lawyer, fighting in the court of public opinion to persuade others of the elephant's point of view.

In his follow-up book, *The Righteous Mind*[458], Haidt builds upon that metaphor to propose a cornerstone principle[459] of moral psychology:

Intuitions come first, strategic reasoning second.

Moral intuitions arise automatically and almost instantaneously, long before moral reasoning has a chance to get started, and those first intuitions tend to drive our later reasoning. If you think that moral reasoning is something we do to figure out the truth, you'll be constantly frustrated by how foolish, biased, and illogical people become when they disagree with you. But if you think about moral reasoning as a skill we humans evolved to further our social agendas – to justify our own actions and to defend the teams we belong to – then things will make a lot more sense. Keep your eye on the intuitions, and don't take people's moral arguments at face value. They're mostly post-hoc constructions made up on the fly, crafted to advance one or more strategic objectives.

The central metaphor... is that *the mind is divided, like a rider on an elephant, and the rider's job is to serve the elephant.* The rider is our conscious reasoning – the stream of words and images that hogs the stage of our awareness. The elephant is the other 99% of mental processes – the ones that occur outside of awareness but that actually govern most of our behaviour.

On the face of things, that's a depressing conclusion. It indicates why our attempts at rational dialogue often flop, when they cover matters of fundamental importance to someone's sense of identity and purpose.

However, Haidt extends his model of the divided mind to identify some practical steps forwards. The following is from the third chapter, "Elephants Rule", of *The Righteous Mind*:

The elephant is far more powerful than the rider, but it is not an absolute dictator.

When does the elephant listen to reason? The main way that we change our minds on moral issues is by interacting with other people. We are terrible at seeking evidence that challenges our own beliefs, but other people do us this favour, just as we are quite good at finding errors in other people's beliefs. When discussions are hostile, the odds of change are slight. The elephant leans away from the opponent, and the rider works frantically to rebut the opponent's charges. But if there is affection, admiration, or a desire to please the other person, then the elephant leans toward that person and the rider tries to find the truth in the other person's arguments. The elephant may not often change its direction in response to objections from its own rider, but it is easily steered by the mere presence of friendly elephants or by good arguments given to it by the riders of those friendly elephants…

Under normal circumstances the rider takes its cue from the elephant, just as a lawyer takes instructions from a client. But if you force the two to sit around and chat for a few minutes, the elephant actually opens up to advice from the rider and arguments from outside sources. Intuitions come first, and under normal circumstances they cause us to engage in socially strategic reasoning, but there are ways to make the relationship more of a two-way street…

The elephant (automatic processes) is where most of the action is in moral psychology. Reasoning matters, of course, particularly between people, and particularly when reasons trigger new intuitions. Elephants rule, but they are neither dumb nor despotic. Intuitions can be shaped by reasoning, especially when reasons are embedded in a friendly conversation or an emotionally compelling novel, movie, or news story.

This provides us with three ways to change the elephant's opinion, on a matter as controversial as political conviction. People are more likely to accept advice, on potentially difficult topics, if that advice:

1. Comes from someone perceived as being "one of us" – that is, a friend, from a similar demographic, rather than a strange outsider
2. Is supported by "an emotionally compelling novel, movie, or news story"
3. Exists in a context where the elephant feels that its own needs are well understood and well supported.

The first of these three conditions matches a well-known principle of technology marketing – that of companies needing to change their marketing approach while "crossing the chasm" from the set of visionary early adopters of a new technology, to the larger market of "early majority" pragmatists. Geoffrey Moore brought attention to this idea in his 1991 book *Crossing the Chasm*[460], which in turn drew on rich observations in Everett Walker's 1962 work *Diffusion of Innovation*[461]. The key insight is as follows: whereas early adopters of a new idea are often impressed by unorthodox theoretical ideas, access to the mainstream market is controlled instead by *pragmatists* whose strong instinct is to "stick with the herd". In general, such people will only adopt a solution (or an idea) if they see others from their own herd who have already adopted it and endorse it.

There's an important implication here. Advocates and slogans that were successful in attracting an *initial* community of supporters to a new cause – such as transhumanism – often need to be changed, before potential *mainstream* supporters will be prepared to listen. Breathless talk of, for example, immortality, or mind uploading, which appealed to early supporters of transhumanism, can be counterproductive as the movement seeks to gain a wider circle of supporters.

The second of the three conditions is a reminder of the importance but also the danger of developing and using multiple styles of communication. A movement should not allow itself to become bogged down in just one type of messaging. But in the resulting variety, a careless cold word can undo all the good progress of prior warm overtures. Just as an elephant is inclining in our direction, it might take alarm at a perceived threat, and stampede away.

The third of the conditions mentioned might be the most important of all. It can be re-expressed in the phrase, "people don't care how much you know, until they know how much you care"[462].

Building bridges across warring political tribes requires finding a shared underlying foundation. When someone with strong pro-market sentiments clashes with someone with strong pro-equality sentiments, they're unlikely to be able to reach a meaningful common understanding simply by weighing up market considerations versus equality considerations. They need instead to reach a common set of goals from which both market considerations and equality considerations can be derived.

To my mind, it is the concept of human flourishing, set out in the previous pages of this book – a sustainable Humanity+ abundance of human flourishing for everyone, with no-one left behind – which can provide the required common set of goals.

But to turn this vision of agreement into tangible collaboration will require more than just ideas. It will require people from all communities to live up to the best characteristics of human nature – patience, tolerance, encouragement, renewal, creativity, appreciation, and kindness.

Transhumanists of the world, are you up for this challenge?

Afterword

Communities well worth joining

Faster progress with tasks can take place if you connect into suitable communities. Let me share some brief descriptions of communities that you may find to your taste. I've chosen communities that, at time of writing:

- Are broadly aligned with the technoprogressive vision – though they might not use that particular word to describe themselves
- Are engaged in a number of promising projects – rather than just being a "talking shop"
- Are primarily motivated to improve the prospects for humanity as a whole – rather than making money or joy-riding
- Are open to participation from general members of the public – without any large membership fee or other restrictive selection criterion
- Consider not just the technological dimensions of change, but also the political and social dimensions
- Show real awareness of the radical disruptions ahead; they're fast-paced futurists rather than slow-paced futurists.

I'll start with three communities that each have significant links to prominent academic institutions.

The Future of Life Institute (FLI), futureoflife.org, has close associations with both MIT and Harvard. It has this mission statement:

> To catalyze and support research and initiatives for safeguarding life and developing optimistic visions of the future, including positive ways for humanity to steer its own course considering new technologies and challenges.

The FLI carries this description on its website[463]:

> We have technology to thank for all the ways in which today is better than the stone age, and technology is likely to keep improving at an accelerating pace. We are a charity and outreach organization working to ensure that tomorrow's most powerful technologies are beneficial for humanity. With less powerful technologies such as fire, we learned to minimize risks largely by learning from mistakes. With more powerful technologies such

as nuclear weapons, synthetic biology and future strong artificial intelligence, planning ahead is a better strategy than learning from mistakes, so we support research and other efforts aimed at avoiding problems in the first place.

We are currently focusing on keeping artificial intelligence beneficial and we are also exploring ways of reducing risks from nuclear weapons and biotechnology. FLI is based in the Boston area, and welcomes the participation of scientists, students, philanthropists, and others nearby and around the world.

The Future of Humanity Institute (FHI), fhi.ox.ac.uk, is part of Oxford University. According to its website[464]:

FHI investigates what we can do now to ensure a long flourishing future.

FHI is a multidisciplinary research institute at the University of Oxford. Academics at FHI bring the tools of mathematics, philosophy and social sciences to bear on big-picture questions about humanity and its prospects. The Institute is led by Founding Director Professor Nick Bostrom.

Humanity has the potential for a long and flourishing future. Our mission is to shed light on crucial considerations that might shape that future.

The Centre for the Study of Existential Risk (CSER), cser.ac.uk, is part of Cambridge University[465]:

We are an interdisciplinary research centre within the University of Cambridge dedicated to the study and mitigation of existential risks.

Now is an important time for efforts to reduce existential risk. There are new and largely unstudied risks associated with powerful emerging technologies and the impacts of human activity, which in the worst case might pose existential risks. We want to reap the enormous benefits of technological progress while safely navigating these catastrophic pitfalls. These threaten everyone – we can only tackle them together.

Next, I'll mention a community which is organised around a widely-read online blog, but also has physical meetups around the world[466].

Less Wrong (LW), lesswrong.com, describes itself as "A community blog devoted to refining the art of human rationality"[467]:

Interested in improving your reasoning and decision-making skills? Then you've come to the right place. We're an online community dedicated to the study of human rationality, the general field of improving our decisions. Less Wrong pulls together a variety of material from mathematics, economics, cognitive science, and other disciplines which can all be relevant when considering how we think. We're also interested in technology, the long-term future of humanity, and philosophy…

Less Wrong dates back to 2006 when Eliezer Yudkowsky starting writing about rationality on economist Robin Hanson's blog *Overcoming Bias*. In February 2009, those posts were used as the seed material for Less Wrong. Since 2006 we have collected many friends.

A number of organisations that spun off from the Less Wrong community deserve mention:

- **The Center For Applied Rationality (CFAR)**[468], with its mission statement of "Actually trying to figure things out"

- **The Machine Intelligence Research Institute (MIRI)**[469], with its mission statement of "We do foundational mathematical research to ensure smarter-than-human artificial intelligence has a positive impact".

Effective Altruism (EA), effectivealtruism.org, is another outgrowth from Less Wrong that has arguably become at least as significant in its own right. It runs a large number of events worldwide, including public presentations and smaller meetups[470]. Here's how the community describes itself[471]:

Effective altruism is changing the way we do good.

Effective altruism is about answering one simple question: how can we use our resources to help others the most?

Rather than just doing what feels right, we use evidence and careful analysis to find the very best causes to work on.

But it's no use answering the question unless you act on it. Effective altruism is about following through. It's about being generous with your time and your money to do the most good you can.

This extract from their website gives a flavour of the kind of thinking that Effective Altruism promotes[472]:

History contains many examples of people who have had a huge positive impact on the world.

Irena Sendler saved 2500 Jewish children from the Holocaust by providing them with false identity documents and smuggling them out of the Warsaw ghetto. Norman Borlaug's research into disease-resistant wheat precipitated the 'Green Revolution'. He has been credited with saving hundreds of millions of lives. Stanislav Petrov prevented all-out nuclear war simply by being calm under pressure and being willing to disobey orders.

These people might seem like unrelatable heroes, who were enormously brave, or skilled, or who just happened to be in the right place at the right time. But many people in developed countries can also have a tremendous positive impact on the world, if they choose wisely.

The next community I'll mention grew out of a three year project involving the United Nations University in the final years of the last millennium. This community is led by Jerome Glenn, and has chapters ("nodes") around the world[473].

The Millennium Project, millennium-project.org, regularly publishes one of the most useful reports on the "State of the Future". This provides updates on what the project calls "The 15 global challenges"[474]. The most recent edition of this report is version 19.1, described as follows[475]:

The State of the Future v.19.1 is a compelling overview of humanity's present situation, challenges and opportunities, potentials for the future, and actions and policies that could improve humanity's outlook – in clear, precise, and readable text with unparalleled breadth and depth. "We need hard-headed pragmatic idealists willing to understand the depths of human depravity and heights of human wisdom. We need serious, coherent, and integrated understandings of mega-problems and mega-opportunities to identify and implement strategies on the scale necessary to address global challenges", says the Conclusions of the report.

The Millennium Project also maintains an online "Global Futures Intelligence System"[476].

The communities I've listed so far, whilst all being aware of political issues, don't especially prioritise politics. The remaining communities put a greater focus on politics.

The Democracy in Europe Movement 2025 (DiEM25), diem25.org, is advocating a "new deal for Europe". It is active throughout Europe, and is developing a rich set of policy proposals. Here's how it describes itself[477]:

DiEM25 is a pan-European, cross-border movement of democrats.

We believe that the European Union is disintegrating. Europeans are losing their faith in the possibility of European solutions to European problems. At the same time as faith in the EU is waning, we see a rise of misanthropy, xenophobia and toxic nationalism.

If this development is not stopped, we fear a return to the 1930s. That is why we have come together despite our diverse political traditions – Green, radical left, liberal – in order to repair the EU. The EU needs to become a realm of shared prosperity, peace and solidarity for all Europeans. We must act quickly, before the EU disintegrates.

DiEM25, which was co-founded in February 2016 by Croat political philosopher Srećko Horvat and former Greek Finance Minister Yanis Varoufakis, include these sentiments in its online Manifesto[478]:

The European Union was an exceptional achievement, bringing together in peace European peoples speaking different languages, submersed in different cultures, proving that it was possible to create a shared framework of human rights across a continent that was, not long ago, home to murderous chauvinism, racism and barbarity. The European Union could have been the proverbial Beacon on the Hill, showing the world how peace and solidarity may be snatched from the jaws of centuries-long conflict and bigotry.

Alas, today, a common bureaucracy and a common currency divide European peoples that were beginning to unite despite our different languages and cultures. A confederacy of myopic politicians, economically naïve officials and financially incompetent 'experts' submit slavishly to the edicts of financial and industrial conglomerates, alienating Europeans and stirring up a dangerous anti-European backlash. Proud peoples are being turned against each other. Nationalism, extremism and racism are being re-awakened...

Realism demands that we work toward reaching milestones within a realistic timeframe. This is why DiEM25 will aim for four breakthroughs at regular intervals in order to bring about a fully democratic, functional Europe by 2025...

- *Immediately*: Full transparency in decision-making...

- *Within twelve months*: Address the on-going economic crisis utilising existing institutions and within existing EU Treaties...

- *Within two years*: Constitutional Assembly...

- *By 2025*: Enactment of the decisions of the Constitutional Assembly.

The comprehensive set of "aspirations" at the end of the DiEM25 Manifesto resonates with many of the principles covered throughout this book:

We aspire to:

- *A Democratic Europe* in which all political authority stems from Europe's sovereign peoples

- *A Transparent Europe* where all decision-making takes place under the citizens' scrutiny

- *A United Europe* whose citizens have as much in common across nations as within them

- *A Realistic Europe* that sets itself the task of radical, yet achievable, democratic reforms

- *A Decentralised Europe* that uses central power to maximise democracy in workplaces, towns, cities, regions and states

- *A Pluralist Europe* of regions, ethnicities, faiths, nations, languages and cultures

- *An Egalitarian Europe* that celebrates difference and ends discrimination based on gender, skin colour, social class or sexual orientation

- *A Cultured Europe* that harnesses its people's cultural diversity and promotes not only its invaluable heritage but also the work of Europe's dissident artists, musicians, writers and poets

- *A Social Europe* that recognises that liberty necessitates not only freedom from interference but also the basic goods that render one free from need and exploitation

- *A Productive Europe* that directs investment into a shared, green prosperity

- *A Sustainable Europe* that lives within the planet's means, minimising its environmental impact, and leaving as much fossil fuel in the earth

- *An Ecological Europe* engaged in genuine world-wide green transition

- *A Creative Europe* that releases the innovative powers of its citizens' imagination

- *A Technological Europe* pressing new technologies in the service of solidarity

- *A Historically-minded* Europe that seeks a bright future without hiding from its past

- *An Internationalist Europe* that treats non-Europeans as ends-in-themselves

- *A Peaceful Europe* de-escalating tensions in its East and in the Mediterranean, acting as a bulwark against the sirens of militarism and expansionism

- *An Open Europe* that is alive to ideas, people and inspiration from all over the world, recognising fences and borders as signs of weakness spreading insecurity in the name of security

- *A Liberated Europe* where privilege, prejudice, deprivation and the threat of violence wither, allowing Europeans to be born into fewer stereotypical roles, to enjoy even chances to develop their potential, and to be free to choose more of their partners in life, work and society.

For a political community with a somewhat different focus – on improving political imagination and political reinvention rather than democracy per se – check out "The Alternative". This has existed in Denmark since 2013, as Alternativet[479], and in the UK since 2017 as "The Alternative UK".

The Alternative UK, thealternative.org.uk, poses a stark question on its website[480]:

Politics is broken; what's the alternative?

It then invites potential supporters:

Let's begin the job of imagining politics.

The website continues:

We are a political platform, not a political party.

Our purpose is to catalyse a new politics that goes far beyond our current reality. We focus on engagement more than elections, on values over ideology, on futures that include, not exclude. We care about solutions, challenges – and great questions.

Beneath the democratic deficit lies an *imagination deficit*.

Through political laboratories, creative practice and sociable meet-ups we are launching a "friendly revolution", where we support all citizens to engage deeply with the complex issues that face our society.

The Alternative UK positions itself as "a network of networks"[481]:

The Alternative (UK) is a network of networks, curated along these lines:

- Those who explore the challenge of how to be fully human

- Those who are grappling with power and agency for communities at all levels

- Those who can look at the world and see it as an interdependent whole, looking for ways to work better together…

As a backdrop to those realms, we bring

- Techno-progressives – those who can look at the future with optimism, seeing the possibility of new resources, cultures and ways of being that create value for all of us

- Creatives of all kinds: those who know better than to look for fixes from within the current systems and are up for digging deep to find new resources for imagination.

Another recently formed political community takes its inspiration from discussion of the fourth industrial revolution.

The Fourth Group, thefourthgroup.org, sets itself the mission of "Creating a new politics for the fourth industrial revolution". The website for the organisation lists four main tasks[482]:

What we do:

- *Community*: We are building a global community of people who are working together to create a new politics.

- *Politech*: We create politech (political technology) to exponentially improve politics worldwide.

- *Education*: We inform people about the impact of technological advancements on politics, society, and the global economy.

- *Philosophy*: We are creating a new political philosophy which is rooted in the realities of our world today.

It's noteworthy that the Fourth Group speaks of the need for "a new political philosophy". They have suggested the name "forward" for this philosophy, stating that[483]:

We are not left, nor right, we are forward.

I personally anticipate that, as the concept of "forward" is developed, it will adopt an increasing number of the themes I've highlighted in this book as "transhumanist" and "technoprogressive".

That takes me to a community that explicitly positions itself as a transhumanist political initiative.

The Transhumanist Party, transhumanist-party.org, was created in the USA in October 2014 by Zoltan Istvan, and passed into the leadership of Gennady Stolyarov in November 2016. It maintains a particular interest in US politics, as evident in its mission statement[484]:

> Putting Science, Health, and Technology at the Forefront of American Politics

However, the party welcomes members from overseas, and many of the policies it has adopted are in principle applicable outside the US as well as inside it. Moreover, the party has a set of relationships (some formal, some informal) to other transhumanist political organisations around the world.

In its online constitution, the Transhumanist Party sets out three core ideals[485]:

> The United States Transhumanist Party is defined at its core by the following principles...

- Ideal 1. The Transhumanist Party supports significant life extension achieved through the progress of science and technology.

- Ideal 2. The Transhumanist Party supports a cultural, societal, and political atmosphere informed and animated by reason, science, and secular values.

- Ideal 3. The Transhumanist Party supports efforts to use science, technology, and rational discourse to reduce and eliminate various existential risks to the human species.

A distinguishing feature of the Transhumanist Party is the rich collection of "platform planks" that have been proposed, debated, voted, and selected by members[486].

The final four communities on my list are ones with which I have a direct personal involvement.

Humanity+, humanityplus.org, declares in its mission statement[487] that it "advocates the ethical use of technology to expand human capacities". Created in 1998 under the previous name of "World Transhumanist Association", the organisation at present has the following main activities:

- Distribution of a newsletter "Humanity+ Transhumanist News"

- An internal mailing list, restricted to members, covering transhumanist policy and initiatives

- Maintenance of the agreed versions of the Transhumanist Declaration and the Transhumanist FAQ

- Supporting the Humanity+ and TransVision series of international conferences[488]

- Supporting the H+Pedia knowledge aggregation project (covered below).

The Institute for Ethics and Emerging Technologies (IEET), ieet.org, is the organisation which has been associated for the longest time with the concept of "technoprogressive"[489]. James Hughes, Executive Director of the IEET, developed this set of ideas (at the time under the label "democratic transhumanism") in his 2004 book *Citizen Cyborg: Why Democratic Societies Must Respond to the Redesigned Human of the Future*[490] – a book that did a great deal to influence my own thinking[491].

The activities of the IEET are described as follows on its website[492]:

The Institute for Ethics and Emerging Technologies was formed to study and debate vital questions such as:

- Which technologies, especially new ones, are likely to have the greatest impact on human beings and human societies in the 21st century?

- What ethical issues do those technologies and their applications raise for humans, our civilization, and our world?

- How much can we extrapolate from the past and how much accelerating change should we anticipate?

- What sort of policy positions can be recommended to promote the best possible outcomes for individuals and societies?

The Institute for Ethics and Emerging Technologies... promotes ideas about how technological progress can increase freedom, happiness, and human flourishing in democratic societies. We believe that technological progress can be a catalyst for positive human development so long as we ensure that technologies are safe and equitably distributed. We call this a "technoprogressive" orientation.

Focusing on emerging technologies that have the potential to positively transform social conditions and the quality of human lives – especially "human enhancement technologies" – the IEET seeks to cultivate academic, professional, and popular understanding of their implications, both positive and negative, and to encourage responsible public policies for their safe and equitable use.

London Futurists, londonfuturists.com, is a meetup organisation with the mission statement "Serious analysis of radical scenarios for the next 3-40 years". Here's an extract from the organisation's website[493]:

The next few years are likely to bring unprecedented change. Humanity is facing:

- Accelerating changes in numerous fields of technology

- Deepening impacts of technologies into many new areas of life and society

- Stresses and strains of rapidly increasing resource usage

- Untested ideas and fads, often with little substance, spreading like wildfire

- Swiftly changing lifestyles, with unforeseeable consequences

- Gridlock in the mechanisms for international collaboration, being challenged by intense pent-up pressures...

Thanks to technology, we seem poised to gain god-like powers, such as super-intelligence and super-longevity. But at the same time, we risk losing sight of our humanity, and destroying everything that we used to hold dear.

There are many interconnections between technologies, economies, the environment, politics, cultures, and philosophies. We cannot predict with any certainty how these interconnections will unfold. We must consider, not just one possible scenario for the future, but many...

London Futurist meetings and projects explore both the potential upsides, and the potential downsides, of these scenarios.

We aim to set aside hype and sensationalism, over-optimism and over-pessimism. We want to explore and highlight information about future scenarios that is trustworthy and clear. This information can guide our actions, individually and collectively, as we seek to find our place in the future, and even to help create that future.

So, let's pool our best insights into what's technically feasible, and what's desirable. Given the gravity of the changes that may soon befall us, it's well worth debating, beforehand, what we can do so that technology deeply enhances humanity rather than deeply diminishes humanity.

I've been chairing London Futurists meetings since March 2008[494]. Our physical meetings take place in central London but are generally recorded and made available for wider viewing afterwards[495]. A newsletter is sent to members roughly once a month[496]. There are also online video meetings in which audience members around the world can raise questions and comments in real time[497]. Topics covered in this book frequently surface in London Futurists meetings, with the dual goals of reaching a better understanding and sparking positive action.

H+Pedia, hpluspedia.org, is a project that draws on support from a number of organisations, including London Futurists and Humanity+. As the website makes clear, the project takes inspiration from Wikipedia[498]:

> H+Pedia is a Humanity+ project to spread accurate, accessible, non-sensational information about transhumanism, radical life extension and futurism among the general public. H+Pedia is also an opportunity for transhumanist, radical life extensionist and futurist enthusiasts to work together, thereby strengthening the transhumanist community…

> H+Pedia aims to follow the principles of Wikipedia. At the same time, the H+Pedia editorial team seek to demonstrate greater awareness and appreciation of transhumanism and radical futurism. This will be reflected by the inclusion in H+Pedia of material which might not pass the Wikipedia tests for notability, as currently applied by Wikipedia editors.

The site maintains a "community portal" landing page that makes suggestions for where potential contributors might focus their attention[499]. As well as ideas for new articles, these suggestions include outreach, reviews, editorial, site mergers, and other admin tasks.

What makes the H+Pedia project particularly useful, in my view, is its careful aggregation and analysis of the overall mix of ideas relevant to the success of the technoprogressive initiative. As I write these words, the quality of H+Pedia articles remains variable. In some areas, the coverage remains threadbare. Evidently, the project will benefit from additional contributors. *Come on in!*

Acknowledgements

The superb design on the front cover is by Kevin Hawkes. Contact Kevin via inquiries@22creative.co.uk.

People who gave their time generously to provide feedback on draft material for this book include (in alphabetical order) Andrea Casalotti, Andrew Vladimirov, Anton Kulaga, Dalton Murray, Dana Edwards, Fabian Schneider, Gareth John, George Pór, Indra Adnan, John G Messerly, Jon Twigge, José Cordeiro, Kasim Khorasanee, Lee Andercheck, Mathieu Gosselin, Michael Haupt, Seth Weisberg, Stuart Dambrot, Ted Howard, Toby Unwin, and Yates Buckley. To all of them, I express my heartfelt thanks.

I'm also extremely grateful to all my colleagues and contacts in different organisations, for putting up with my slow communications as I prioritised writing this book. Many thanks for your patience and support!

About the author

David W. Wood, D.Sc., was one of the pioneers of the smartphone industry. He is now a futurist consultant, speaker and writer.

Wood spent 25 years envisioning, architecting, designing, implementing, and avidly using smart mobile devices. This includes ten years with PDA manufacturer Psion PLC, and ten more with smartphone operating system specialist Symbian Ltd, which he co-founded in 1998. At different times, his executive responsibilities included software development, technical consulting, developer evangelism, partnering and ecosystem management, and research and innovation. His software for UI and application frameworks was included on 500 million smartphones from companies such as Nokia, Samsung, LG, Motorola, Sony Ericsson, Fujitsu, Sharp, Siemens, and Panasonic.

From 2010 to 2013, Wood was Technology Planning Lead (CTO) of Accenture Mobility. During this time, he also co-led Accenture's "Mobility Health" business initiative.

Wood is CEO of the independent futurist consultancy and publisher Delta Wisdom. Delta Wisdom helps clients to anticipate the dramatic impact of rapidly changing technology on human individuals and communities, and highlights opportunities to apply technology in new solutions to deep-rooted problems. Clients of Delta Wisdom include individuals, businesses, organisations, and governments around the world.

As chair of London Futurists, Wood has organised regular meetings in London since March 2008 on futurist and technoprogressive topics. Membership of London Futurists reached 7,000 in February 2018.

Wood's previous books include *Smartphones and Beyond: Lessons from the remarkable rise and fall of Symbian* (published in September 2014) and *The Abolition of Aging: The forthcoming radical extension of healthy human longevity* (May 2016). He was also the lead editor of the volume *Anticipating 2025: A guide to the radical changes that may lie ahead, whether or not we're ready* (June 2014), and two collections of essays by Transpolitica consultants: *Anticipating Tomorrow's Politics* (March 2015) and *Envisioning Politics 2.0* (June 2015).

Wood founded the political think tank Transpolitica in January 2015. The declared goals of Transpolitica are to:

- Enable society to transcend the limitations and constraints of today's political models

- Anticipate the better political practices of an envisaged technoprogressive future

- Advocate the practical policies that will advance that future

- Engage people at all levels of politics and society around the world, to support and implement these policies

- Support transhumanists within political parties of all shapes and stripes.

Wood has a triple first class mathematics degree from Cambridge and undertook doctoral research in the Philosophy of Science. He has an honorary Doctorate in Science from Westminster University. In 2009 he was included in T3's list of "100 most influential people in technology". He has been a Fellow of the Royal Society of Arts (FRSA) in London since 2005, a Director of Humanity+ since November 2013, and a Fellow of the IEET (Institute for Ethics and Emerging Technologies) since January 2015.

He blogs at dw2blog.com and tweets as @dw2.

Endnotes

Note: for the convenience of readers, the online page https://transpolitica.org/projects/transcending-politics/endnotes/ provides an easily clickable version of the contents of the following list of endnotes.

[1] "An Intellectual Entente" http://harvardmagazine.com/breaking-news/james-watson-edward-o-wilson-intellectual-entente
[2] "A Letter to Mother Nature: Amendments to the Human Constitution" http://strategicphilosophy.blogspot.co.uk/2009/05/its-about-ten-years-since-i-wrote.html
[3] "Definitions of Transhumanism" https://web.archive.org/web/19970712091927/http://www.aleph.se/Trans/Intro/definitions.html
[4] "Extropy Institute Neologisms" https://web.archive.org/web/19980110162302/http:/www.extropy.com/neologo.htm
[5] "The Transhumanist Reader: Classical and Contemporary Essays on the Science, Technology, and Philosophy of the Human Future" https://www.goodreads.com/book/show/16287039-the-transhumanist-reader.
[6] "Transhumanism" https://hpluspedia.org/wiki/Transhumanism
[7] "An Introduction to Transhumanism" https://www.youtube.com/watch?v=bTMS9y8OVuY
[8] "2017 update to the Technoprogressive Declaration" https://transvision-conference.org/tpdec2017/
[9] "Lord Acton Quote Archive" https://acton.org/research/lord-acton-quote-archive
[10] This saying is from the New Testament: http://biblehub.com/matthew/16-26.htm
[11] "An Intellectual Entente" http://harvardmagazine.com/breaking-news/james-watson-edward-o-wilson-intellectual-entente
[12] This phrase is an adaptation of a similar saying by Marc Andreessen: https://www.wsj.com/articles/SB10001424053111903480904576512250915629460
[13] "Joseph de Maistre" https://en.wikiquote.org/wiki/Joseph_de_Maistre
[14] "Up-Wingers: A Futurist Manifesto" https://www.goodreads.com/book/show/931652.Up_Wingers

15 "The Proactionary Imperative: A Foundation for Transhumanism" https://www.goodreads.com/book/show/20696118-the-proactionary-imperative

16 "Plato's Philosopher Kings" https://www.youtube.com/watch?v=ALXsaT6bqL0

17 "What about technocracy?" http://www.technocracyinc.org/what-about-technocracy/

18 "Scientocracy: Policy making that reflects human nature" https://www.psychologytoday.com/blog/scientocracy/200901/scientocracy-policy-making-reflects-human-nature

19 "Britain has had enough of experts, says Gove" https://www.ft.com/content/3be49734-29cb-11e6-83e4-abc22d5d108c

20 "Trofim Lysenko" http://www.nndb.com/people/828/000050678/

21 "Techies have been trying to replace politicians for decades" https://www.wired.com/2015/06/technocracy-inc/

22 An archive of the first Transpolitica newsletter is available at https://transpolitica.org/2015/01/28/transpolitica-news-1/

23 "Preamble" https://transpolitica.org/manifesto/

24 "Transpolitica: Anticipating tomorrow's politics" https://transpolitica.org/

25 For example, that statement was made at a conference in New York in October 2014, by Alexis Ohanian, the founder of Reddit: http://www.bbc.com/future/story/20141022-are-we-getting-smarter

26 "Political Lying" http://www.bartleby.com/209/633.html

27 "President Trump has made 1,628 false or misleading claims over 298 days" https://www.washingtonpost.com/news/fact-checker/wp/2017/11/14/president-trump-has-made-1628-false-or-misleading-claims-over-298-days/

28 "Trump's Lies vs. Obama's" https://www.nytimes.com/interactive/2017/12/14/opinion/sunday/trump-lies-obama-who-is-worse.html

29 "Killing the Truth: How Trump's Attack on the Free Press Endangers Democracy" https://www.huffingtonpost.com/entry/killing-the-truth-how-trumps-attack-on-the-free-press_us_58ba1469e4b02eac8876cebf

30 "Why Trump's supporters will never abandon him" http://www.bbc.co.uk/news/world-us-canada-41028733

31 "Upton Sinclair" https://en.wikiquote.org/wiki/Upton_Sinclair

32 "Burn the rich: a recent study suggests that envy comes naturally": http://reason.com/archives/2002/06/19/burn-the-rich

33 "Are People Willing to Pay to Reduce Others' Incomes?" http://www2.warwick.ac.uk/fac/soc/economics/staff/ajoswald/finaljuly13paris.pdf (PDF)

[34] "My Final Answer – 'Kill My Neighbour's Goat'" http://www.rferl.org/a/1052770.html

[35] "Meditation 17", quoted in https://qz.com/716088/john-donnes-solemn-400-year-old-poem-against-isolationism-is-resonating-with-brits-today/

[36] "Pence's Past" http://www.snopes.com/mike-pences-gay-past/

[37] "List of cognitive biases" https://en.wikipedia.org/wiki/List_of_cognitive_biases

[38] "Only the Paranoid Survive" https://www.goodreads.com/book/show/66863.Only_the_Paranoid_Survive

[39] "The Better Angels of Our Nature: Why Violence Has Declined" https://www.goodreads.com/book/show/11107244-the-better-angels-of-our-nature

[40] "Homo Deus: A Brief History of Tomorrow" https://www.goodreads.com/book/show/31138556-homo-deus

[41] "Abundance: The Future is Brighter Than You Think" http://www.diamandis.com/abundance

[42] "A Single Death is a Tragedy; a Million Deaths is a Statistic" http://quoteinvestigator.com/2010/05/21/death-statistic/

[43] "Brave New World: A defence of paradise-engineering", by David Pearce: https://www.huxley.net/

[44] "Statement from the new Prime Minister Theresa May" https://www.gov.uk/government/speeches/statement-from-the-new-prime-minister-theresa-may

[45] "The greatest motivational poster ever?" http://news.bbc.co.uk/1/hi/magazine/7869458.stm

[46] "It was the best of times" http://www.nationalreview.com/article/443374/2016-best-year-ever

[47] "Was 2016 the Best Year Ever?" https://www.project-syndicate.org/commentary/inequality-and-climate-change-exaggeration-by-bjorn-lomborg-2016-12

[48] "The Infinite Resource" http://rameznaam.com/the-infinite-resource/

[49] "State of the Future version 19.1" http://www.millennium-project.org/state-of-the-future-version-19-1/

[50] "State of the Future Index" http://www.millennium-project.org/millennium/SOFI.html

[51] "The Great Illusion" https://www.goodreads.com/book/show/2462426.The_Great_Illusion

[52] "World War One: First war was impossible, then inevitable" http://blogs.reuters.com/anatole-kaletsky/2014/06/27/world-war-one-first-war-was-impossible-then-inevitable/

53 Quote included in "A mirror on the crisis" http://www.independent.co.uk/arts-entertainment/books/reviews/the-ascent-of-money-by-niall-ferguson-980013.html

54 "The Executive Who Brought Down AIG" http://abcnews.go.com/Blotter/story?id=7210007

55 "Accidental Nuclear War: A Timeline of Close Calls" http://futureoflife.org/background/nuclear-close-calls-a-timeline/

56 "Science Debunked Meteorites" https://www.sott.net/article/238325-Science-Debunked-Meteorites

57 "Scientific group-think: the meteorite case" http://arthur.shumwaysmith.com/life/content/scientific_group_think_the_meteorite_case

58 "Museums that threw away their meteorite collections" http://ersby.blogspot.co.uk/2013/02/museums-that-threw-away-their-meteorite.html

59 "As Hiroshima smouldered, our atom bomb scientists suffered remorse" http://www.newsweek.com/hiroshima-smouldered-our-atom-bomb-scientists-suffered-remorse-360125

60 "Hiroshima: The medical aftermath of the day that changed the world" http://hiroshima.australiandoctor.com.au/

61 "Sidelining Science Since Day One" https://www.ucsusa.org/center-science-and-democracy/promoting-scientific-integrity/sidelining-science-from-day-one

62 "The 7 biggest problems facing science, according to 270 scientists" https://www.vox.com/2016/7/14/12016710/science-challeges-research-funding-peer-review-process

63 "Unweaving the Rainbow: Science, Delusion and the Appetite for Wonder" https://www.goodreads.com/book/show/31487.Unweaving_the_Rainbow

64 "The 20th Century Transformation of U.S. Agriculture and Farm Policy" http://www.ers.usda.gov/media/259572/eib3_1_.pdf

65 "The Demographics of the U.S. Equine Population" http://www.humanesociety.org/assets/pdfs/hsp/soaiv_07_ch10.pdf

66 "Technology and people: The great job-creating machine" https://www2.deloitte.com/uk/en/pages/finance/articles/technology-and-people.html

67 "Technology has created more jobs than it has destroyed, says 140 years of data" https://www.theguardian.com/business/2015/aug/17/technology-created-more-jobs-than-destroyed-140-years-data-census

68 https://www.goodreads.com/book/show/949299.The_New_Division_of_Labor

69 "Uber's Self-Driving Truck Makes Its First Delivery: 50,000 Beers" https://www.wired.com/2016/10/ubers-self-driving-truck-makes-first-delivery-50000-beers/

70 "Microsoft, Google Beat Humans at Image Recognition" http://www.eetimes.com/document.asp?doc_id=1325712

71 "The Master Algorithm: How the Quest for the Ultimate Learning Machine Will Remake Our World" https://www.goodreads.com/book/show/24612233-the-master-algorithm

72 "A welcome from the President, David Levy" http://icga.leidenuniv.nl/?page_id=24

73 "David Levy speaker preview of Anticipating 2025" https://www.youtube.com/watch?v=q-Rk6rtLc-E

74 "'Huge leap forward' Computer that mimics human brain beats professional at game of Go" http://www.sciencemag.org/news/2016/01/huge-leap-forward-computer-mimics-human-brain-beats-professional-game-go

75 "The Mystery of Go, the Ancient Game That Computers Still Can't Win" https://www.wired.com/2014/05/the-world-of-computer-go/

76 "The Mystery of Go, the Ancient Game That Computers Still Can't Win" https://www.wired.com/2014/05/the-world-of-computer-go/

77 "Artificial Intuition: The Improbable Deep Learning Revolution" https://gumroad.com/l/IHDj

78 "What the AI Behind AlphaGo Can Teach Us About Being Human" https://www.wired.com/2016/05/google-alpha-go-ai/

79 "Heart of the Machine: Our Future in a World of Artificial Emotional Intelligence" https://www.goodreads.com/book/show/31213179-heart-of-the-machine

80 "Rise of the robots: 60,000 workers culled from just one factory as China's struggling electronics hub turns to artificial intelligence" http://www.scmp.com/news/china/economy/article/1949918/rise-robots-60000-workers-culled-just-one-factory-chinas

81 "Japanese company replaces office workers with artificial intelligence" https://www.theguardian.com/technology/2017/jan/05/japanese-company-replaces-office-workers-artificial-intelligence-ai-fukoku-mutual-life-insurance

82 "Khosla explains his 'robots replacing doctors' comment" http://venturebeat.com/2013/12/05/khosla-explains-his-robots-replacing-doctors-comment-and-goes-on-the-hunt-for-data-scientists/

83 "Speculations and musings of a technology optimist" http://www.khoslaventures.com/20-percent-doctor-included-speculations-and-musings-of-a-technology-optimist

84 "The Future of the Professions: How Technology Will Transform the Work of Human Experts" https://www.goodreads.com/book/show/23462787-the-future-of-the-professions

85 "Google a step closer to developing machines with human-like intelligence" https://www.theguardian.com/science/2015/may/21/google-a-step-closer-to-developing-machines-with-human-like-intelligence

86 "James Bessen on Learning by Doing" http://www.econtalk.org/archives/2016/05/james_bessen_on.html

87 "Why Robots Will Be The Biggest Job Creators In World History" http://www.forbes.com/sites/johntamny/2015/03/01/why-robots-will-be-the-biggest-job-creators-in-history

88 "Occupational outlook handbook" https://www.bls.gov/ooh/office-and-administrative-support/tellers.htm#tab-6

89 "The Horses, 'going to the Dogs', from George Cruikshank's Scraps and Sketches" https://www.bl.uk/collection-items/the-horses-going-to-the-dogs-from-george-cruikshanks-scraps-and-sketches

90 Quoted in "Horses at Work: Harnessing Power in Industrial America" https://www.goodreads.com/book/show/5972226-horses-at-work

91 "The Rise and Fall of American Growth: The U.S. Standard of Living Since the Civil War" https://www.goodreads.com/book/show/26634594-the-rise-and-fall-of-american-growth

92 "Museum of the City of New York" http://collections.mcny.org

93 "5th Ave. – Easter, '13" http://www.loc.gov/pictures/resource/ggbain.11656/

94 "Technology and inequality" http://www.technologyreview.com/featuredstory/531726/technology-and-inequality/

95 "The Second Machine Age" http://secondmachineage.com/

96 "The Economics of Superstars" http://home.uchicago.edu/~vlima/courses/econ201/Superstars.pdf

97 "The Pitchforks Are Coming... For Us Plutocrats" http://www.politico.com/magazine/story/2014/06/the-pitchforks-are-coming-for-us-plutocrats-108014.html

98 "Why Robots Will Be The Biggest Job Creators In World History" http://www.forbes.com/sites/johntamny/2015/03/01/why-robots-will-be-the-biggest-job-creators-in-history

99 "Utopia for Realists: And How We Can Get There" https://www.goodreads.com/book/show/36690518-utopia-for-realists

[100] "A Commitment to Philanthropy" https://givingpledge.org

[101] "The iPhone at 10: How the smartphone became so smart" http://www.bbc.co.uk/news/business-38320198

[102] "Economic Possibilities for our Grandchildren" http://www.econ.yale.edu/smith/econ116a/keynes1.pdf

[103] "Roy Amara, forecaster, RIP" http://boingboing.net/2008/01/03/roy-amara-forecaster.html

[104] "A Conversation with Kevin Kelly" http://edge.org/conversation/the-technium

[105] "Know Your Baby is Okay" http://www.owletcare.com/

[106] "Consumer Alert: Consumer Affairs Warns Parents to Secure Video Baby Monitors" http://www1.nyc.gov/site/dca/media/pr012716.page

[107] "Hacker disables more than 100 cars remotely" https://www.wired.com/2010/03/hacker-bricks-cars/

[108] "Pacemaker hack can deliver deadly 830-volt jolt" http://www.computerworld.com/article/2492453/malware-vulnerabilities/pacemaker-hack-can-deliver-deadly-830-volt-jolt.html

[109] "Dick Cheney's Heart" http://www.cbsnews.com/news/dick-cheneys-heart/

[110] "China Hackers Hit U.S. Chamber" https://www.wsj.com/articles/SB10001424052970204058404577110541568535300

[111] "CIA Chief: We'll Spy on You Through Your Dishwasher" https://www.wired.com/2012/03/petraeus-tv-remote/

[112] "Another IoT botnet with pieces of Mirai embedded can do DDoS from 100k devices" https://www.networkworld.com/article/3195900/security/another-iot-botnet-with-pieces-of-mirai-embedded-can-do-ddos-from-100k-devices.html

[113] "Google's DeepMind AI can lip-read TV shows better than a pro" https://www.newscientist.com/article/2113299-googles-deepmind-ai-can-lip-read-tv-shows-better-than-a-pro/

[114] "How Web Sites Vary Prices Based on Your Information (and What You Can Do About It)" https://lifehacker.com/5973689/how-web-sites-vary-prices-based-on-your-information-and-what-you-can-do-about-it

[115] "State of the Future": http://millennium-project.org/millennium/201314SOF.html

[116] https://twitter.com/tom_peters/status/820440755214827521

[117] https://twitter.com/tom_peters/status/820441228101591042

[118] https://twitter.com/tom_peters/status/820463464057446400

[119] https://twitter.com/tom_peters/status/820462055601762304

[120] "About Bruce Schneier" https://www.schneier.com/blog/about/

121   "Click   Here   to   Kill   Everyone"
http://nymag.com/selectall/2017/01/the-internet-of-things-dangerous-future-bruce-schneier.html

122 "Future Crimes" http://www.futurecrimesbook.com/

123 "About Marc Goodman" http://www.marcgoodman.net/about/

124   "Singularity   1on1:   Marc   Goodman   on   Future   Crimes"
https://www.singularityweblog.com/marc-goodman-on-future-crimes-2/

125   "We   Need   a   Manhattan   Project   for   Cyber   Security"
http://www.marcgoodman.net/2014/11/14/medium-we-need-a-manhattan-project-for-cyber-security/

126 "March of the terminators: Robot warriors are no longer sci-fi but reality. So what happens when they turn their guns on us?"
http://www.dailymail.co.uk/sciencetech/article-1182910/March-terminators-Robot-warriors-longer-sci-fi-reality-So-happens-turn-guns-us.html

127 "The problem" http://www.stopkillerrobots.org/the-problem/

128 See for example the points made by Calum Chace in "The killer robots have   arrived: but   could   they   also   save   your   life?"
http://metro.co.uk/2018/01/29/the-killer-robots-have-arrived-but-could-they-also-save-your-life-7265785/

129 "Autonomous weapons: An open letter from AI & robotics researchers"
https://futureoflife.org/open-letter-autonomous-weapons/

130   "Click   Here   to   Kill   Everyone"
http://nymag.com/selectall/2017/01/the-internet-of-things-dangerous-future-bruce-schneier.html

131 "Life 3.0: Being Human in the Age of Artificial Intelligence"
https://www.goodreads.com/book/show/34272565-life-3-0

132 "Our Final Invention: Artificial Intelligence and the End of the Human Era"   https://www.goodreads.com/book/show/17286699-our-final-invention

133 "Surviving AI: The promise and peril of artificial intelligence"
https://www.goodreads.com/book/show/26254196-surviving-ai

134   "The   Technological   Singularity"
https://www.goodreads.com/book/show/26017445-the-technological-singularity

135   "Superintelligence: Paths,   Dangers,   Strategies"
https://www.goodreads.com/book/show/20527133-superintelligence

136   "Defining   Intelligence"
https://www.edge.org/conversation/stuart_russell-defining-intelligence

137   "Artificial   Intelligence: A   modern   approach"
https://www.goodreads.com/book/show/27543.Artificial_Intelligence

[138] "Anniversary – 80 years ago, Leo Szilard envisioned neutron chain reaction" http://ansnuclearcafe.org/2013/09/17/anniversary-80-years-ago-leo-szliard-envisioned-neutron-chain-reaction

[139] "AI: The Story So Far", slides by Stuart Russell https://intelligence.org/files/csrbai/russell-slides.pdf

[140] "Thinking about the unthinkable" https://www.goodreads.com/book/show/179016.Thinking_about_the_Unthinkable

[141] "'Whoever leads in AI will rule the world': Putin to Russian children on Knowledge Day" https://www.rt.com/news/401731-ai-rule-world-putin/

[142] "World Economic Forum Annual Meeting" https://www.weforum.org/events/world-economic-forum-annual-meeting-2017

[143] "Future of life institute" https://futureoflife.org/

[144] "Beneficial AI 2017" https://futureoflife.org/bai-2017/

[145] "Asilomar AI principles" https://futureoflife.org/ai-principles/

[146] "AI safety conference in Puerto Rico" https://futureoflife.org/2015/10/12/ai-safety-conference-in-puerto-rico/

[147] https://www.partnershiponai.org/

[148] "China's Artificial-Intelligence Boom" https://www.theatlantic.com/technology/archive/2017/02/china-artificial-intelligence/516615/

[149] "Get serious about obesity or bankrupt the NHS – Simon Stevens" https://www.england.nhs.uk/2014/09/serious-about-obesity/

[150] "Billions wasted as drugs bill threatens to bankrupt the NHS, experts say" http://www.express.co.uk/news/uk/736856/Billions-wasted-drugs-bill-threatens-bankrupt-NHS-experts-say

[151] "Dear Prime Minister: Final Letter" https://www.scribd.com/document/368914596/Final-Letter

[152] "NHS waiting list could soar to 5m without urgent cash, chief warns" https://www.theguardian.com/society/2017/nov/08/nhs-chief-warns-waiting-lists-could-hit-5m-without-extra-cash

[153] "This is the No. 1 reason Americans file for bankruptcy" https://www.usatoday.com/story/money/personalfinance/2017/05/05/this-is-the-no-1-reason-americans-file-for-bankruptcy/101148136/

[154] "The Digital Doctor: Hope, Hype, and Harm at the Dawn of Medicine's Computer Age" https://www.goodreads.com/book/show/23131174-the-digital-doctor

[155] "NHS pulls the plug on its 11bn IT system" http://www.independent.co.uk/life-style/health-and-families/health-news/nhs-pulls-the-plug-on-its-11bn-it-system-2330906.html

156 "Oh dear, is this another costly IT failure?" http://www.telegraph.co.uk/news/politics/10986642/Oh-dear-is-this-another-costly-IT-failure.html

157 "Now, Cancer becomes one of the most expensive and riskiest diseases to treat" http://www.nationaldailypress.com/2016/05/01/now-cancer-become-one-of-the-most-expensive-and-riskiest-diseases-to-treat/

158 "Low-Income Diabetics Paying High Price For Insulin" http://c-hit.org/2016/04/10/low-income-diabetics-paying-high-price-for-insulin/

159 "The Cost of Sequencing a Human Genome" https://www.genome.gov/sequencingcosts/

160 "Diagnosing the decline in pharmaceutical R&D efficiency" http://www.nature.com/nrd/journal/v11/n3/full/nrd3681.html

161 "Gompertz–Makeham law of mortality" https://en.wikipedia.org/wiki/Gompertz%E2%80%93Makeham_law_of_mortality

162 Analysis from https://www.ons.gov.uk/peoplepopulationandcommunity/birthsdeathsandmarriages/lifeexpectancies/datasets/nationallifetablesunitedkingdomreferencetables

163 "The Innovator's Prescription: A Disruptive Solution for Health Care" https://www.goodreads.com/book/show/3487850-the-innovator-s-prescription

164 "Factors in the Drop in United States Infant Mortality: 1900-1940" http://repository.cmu.edu/cgi/viewcontent.cgi?article=1070&context=hss honors

165 "Infant mortality decline in the late 19th and early 20th centuries: the role of market milk" https://www.ncbi.nlm.nih.gov/pubmed/17951891

166 "American Amnesia: Business, Government, and the Forgotten Roots of Our Prosperity" https://www.goodreads.com/book/show/25814409-american-amnesia

167 "Dr. Semmelweis' Biography" http://semmelweis.org/about/dr-semmelweis-biography/

168 "Views on puerperal fever" https://en.wikipedia.org/wiki/Carl_Braun_(obstetrician)#Views_on_puerperal_fever

169 "Cigarettes were once 'physician' tested, approved" http://www.healio.com/hematology-oncology/news/print/hemonc-today/%7B241d62a7-fe6e-4c5b-9fed-a33cc6e4bd7c%7D/cigarettes-were-once-physician-tested-approved

170 "The Abolition of Aging: The forthcoming radical extension of healthy human longevity" https://theabolitionofaging.com/

[171] "Ending Aging: The Rejuvenation Breakthroughs That Could Reverse Human Aging in Our Lifetime" https://www.goodreads.com/book/show/519781.Ending_Aging

[172] "Juvenescence: Investing in the Age of Longevity" https://www.juvenescence-book.com/

[173] "In pursuit of the Longevity Dividend" http://sjayolshansky.com/sjo/Background_files/TheScientist.pdf

[174] "The Value of Health and Longevity" https://web.archive.org/web/20061018172529/http://www.econ.yale.edu/seminars/labor/lap04-05/topel032505.pdf

[175] "Estimates of Funding for Various Research, Condition, and Disease Categories" https://report.nih.gov/categorical_spending.aspx

[176] "SENS Research Foundation" http://www.sens.org/

[177] "How Much Does It Cost To Find A Higgs Boson?" http://www.forbes.com/sites/alexknapp/2012/07/05/how-much-does-it-cost-to-find-a-higgs-boson/

[178] "Why Not Artificial Wombs?" http://www.thenewatlantis.com/docLib/TNA03-Rosen.pdf

[179] "Transhumanism" https://hpluspedia.org/wiki/Transhumanism

[180] "Humanity+" http://humanityplus.org/

[181] "Updated planetary boundaries framework shows four of nine boundaries now crossed" http://www.futureearth.org/news/updated-planetary-boundaries-framework-shows-four-nine-boundaries-now-crossed

[182] "Powering the planet: Chemical challenges solar energy utilization" http://www.pnas.org/content/103/43/15729.long

[183] "Could the desert sun power the world?" https://www.theguardian.com/environment/2011/dec/11/sahara-solar-panels-green-electricity

[184] "Total Surface Area Required to Fuel the World With Solar" http://landartgenerator.org/blagi/archives/127

[185] "Growth of photovoltaics" https://en.wikipedia.org/wiki/Growth_of_photovoltaics

[186] "Sunny uplands: Alternative energy will no longer be alternative" http://www.economist.com/news/21566414-alternative-energy-will-no-longer-be-alternative-sunny-uplands

[187] "Utility-Scale Solar 2015: An Empirical Analysis of Project Cost, Performance, and Pricing Trends in the United States" https://emp.lbl.gov/publications/utility-scale-solar-2015-empirical

[188] "H2 2016 LCOE: Giant fall in generating costs" https://about.bnef.com/blog/h2-2016-lcoe-giant-fall-generating-costs-offshore-wind/

189 "Abu Dhabi confirms USD 24.2/MWh bid in solar tender" https://renewablesnow.com/news/update-abu-dhabi-confirms-usd-24-2-mwh-bid-in-solar-tender-540324/

190 "Seeing the light: How India is embracing solar power" http://www.bbc.co.uk/news/business-39844446

191 "European Energy Auctions Yield Ever-Lower Wind Energy Prices In Germany & Spain" https://cleantechnica.com/2017/05/22/european-energy-auctions-yield-ever-lower-wind-energy-prices-germany-spain/

192 "Graph of the Day: Germany's record 85% renewables over weekend" http://reneweconomy.com.au/graph-of-the-day-germanys-record-85-renewables-over-weekend-60743/

193 "Solar power breaks UK records thanks to sunny weather" https://www.theguardian.com/environment/2017/may/26/solar-power-breaks-uk-records-thanks-sunny-weather

194 "100% renewable energy" https://en.wikipedia.org/wiki/100%25_renewable_energy

195 "Key world energy statistics" https://www.iea.org/publications/freepublications/publication/KeyWorld2016.pdf.

196 "REN21 Renewables Global Futures Report" http://www.ren21.net/future-of-renewables/global-futures-report/

197 "Merchants of Doubt: How a Handful of Scientists Obscured the Truth on Issues from Tobacco Smoke to Global Warming" https://www.goodreads.com/book/show/7799004-merchants-of-doubt

198 "Russian Combat Medals Put Lie To Putin's Claim Of No Russian Troops In Ukraine" https://www.forbes.com/sites/paulroderickgregory/2016/09/06/russian-combat-medals-put-lie-to-putins-claim-of-no-russian-troops-in-ukraine

199 "The Press and immigration: reporting the news or fanning the flames of hatred?" http://www.sub-scribe.co.uk/2016/09/the-press-and-immigration-reporting.html

200 "Cameron vows 'green revolution'" http://news.bbc.co.uk/1/hi/uk/4917516.stm

201 "David Cameron at centre of 'get rid of all the green crap' storm" https://www.theguardian.com/environment/2013/nov/21/david-cameron-green-crap-comments-storm

202 "UK Lobbied European Union To Weaken Climate Rules" https://cleantechnica.com/2017/05/31/uk-lobbied-european-union-weaken-climate-rules/

203 "How Large Are Global Energy Subsidies?" http://www.imf.org/external/pubs/cat/longres.aspx?sk=42940.0

[204] "Fossil fuels subsidised by $10m a minute, says IMF" https://www.theguardian.com/environment/2015/may/18/fossil-fuel-companies-getting-10m-a-minute-in-subsidies-says-imf

[205] "Wind farm subsidies axed 'to stop turbines covering beautiful countryside'" http://www.telegraph.co.uk/news/earth/energy/windpower/11685082/Wind-farm-subsidies-axed-to-stop-turbines-covering-beautiful-countryside.html

[206] "ELF09: energy, sustainability, and more" https://dw2blog.com/2009/11/19/elf09-energy-sustainability-and-more/

[207] "Advances and slowdowns in Carbon Capture and Storage technology development" http://www.iccgov.org/wp-content/uploads/2016/05/48_CCS_Aurora.pdf

[208] "Sustainable Energy - Without the Hot Air" https://www.goodreads.com/book/show/4070074-sustainable-energy---without-the-hot-air

[209] "Saving the planet by numbers" http://news.bbc.co.uk/1/hi/sci/tech/8014484.stm

[210] "Archive of press releases" http://www.desertec.org/press

[211] "Carbon Dioxide Set an All-Time Monthly High" http://www.climatecentral.org/news/carbon-dioxide-all-time-monthly-high-21507

[212] "Historic Heat Wave Sweeps Asia, the Middle East and Europe" https://www.wunderground.com/cat6/historic-heat-wave-sweeps-asia-middle-east-and-europe

[213] "The Younger Dryas" https://www.ncdc.noaa.gov/abrupt-climate-change/The%20Younger%20Dryas

[214] "How to kill (almost) all life: the end-Permian extinction event" http://palaeo.gly.bris.ac.uk/Benton/reprints/2003TREEPTr.pdf

[215] "83-year-old man isn't shaken by Mount St Helens earthquakes" https://news.google.com/newspapers?id=50MyAAAAIBAJ&sjid=T-cFAAAAIBAJ&pg=3106,4578982

[216] "1980 eruption of Mount St. Helens" https://en.wikipedia.org/wiki/1980_eruption_of_Mount_St._Helens

[217] "Advances and slowdowns in Carbon Capture and Storage technology development" http://www.iccgov.org/wp-content/uploads/2016/05/48_CCS_Aurora.pdf

[218] "How Large Are Global Energy Subsidies?" http://www.imf.org/external/pubs/cat/longres.aspx?sk=42940.0

[219] "Congestion charge" https://tfl.gov.uk/modes/driving/congestion-charge

220 "CBO Testimony" https://web.archive.org/web/20080214064914/http://www.cbo.gov/ftpd oc.cfm?index=4197

221 "London to introduce £10 vehicle pollution charge, says Sadiq Khan" https://www.theguardian.com/environment/2017/feb/17/london-to-introduce-vehicle-pollution-charge-in-october-says-mayor-sadiq-khan

222 "What Would Milton Friedman Do About Climate Change? Tax Carbon" https://www.forbes.com/sites/jeffmcmahon/2014/10/12/what-would-milton-friedman-do-about-climate-change-tax-carbon

223 "What Would Milton Friedman Do About Climate Change? Tax Carbon" https://www.forbes.com/sites/jeffmcmahon/2014/10/12/what-would-milton-friedman-do-about-climate-change-tax-carbon

224 "Investor lessons from a market bubble that cost Isaac Newton a bundle": http://www.marketwatch.com/story/investor-lessons-from-a-market-bubble-that-cost-isaac-newton-a-bundle-2016-08-25

225 "The Myths of the South Sea Bubble": http://discovery.ucl.ac.uk/12397/1/12397.pdf

226 "How Isaac Newton went flat broke chasing a stock bubble": https://www.sovereignman.com/finance/how-isaac-newton-went-flat-broke-chasing-a-stock-bubble-13268/

227 "Panic of 1857": https://en.wikipedia.org/wiki/Panic_of_1857

228 "The slumps that shaped modern finance": http://www.economist.com/news/essays/21600451-finance-not-merely-prone-crises-it-shaped-them-five-historical-crises-show-how-aspects-today-s-fina

229 "Economy in the great depression": http://www.shmoop.com/great-depression/economy.html

230 "On the Brink": https://www.goodreads.com/book/show/7098979-on-the-brink

231 "Bank of Cyprus haircut could reach 60%": https://www.ft.com/content/4a1bb1d6-9926-11e2-af84-00144feabdc0

232 "Remarks by Chairman Alan Greenspan" https://www.federalreserve.gov/boarddocs/speeches/1996/19961205.htm

233 "This Time Is Different: Eight Centuries of Financial Folly": https://www.goodreads.com/book/show/6372440-this-time-is-different

234 "The Mississippi Bubble of 1718-1720": http://www.thebubblebubble.com/mississippi-bubble/

235 "The Plot Between Ignorance and Arrogance": https://economix.blogs.nytimes.com/2009/09/30/the-plot-between-ignorance-and-arrogance/

236 "1927-1933 Chart of Pompous Prognosticators": http://www.gold-eagle.com/article/1927-1933-chart-pompous-prognosticators

[237] "Herbert Hoover": https://en.wikiquote.org/wiki/Herbert_Hoover

[238] "Macroeconomic Priorities": http://pages.stern.nyu.edu/~dbackus/Taxes/Lucas%20priorities%20AER%2003.pdf

[239] "This is how we let the credit crunch happen, Ma'am ...": https://www.theguardian.com/uk/2009/jul/26/monarchy-credit-crunch

[240] "The economic forecasters' failing vision": https://www.ft.com/content/50007754-ca35-11dd-93e5-000077b07658?mhq5j=e3

[241] "Greenspan – I was wrong about the economy. Sort of": https://www.theguardian.com/business/2008/oct/24/economics-creditcrunch-federal-reserve-greenspan

[242] "The End of Alchemy": https://www.goodreads.com/book/show/30231791-the-end-of-alchemy

[243] "Interview with Dr. Rudi Dornbusch": http://www.pbs.org/wgbh/pages/frontline/shows/mexico/interviews/dornbusch.html

[244] "The Hemingway Law of Motion: Gradually, then Suddenly": http://conversableeconomist.blogspot.co.uk/2015/01/the-hemingway-law-of-motion-gradually.html

[245] "Four Dumb Things Smart Leaders Say (And What You Can Learn From Them)": https://www.forbes.com/sites/forbescoachescouncil/2017/02/22/four-dumb-things-smart-leaders-say-and-what-you-can-learn-from-them/

[246] "Technology vs. Humanity: Futurist Gerd Leonhard's new Book": http://www.techvshuman.com/read-preview/

[247] "How Did You Go Bankrupt? Hemingway, China And The EU": http://www.valuewalk.com/2014/06/how-did-you-go-bankrupt/?all=1

[248] That term was coined in 2003 by Warren Buffett: http://www.fintools.com/docs/Warren%20Buffet%20on%20Derivatives.pdf

[249] "Can We Avoid Another Financial Crisis?" https://www.goodreads.com/book/show/35121849-can-we-avoid-another-financial-crisis

[250] "Flash Crash – Don't Fall for Market 'Spoofers'": http://www.valuewalk.com/2017/05/flash-crash-dont-fall-for-market-spoofers/

[251] "The Coming Cryptocurrency Crash": https://www.forbes.com/sites/robertwolcott/2017/07/07/the-coming-cryptocurrency-crash-and-why-its-a-good-thing/

[252] "What's the ultimatum game?" http://money.howstuffworks.com/ultimatum-game.htm

253 "Fixing Economics": https://www.goodreads.com/book/show/31436895-fixing-economics

254 "The Role of Fairness in Wage Determination": https://www.jstor.org/stable/2535192

255 "Misbehaving: The Making of Behavioral Economics": https://www.goodreads.com/book/show/26530355-misbehaving

256 "The enduring certainty of radical uncertainty": https://www.ft.com/content/ec5520c4-fb23-11e5-8f41-df5bda8beb40

257 "The key to industrial capitalism: limited liability": http://www.economist.com/node/347323

258 "Monetary metamorphosis": http://www.economist.com/node/242113

259 1 Timothy 6:10: http://biblehub.com/1_timothy/6-10.htm

260 "Celebrity Chef Mario Batali Says Bankers As Bad As Hitler, Stalin": https://www.forbes.com/sites/jeffbercovici/2011/11/08/celebrity-chef-mario-batali-says-bankers-as-bad-as-hitler-stalin

261 "Adults In The Room: My Battle With Europe's Deep Establishment": https://www.goodreads.com/book/show/34673467-adults-in-the-room

262 "What Happens When Money Breaks the Rules?" http://www.slate.com/articles/business/the_next_20/2016/09/saving_glut_and_the_failure_of_capital_in_the_21st_century.html

263 "The sequel to the global financial crisis is here: High credit ratings have hidden a structural instability": https://www.ft.com/content/95808118-662e-11e7-9a66-93fb352ba1fe

264 "Other People's Money: The Real Business of Finance": https://www.goodreads.com/book/show/24612279-other-people-s-money

265 Genesis 1:31 http://biblehub.com/genesis/1-31.htm

266 "Adam Smith" https://en.wikiquote.org/wiki/Adam_Smith

267 "The Great Lightbulb Conspiracy" http://spectrum.ieee.org/geek-life/history/the-great-lightbulb-conspiracy

268 "Operators blame roaming charges on handset subsidies" http://www.zdnet.com/article/operators-blame-roaming-charges-on-handset-subsidies/

269 "Court's Finding of Fact" http://www.webcitation.org/query?id=1298665666970544

270 "Standard Oil" https://en.wikipedia.org/wiki/Standard_Oil#Monopoly_charges_and_anti-trust_legislation

271 "Richard Oastler's letter on 'Yorkshire slavery', 1830" http://webarchive.nationalarchives.gov.uk/20170405151432/http://www.makingthemodernworld.org.uk/learning_modules/history/01.TU.01/?style=expander_popup&filename=expandables/01.EX.18.xml

272 "Evidence of Richard Oastler on 'Yorkshire Slavery'"
http://www.victorianweb.org/history/yorkslav.html
273 "A Cotton Manufacturer on Hours of Labor"
http://www.victorianweb.org/history/workers2.html
274 Quoted in "The Factory System"
https://www.goodreads.com/book/show/5351760-the-factory-system
275 "The Jungle"
https://www.goodreads.com/book/show/41681.The_Jungle
276 "The Dissipated Life of William A. Rockefeller"
https://www.americanhistoryusa.com/strange-life-of-william-rockefeller/
277 "The Great American Fraud by Samuel Hopkins Adams, 1905"
http://college.cengage.com/history/ayers_primary_sources/americanfraud
_adams_1905.htm
278 "Pure Food and Drug Act of 1906"
https://en.wikisource.org/wiki/Pure_Food_and_Drug_Act_of_1906
279 "Natural Capital at Risk: The 100 top externalities of business"
https://web.archive.org/web/20160605043250/http://www.trucost.com/
_uploads/publishedResearch/TEEB%20Final%20Report%20-
%20web%20SPv2.pdf
280 "The Economics of Ecosystems and Biodiversity"
http://www.teebweb.org/
281 "Max Born: The Nobel prize winning physicist's advice on what causes
'all evil'" http://www.independent.co.uk/news/science/max-born-
quantum-physics-rule-google-doodle-single-truth-ceremony-knowledge-
nazis-germany-evil-a8103961.html
282 "Pharmocracy: How Corrupt Deals and Misguided Medical Regulations
Are Bankrupting America--And What to Do about It"
https://www.goodreads.com/book/show/12615698-pharmocracy
283 "How Regulation of Medicine is Bankrupting the United States and
What Congress Can Do to Stop It"
http://www.lifeextension.com/magazine/2011/10/Regulation-of-
Medicine-is-Bankrupting-the-United-States-What-Congress-Can-Do-to-
Stop-It/Page-01
284 "Ashes to Ashes: America's Hundred-Year Cigarette War, the Public
Health, and the Unabashed Triumph of Philip Morris"
https://www.goodreads.com/book/show/335451.Ashes_to_Ashes
285 "Number of smokers in England drops to all-time low"
https://www.theguardian.com/society/2016/sep/20/number-of-uk-
smokers-falls-to-lowest-level
286 "Big Tobacco: A history of its decline"
http://edition.cnn.com/2009/POLITICS/06/19/tobacco.decline/index.ht
ml

287 "Are Teenagers Replacing Drugs With Smartphones?" https://www.nytimes.com/2017/03/13/health/teenagers-drugs-smartphones.html?_r=0

288 "How Big Tobacco got away with the Crime of the Century" https://theloungeisback.wordpress.com/2011/03/28/how-big-tobacco-got-away-with-the-crime-of-the-century/

289 "Andrew S. Fastow – Enron Corp" https://web.archive.org/web/20040820122148/http://www.cfo.com/printable/article.cfm/2989389

290 "Enron's many strands" http://www.nytimes.com/2002/01/30/business/enron-s-many-strands-the-accounting-fuzzy-rules-of-accounting-and-enron.html?mcubz=1

291 "Enron's collapse: The relationships" http://www.nytimes.com/2002/01/12/business/enron-s-collapse-the-relationships-bush-and-democrats-disputing-ties-to-enron.html?mcubz=1

292 "Enron's collapse: The politicians" http://www.nytimes.com/2002/01/21/us/enron-s-collapse-politicians-enron-spread-contributions-both-sides-aisle.html?mcubz=1

293 "Iceland Has Jailed 29 Bankers" http://www.huffingtonpost.com/stefan-simanowitz/iceland-has-jailed-29-bankers_b_8908536.html

294 "Samsung heir sentenced to five years in jail after corruption conviction" https://www.theguardian.com/world/2017/aug/25/samsung-heir-lee-jae-yong-found-guilty-of-corruption

295 "Crowds vs Swarms – which is smarter?" http://unanimous.ai/crowds-vs-swarms-which-is-smarter/

296 "German federal election, March 1933" https://en.wikipedia.org/wiki/German_federal_election,_March_1933

297 "Was Hitler democratically elected?" http://diebesteallerzeiten.de/blog/2009/02/19/was-hitler-democratically-elected/

298 "German referendum, 1934" https://en.wikipedia.org/wiki/German_referendum,_1934

299 "Hitler Was Elected President in a Democratic Election: Myth" http://factmyth.com/factoids/hitler-was-elected-in-a-democratic-election/

300 "History of Venezuela (1999–present)" https://en.wikipedia.org/wiki/History_of_Venezuela_(1999%E2%80%93present)

301 "Venezuela: Chávez's Authoritarian Legacy" https://www.hrw.org/news/2013/03/05/venezuela-chavezs-authoritarian-legacy

302 "Algerian legislative election, 1991" https://en.wikipedia.org/wiki/Algerian_legislative_election,_1991

303 "Algerian lessons for the Tunisian crisis" https://www.opendemocracy.net/north-africa-west-asia/hicham-yezza/how-to-be-different-together-algerian-lessons-for-tunisian-crisis

304 "Theodore Parker" https://en.wikipedia.org/wiki/Theodore_Parker

305 "Gettysburg Address" https://en.wikipedia.org/wiki/Gettysburg_Address

306 "10 of the best Tony Benn quotes - as picked by our readers" https://www.theguardian.com/politics/2014/mar/15/10-of-the-best-tony-benn-quotes-as-picked-by-our-readers

307 "Tony Benn and the Five Essential Questions of Democracy" https://www.thenation.com/article/tony-benn-and-five-essential-questions-democracy/

308 "Lord Acton Quote Archive" https://acton.org/research/lord-acton-quote-archive

309 "Famous Words Churchill Never Said" https://www.winstonchurchill.org/publications/finest-hour/finest-hour-141/history-detectives-red-herrings-famous-words-churchill-never-said

310 "The right to vote should be restricted to those with knowledge" https://aeon.co/ideas/the-right-to-vote-should-be-restricted-to-those-with-knowledge

311 "Don't let ignorant people vote" http://edition.cnn.com/2011/OPINION/04/12/granderson.ignorant.vote/index.html

312 "Democracy vs. Epistocracy" https://www.washingtonpost.com/news/volokh-conspiracy/wp/2016/09/03/democracy-vs-epistacracy/

313 "Against Epistocracy: For True Democracy" http://www.thecritique.com/articles/against-epistocracy/

314 "Chartism" on the Victorian Web: https://web.archive.org/web/20080219044548/http://www.victorianweb.org/history/chartism.html

315 "Our democracy no longer represents the people; here's how we fix it" https://www.youtube.com/watch?v=PJy8vTu66tE

316 "Testing Theories of American Politics: Elites, Interest Groups, and Average Citizens" https://www.cambridge.org/core/journals/perspectives-on-politics/article/testing-theories-of-american-politics-elites-interest-groups-and-average-citizens/62327F513959D0A304D4893B382B992B

317 "Is America an Oligarchy?" https://www.newyorker.com/news/john-cassidy/is-america-an-oligarchy

318 "Daring Democracy: Igniting Power, Meaning, and Connection for the America We Want" https://www.goodreads.com/book/show/34002224-daring-democracy

319 "Electoral System (Chamber 1)" http://aceproject.org/epic-en/CDTable?question=ES005&set_language=en

320 "Democracy in crisis" https://freedomhouse.org/report/freedom-world/freedom-world-2018

321 "Electoral Systems around the World" http://www.fairvote.org/research_electoralsystems_world

322 "Electoral reform" https://www.electoral-reform.org.uk/campaigns/electoral-reform/

323 "Athenian Democracy" https://www.ancient.eu/Athenian_Democracy/

324 "Allotment and Democracy in Ancient Greece" http://www.booksandideas.net/Allotment-and-Democracy-in-Ancient.html

325 "The End of Politicians: Time for a Real Democracy" https://www.goodreads.com/book/show/34518675-the-end-of-politicians

326 "The Sortition Foundation" http://www.sortitionfoundation.org/

327 "What is sortition?" http://www.sortitionfoundation.org/what_is_sortition

328 "Should there be juries in fraud cases?" http://www.bbc.co.uk/news/uk-scotland-39877171

329 "Why Nations Fail: The Origins of Power, Prosperity, and Poverty" https://www.goodreads.com/book/show/12158480-why-nations-fail

330 "Why Nations Fail – Schwartz Lecture" http://economics.mit.edu/files/6699

331 "Creative destruction" https://economics.mit.edu/files/1785

332 "Prisoner's Dilemma: John Von Neumann, Game Theory and the Puzzle of the Bomb" https://www.goodreads.com/book/show/29506.Prisoner_s_Dilemma

333 "Leviathan", Chapter XIII: http://www.bartleby.com/34/5/13.html

334 "Leviathan", Chapter XVII: http://studymore.org.uk/xhob17.htm

335 "The End of History and the Last Man" https://www.goodreads.com/book/show/57981.The_End_of_History_and_the_Last_Man

336 "The history at the end of history" https://www.theguardian.com/commentisfree/2007/apr/03/thehistoryattheendofhist

337 "The World Is Flat: A Brief History of the Twenty-first Century" https://www.goodreads.com/book/show/1911.The_World_Is_Flat

[338] "Red Spy Queen – the story of Elizabeth Bentley" http://scandalouswoman.blogspot.com/2008/07/elizabeth-bentley-red-spy-queen.html

[339] "Judge Kaufman's Statement Upon Sentencing the Rosenbergs" http://www.law.umkc.edu/faculty/projects/ftrials/rosenb/ROS_SENT.HTM

[340] "Reds under the bed" http://alphahistory.com/coldwar/reds-under-the-bed/

[341] "Edward R. Murrow: A Report on Senator Joseph R. McCarthy, See it Now (CBS-TV, March 9, 1954)" http://www.lib.berkeley.edu/MRC/murrowmccarthy.html

[342] "Comments on John Earl Haynes' 'The Cold War Debate Continues'" https://sites.fas.harvard.edu/~hpcws/comment15.htm

[343] "McCarthyism: Critical reactions" https://en.wikipedia.org/wiki/McCarthyism#Critical_reactions

[344] "TWE Remembers: Joseph McCarthy's Wheeling Speech" https://www.cfr.org/blog/twe-remembers-joseph-mccarthys-wheeling-speech

[345] "Inaugural Address, 20 January 1961" https://www.jfklibrary.org/Asset-Viewer/BqXIEM9F4024ntFl7SVAjA.aspx

[346] "Fourteen Points Speech" https://en.wikisource.org/wiki/Fourteen_Points_Speech

[347] "Ho Chi Minh Documents on the Era of the First World War" http://vietnamwar.lib.umb.edu/origins/docs/Lansing.html

[348] "Will Dyson" https://en.wikipedia.org/wiki/Will_Dyson

[349] "The UN and the Hypocrisy of Power" http://www.consortiumnews.com/2010/111310a.html

[350] "Eisenhower's Farewell Address to the Nation" http://mcadams.posc.mu.edu/ike.htm

[351] "Intelligence Report on Russian Hacking" https://www.nytimes.com/interactive/2017/01/06/us/politics/document-russia-hacking-report-intelligence-agencies.html

[352] "Russia used Twitter bots and trolls 'to disrupt' Brexit vote" https://www.thetimes.co.uk/edition/news/russia-used-web-posts-to-disrupt-brexit-vote-h9nv5zg6c

[353] "Russian troll describes work in the infamous misinformation factory" https://www.nbcnews.com/news/all/russian-troll-describes-work-infamous-misinformation-factory-n821486

[354] "J.J. Patrick" https://www.byline.com/journalist/jamespatrick/column

[355] "British Journalism Awards 2017" http://www.pressgazette.co.uk/british-journalism-awards-2017-nick-ferrari-is-journalist-of-the-year-full-list-of-winners/

356 "Carole Cadwalladr" https://www.theguardian.com/profile/carolecadwalladr

357 "No Is Not Enough: Resisting Trump's Shock Politics and Winning the World We Need" https://www.goodreads.com/book/show/34814047-no-is-not-enough

358 "2017 Lie of the Year: Russian election interference is a 'made-up story'" http://www.politifact.com/truth-o-meter/article/2017/dec/12/2017-lie--year-russian-election-interference-made-s/

359 "A history of Donald Trump's business dealings in Russia" https://www.washingtonpost.com/opinions/a-history-of-donald-trumps-business-dealings-in-russia/2017/11/02/fb8eed22-ba9e-11e7-be94-fabb0f1e9ffb_story.html

360 "Revealed: the $2bn offshore trail that leads to Vladimir Putin" https://www.theguardian.com/news/2016/apr/03/panama-papers-money-hidden-offshore

361 "Why Does the Kremlin Care So Much About the Magnitsky Act?" https://www.theatlantic.com/international/archive/2017/07/magnitsky-act-kremlin/535044/

362 "How far do EU-US sanctions on Russia go?" http://www.bbc.co.uk/news/world-europe-28400218

363 "What Caused the Russian Financial Crisis of 2014 and 2015" https://www.thebalance.com/what-caused-the-russian-financial-crisis-of-2014-and-2015-1979012

364 For example, see "America's long history of meddling in other countries' elections" https://www.channel4.com/news/factcheck/americas-long-history-of-meddling-in-other-countries-elections

365 "Highest death toll from a civil war" http://www.guinnessworldrecords.com/world-records/highest-death-toll-from-a-civil-war

366 "Special Operations Forces (SOF) and CIA Paramilitary Operations: Issues for Congress" https://web.archive.org/web/20160303045342/http://ftp.fas.org/sgp/crs/intel/RS22017.pdf

367 "Key Figures In CIA-Crack Cocaine Scandal Begin To Come Forward" http://www.huffingtonpost.co.uk/entry/gary-webb-dark-alliance_n_5961748

368 "Stealing Elections Is All in the Game" http://foreignpolicy.com/2017/01/10/stealing-elections-is-all-in-the-game-russia-trump/

369 "Americans can spot election meddling because they've been doing it for years"

https://www.theguardian.com/commentisfree/2017/jan/05/americans-spot-election-meddling-doing-years-vladimir-putin-donald-trump

[370] "Red Notice: A True Story of High Finance, Murder, and One Man's Fight for Justice" https://www.goodreads.com/book/show/22609522-red-notice

[371] "Red Notice: How I Became Putin's No 1 Enemy by Bill Browder" https://www.theguardian.com/books/2015/mar/26/red-notice-how-i-became-putin-no-1-enemy-bill-browder-review

[372] "It Takes A Village To Determine The Origins Of An African Proverb" https://www.npr.org/sections/goatsandsoda/2016/07/30/487925796/it-takes-a-village-to-determine-the-origins-of-an-african-proverb

[373] "Smartphones and Beyond" https://smartphonesandbeyond.com/

[374] See especially Chapter 26, "February 11th" https://smartphonesandbeyond.com/chapters/part-iii/february-11th/

[375] "Did the Mail and Sun help swing the UK towards Brexit?" https://www.theguardian.com/media/2016/jun/24/mail-sun-uk-brexit-newspapers

[376] "The Press and immigration: reporting the news or fanning the flames of hatred?" http://www.sub-scribe.co.uk/2016/09/the-press-and-immigration-reporting.html

[377] "Stay or go – the lack of solid facts means it's all a leap of faith" https://www.standard.co.uk/comment/comment/anthony-hilton-stay-or-go-the-lack-of-solid-facts-means-it-s-all-a-leap-of-faith-a3189151.html

[378] "Rupert Murdoch: 'I've never asked any prime minister for anything'" https://www.theguardian.com/media/2016/dec/19/rupert-murdoch-ive-never-asked-any-prime-minister-for-anything

[379] "How To Stop Brexit – And Make Britain Great Again" https://www.goodreads.com/book/show/35720126-how-to-stop-brexit---and-make-britain-great-again

[380] "The Brexiters who put their money offshore" https://www.theguardian.com/news/2017/nov/09/brexiters-put-money-offshore-tax-haven

[381] "Everything you need to know about Lexit in five minutes" http://www.politics.co.uk/blogs/2017/11/17/everything-you-need-to-know-about-lexit-in-five-minutes

[382] "Internal market and free movement – freedom of establishment and collective action initiated by a trade union" http://ec.europa.eu/dgs/legal_service/arrets/05c438_en.pdf

[383] "Dominic Cummings: how the Brexit referendum was won" https://blogs.spectator.co.uk/2017/01/dominic-cummings-brexit-referendum-won/

384 "Apollo 11 moon landing: top 15 Nasa inventions" http://www.telegraph.co.uk/news/science/space/5893387/Apollo-11-moon-landing-top-15-Nasa-inventions.html

385 "Marshall Plan, 1948" https://history.state.gov/milestones/1945-1952/marshall-plan

386 "NHS Expenditure" http://researchbriefings.parliament.uk/ResearchBriefing/Summary/SN00724

387 "Genocide in the 20th century" http://www.historyplace.com/worldhistory/genocide/index.html

388 Links purposely omitted

389 Ephesians 4:32: https://www.biblegateway.com/passage/?search=Ephesians+4%3A32

390 "Marx's theory of alienation" https://en.wikipedia.org/wiki/Marx%27s_theory_of_alienation

391 "Literature and Revolution" https://books.google.co.uk/books?id=MG-981usVQEC

392 "Communism & Democratic Socialism & the 'New Man'" https://www.ourcivilisation.com/cooray/westdem/chap13.htm

393 "Cogs in the Wheel: The Formation of Soviet Man" https://www.goodreads.com/book/show/1278847.Cogs_in_the_Wheel

394 "This Day in History: Down to the Countryside Movement" http://www.thatsmags.com/china/post/8077/china-chronicles-up-to-the-mountains-and-down-to-the-countryside

395 "China's 'lost generation' recall hardships of Cultural Revolution" http://edition.cnn.com/2012/10/24/world/asia/china-lost-generation/index.html

396 "The Cultural Revolution: all you need to know about China's political convulsion" https://www.theguardian.com/world/2016/may/11/the-cultural-revolution-50-years-on-all-you-need-to-know-about-chinas-political-convulsion

397 "Mao's Great Leap Forward 'killed 45 million in four years'" http://www.independent.co.uk/arts-entertainment/books/news/maos-great-leap-forward-killed-45-million-in-four-years-2081630.html

398 "Mao's Great Famine: The History Of China's Most Devastating Catastrophe, 1958-62" https://www.goodreads.com/book/show/8410925-mao-s-great-famine

399 "Looking back on the Great Leap Forward" http://www.historytoday.com/frank-dik%C3%B6tter/looking-back-great-leap-forward

400 "Chinese Support for Khmer Rouge Grows Cooler" http://www.nytimes.com/1993/05/09/world/chinese-support-for-khmer-rouge-grows-cooler.html

401 "Literacy and Education under the Khmer Rouge" https://gsp.yale.edu/literacy-and-education-under-khmer-rouge

402 "The Khmer Rouge" http://content.time.com/time/world/article/0,8599,1879785,00.html

403 "How two men survived a prison where 12,000 were killed" http://www.bbc.co.uk/news/magazine-33096971

404 "The Killing Fields" http://www.imdb.com/title/tt0087553/

405 "Court Revives Convictions in Murder of 'Killing Fields' Survivor" http://www.metnews.com/articles/2005/tanx070805.htm

406 "Khmer Rouge chief: babies were 'smashed to death'" http://www.independent.co.uk/news/world/asia/khmer-rouge-chief-babies-were-smashed-to-death-1700196.html

407 This example is discussed more fully in Chapter 3 of "The abolition of aging" https://theabolitionofaging.com/contents/

408 "Extropy Magazines" https://hpluspedia.org/wiki/Extropy_Magazines

409 "The Extropian Principles version 3.0" http://vency.com/EXtropian3.htm

410 "Principles of Extropy version 3.11" https://web.archive.org/web/20110806105153/http://www.extropy.org/principles.htm

411 "H+: True Transhumanism" http://www.metanexus.net/essay/h-true-transhumanism

412 "US military successfully tests electrical brain stimulation to enhance staff skills" https://www.theguardian.com/science/2016/nov/07/us-military-successfully-tests-electrical-brain-stimulation-to-enhance-staff-skills

413 "Moral Enhancement" https://philosophynow.org/issues/91/Moral_Enhancement

414 "The abolition of aging" https://theabolitionofaging.com/

415 "Why Cryonics Makes Sense" https://waitbutwhy.com/2016/03/cryonics.html

416 "Technological Resurrection: An idea ripe for discussion" https://dw2blog.com/2017/11/30/technological-resurrection-an-idea-ripe-for-discussion/

417 "Criticism of transhumanism" https://hpluspedia.org/wiki/Criticism_of_transhumanism

418 "The pope of transhumanism" https://www.actualized.org/forum/topic/951-transhumanism/

419   "The   Transhumanist   Declaration   (2.4)"
https://web.archive.org/web/19980702105748/http://www.transhumanis
m.com/declaration.htm

420   "Transhumanist   Art   Statement"
https://web.archive.org/web/19980523093459/http://www.extropic-
art.com/transart.htm

421   "Transhumanist   Declaration"
https://hpluspedia.org/wiki/Transhumanist_Declaration

422 "Biohacker Summit Program" http://biohackersummit.com/stockholm-
2017/program/

423   "Search   Inside   Yourself"
https://www.goodreads.com/book/show/12921211-search-inside-yourself

424 "Search Inside Yourself" http://siybook.com/

425 "Results" https://siyli.org/results

426 "Stealing Fire" https://www.goodreads.com/book/show/30317415-
stealing-fire

427   "Democratize   Nirvana"
https://www.youtube.com/watch?v=Ao1jztX7Wws

428 "Frequently Asked Questions" https://nootropics.com/frequently-
asked-questions/

429   "Psychoactive   Substances   Act   2016"
https://www.gov.uk/government/collections/psychoactive-substances-
bill-2015

430   "Re: Psychoactive   Substances   Bill"
https://www.gov.uk/government/uploads/system/uploads/attachment_d
ata/file/441400/2-7-15-_ACMD_advice_on_PS_Bill.pdf

431 "You're not hallucinating, MPs really did pass crazy bad drug law"
https://www.newscientist.com/article/2074813-youre-not-hallucinating-
mps-really-did-pass-crazy-bad-drug-law/

432 "David Nutt: 'The government cannot think logically about drugs'"
https://www.theguardian.com/uk/2010/dec/06/david-nutt-drugs-alcohol

433 "Theresa May's Religion Has Made Her An 'Extremist' On Drugs
Policy,   Professor   David   Nutt   Says"
http://www.huffingtonpost.co.uk/entry/theresa-mays-religion-has-made-
her-an-extremist-on-drugs-professor-david-nutt-
says_uk_58a6e850e4b07602ad53a8a7

434 "Nick Clegg accuses Theresa May of tampering with drug report"
https://www.theguardian.com/politics/2016/apr/17/nick-clegg-accuses-
theresa-may-drug-report-conservatives

435   "Lifespans   Are   Long   Enough"
https://www.intelligencesquaredus.org/debates/lifespans-are-long-enough

436 "Transhumanism" http://foreignpolicy.com/2009/10/23/transhumanism/

437 "Socrates' objections to writing" http://outofthejungle.blogspot.co.uk/2007/11/socrates-objections-to-writing.html

438 "Memorial: Karl Marx grave" https://www.londonremembers.com/memorials/karl-marx-grave

439 "Tasks awaiting volunteers" https://transpolitica.org/projects/

440 "The Starfish and the Spider: The Unstoppable Power of Leaderless Organizations" https://www.goodreads.com/book/show/21314.The_Starfish_and_the_Spider

441 "10 interesting open source software forks and why they happened" http://royal.pingdom.com/2008/09/11/10-interesting-open-source-software-forks-and-why-they-happened/

442 "Bitcoin security model: trust by computation" http://radar.oreilly.com/2014/02/bitcoin-security-model-trust-by-computation.html

443 "About R3" https://www.r3.com/about/

444 "How Blockchain Can Improve Politics" https://medium.com/@shivagbhaskar/how-blockchain-can-improve-american-politics-9a2016680f10

445 "Blockchain Technology and Decentralized Governance: Is the State Still Necessary?" https://papers.ssrn.com/sol3/papers.cfm?abstract_id=2709713

446 "A Brief History of Blockchain" https://hbr.org/2017/02/a-brief-history-of-blockchain

447 "Transcending Politics With Vinay Gupta" https://www.youtube.com/watch?v=gwNloQctV60

448 "Vinay Gupta – Blockchain Beyond Bitcoin" https://www.youtube.com/watch?v=YaH5HDhtWo4

449 "Fundamental challenges with public blockchains" https://medium.com/@preethikasireddy/fundamental-challenges-with-public-blockchains-253c800e9428

450 See also "Buckminster Fuller is Idiotic" https://medium.com/cognitive-computing-singularity-futurology/buckminster-fuller-is-idiotic-6233e1f8b3b3

451 "Code Is Law: On Liberty in Cyberspace" https://harvardmagazine.com/2000/01/code-is-law-html

452 "Blockchain Technology and Decentralized Governance: Is the State Still Necessary?" https://papers.ssrn.com/sol3/papers.cfm?abstract_id=2709713

453 "The Singularity" https://hpluspedia.org/wiki/The_Singularity

454 "The 7 Habits of Highly Effective People: Powerful Lessons in Personal Change" (Covey spoke about finding the right ladder to climb, rather than finding the right rope to pull) https://www.goodreads.com/book/show/36072.The_7_Habits_of_Highly _Effective_People

455 "Official Jim Rohn Facebook page" https://www.facebook.com/OfficialJimRohn/posts/10154545230540635

456 "The Happiness Hypothesis: Finding Modern Truth in Ancient Wisdom" http://www.happinesshypothesis.com/

457 "The Divided Self" http://www.happinesshypothesis.com/happiness-hypothesis-ch1.pdf

458 "The Righteous Mind" http://righteousmind.com/

459 "Introductory Chapter" http://righteousmind.com/about-the-book/introductory-chapter/

460 "Crossing the Chasm: Marketing and Selling High-Tech Products to Mainstream Customers" https://www.goodreads.com/book/show/61329.Crossing_the_Chasm

461 "Diffusion of Innovations" https://www.goodreads.com/book/show/134781.Diffusion_of_Innovatio ns

462 "Theodore Roosevelt Quotes" http://www.theodorerooseveltcenter.org/Learn-About-TR/TR-Quotes?page=3

463 "The Future of Life Institute (FLI)" https://futureoflife.org/team/

464 "Future of Humanity Institute" https://www.fhi.ox.ac.uk/

465 "Centre for the Study of Existential Risk" https://www.cser.ac.uk/about-us/

466 "Less Wrong Meetup Groups" https://wiki.lesswrong.com/wiki/Less_Wrong_meetup_groups

467 "About Less Wrong" http://lesswrong.com/about/

468 "Center for Applied Rationality" http://www.rationality.org/

469 "Machine Intelligence Research Institute" https://intelligence.org/

470 "Effective Altruism Global Events" https://www.eaglobal.org/events/

471 "Effective Altruism" https://www.effectivealtruism.org/

472 "Introduction to Effective Altruism" https://www.effectivealtruism.org/articles/introduction-to-effective-altruism/

473 "Nodes" http://www.millennium-project.org/about-us/nodes/

474 "Challenges" http://www.millennium-project.org/projects/challenges/

475 "State of the Future version 19.1" http://www.millennium-project.org/state-of-the-future-version-19-1/

476 "Global Futures Intelligence System" http://www.millennium-project.org/projects/global-futures-intelligence-system/

477 "What is DiEM25?" https://diem25.org/what-is-diem25/

478 "Manifesto for Democratising Europe" https://diem25.org/manifesto-long/

479 "The Alternative" https://alternativet.dk/en

480 "The Alternative UK" https://www.thealternative.org.uk/

481 "A global network of networks" https://www.thealternative.org.uk/who-is-the-alternative/

482 "The Fourth Group" http://thefourthgroup.org/

483 "Community values" http://thefourthgroup.org/community-values/

484 "Frequently Asked Questions" http://transhumanist-party.org/faq/

485 "Constitution of the United States Transhumanist Party" http://transhumanist-party.org/constitution/

486 "Category: Platform" http://transhumanist-party.org/category/platform/

487 "Mission" http://humanityplus.org/about/mission/

488 "TransVision" https://hpluspedia.org/wiki/TransVision

489 "Technoprogressivism" https://ieet.org/index.php/tpwiki/Technoprogressivism/

490 "Citizen Cyborg: Why Democratic Societies Must Respond to the Redesigned Human of the Future" https://www.goodreads.com/book/show/111902.Citizen_Cyborg

491 "Top of the list: the biggest impact" https://dw2blog.com/2010/01/13/top-of-the-list-the-biggest-impact/

492 "The Institute for Ethics and Emerging Technologies" https://ieet.org/index.php/IEET2/about

493 "Welcome to London Futurists" https://londonfuturists.com/

494 "History of London Futurists" https://londonfuturists.com/2016/07/10/about-london-futurists/

495 "Videos" https://londonfuturists.com/videos/

496 "Newsletters" https://londonfuturists.com/newsletters/

497 "Hangouts on Air" https://londonfuturists.com/videos/hangouts-on-air/

498 "Welcome to H+Pedia!" https://hpluspedia.org/wiki/Main_Page

499 "Community portal" https://hpluspedia.org/wiki/Community_portal